1170	Assassination of Thomas Becket [at] Canterbury
1189–1192	Third Crusade; height of crusad[ing]
1204	Fourth Crusade establishes Latin Empire at Constantinople
1215	English barons force King John to grant Magna Carta
1237–1241	Mongols invade Russia and Hungary; establishment of the Empire of the Golden Horde
1337–1453	Hundred Years' War between England and France
1415	Henry V of England wins Battle of Agincourt
1431	Joan of Arc burned at the stake at Rouen
1453	Fall of Constantinople to the Ottomans; end of the Byzantine Empire
1455–1485	Wars of the Roses in England
1478–1492	Lorenzo the Magnificent, ruler of Florence
1492	Fall of Granada, last Muslim stronghold in Spain
1494	Treaty of Tordesillas divides the world between Portugal and Spain
1519	**Cortés's expedition to Mexico**; Charles V becomes Holy Roman Emperor
1529	Suleiman besieges Vienna; high-water mark of Ottoman expansion into Europe
1558	**Elizabeth I becomes queen of England**
1643	**Louis XIV succeeds to throne of France under a regency**
1661	**Beginning of Louis XIV's personal government**
1688–1689	Glorious Revolution in England
1702–1713	War of the Spanish Succession; Treaty of Utrecht
1715	**Death of Louis XIV**

Social/Economic

B.C.

776	First Olympic games
750–600	Greek renaissance
332–331	Alexandria founded in Egypt

A.D.

c. 120	Hadrian attempts to codify laws
250–311	Age of persecution of Christians
311	Edict of toleration for Christians
632–732	Muslim conquests jeopardize Mediterranean trade
1086	English population 1.1 million, based on *Domesday Book*
1275–1292	Marco Polo travels in China
1348	Black Death strikes mainland Europe
c. 1450	Gutenberg prints with movable type
1492	Columbus's first voyage to America; expulsion of the Jews from Spain

(Continued inside the back cover)

MAKERS OF THE WESTERN TRADITION

Portraits from History
Volume One

SEVENTH EDITION

Edited by

J. Kelley Sowards

Wichita State University

BEDFORD/ST. MARTIN'S   Boston ◆ New York

To my sons, Steve and Mike, and their families

For Bedford/St. Martin's
President and Publisher: Charles H. Christensen
General Manager and Associate Publisher: Joan E. Feinberg
History and Developmental Editor: Katherine E. Kurzman
Editorial Assistant: Charisse Kiino
Managing Editor: Elizabeth M. Schaaf
Copyeditor: Cynthia Benn
Cover Design: Hannus Design Associates
Cover Art: Elizabeth I, Armada Portrait (version 2), attributed to George
Gower (1540–1596). Woburn Abbey, Bedfordshire/Bridgeman Art Library,
London.

Manufactured in the United States of America.

9 8 7 6
i h g f

For information, write: Bedford/St. Martin's, 75 Arlington Street, Boston,
MA 02116 (617–399–4000)

ISBN: 0–312–14252–8

Acknowledgments

MOSES: Portrait: Stock Montage. "The Moses of Exodus" from *Revised Standard Bible* (Oxford: Oxford University Press, 1971). Copyright 1946, 1952, ©
1971 by the Division of Christian Education of the National Council of the
Churches of Christ in the USA. Reprinted by permission. Daniel Jeremy
Silver, "Moses and the Modern World." Selected excerpt from *Images of Moses*
by Daniel Jeremy Silver. Copyright © 1982 by Basic Books, Inc. Reprinted by
permission of Basic Books, a division of HaperCollins Publishers, Inc.

*Acknowledgments and copyrights are continued at the back of the book on pages 317–
19, which constitute an extension of the copyright page. It is a violation of the law to
reproduce these selections by any means whatsoever without the written permission of
the copyright holder.*

Preface
for Instructors

Are individual men and women capable of altering the course of history by their actions, or are they simply caught in the grinding process of great, impersonal forces over which they have no control? Historians, along with theologians, philosophers, and scientists, have long been fascinated by this question. People in every age and at every level of society have recognized larger forces at work in their lives, whether they interpreted those forces as divine, ecological, sociological, or economic. While most of us remain largely spectators, a few individuals in history—such as Alexander the Great, Elizabeth I, and Hitler—have been able to seize the opportunities of their time and direct the course of events. Still others—like Dante, Martin Luther, Darwin, and Freud—were able, solely by the power of their thought or vision, to affect the way people understood their own world. These accomplishments continue to reverberate in the twentieth century with as much or more impact than the military conquests and treaties that mean "history" to the average student.

First and foremost, this is a book for students. I have learned over my years of teaching that they love a good story and that it helps them to focus on individuals at regular points in the huge sweep of Western Civilization. The twenty-seven individuals chosen for *Makers of the Western Tradition*, Seventh Edition, are those of whom students already have a brief knowledge; most have an image of Caesar, borrowed from film, and many can match ego and id with Sigmund Freud. Building on their inherent interest in people, I have sought with these books to introduce students to the methods historians use to deepen their own understanding of these complex personalities, constructing chapters with a variety of sources and questions to encourage critical thinking.

Purpose and Organization

Few personalities or events stand without comment in the historical record; contemporary accounts and documents—the original sources—no less than later scholarly interpretations are crafted by people with a distinct point of view and interpretation of what they see. Problems of interpretation are inseparable from the effort to achieve an understanding of the past. It is my goal in these volumes to make apparent to students what is implicitly understood by all historians: that history is composed of many stories, all of which deserve a hearing.

Makers of the Western Tradition is set up to make this truth apparent: Each chapter includes a portrait or bust of the figure and then pairs a primary account with two often conflicting secondary interpretations. The first secondary source presents the "standard" reading. For example, to introduce students to Charles Darwin, I first have them read from Alan Moorehead's narrative about Darwin as a young and ambitious naturalist just beginning to form his opinions and theories on evolution. I then offer an excerpt from Stephen Jay Gould, who boldly defends Darwin's theory of evolution against the belief of "scientific creationism." This second historical interpretation is included to complete *and* complicate the picture, to stretch students by showing them another compelling interpretation of the legacy and mark a particular "maker" left on the world. These sources—visual, primary, and secondary—combine to create a portrait of a major individual from the past, suggesting more questions than answers about that figure's achievements and ultimate importance.

New to This Edition

In this seventh edition I have made several changes with an aim to fitting *Makers* more clearly into the standard Western Civilization curriculum and to provide students with the support they need to begin asking good questions. I assume that for most classes these are supplementary reading; as such, these volumes need to work in tandem with the textbook's coverage and the instructor's lectures to create a consistent picture of the past. I have tried to do so clearly and simply, enabling teachers to jump into and out of the readings without disturbing the flow of their courses.

Based on requests from fourteen reviewers, many of them long-term users of the books, I have changed the lineup of twenty-seven figures. Those familiar with the book were consistent in one request: that I not stretch the interpretation of "makers" for political or nonpedagogical concerns. To maintain my goal of creating a book for students, I have thus concentrated on the acknowledged leaders of the past, knowing that others will lead the charge in redefining this canon in their scholarly publications. It is the role of this book to follow that path, not to lead the efforts at reform.

In Volume One, I have two new chapters, one on Homer and one on Cortés; both Constantine and Dante have been revived from past editions at the request of loyal users. In Volume Two, Nelson Mandela is new, bringing the final chapter right into the present. Gandhi is new to these volumes, borrowed from my book *Makers of World History,* as traditional Western Civilization courses expand their definitions of what constitutes the West. Cecil Rhodes, again at the request of users, has been brought back from a previous edition.

Students always need context; in this edition I have tried to provide more. For the first time in twenty-two years we have included maps; eleven appear, with five or six in each volume, to help students trace military campaigns and understand the extent of influence a ruler like Catherine the Great had over incredibly vast areas of Europe. In an effort to help tie the books and figures clearly back into the scheme of the survey course, I have also included timelines in each volume. These list selected major events, people, and trends, highlighting where each volume's fourteen individuals fall in the larger picture.

To encourage critical thinking I have reviewed the Questions for Review and Study for all the chapters and revised many. These are now accompanied by Questions for Comparison that ask students to consider commonalties and differences between figures, and ultimately, their legacies. As study aids, these questions will help students return to the texts with a critical eye and provide a start for classroom discussion.

The bibliographies have all been updated and now appear in a new format. These have been reorganized to look less daunting to students who wish to read further or who need to pursue full scholarly discussions for writing assignments. All the portraits have also been reexamined and many replaced to deepen their usefulness as visual "documents." All chronologies have been reviewed and many revised to include more detail.

Acknowledgments

A project like this requires a lot of work and input—from reviewers and users to development and production editors. I would like to express my gratitude to colleagues across the country who have used and stayed with these books for some segment of the twenty-two years the books have been in existence. Their comments about which sections work in class and appeal to students have always been my guiding principle in revisions; it is certainly clear to me that because of this help the books have gotten much better over time. I am indebted to Timothy Sarbaugh, Gonzaga University; Sheldon Hanft, Appalachian State University; George Vascik, Miami University; Richard Nelson, Augsberg College; Carol Carbine, Loyola University; Donald Kaiper, Los Medanos College; Donald Sullivan, University of New Mexico; Carol Putko, San Diego State University; Nancy Bjorkland, Fullerton College; Kay Slocum, Capitol University; and Suzanne Hamner, Northeastern University.

Finally, I must thank the people at Bedford Books. After six editions, there is still room for new ideas. Charles Christensen, Publisher, I thank for his faith and vision. Joan Feinberg, Associate Publisher, also deserves my gratitude for her expertise and sound advice. Both Katherine Kurzman, Developmental Editor, and Charisse Kiino, Editorial Assistant, guided my efforts to renew these books, and I am grateful for their contributions as well. Elizabeth Schaaf, Managing Editor, has kept the book on schedule and gotten all the details right. Susan Pace in Promotion and Dick Hannus, the cover designer, made *Makers* a thing of beauty; thanks to them, I have the two most beautiful covers ever. I could not have asked for a more thorough and dependable copyeditor; Cynthia Benn fine-tuned and polished the manuscript into tiptop shape. I also owe thanks to Fred Courtright for clearing permissions and Bruce Jones for rendering the maps.

J. K. S.

Introduction
for Students

The book you are holding in your hands, *Makers of the Western Tradition*, Seventh Edition, is a set of readings for use in any Western Civilization class. This "reader" is meant to accompany a core textbook, which will serve as a comprehensive reference for the class. As a supplement, then, *Makers of the Western Tradition* permits a deeper treatment of fewer topics, in this case, people. All those discussed here—Socrates, Alexander the Great, Louis XIV, Catherine the Great, and Hitler—will play a major role in your course. You are probably familiar with some of the events, theories, and campaigns that are synonymous with many of these names. Here you will be asked to study them with the eye of a historian, questioning evidence and coming to your own conclusions. These are the individuals who have *made* our Western tradition and these readings should provide a glimpse into the legacy they have left.

Format of the Book

Every chapter focuses on a person, and each chapter is organized in the same way. Each chapter opens with a portrait or bust of the featured figure, giving you an image to start with. Next is a brief overview, outlining the figure's accomplishments in the context of his or her day. The first reading, introduced with a headnote, is a "primary" source. This source, written either by the figure or a contemporary, places you squarely in the past, surrounded by the language and concerns of the day. The next selection is usually by a historian and gives a "classic" interpretation of the figure in question. The last piece in every chapter is a more modern reading by a living scholar, and in many cases it presents a contrasting view. The primary source should suggest to you the difficulty a modern reader encounters when evaluating events so far distant geographically and temporally. It is no

ix

surprise, then, that so many different opinions exist today when historians look at the same, often limited, sources.

The real lesson of this book is that history is a story that continues to be told and retold. New evidence, both documentary and archaeological, surfaces regularly, and new generations of historians learn to evaluate it in different ways. One of the most important figures in our own national history, Christopher Columbus, has recently become a source of debate. Was he a brave and determined man who helped launch Europe to world dominance with his discovery and settlement of the Americas? Scholars in recent years have brought this standard interpretation into question, suggesting instead that Columbus had selfish, rather than noble, reasons for the voyages and citing his "accomplishments" as the precursor to the annihilation of millions of natives. New discoveries and conclusions continually force new investigations. This is what constantly renews the excitement of reading and studying history.

The Different Types of Sources

Historians, however, are not fiction writers; every opinion must be supported by facts. The evidence with which historians work are called *primary sources;* these are the direct commentary of past people on their own lives and events of their day. They are as close as we can get to the past and serve as the *raw data* of history. Since this is where historians start their investigations, this is also where you should begin. The first reading of every chapter is a primary source, a document written by the figure under study or by a contemporary who had direct contact with the figure. These firsthand accounts were written by people with various motives and prejudices and should be read with this in mind. Whatever their motives, however, the writers were conditioned by the events and concerns that surrounded a person living in a particular century, under the conditions of the day. We at the end of the twentieth century cannot hope to see with the same clarity and sympathy; that is why we attempt to listen to the voices of the past and see their world through their eyes.

Historians also write for a purpose, and thus their interpretations of the primary documents always take an angle that excludes as much as it includes. These writings, based on primary materials, constitute our secondhand knowledge of the past and are called *secondary sources*. Historians are constantly looking over the primary materials and reconsidering their meaning; this process of reevaluation and reinterpretation is reflected in the second and third selections in each chapter. These writings are by individuals (often historians) who neither experienced the events about which they are writing nor are embroiled in the subjective concerns of participants. Even primary accounts of an event can differ; so it is a given that secondary interpretations do. As you read the second and third pieces in each chapter, it is important to consider why they sometimes differ and what the writer might be suggesting with a particular approach.

You need to bring a certain amount of skepticism to your reading; this is precisely what historians themselves do and is why, for example, even the history of the United States' founding continues to be so hotly debated. Every writer has an agenda, and you need to evaluate it to gain the fullest possible understanding of the past. Critical judgment is what underlies all historical research and what continues to make the stories worth retelling. This retelling too is worth thinking about.

Support for Students

A large variety of apparatus throughout *Makers of the Western Tradition* will guide you in this endeavor. *Headnotes* precede every selection, providing context about the reading and its writer. *Maps* are often included, and brief *chronologies* for each historical figure featured show the where and when needed to help you start framing questions. The *timelines* inside the front and back covers of the book show the temporal context and ask you to begin considering how the events preceding and following those under discussion show what may have influenced the figure of interest and what that figure later influenced in history. *Questions for Review and Study* follow the final reading of every chapter and provide a start for evaluating both the writings and their writers. Finally, *Questions for Comparison* ask you to examine the figure's legacy for yourself by contrasting him or her with another profiled in the book. Having read the primary accounts and two (perhaps differing) secondary interpretations, you may have begun formulating your own interpretation. These questions invite you to attempt just that.

This reading should be an enjoyable, exciting foray into history. In each chapter there should be enough context to help you start asking questions, just as historians themselves do, and to appreciate how complex the answers are. This is very likely the first course you have taken in college-level history; if these books are successful, it won't be the last.

Contents

Preface for Instructors   v
Introduction for Students   ix

MOSES: THE SERVANT OF YAHWEH   3
The Moses of Exodus   5
Ernest Renan, *Moses between Myth and History*   9
Daniel Jeremy Silver, *Moses and the Modern World*   14
QUESTIONS FOR REVIEW AND STUDY   19
QUESTIONS FOR COMPARISON   19
SUGGESTIONS FOR FURTHER READING   19

HOMER AND THE BEGINNING OF GREEK POETRY   23
Aristotle, *The Poetics*   25
Milman Parry, *Homer and the Oral Tradition*   28
William A. Camps, *How the Stories Are Told*   31
QUESTIONS FOR REVIEW AND STUDY   35
QUESTIONS FOR COMPARISON   35
SUGGESTIONS FOR FURTHER READING   35

THE IMAGE OF SOCRATES: MAN OR MYTH?   39
Aristophanes, *The Clouds*   41
Plato, *The Apology*   52
Moses Hadas and Morton Smith, *Socrates: A Modern
    Perspective*   58

xiii

QUESTIONS FOR REVIEW AND STUDY   62

QUESTIONS FOR COMPARISON   62

SUGGESTIONS FOR FURTHER READING   63

THE "PROBLEM" OF ALEXANDER THE GREAT   67

The Ancient Sources: Arrian, Eratosthenes, and Plutarch   71

W. W. Tarn, *Alexander the Great and the Unity of Mankind*   74

N. G. L. Hammond, *The New Alexander*   81

QUESTIONS FOR REVIEW AND STUDY   88

QUESTIONS FOR COMPARISON   88

SUGGESTIONS FOR FURTHER READING   88

JULIUS CAESAR: THE COLOSSUS THAT BESTRODE THE NARROW WORLD   93

Suetonius, *The Life of Caesar*   97

Theodor Mommsen, *The Heroic Image of Caesar*   102

Ronald Syme, *Caesar the Politician*   106

QUESTIONS FOR REVIEW AND STUDY   112

QUESTIONS FOR COMPARISON   112

SUGGESTIONS FOR FURTHER READING   113

THE CONVERSION OF CONSTANTINE   117

Eusebius of Caesarea, *The Life of Constantine*   119

Edward Gibbon, *The Christian Fable*   123

Peter Brown, *Constantine and the "Great Thaw"*   127

QUESTIONS FOR REVIEW AND STUDY   129

QUESTIONS FOR COMPARISON   130

SUGGESTIONS FOR FURTHER READING   130

CHARLEMAGNE AND THE FIRST EUROPE   133

Einhard, *The Emperor Charlemagne*   136

Heinrich Fichtenau, *A New Portrait of the Emperor*   141

F. L. Ganshof, *A More Somber Light*   146

QUESTIONS FOR REVIEW AND STUDY   152

QUESTIONS FOR COMPARISON   152

SUGGESTIONS FOR FURTHER READING   152

ELEANOR OF AQUITAINE AND THE WRATH OF GOD   157

William of Tyre and John of Salisbury, *Eleanor and the Chroniclers*   160

Amy Kelly, *Eleanor, the Queen of Hearts*   163

Marion Meade, *Eleanor the Regent*   169

QUESTIONS FOR REVIEW AND STUDY   175

SUGGESTIONS FOR FURTHER READING   175

THE MEANING OF DANTE   179

Boccaccio, *The Life of Dante*   181

Henry Osborn Taylor, *The Historical Dante*   187

Philip McNair, *Dante's Relevance Today*   191

QUESTIONS FOR REVIEW AND STUDY   196

SUGGESTIONS FOR FURTHER READING   197

LEONARDO DA VINCI: UNIVERSAL MAN OF THE RENAISSANCE   201

Giorgio Vasari, *In Praise of Leonardo*   204

John Herman Randall Jr., *Leonardo the Scientist*   209

Ladislao Reti, *Leonardo the Technologist*   213

QUESTIONS FOR REVIEW AND STUDY   219

QUESTIONS FOR COMPARISON   219

SUGGESTIONS FOR FURTHER READING   220

CORTÉS AND THE CONQUEST OF MEXICO   225

Hernán Cortés, *The Second Letter to Emperor Charles V*   228

William H. Prescott, *An Heroic Cortés*   232

J. H. Elliott and Anthony Pagden, *A New Explanation*   237

QUESTIONS FOR REVIEW AND STUDY   244

QUESTIONS FOR COMPARISON   244

SUGGESTIONS FOR FURTHER READING   244

MARTIN LUTHER: PROTESTANT SAINT OR "DEVIL IN THE HABIT OF A MONK"? 249

Martin Luther, *The Protestant Luther* 252

Erik H. Erikson, *Young Man Luther* 255

Erwin Iserloh, *Luther between Reform and Reformation* 260

QUESTIONS FOR REVIEW AND STUDY 265

QUESTIONS FOR COMPARISON 265

SUGGESTIONS FOR FURTHER READING 266

ELIZABETH I, THE ARMADA, AND "THE BLACK LEGEND" 271

Sir Francis Bacon, *The Legendary Elizabeth* 273

James Anthony Froude, *The "New" Elizabeth* 277

Garrett Mattingly, *Elizabeth and the "Invincible" Armada* 283

QUESTIONS FOR REVIEW AND STUDY 288

QUESTIONS FOR COMPARISON 288

SUGGESTIONS FOR FURTHER READING 288

LOUIS XIV: "THE SUN KING" 293

Louis, Duc de Saint-Simon, *The Memoirs* 297

Voltaire, *A Rationalist View of Absolutism* 303

Pierre Goubert, *Louis XIV and the Larger World* 308

QUESTIONS FOR REVIEW AND STUDY 313

QUESTIONS FOR COMPARISON 313

SUGGESTIONS FOR FURTHER READING 314

MAKERS OF THE WESTERN TRADITION

Portraits from History
Volume One

SEVENTH EDITION

MOSES:
THE SERVANT
OF YAHWEH

?	Born
C. 1280 B.C.	Led Exodus of the Jewish people from Egypt
C. 1240 B.C.	Died

The history of the ancient Hebrews crisscrossed the histories of the other peoples of the ancient Near East throughout antiquity. The patriarch Abraham came from the Sumerian city of Ur. The "promised land" to which he went was that of the Canaanites, a people clearly documented in the nonbiblical sources of the second millennium B.C. Abraham and his people contended with such historical nations as the Amorites, the Hittites, the Assyrians, and the Philistines. Jacob served Laban "the Aramean" and married his daughters Leah and Rachel. Joseph was sold into slavery in Egypt by his jealous brothers but found favor with the pharaoh, who proclaimed, "Behold, I have set you over all the land of Egypt."

Yet in none of the records of these other historical peoples is there any reference to the ancient Hebrews, to any of their leaders' names, or to any of the events so graphically depicted in the opening books of the Old Testament—not a single contemporary document, not a stele nor a carving, not even a scribbled reference on a dusty shard. There is no Egyptian record of a pharaoh who raised Joseph up nor of a successor "which knew not Joseph," neither a reference to any Egyptian vizier or court figure whose name might possibly have been Joseph nor a single Egyptian reference to the Hebrew tribes descended from Joseph's brothers, who came at his behest to dwell in the land of Goshen.

But despite the maddening silence of the nonbiblical sources, the biblical history of the early Hebrews remains a history. It moves

3

through time, generation after generation; events have the ring of authenticity about them, the "thickness" and stubborn uniqueness of genuine historical events; and the characters, both major and minor, have the solid individuality of historical personalities. The history of these people and events is, in the phrase of Martin Buber, a "saga history,"[1] a history that is partially visible and susceptible to modern historical analysis, but partially hidden in what Abram Leon Sachar calls "the grey morning of folk-memory and fable."[2]

This is the case not only with the patriarchs but also with the great hero figure who stands between the patriarchs and historical Israel: Moses, the founder of the Hebrew nation. The events surrounding the figure and the accomplishments of Moses are the watershed of Hebrew history, of the religion of Judaism, and of the Judaeo-Christian tradition. To quote Martin Buber again, "The meeting of a people with events so enormous that it cannot ascribe them to its own plans and their realisation, but must perceive in them deeds performed by heavenly powers, is of the genuine substance of history."[3]

---

[1]Martin Buber, *Moses, the Revelation and the Covenant* (New York: Harper, 1958), pp. 15–19.

[2]Abram Leon Sachar, *A History of the Jews*, 5th. ed. rev. and enlarged (New York: Knopf, 1968), p. 9.

[3]Buber, *Moses*, p. 16.

The Moses of Exodus

The only source for the story of Moses and the enormous events surrounding him is the Old Testament book of Exodus. For Moses, like the patriarchs before him, is not mentioned in any nonbiblical source or record. The account in Exodus begins with that nameless Egyptian pharaoh "which knew not Joseph," and with a drastic change in the fortunes of those Hebrews who had come to Egypt at Joseph's invitation. No longer did they enjoy "the fat of the land." This pharaoh was fearful of their numbers and enslaved them to build "store cities" for him, Pithom and Ramses. But the Hebrews increased even in affliction until the pharaoh decreed that every male Hebrew baby be cast into the Nile; daughters were to be spared. It was at this crucial juncture of events that Moses was born, to parents both of whom were of the house of Levi. After three months, when she could hide him no longer, his mother laid the infant in a basket of bulrushes daubed with bitumen and pitch, and placed it in the reeds at the river's edge. Here the baby was discovered by the pharaoh's daughter, taken by her, given the name Moses, and raised in her household as her own son.

One day, when Moses had grown up, he went out to his people and looked on their burdens; and he saw an Egyptian beating a Hebrew, one of his people. He looked this way and that, and seeing no one he killed the Egyptian and hid him in the sand. When he went out the next day, behold, two Hebrews were struggling together; and he said to the man that did the wrong, "Why do you strike your fellow?" He answered, "Who made you a prince and a judge over us? Do you mean to kill me as you killed the Egyptian?" Then Moses was afraid, and thought, "Surely the thing is known." When Pharaoh heard of it, he sought to kill Moses.

But Moses fled from Pharaoh, and stayed in the land of Mid'ian; and he sat down by a well. Now the priest of Mid'ian had seven daughters; and they came and drew water, and filled the troughs to water their father's flock. The shepherds came and drove them away; but Moses stood up and helped them, and watered their flock. When they came to their father Reu'el, he said, "How is it that you have come so soon today?" They said, "An Egyptian delivered us out of the hand of the shepherds, and even drew water for us and watered the flock." He said to his daughters, "And where is he? Why have you left the man? Call him, that he may eat bread." And Moses was content to dwell with the man, and he gave Moses his daughter Zippo'rah. . . .

Now Moses was keeping the flock of his father-in-law, Jethro, the priest of Mid'ian; and he led his flock to the west side of the wilderness, and came to Horeb, the mountain of God. And the angel of the Lord appeared to him in a flame of fire out of the midst of a bush; and he looked, and lo, the bush was burning, yet it was not consumed. And Moses said, "I will turn aside and see this great sight, why the bush is not burnt." When the Lord saw that he turned aside to see, God called to him out of the bush, "Moses, Moses!" And he said, "Here am I." Then he said, "Do not come near; put off your shoes from your feet, for the place on which you are standing is holy ground." And he said, "I am the God of your father, the God of Abraham, the God of Isaac, and the God of Jacob." And Moses hid his face, for he was afraid to look at God.

Then the Lord said, "I have seen the affliction of my people who are in Egypt, and have heard their cry because of their taskmasters; I know their sufferings and I have come down to deliver them out of the hand of the Egyptians, and to bring them up out of that land to a good and broad land, a land flowing with milk and honey, to the place of the Canaanites, the Hittites, the Amorites, the Per'izzites, the Hivites, and the Jeb'usites. And now, behold, the cry of the people of Israel has come to me, and I have seen the oppression with which the Egyptians oppress them. Come, I will send you to Pharaoh that you may bring forth my people, the sons of Israel, out of Egypt."

At first Moses was reluctant to accept God's mission: he was neither worthy nor eloquent enough. But God convinced him by miracles, by the promise of his own divine support, and commanded Moses' brother Aaron to go with him. So Moses and his family and his brother Aaron returned to Egypt and to yet another pharaoh and put God's command to him. But not only did the pharaoh refuse to let the enslaved Hebrews go, he increased their misery: "Let heavier work be laid upon the men that they may labor at it and pay no regard to lying words" (5:9).

Once more Moses and Aaron went to the pharaoh. Once more the pharaoh contemptuously refused. And God brought upon the land a series of plagues, including a plague of frogs, one of gnats and flies, and a plague that felled the Egyptians' flocks and herds but spared those of the Hebrews. Each time the pharaoh would promise to comply, only to recant and be set upon by yet another plague—hail and locusts and a "thick darkness." At last God brought the most terrible plague of all: "The Lord slew all the first-born in the land of Egypt, both the first-born of man and the first-born of cattle" (13:15). Again the children of Israel were spared, and the ceremony of Passover thereupon established, for the vengeful Lord "passed over" their houses with the doorposts marked with the blood of sacrificial lambs. Among the Egyptian dead was the pharaoh's own first-born son. He was at last ready to let the Israelites go. He summoned Moses and Aaron and said, "Rise up, go forth from among my people, both you and the people of Israel" (12:31).

When Pharaoh let the people go, God did not lead them by way of the land of the Philistines,[4] although that was near; for God said, "Lest the people repent when they see war, and return to Egypt." But God led the people round by the way of the wilderness toward the Red Sea. . . .

And the Lord went before them by day in a pillar of cloud to lead them along the way, and by night in a pillar of fire to give them light, that they might travel by day and by night; the pillar of cloud by day and the pillar of fire by night did not depart from before the people. . . .

Then Moses stretched out his hand over the sea; and the Lord drove the sea back by a strong east wind all night, and made the sea dry land, and the waters were divided. And the people of Israel went into the midst of the sea on dry ground, the waters being a wall to them on their right hand and on their left. The Egyptians pursued, and went in after them into the midst of the sea, all Pharaoh's horses, his chariots, and his horsemen. And in the morning watch the Lord in the pillar of fire and of cloud looked down upon the host of the Egyptians, and discomfited the host of the Egyptians, clogging their chariot wheels so that they drove heavily; and the Egyptians said, "Let us flee from before Israel, for the Lord fights for them against the Egyptians."

Then the Lord said to Moses, "Stretch out your hand over the sea, that the water may come back upon the Egyptians, upon their chariots, and upon their horsemen." So Moses stretched forth his hand over the sea, and the sea returned to its wonted flow when the morning appeared; and the Egyptians fled into it, and the Lord routed the Egyptians in the midst of the sea. The waters returned and covered the chariots and the horsemen and all the host of Pharaoh that had followed them into the sea; not so much as one of them remained. But the people of Israel walked on dry ground through the sea, the waters being a wall to them on their right hand and on their left.

Thus the Lord saved Israel that day from the hand of the Egyptians; and Israel saw the Egyptians dead upon the seashore. And Israel saw the great work which the Lord did against the Egyptians, and the people feared the Lord; and they believed in the Lord and in his servant Moses.

Once across the Red Sea and in the wilderness of Sinai, the people suffered hunger and thirst. In spite of God's gifts of manna from heaven, of flights of quail and

---

[4]The land of the Philistines was in Canaan, along the eastern Mediterranean from Egypt to Ekron. [All notes are the editor's unless identified otherwise.]

bitter springs that he changed to sweet water, the people "murmured against Moses" and against God. They had to fight against the Amalekites, and Moses struggled to develop among them a sense of nationhood and a government.

On the third new moon after the people of Israel had gone forth out of the land of Egypt, on that day they came into the wilderness of Sinai . . . and there Israel encamped before the mountain. And Moses went up to God, and the Lord called to him out of the mountain, saying, "Thus you shall say to the house of Jacob, and tell the people of Israel: You have seen what I did to the Egyptians, and how I bore you on eagles' wings and brought you to myself. Now therefore, if you will obey my voice and keep my covenant, you shall be my own possession among all peoples; for all the earth is mine, and you shall be to me a kingdom of priests and a holy nation. These are the words which you shall speak to the children of Israel."

So Moses came and called the elders of the people, and set before them all these words which the Lord had commanded him. And all the people answered together and said, "All that the Lord has spoken we will do." And Moses reported the words of the people to the Lord. And the Lord said to Moses, "Lo, I am coming to you in a thick cloud, that the people may hear when I speak to you, and may also believe you for ever." . . .

On the morning of the third day there were thunders and light-nings, and a thick cloud upon the mountain, and a very loud trumpet blast, so that all the people who were in the camp trembled. Then Moses brought the people out of the camp to meet God; and they took their stand at the foot of the mountain. And Mount Sinai was wrapped in smoke, because the Lord descended upon it in fire; and the smoke of it went up like the smoke of a kiln, and the whole mountain quaked greatly. And as the sound of the trumpet grew louder and louder, Moses spoke, and God answered him in thunder. And the Lord came down upon Mount Sinai, to the top of the moun-tain; and the Lord called Moses to the top of the mountain, and Moses went up. . . .

And God spoke all these words, saying,

"I am the Lord your God, who brought you out of the land of Egypt, out of the house of bondage.

"You shall have no other gods before me.

"You shall not make for yourself a graven image, or any like-ness of anything that is in heaven above, or that is in the earth beneath, or that is in the water under the earth; you shall not bow down to them or serve them; for I the Lord your God am a jealous God, visiting the iniquity of the fathers upon the children to the third and the fourth generation of those who hate me, but showing steadfast love to thousands of those who love me and keep my commandments.

"You shall not take the name of the Lord your God in vain; for the Lord will not hold him guiltless who takes his name in vain.

"Remember the sabbath day, to keep it holy. Six days you shall labor, and do all your work; but the seventh day is a sabbath to the Lord your God; in it you shall not do any work, you, or your son, or your daughter, your manservant, or your maidservant, or your cattle, or the sojourner who is within your gates; for in six days the Lord made heaven and earth, the sea, and all that is in them, and rested the seventh day; therefore the Lord blessed the sabbath day and hallowed it.

"Honor your father and your mother, that your days may be long in the land which the Lord your God gives you.

"You shall not kill.

"You shall not commit adultery.

"You shall not steal.

"You shall not bear false witness against your neighbor.

"You shall not covet your neighbor's house; you shall not covet your neighbor's wife, or his manservant, or his maidservant, or his ox, or his ass, or anything that is your neighbor's."

Now when all the people perceived the thunderings and the lightnings and the sound of the trumpet and the mountain smoking, the people were afraid and trembled; and they stood afar off, and said to Moses, "You speak to us, and we will hear; but let not God speak to us, lest we die." And Moses said to the people, "Do not fear; for God has come to prove you, and that the fear of him may be before your eyes, that you may not sin."

Moses between Myth and History

ERNEST RENAN

Through the long historical development of Judaism and of Christian history, the main line of those traditions tended to accept without serious question the absolute truth of the biblical narrative and raised no questions about the historicity of biblical people and events. It was only in the age of the Enlightenment that such questions began to be raised. In the late seventeenth century, Spinoza had cast doubt on the Mosaic authorship of the Pentateuch, the first five books of the Old Testament, and advocated a rational and historical interpretation of the Bible. In the course of the late eighteenth century and especially the nineteenth, the notion of the historical interpretation of the Bible became commonly accepted, prompted in part by the nineteenth-century enthusiasm for the new "scientific" historiography and in part by the popularity of Near Eastern archaeology. But even as these trends developed, religious fundamentalism had reached an almost frantic pitch; and one of its cardinal principles was biblical literalism. At the center of the resulting whirlwind of controversy stood the French historian Ernest Renan (1823–1892).

As a young man, Renan had trained for the priesthood, but he left his training and the Catholic church in 1845 over the question of the incompatibility of the church's teaching with modern historical criticism. Renan's dedication to historical criticism, in particular as it applied to the history of religion, dated from this time. He went on to become a distinguished Semitic scholar and professor of Hebrew Studies at the Collège de France and eventually a member of the French Academy. He also became one of the most controversial public figures of his time. In 1863 he wrote his most famous book, a massive Life of Jesus. *It was a thoroughgoing piece of rational skepticism in which he interpreted Jesus as "an incomparable man," but a man nevertheless. The book and the author were vilified by orthodox critics both Catholic and Protestant, and both the book and Renan became celebrated, even notorious.*

In the next twenty years, Renan returned to his Semitic studies and began work on his most important book, a five-volume History of the People of Israel. *By this time he had somewhat tempered the sharp-edged rationalism that had characterized his* Life of Jesus. *He saw instead the process of Hebrew history evolving as a demonstration of the human capacity for faith. He was, in short, a scholar yearning to believe, to find a way for the historian to accept the myth and folklore that stood as so much of the history of the ancient Hebrews. One of his critics has characterized his* History of the People of Israel *as "providing less a history than a half imaginative reconstruction of society and religion before the historical period."[5] Renan himself wrote in the preface of the book, "We do not need to know, in histories of this kind, how things happened; it is sufficient for us to know how they might have happened" (p. xvii).*

We turn now to his account in History of the People of Israel *of Moses and his age.*

———————

Moses is completely buried by the legends which have grown up over him, and though he very probably existed, it is impossible to speak of him as we do of other deified or transformed men. His name appears to be Egyptian. *Mosé* is probably the name of Ahmos, Amosis, shortened at the beginning. According to the prevalent tradition, Moses was a *Levi*, and . . . this name probably was used to designate the Egyptians whose services were required for the worship and who followed Israel into the desert. The name of Aharon, perhaps, is derived in a similar way. Moses appears to us at first as having been

———————

[5]G. P. Gooch, *History and Historians in the Nineteenth Century* (London: Longmans, 1928), p. 528.

brought up by, and being a functionary of, the Egyptians. The fact of his killing an Egyptian in a moment of instinctive indignation has nothing improbable about it. His relations with the Arab Midianites, a species of Hebrews not reduced to servitude by Egypt, and with the Idumean Kenites, especially with a certain Ieter or Jethro, whose daughter he is said to have married, also seem to have a semi-historical character. With regard to whether he was really the leader of the revolt and the guide of fugitive Israel, it is unquestionably quite possible that an Egyptian functionary of mixed race, told to keep watch over his brethren, may have . . . been the author of the deliverance. But it is also possible that all these narratives of the Exodus, into which fable has penetrated so deeply, may be even more mythical than is generally supposed, and that the only fact which can be depended upon out of them all is the departure from Egypt of Israel and its entry into the peninsula of Sinai.

It does not seem as if the Israelites and their companions had any other object in view, before they left Pa-Rameses, except to escape the tyranny of Pharaoh. . . .

Having escaped from what they always called "the house of bondage," the people of Israel found themselves face to face with what is perhaps the most inhospitable desert under heaven. . . .

The narratives of the incidents which occurred during this march, which afterwards became the basis of a religion, or, to speak more correctly, of universal religion, all of them attribute the principal part to Mosé. I have already pointed out that this theory can only be accepted with considerable reserve, but it is probable, nevertheless, that the activity of the semi-Egyptian Hebrew, who seems to have had much to do with the preparations for the exodus, was again manifested during the marches through the desert. Another *Levite*, named Ahron, or Aharon (an Egyptian name, perhaps), stands out side by side with him, as well as a woman named Miriam, who, according to the legend, were his brother and sister. Some narratives attached more importance to these persons than do the versions which have come down to us.

There is perhaps some foundation for what we are told as to the relations which Moses established with the tribes to the east of Egypt, and these relations would have been useful to him in the difficult task which he had assumed. But one hesitates about speaking of the shadows dimly outlined in the darkness of profound night as real personages. . . .

The voyage of Israel through the desert was a passage, not a sojourn; but the impression which this short period of miserable existence left upon the minds of the people was very deep. All the circumstances, of which a more or less distorted recollection was preserved, were regarded as sacramental, and the theocratic caste afterwards moulded them to the purposes of its religious policy. The slightest incidents were magnified, and the manna and the quails were adduced as proofs that the people had been miraculously fed, and that God himself had been their guide, and had marched before them in the way. Upon these vast solitary plains, where the atmosphere is so luminous, the presence of a tribe can be detected from afar by the smoke which ascends straight up towards the sky. Night time is often chosen for a march, and in that case a lighted lantern, fastened on to the end of a long pole, is often used as a rallying sign. This column, invisible by day, luminous by night, was the very God of Israel, guiding his people through these solitudes. This good genius of the desert had shown such a special affection for Israel that the people came to invoke him in a quite personal way. The God who had brought Israel out of Egypt and enabled them to live in "the land of thirst" was not the absolute Elohim, the great God, King, and Providence of the whole universe. He was a god who had a special affection for Israel, who had bought them as merchandise. How far we are here from the ancient patriarchal God, just and universal![6] The new god of whom I am speaking is in the highest degree partial. His providence has only one aim, and that is to watch over Israel. He is not as yet the god of a nation, for a nation is the produce of the marriage of a group of men with some land, and Israel has no land; but he is the god of a tribe in every sense of the word. . . .

A protecting god needs a proper name, for the protecting god is a person; he becomes identified with those whom he protects. . . .

By a process of ideas which it is impossible now to follow out, the protecting god of Israel was called Iahveh. Each step towards the formation of the national idea was, it will be seen, accompanied by a degradation in the theology of Israel. The national idea was in favour of a god who would think only of the nation, who in the interests of the nation would be cruel, unjust, and hostile to the whole human race. Iahvéism commenced, to all intents and purposes, the day that Israel became egotistical as a nation principle; and it grew with the nation, becoming an obliteration of the sublime and true idea of the primitive Elohism. Fortunately there was in the genius of Israel something superior to national prejudices. The old Elohism was never to die; it was to survive Iahvéism, or rather to assimilate it. . . .

The people clamoured for Mnévis and Hathor. It is doubtful whether Mosé was so much opposed to this idolatrous worship as was afterwards asserted, for we find that a brazen serpent said to have

---

[6]Renan is here making a distinction that other scholars make too between Yahweh, the God of Moses, and El or Elohim, the earlier God of the patriarchs.

been set up by him was in existence until the reign of Hezekiah, who broke it in pieces. . . .

At a later date it was asserted that Moses had lifted up and placed upon a pole, as a talisman against the bite of the serpents, this mysterious *Nehustan*. Both versions may be true, for it is not at all impossible that Moses may have been, in some ways, one of those sorcerers whom Egypt possessed, or who came from the banks of the Euphrates. No alterations are too great to have taken place after the lapse of five or six centuries, when a religious genius as powerful as that of the Hebrews is working upon an oral tradition which is above all things non-resistant and susceptible of any degree of transformation. . . .

Horeb, or Sinai, from the most remote antiquity, was the object of religious worship on the part of the people of Hebrew or of Arab origin who roamed about those parts. They made pilgrimages there. The Semites of Egypt went there frequently to offer up sacrifices. They believed that their god resided there. The holy mountain spread terror a long way around it. It was called *par excellence* "the mountain of Elohim," or "the mountain of God." It was admitted that the Elohim resided on its summits, snowy or shining, limpid as crystal or gloomy and enveloped with a terrible covering of mist. . . .

Sinai was therefore above all a mountain of terror. Certain spots were considered holy, and one could not walk on them without taking off one's shoes. The general belief was that one could not see the god and live. Even his presence killed. The common people could not approach him. . . .

Even those who enjoyed the honour of conversing with him face to face expiated that honour by death. It was related that one day, in Horeb, Moses wished to see the glory of this terrible god. The god took him, placed him in the cleft of a rock, made him stand up, covered him with his large open hand, and passed by. Then he withdrew his hand so that Moses saw his back parts. Had Moses seen his face he would have died. . . .

The god of Sinai, it will be seen, was a god of lightning. His *theophanies* took place in the storm, in the midst of the flashing of lightning. The ancient Iahveh had already perhaps possessed some of these characteristics. Iahveh besides was decidedly beginning to play the part of the tutelary god of Israel, and was replacing the old *elohim* in the imagination of the people. It was therefore only natural that they should identify Iahveh with the god through whose lands they were passing and whose terrible influence they thought that they felt. . . .

What really happened when, from the camp of Rephidim, the tribe entered the rocky defiles of the Horeb? Impossible to say. . . .

Two things only can be perceived. The first is that from the commencement of the Sinaitic epoch it became the custom to regard

Iahveh as appearing in the form of a vision of flame. For clothing he had a thick cloud, for voice the thunder. In the storm he rode upon the wind and made the clouds his chariot. . . .

A second well-ascertained fact, not less remarkable, is that the Iahveh of the Hebrews, when definitely constituted, lived in Sinai, as Jupiter and the Grecian gods lived in Olympus. His dwelling was on the mountain top, especially when the summit was hidden from sight by heavy clouds. From thence he burst forth with horrible sounds, lightning, flames of fire, and thunder. The fundamental image of the Hebrew religion and poetry is the *theophany* of Iahveh appearing like an aurora borealis to judge the world. . . .

Sinai became therefore the Olympus of Israel, the place from whence all the luminous apparitions of Iahveh issued. It was only natural that when they desired a Thora from Iahveh they made him reveal it on Mount Sinai or Mount Horeb. At this remote epoch, that is to say when Israel went up to the mountain of God, did the people think that they heard some lesson? Did Moses take advantage of the circumstance to inculcate certain precepts? The little influence exercised by those precepts in the daily life of Israel, during the six or seven hundred years which followed, favours the belief that they never existed. It appears probable at least that the people left the holy mountain filled with terror and persuaded that a powerful god inhabited its peaks. There were no doubt sacrifices offered and altars erected. There was, above all, a startling recollection. The people had really seen the god of the holy mountain.

Moses and the Modern World

DANIEL JEREMY SILVER

In the foregoing selection we sampled the nineteenth-century historian Ernest Renan's historical scholarship moving to accept the myth and folklore "that stood as so much of the history of the ancient Hebrews" and of Moses. The debate that Moses was the leader of the biblical Hebrews, was exiled in Sinai for forty years, and received the Ten Commandments from God has continued into the twentieth century. The following selection is from Images of Moses, *by Daniel Jeremy Silver. A rabbi's son who was himself a rabbi and a distinguished scholar of Hebrew studies, Silver examines, as one reviewer of the book states it, "the diverse literary, artistic, pietistic, and historical treatment of the biblical Moses."[7] Silver*

---

[7]Egon Mayer, in *Library Journal* (November 1, 1982), vol. 107, p. 2102.

*goes on to point out that the successive treatments of Moses reflect the values and
the ethnic/political strategies of the various authors.*

———————————

The past is irretrievable, but ideas and artifacts live on as constitutive
elements in civilization. Moses is dead but an ideal of Moses lives.
Ahad Ha-Am[8] says, in effect, Turn away from what cannot be accomplished. It doesn't matter that Jews can't resurrect Moses; what matters is that they understand and respond to the Moses who lives in the
hearts of the Jewish people.

The modern spirit is existential. It researches the dead Moses but
cares about the living Moses. History cannot establish meaning—the
meaning is in the moment, existentialism insists—but modern thought
has used the discipline of history quite effectively to free itself from the
grip of the past. Medieval thought valued order, assumed a static
universe governed by eternal truths, and consecrated the prerogatives
of class and status as elemental parts of God's design. Modernists used
history to prove that God's design is dynamic, not static, and that all
claims to privilege based on the authority of the tradition have no
foundation in God's design.

When Jews were allowed to enter the modern world they willingly
subjected their tradition to historical analysis. History was the basic
discipline of the Haskalah, the Jewish Enlightenment. The early
Haskalah concentrated on non-Biblical subjects like the synagogue,
the sermon, and the liturgy, issues which were being debated between
traditionalists and reformers. But it was not long before the Bible was
subjected to similar analyses. The rabbis had tended to treat Judaism
as a conclusion, a single tradition since Sinai. Haskalah saw Judaism
as process. The more historical research was pursued the more apparent it became that Judaism was and is the organic, therefore ever-
changing, religious civilization of the Jewish people.

As long as Jews lived in cultures dominated by the Muslim and
Christian traditions, critical theories suggesting that Moses may never
have lived received little or no support. However bitter the religious
polemic between the religious communities, the existence of Moses or
his virtue as a leader never became a controversial issue. The New
Testament had used Moses as a witness to Jesus' mission. The Quran
had listed Moses among God's apostles. In modern times the emergence of religiously neutral pockets of population in Western society,
particularly in the universities, removed Moses from the list of historic figures whose life and worth scholars could take for granted.
The more the Torah texts were analyzed, the more questions were
raised about the life and work of the original Moses. In 1905 the

———————————

[8]A contemporary Mosaic scholar.

German historian Eduard Meyer (1835–1930), who had gained international fame for his work in Pharaonic chronology, lent the weight of his scholarly distinction to those who argued that search for the historical Moses would never be successful because the existing texts do not provide the kind of material a researcher would need to recover a historic figure (*Die Mose Sagen und die Lewiten*, 1905). An equally famed disciple, Martin Noth, took the same position. Pending any unexpected discoveries, studied agnosticism remains today the most creditable scholarly stance.

History brings all certainties into question, including all the certainties which have developed around the Torah. If there was no Moses, how could there be a *Torat Moshe*? One would have expected scholarly agnosticism about Moses to cause an angry defensive reaction throughout the Jewish world. Actually, the reaction was milder than might have been anticipated. The traditionalists simply declared that as the Word of God the Torah was a unique document which could not be subjected to the forms of analysis useful in understanding all other literature; and the modernists simply declared that, however the Torah came into being, it was a new force in the world whose results were far-reaching and culturally seminal, and that no reinterpretation of Moses' role would increase or diminish the Torah's value. Martin Noth put it this way, "The core of the Sinai tradition was a historical occurrence, however little it may be historically grasped in detail. . . . The gradually developing tradition of the Pentateuch, the religious content of which is quite without parallel, becomes a clear token of the particularity and qualitative uniqueness of Israel's position among the nations" (Noth 136–37). The *Midrashic* cast of mind which Jews had developed over the centuries predisposed them to look behind the surface meaning of a text, the so-called facts, to its philosophic or psychological implications and to value these implications as much as the facts. As we have seen, the *Midrash* had for centuries been presenting the Moses who lived in each generation's soul. Since Moses had never died in Jewish consciousness, the exhumation of the original Moses did not seem to be an urgent issue and the academic search for the historical Moses began as and remained an almost entirely non-Jewish enterprise pursued by such scholars as Hugo Gressmann (*Mose und Seine Zeit*, 1913) and Paul Volz (*Mose*, 1907). . . .

Using similar philosophic tools, Martin Buber (1878–1965) expanded on this approach in his book, *Moses* (1944). *Moses* is not, as the title suggests, a biography but, rather, an essay in Biblical appreciation. Buber assumes the existence of a historic Moses and offers as proof the inescapable impression, which he feels any sympathetic reader will come away with, of a sensitive and powerful spirit behind and within various Torah narratives. Buber's approach rests on a postulate he took over from the studies of philologists and students of ancient languages and literatures (particularly the Iranologist, Ernst Herzfeld) who had concluded that the classic sagas were not purely literary inventions but literary elaborations of someone's dramatic personal experience, particularly the radical surprise a writer or singer felt at some unexpected event he had participated in or witnessed. . . .

Buber's Moses is a God-intoxicated man, a mystic, an active leader always conscious of the responsibilities of office, and "an undivided entire person who, as such, receives the message and as such endeavors to establish that message in life" (Buber 200). In this last respect Moses is unique. There are many leaders of men, but few who, like Moses, are possessed of an original vision and able to transform their society according to it. . . .

The Burning Bush episode becomes a classic model of the moment of tension when one feels prudence war with commitment in his soul, when "God commands and man resists" (Buber 46). The Torah language captures and refracts the moment of recognition when Moses becomes aware of a compelling mission and aware that he must choose to respond to it. Sinai becomes a collective moment of recognition when the community under Moses' guidance senses its destiny. Buber thought of himself as an analytical scholar, but in reality he was an old-fashioned *Midrashist* who uses throughout the old technique of interpreting the text from within the text; he does so brilliantly and reveals much, but his conclusions are impressionistic, not historical. The Torah text simply does not reveal to every sensitive reader the afterglow of a series of I-Thou meetings between the prophet and God. . . . I discover little of Moses' personal experience in the Torah. What I discover there is a record of the community's meeting with God and its awe before God's redemptive power. I find it unlikely that a text which consistently diminishes Moses' role would be shaped around Moses' personal experiences. . . .

I was forcibly struck by the tendency of Jews to push aside the historical questions in favor of the *Midrashic* approach when my father, Abba Hillel Silver (1893–1963), published a historical evaluation of Moses, *Moses and the Original Torah.* His arguments apart, what fascinated me at the time and since was the resounding silence which greeted the book's publication (1959). Despite his worldwide fame as a scholar and leader in the Jewish world, the book sold poorly and was rarely reviewed in the Jewish press. I read this silence as a way of saying that the historical question he posed did not merit the effort he had invested in trying to answer it and perhaps should not have been asked at all. I came to believe that most Jews shy away from the search for the historical Moses out of an instinctive feeling that Judaism's credibility does not depend on, and cannot be allowed to appear to depend on, the historical accuracy of the Torah's narrative.

Using the judgments and tools of Biblical criticism, Silver sought to
recover the original Moses and the original Torah, the actual teaching
of Moses. He argues that Moses' original words dealt with the unity of
God and righteousness and are found in the familiar Decalogue
(Exod. 20; Deut. 5) and various other parts of the law, specifically
those apodictic oracles (*devarim*) which are the "you shall" and "you
shall not" commandments. He describes Moses as a religious pioneer
who refined the basically monotheistic faith of the patriarchs by adding to it the covenant of righteousness, a thorough-going opposition
to idolatry, and a sense of national mission.

According to Silver, the birth stories are legends. Moses was actually born in Egypt, and Egyptian religion and culture were essential
parts of his upbringing. Moses, he writes, was affected by the religious ferment of the thirteenth century B.C.E. which centered on
Akhenaten, the Pharaoh who destroyed many of Egypt's shrines and
made the worship of Aten, the sun god, into a state religion. Moses'
religious teachings go beyond Akhenaten's short-lived reformation,
far beyond this Pharaoh who sensed a single high God but never
abandoned a symbolized god, never denied the divinity of other
gods, and never rejected the divinity of the pharaohs and pharaonic
claims to absolute power. In many ways Moses' Torah represents a
reaction to what he had seen in Egypt. It outlaws incest, a common
feature of Egyptian society, and puts an end to lifelong slavery. It
rejects the idea of kings who claim to be gods incarnate and wield
unlimited power. The God to whom Moses bound himself and his
people is a zealous God intolerant of the worship of other gods and
the making of images, but in relation to His people a "God merciful
and just, slow to anger, and abounding in steadfast love and faithful-
ness" (Silver 29). Moses' major theological insight, which catalyzed a
radical shift in religious history, is a vision of God which denies that
dread and implacability are the essential attributes of His being. In
his view this newfound faith in a dependable and caring God made
possible the study of science and of political philosophies with some
expectation of useful findings about society's future. The argument
is close and scholarly, but it is doubtful that a dispassionate outside
observer would accept the author's arguments as ineluctable. The
more interesting question is why Silver broke with the general Jewish silence and explored the historical questions which surround
Moses' life. I have always felt that he did so because he was not
really raising the historical issues. He was convinced in the deepest
recesses of his being that Moses was "the foremost religious genius
of all times," the creator of the Jewish people, and the effective
founder of the faith. Therefore, the problem, as he saw it, was not
whether Moses had lived but what was the nature of Moses' accom-
plishment, which is really the question, In what does Judaism's
uniqueness consist?

Questions for Review and Study

1. Write an essay dealing with Mosaic criticism in the eighteenth century; in the nineteenth century; in the twentieth century.
2. Was Moses a figure of myth or a figure of history? Discuss.
3. Discuss the Ten Commandments. How do they relate to the age of the ancient Hebrews? How do they relate to contemporary society?
4. In what setting did God convey his Holy Law to Moses and the people of Israel? What is the significance of this setting?
5. Are there any obvious borrowings in Mosaic Judaism from the religion of Egypt?

Questions for Comparison

1. Compare Moses and Socrates (pp. 39–65) as creators of distinctively Hebrew and Greek attitudes. Of whom do we know most, and by what means? What were their messages, for whom were they meant, and what were the sources of their truths? How did each define the virtuous life? To what extent did each represent a break from his culture's past? What problems do interpreters face when defining the "true" Moses and Socrates? Whose thought exerts a greater influence on (y)our culture? Explain.

Suggestions for Further Reading

There are several attractive modern synthetic biographical-historical treatments of Moses, among the most readable is the *Moses* by David Daiches. Elias Auerbach's *Moses* is a more controversial and technical book by an established authority. Also see *Kings without Privilege*, by A. Graeme Auld, and *Moses and Pharao*, by Gary North. *Moses, the Revelation and the Covenant*, by Martin Buber, one of the most influential figures in modern religious history, is the first book to create a Moses of history.

Three works of interpretation may also be recommended. Daniel Jeremy Silver's *Images of Moses* is a well-written, fascinating history and historiography of Moses; students will find the first five chapters particularly useful. It is excerpted in this chapter. Robert Polzin's *Moses and the Deuteronomist* is a more detailed and scholarly work of interpretation, especially the first two chapters, which deal with Moses as he appears in the biblical book of Deuteronomy. Aaron Wildavsky's *The Nursing Father,* although not an especially profound scholarly book, is an interesting essay on the theme of Moses as a political leader. Baruch Halpern's "The Development of Israelite Monotheism," is also an interesting interpretive essay.

Most of the books of William Foxwell Albright can be recommended, especially *From the Stone Age to Christianity* and *The Archaeology of Palestine.*

Among the many histories of Israel, three are especially appropriate for students: *Ancient Israel,* by Harry M. Orlinsky, *A History of the Jews,* by Abram Leon Sachar, and *A History of Israel,* by John Bright. Two further works by great European authorities are also excellent, though they are somewhat technical and detailed: Roland de Vaux's *The Early History of Israel* and Martin Noth's *The History of Israel.* See also Noth's *Exodus.* Finally, there is the famous and controversial work by Sigmund Freud, *Moses and Monotheism,* which, though it has been bitterly criticized, is Freud's own pioneer work in psychohistory. (Titles with an asterisk are out of print.)

Albright, William Foxwell. *The Archaeology of Palestine.* Rev. ed. Baltimore: Penguin, 1954.

————. *From the Stone Age to Christianity: Monotheism and the Historical Process.* 2nd ed. Garden City, N.Y.: Anchor, 1957.*

Auerbach, Elias. *Moses.* Trans. and ed. Robert A. Barclay and Israel O. Lehman. Detroit: Wayne State University Press, 1975.

Auld, A. Graeme. *Kings without Privilege: David and Moses in the Story of the Bible's Kings.* Edinburgh: Tat Clark, 1994.

Bright, John. *A History of Israel.* 2nd ed. Philadelphia: Westminster, 1974.

Buber, Martin. *Moses, the Revelation and the Covenant.* New York: Harper, 1946, 1958.

Daiches, David. *Moses: The Man and His Vision.* New York: Praeger, 1975.

De Vaux, Roland. *The Early History of Israel.* Trans. David Smith. Philadelphia: Westminster, 1978.

Freud, Sigmund. *Moses and Monotheism.* New York: Knopf, 1939.

Halpern, Baruch. "The Development of Israelite Monotheism." In *Judaic Perspectives on Ancient Israel,* ed. Jacob Neusner, Baruch A. Levine, and Ernest S. Fredricks. Philadelphia: Fortress Books, 1987.

North, Gary. *Moses and Pharao: Dominion Religion versus Power Religion.* Tyler, Tex.: Institute for Christian Economies, 1985.

Noth, Martin. *Exodus: A Commentary.* Trans. J. S. Bowden. Philadelphia: Westminster, 1962.

————. *The History of Israel.* Trans. Stanley Godman. 2nd ed. New York: Harper, 1960.

Orlinsky, Harry M. *Ancient Israel.* Ithaca, N.Y.: Cornell University Press, 1960.

Polzin, Robert. *Moses and the Deuteronomist: A Literary Study of the Deuteronomic History, Part One.* New York: Seabury Press, 1980.

Sachar, Abram Leon. *A History of the Jews.* 5th ed., revised and enlarged. New York: Knopf, 1968.

Silver, Daniel Jeremy. *Images of Moses.* New York: Basic Books, 1982.

Wildavsky, Aaron. *The Nursing Father: Moses as a Political Leader.* Tuscaloosa: University of Alabama Press, 1984.

J. Chapman, Sc.

HOMER.

HOMER AND THE BEGINNING OF GREEK POETRY

13th–12th centuries B.C.	Age of Mycenaean civilization
2nd half of 8th century B.C.	Probable date of Homer's birth
c. 1185 B.C.	Probable end of the Trojan War
c. 600–480 B.C.	Rise of Athens
3rd and 2nd centuries B.C.	Development of Alexandrian Homeric scholarship

Homer is the name the Greeks gave to the greatest epic poet of antiquity, author of the *Iliad* and the *Odyssey*. Little more than attribution of authorship of those famous epics was known about him in antiquity, and what was known came not from any authentic history of the man but from Homeric tradition. That tradition makes him a blind poet and places him in Ionia, where he was supposedly born in the ninth century B.C. Tradition attributes to Homer, in addition to the *Iliad* and the *Odyssey*, an *Epic Cycle* dealing with other aspects of the Trojan War and surviving only in a few fragmentary citations; two comic poems, *Margites* and the *Battle of Frogs and Mice;* and the *Homeric Hymns*. These attributions were questioned even in antiquity and are today generally believed to be false.

Scholars now believe the historic Homer was born in the last half of the eighth century B.C. Some scholars believe that the *Iliad* and the *Odyssey* took shape over a long period of time rather than being the work of a single author, though some version of the stories' texts may in fact have originated with a single "Homer." Others hold to a "unitarian" theory, pointing to the rich and complex structure of the poems and to the fact that oral poetry often contains incongruities of plot and characters.

The discoveries by Heinrich Schliemann, in the late nineteenth century, of ancient Troy, Mycenae, and Tiryns provided a historic context for the Homeric age that had not existed before. These great civilizations of the Bronze Age had indeed existed in something like the grandeur with which Homer endowed them. The fall of Troy seems to have taken place in the late thirteenth century B.C., according to the excavations there by Carl Blegen.

The historic Homer, thus, took over a vision of Mycenaean Greece handed down by generations of poets and bards and then filled in details of his own time in the late eighth century B.C. in Ionia, where memories of the glories of the Mycenaean age still flourished. The epics were probably first recited at Ionian festivals. They may or may not have been committed to writing at this early time, though they probably were not. But in any case their historic origin is there.

The Poetics

ARISTOTLE

We turn first to a summary of the ancient Greek view of Homeric poetry, a selection from The Poetics, *by Aristotle. Born in 384 B.C., Aristotle arrived late in the Hellenic period of Greek history. Master of a famous school in Athens, the Lyceum, he was the most universal of Greek scholars, writing on a vast range of topics in more than four hundred treatises, some twenty-five of which survive and are considered authentic. He wrote on philosophy, logic, physics and metaphysics, geology, meteorology, zoology, and poetry. The pupil and friend of Plato became late in life the tutor to Alexander of Macedonia and may have written several treatises on political theory for Alexander's instruction. He died in 322 B.C., just a year after Alexander.*

With respect to that species of poetry which imitates by narration, and in hexameter verse, it is obvious that the fable ought to be dramatically constructed like that of tragedy; and that it should have for its subject one entire and perfect action, having a beginning, a middle, and an end; so that, forming like an animal a complete whole, it may afford its proper pleasure, widely differing in its construction from history, which necessarily treats, not of one action, but of one time, and of all the events that happened to one person or to many during that time; events the relation of which to each other is merely casual. For, as the naval action at Salamis, and the battle with the Carthaginians in Sicily, were events of the same time, unconnected by any relation to a common end or purpose; so also in successive events, we sometimes see one thing follow another without being connected to it by such relation. And this is the practice of the generality of poets. Even in this, therefore, as we have observed, the superiority of Homer's genius is apparent, that he did not attempt to bring the whole war, though an entire action with beginning and end, into his poem. It would have been too vast an object, and not easily comprehended in one view; or had he forced it into a moderate compass it would have been perplexed by its variety. Instead of this, selecting one part only of the war, he has from the rest introduced many episodes—such as the catalogue of the ships and others—by which he has diversified his poem. Other poets take for their subject the actions of one person, or of one period of time, or an action which, though one, is composed of too many parts. Thus, the author of the *Cypriacs* and of the Little Iliad. Hence it is that the Iliad and the Odyssey, each of them furnish matter for one tragedy, or two at most. . . .

Again, the epic poem must also agree with the tragic as to its two kinds: it must be simple or complicated, moral or disastrous. Its parts also, setting aside music and decoration, are the same, for it requires revolutions, discoveries, and disasters, and it must be furnished with proper sentiments and diction; of all which Homer gave both the first and the most perfect example. Thus, of his two poems the Iliad is of the simple and disastrous kind, the Odyssey complicated (for it abounds throughout with discoveries) and moral. Add to this, that in language and sentiments he has surpassed all poets.

II

The epic poem differs from tragedy in the length of its plan and in its metre.

With respect to length a sufficient measure has already been assigned. It should be such as to admit of our comprehending at one view the beginning and the end, and this would be the case if the epic poem were reduced from its ancient length, so as not to exceed that of such a number of tragedies as are performed successively at one hearing. But there is a circumstance in the nature of epic poetry which affords it peculiar latitude in the extension of its plan. It is not in the power of tragedy to imitate several different actions performed at the same time; it can imitate only that one which occupies the stage, and in which the actors are employed. But the epic imitation, being narrative, admits of many such simultaneous incidents, properly related to the subject, which swell the poem to a considerable size.

And this gives it a great advantage, both in point of magnificence, and also as it enables the poet to relieve his hearer and diversify his work by a variety of dissimilar episodes; for it is to the satiety naturally arising from similarity that tragedies frequently owe their ill success.

With respect to metre, the heroic is established by experience as the most proper, so that, should any one compose a narrative poem in any other, or in a variety of metres, he would be thought guilty of a great impropriety. For the heroic is the gravest and most majestic of all measures; and hence it is that it peculiarly admits the use of foreign and metaphorical expressions; for in this respect also, the narrative imitation is abundant and various beyond the rest. But the iambic and trochaic have more motion; the latter being adapted to dance, the other to action and business. To mix these different metres, as Chaeremon has done, would be still more absurd. No one, therefore, has ever attempted to compose a poem of an extended plan in any other than heroic verse; nature itself, as we before observed, pointing out the proper choice.

III

Among the many just claims of Homer to our praise, this is one—that he is the only poet who seems to have understood what part in his poem it was proper for him to take himself. The poet, in his own person, should speak as little as possible; for he is not then the imitator. But other poets, ambitious to figure throughout themselves, imitate but little and seldom. Homer, after a few preparatory lines, immediately introduces a man, a woman, or some other character; for all have their character—nowhere are the manners neglected.

IV

The surprising is necessary in tragedy; but the epic poem goes further and admits even the improbable and incredible, from which the highest degree of the surprising results, because there the action is not seen. The circumstances, for example, of the pursuit of Hector by Achilles, are such as, upon the stage, would appear ridiculous—the Grecian army standing still and taking no part in the pursuit, and Achilles making signs to them by the motion of his head not to interfere. But in the epic poem this escapes our notice. Now the wonderful always pleases, as is evident from the additions which men always make in relating anything in order to gratify the hearers.

V

It is from Homer principally that other poets have learned the art of feigning well. It consists in a sort of sophism. When one thing is observed to be constantly accompanied or followed by another, men are apt to conclude that if the latter is, or has happened, the former must also be, or must have happened. But this is an error. For knowing the latter to be true, the mind is betrayed into the false inference that the first is true also.

VI

The poet should prefer impossibilities which appear probable to such things as, though possible, appear improbable. Far from producing a plan made up of improbable incidents, he should, if possible, admit no one circumstance of that kind; or, if he does, it should be exterior to the action itself, like the ignorance of Oedipus concerning the manner in which Laius died; not within the drama, like the narrative of what happened at the Pythian games in the *Electra;* or in the *Mysians,* the man who travels from Tegea to Mysia without speaking.

To say that without these circumstances the fable would have been destroyed is a ridiculous excuse: the poet should take care, from the first, not to construct his fable in that manner. If, however, anything of this kind has been admitted, and yet is made to pass under some colour of probability, it may be allowed, though even in itself absurd. Thus in the Odyssey, the improbable account of the manner in which Ulysses was landed upon the shore of Ithaca is such as in the hands of an ordinary poet would evidently have been intolerable; but here the absurdity is concealed under the various beauties of other kinds with which the poet has embellished it.

The diction should be most laboured in the idle parts of the poem—those in which neither manners nor sentiments prevail; for the manners and the sentiments are only obscured by too splendid a diction.

Homer and the Oral Tradition

MILMAN PARRY

Milman Parry died an accidental death in 1935 at the age of thirty-three. Despite his short life, he had become one of the world's leading classical scholars and an authority on Homer and Homeric verse. An American, he had lived in France for some four years and in 1928 took the coveted degree of Docteur-es-Lettres at the University of Paris. In 1930 he joined the faculty of Harvard University and remained there for the rest of his life. His doctoral thesis had been on a Homeric topic, the traditional epithet in Homer. From this beginning he continued his work on Homer, becoming especially interested in Homer as an oral, traditional poet and in the ancient tradition that produced him.

The poet who composes with only the spoken word a poem of any length must be able to fit his words into the mould of his verse after a fixed pattern. Unlike the poet who writes out his lines—or even dictates them—he cannot think without hurry about his next word, nor change what he has made, nor, before going on, read over what he has just written. Even if one wished to imagine him making his verses alone, one could not suppose the slow finding of the next word, the pondering of the verses just made, the memorizing of each verse. Even though the poet have an unusual memory, he cannot, without paper, make of his own words a poem of any length. He must have for his use word-groups all made to fit his verse and tell what he has to tell. In composing he will do no more than put together for his needs phrases which he has often heard or used himself, and which, grouping themselves in accordance with a fixed pattern of thought, come naturally to make the sentence and the verse; and he will recall his poem easily, when he wishes to say it over, because he will be guided anew by the same play of words and phrases as before. The style of such poetry is in many ways very unlike that to which we are used. The oral poet expresses only ideas for which he has a fixed means of expression. He is by no means the servant of his diction: he can put his phrases together in an endless number of ways; but still they set bounds and forbid him the search of a style which would be altogether his own. For the style which he uses is not his at all: it is the creation of a long line of poets or even of an entire people. No one man could get together any but the smallest part of the diction which is needed for making verses orally, and which is made of a really vast number of word-groups each of which serves two ends: it expresses a given idea in fitting terms and fills just the space in the verse which allows it to be joined to the phrases which go before and after and which, with it, make the sentence. As one poet finds a phrase which is both pleasing and easily used, the group takes it up, and its survival is a further proving of these two prime qualities. It is the sum of single phrases thus found, tried, and kept which makes up the diction. Finally, the poem which is a thing of sound and not of writing is known apart from its author only because it is composed in the same style which others use and so can remember. Writing may be known, and the poem may be dictated and recorded, and the knowledge of writing may thus have some bearing on the text of the poem. But it will not have any upon its style, nor upon its form, nor upon its life in the group of poets and the social group of which its author was a part.

Such in its broadest lines is the composition of oral poetry as it is practiced in our own times in Serbia, among the Tuaregs, in Afghanistan, and in many other places; and it is clear that the best way of knowing whether a style is oral and traditional is to hear it in use, or, lacking that, to compare the recorded work of several poets who have made their verses out of the same formulas. But we cannot do either of these things for the Greek epic. There is too little known about the making of the early poetry in hexameters for us to liken the Singers to the Serbian Guslars without more ado, or to make of Homer a Singer like any other. Moreover, we cannot date the works of this early time at all surely, and we have nothing to show us that any one of the poems we have was made by a Singer. Opinion generally grants a vague body of traditional epic formulas, and we have a certain amount of poetry composed in a style which is either entirely or nearly like that of the *Iliad* and *Odyssey*; but the notion is also current that Homeric phrases found outside these two poems are more or less due to the studied imitation of the style which one poet made. We should be well off if we knew for sure that Homer could not write, but writing may have been known in Ionia in his time, whatever were the uses it was put to. If we are to draw any solid conclusions about the style of Homer, we have only one course to follow. Seeking 'the solution from the text' we must see whether the diction of the *Iliad* and of the *Odyssey* is of a sort which can be understood only as a traditional and oral technique of making verses by means of formulas. The reasoning will be as follows. First, we shall define the formula. Then we shall look to see what means there are of telling whether a formula is traditional or not. The nature of the formula will show us that the more formulas we find in a poet's diction, the smaller is the portion of them which could be the work of that single poet. We shall then be led to a study of the verse of poets who we know wrote, that we may learn how often the formula can appear in written verse. Finally, having seen if the formulas in Homer's verse are so much more common that they suffer no comparison with those of any written poetry, and having thus learned how much of the formulaic element is surely traditional, we shall be able to consider what reasons there are to say that Homer's is an oral style. . . .

The formula in the Homeric poems may be defined as *a group of words which is regularly employed under the same metrical conditions to express a given essential idea*. The essential part of the idea is that which remains after one has counted out everything in the expression which is purely for the sake of style. . . . The word-group is employed regularly when the poet uses it without second thought as the natural means of getting his idea into verse. The definition thus implies the metrical usefulness of the formula. It is not necessary that a poet use one certain formula when he has a given idea to express and a given space of the verse to fill, since there can be formulas of like metrical value and meaning which can take the place of one another, though they are rare in Homer. But if a formula is to be used regularly there must be a steady need for it. . . . The simple number of times the phrase appears is the direct measure of its usefulness, though if one wishes further proof a study of its uses shows it to be part of a fixed device for making hundreds of verses. Kurt Witte's remark that the language of the Homeric poems is the work of the epic verse is by definition true also of the Homeric diction so far as it is made up of formulas. When one has added the factor of the story, since it is this which gives the poet his ideas, and that of the poetic merit of the expression, which also must have its share in the making and the keeping of it, one may state the principle as follows: *the formulas in any poetry are due, so far as their ideas go, to the theme, their rhythm is fixed by the verse-form, but their art is that of the poets who made them and of the poets who kept them*. . . .

There is one other thing to note before leaving this subject: the problem of the formula is not that of literary influence. This fact more than any other has been overlooked by those who have dealt with traditional style.

How the Stories Are Told

WILLIAM A. CAMPS

William A. Camps, master of Pembroke College at Cambridge University, is a classical scholar of considerable reputation. In An Introduction to Homer, *he surveys the contemporary view of Homer and offers a detailed analysis of the* Iliad *and the* Odyssey. *This selection deals with how the stories are actually told and their effect on the hearer. Camps sees the narrative process in the Homerian epics as essentially dramatic rather than narrative, the characters telling their stories rather than the author narrating them. But even in the narration there is dramatic power.*

In the *Iliad* and *Odyssey* the stories are presented partly in dramatic form, the poet's characters speaking in their own persons, and the element of pure narrative being reduced accordingly. This now familiar procedure was remarked by Aristotle (*Poetics* 24.14) as a peculiar merit of the *Iliad* and *Odyssey,* distinguishing them, in the extent of its employment, from all other poetic stories that he knew. In fact, about half of the total extent of the *Iliad* and *Odyssey* consists of direct speech of the participants. Seldom in either are there more than fifty continuous lines of uninterrupted narrative.

Thus even the *Iliad*'s predominantly narrative accounts of battle are diversified at intervals by the utterances of the fighting men, as they challenge or taunt their enemies, or concert action with friends, or shout encouragement or admonition; while in the *Odyssey* the predominantly narrative account of Odysseus' past adventures is punctuated here and there by his exchanges with giant or witch, or his instructions to his men, or (when he is alone on his way from Calypso's island to Phaeacia) by soliloquy. But more forcibly illustrative than this of the truth of Aristotle's remark is the fact that the personal tragedy of Achilles which makes the central theme of the *Iliad* is expressed essentially in four successive scenes of dramatic dialogue: the quarrel with Agamemnon, the rejection of Agamemnon's envoys' appeal, the scene with Thetis after Patroclus' death in which Achilles gives voice to his remorse and his new resolve, and the final scene in which Priam's entreaty wakes his sympathy and restores his humanity. And in the *Odyssey* the greater part of the story unfolds in conversations in domestic settings (Ithaca, Pylos, Sparta, Calypso's island, Phaeacia, and Ithaca again), in which the characters reveal their relations with one another and their reactions to the situation that has resulted from the long absence of Odysseus, and to the emergence of

31

Telemachus into manhood, and to the appearance of the mysterious castaway who will turn out in the end to be Odysseus himself come home.

The dramatic form of presentation animates the stories throughout, because it interweaves with the movement of events a continuous and varied flow of human reactions to them: everything that happens elicits a positive response of human thought or feeling. Especially it intensifies passion and pathos, because terror and pity and grief are expressed directly by the people who experience them: the terror, for instance, of Hector's father and mother as they see him expose himself to certain death, and of his wife as she hears later the groans of the spectators on the wall; the pity of Achilles for Priam; the grief of the survivors of the war at Troy when the talk in Nestor's and Menelaus' houses turns their thoughts to the friends who did not survive. There are also two further particular reasons why the direct speech of the characters in the stories helps to reinforce the impression of their reality. First, because the impression of an extraordinary quality (the beauty of Helen, the magnificence of Menelaus' palace) can be imparted through the mouth of a third party, with the credibility that we attach by instinct to the spontaneous testimony of a witness present in time and place upon the scene: the measure of the remarkable is its effect on the beholder. Secondly, because our poet has the gift of reproducing an accent or manner or habit of speech that an experience of human behaviour which we share with him notes with a certain alacrity of recognition as permanently true to life: the manner of a mother comforting her child, of a woman welcoming a visitor at her door, of a young girl talking to an affectionate father, of an old nurse with her babies now grown up—"dear child" says Eurycleia to the forty-year-old Odysseus as he stands all bloodied among the corpses of the men he has killed. No less exactly recognizable is the crescendo of provocation and counter-provocation that raises the tempers in the quarrel scene that begins the *Iliad;* and the outpouring later of Achilles' long-brooded grievance, with its repetitions, and indignant questions, and insistent accumulated negatives.

This same appeal to experience which we share with the poet distinguishes the narrative as well as the dramatic element in both poems. The poet sees and hears in his imagination the story that he is telling. He sees and hears things and people at rest and in movement. He selects, whether by instinct or conscious purpose, the particulars that will help his hearers to see and hear, and feel, with him the reality of the story that is unfolding. The particulars which he thus selects are often very small, even trivial, in themselves: the hand that plucks a dress to attract attention, the wail of a frightened baby, the gentle disengagement of an embrace, the closing of a door-latch, the sound of a footstep, the glance that a person entering a room casts around in search of somewhere to sit. Of course the particulars chosen are usually less minute, and have often a very evidently distinctive character: an archer standing with bow full drawn, or a drunken giant slumped on his back with head askew. The foremost and commonest consequence of the choice is that it urgently but effortlessly invites us to see and hear with the poet. But sometimes, indeed often, the detail chosen and offered us not only is readily seen or heard in the imagination, but also expresses or illustrates something additional to itself: the gentle movement with which Achilles disengages himself from Priam's suppliant hands is the visible expression of the change of his temper from hate to sympathy, the posture of the giant illustrates the fact of his drunken stupor. Finally, the chosen particular is often one that evokes a quick response from our own experience, so that across the 2,000 years and more that separate us in time we not only see and hear with the poet but enter directly as well into his feelings and those of the people in his story: we share with them our acquaintance with the behaviour of a frightened baby and the slow wagging of an old dog's tail in recognition of a friend, and when we surface from being under water we do just as Odysseus did after his submersion by the wave that swept him from his raft: "at last he came up; and he spat away the salt water that streamed down from his head."

These characteristics of the poet's way of telling his story are important enough to invite documentation with some further instances.

Thus, lame Hephaestus stumping round the table as he serves the gods their wine, or Menelaus dragging Paris by the chin-strap of his helmet, or Ajax wielding his long pike as he strides from deck to deck of the line of ships, or Achilles standing with spear poised over the kneeling Lycaon, or Odysseus emerging naked from the bushes with a spray of foliage held before him, or Odysseus seated with bow drawn and arrow aimed for his dramatic shot through the axes—these all present easily imaginable postures to the mind's eye. And the crash with which the returning Cyclops dumps his load of faggots in the cave, or the clang of the bronze bowl in the silence of the hall when Eurycleia upsets it, or the twang of Odysseus' bowstring as he tests it before the hushed and wondering spectators—these all present easily imaginable sounds to the mind's ear, and do so moreover at dramatically exciting moments of the story. The long battle-scenes of the *Iliad* are full of precisely noted attitudes and movements and mutilations of the combatants, and their battle-cries and shouts and groans, and the ring or clatter of weapon on armour that accompanies the impact of spear or sword or arrow or hurled stone.

This effective but effortless appeal to the hearer's eye and ear is ubiquitous in both poems, and so also is its use in illustration. Achilles half-drawing his sword as his anger rises and slamming it home again in the scabbard as he regains his self-control, Diomede thrusting his spear-point into the ground in sign of peace with the adversary whom he has recognized as a family friend, Hector as he recovers consciousness kneeling and vomiting and then fainting again, Telemachus snatching his hand from the hand of Antinous as he rejects his ingratiating approach, the Phaeacian herald leading the blind bard to his place in the hall and hanging his lyre on a peg and guiding his hand to find it, the Phaeacian spectators ducking as the quoit flies by—in these and similar cases the visual image evoked is in itself sharp and vivid, and in addition is expressive of something beyond itself: the state of mind of Achilles or Diomede or Telemachus, the fact of Hector's disablement or the bard's blindness or the impression made on the bystanders by the power of the quoit-cast. This illustrative or expressive effect of the particular chosen for mention is curiously exemplified in many references to facial expression—the scowls that attend often the opening of an angry speech, and the smiles or laughs that appear in a great variety of qualities, sometimes specified by the poet and sometimes left by him for his hearers' sympathy to supply from the context: smiles grateful, conciliatory, affectionate, grimly confident, amused, ambiguous, satisfied, cruel, indulgent, approving, knowing, contemptuous, and laughs tearful, forced, vague, hysterical, tense, giggling, gleeful, and so on.

When Hector enters Troy on a mission from the battlefield, the women crowd around him in the street with eager questions about the safety of their sons and husbands. When on his way back to the battlefield he and his wife are for a little while together, they find a momentary relief from the tension of parting in shared amusement at their little son's fear of his father's helmet. When Telemachus greets his visitor at the beginning of the *Odyssey* he takes his spear from him and puts it in the spear-stand which still holds the spears Odysseus left when he went to Troy, visible daily reminders of their absent owner. When Odysseus towards the end of the story gets the deadly bow into his hands, he turns it this way and that as he inspects it at leisure, watched by the suitors with attentive curiosity and expectation. The feelings evoked in these situations are instantly and vividly recognizable to us from our own experience in other contexts; we share them with the poet and the people in the story. This is true also of the feeling we associate with being wakened by voices, as Odysseus is by the cry of Nausicaa's maids; or with the sound of voices heard passing in the quiet of night, before sleep comes, as Odysseus on the night before the crisis hears the chatter of the maidservants going out to join their lovers; or with sounds heard while their source is still mysterious or at least unseen, like the bleating of the Cyclops' sheep heard across the strait, or Circe singing inside her house, or the lowing of the fatal cattle that Odysseus and his men hear as his ship approaches the island of the sun-god, or the sound of the lyre within that Odysseus hears as he stands outside his own house, come home after twenty years. In the same way we are invited to enter directly into the feelings of Achilles, as he looks out over the plain and sees from the turn the battle is taking that something disastrous has happened, and fears but does not yet know that this is Patroclus' death; or with the feelings of Andromache, busy with her loom at home, when she hears the groan go up from the Trojans on the wall.

Questions for Review and Study

1. Write an essay comparing the selections from Parry and Camps.
2. What are the two prevailing theories about the origins of the Homeric poems?
3. What was the setting in which the *Iliad* and the *Odyssey* took place?
4. Write an essay analyzing the selection from Aristotle.

Questions for Comparison

1. Discuss Homer and Socrates as representatives of different moments in ancient Greek history. For what audience and purpose was Homer's poetry created: what kind of elite did it suppose, and what qualities did it celebrate? How do the social and cultural conditions of Greek society seem to have changed from Homer's to Socrates' day? What did Socrates most value, and why? How much does Socrates resemble those we now label "rationalists"? Does the term "heroic" apply as well to Socrates as to Homer's epic poetry? Whose achievement represents a finer expression of the human spirit?

Suggestions for Further Reading

Homer was, of course, well known in antiquity and often written of. He was commented on as early as the 5th century B.C. by the philosopher Democritus, speculating on his "divine nature." Aristotle's view of him we have already sampled in the reading from his *Poetics*, the rest of which can be read with considerable profit. Homer was also dealt with by Longinus, Horace, and Quintilian. Plato often cited him. The Roman poet Vergil, in his *Aeneid*, combined the material of the *Iliad* and the *Odyssey*.

Though known imperfectly in the West during the Middle Ages, Homer's poems themselves were recovered in the early Renaissance in Italy. More modern versions of the poems continued to appear. The best modern versions are by Richmond Lattimore: *The Iliad of Homer* and *The Odyssey of Homer*. See also Walter Shewring, *The Odyssey*, and the verse translation of Robert Fitzgerald, *The Iliad*.

There are a large number of biographies and biographical studies of Homer. One of the earliest of these is by William Von Dourn, *Of the Tribe of Homer*. A classic study is by Albert B. Lord, *The Singer of Tales*. One of the best is C. M. Bowra's *Homer.* A specialized study is by Mark W. Edwards, *Homer,* as is *Homer's Original Genius,* by K. Simonsuuri. See also Scott Richardson's *The Homeric Narrater.*

The number of critical editions of Homer and his poems is even greater. Two of the best are excerpted in this chapter: Milman Parry, *The Making of Homeric Verse,* and William A. Camps, *An Introduction to Homer.* A classic work is the course of Harvard lectures by Gilbert Murray, *The Rise of the Greek Epic.* Among the leading Homeric authorities is G. S. Kirk, who has edited a six-volume *Commentaries on the Iliad.* Another work by Kirk is his compilation of thirteen of the best articles published in the previous ten years, *The Language and Background of Homer.* Kirk also has a one-volume work of criticism and interpretation, *The Songs of Homer,* and an abbreviated version, *Homer and the Epic.* He also has a specialized study, *Homer and the Oral Tradition.* Another leading Homeric authority is Denys L. Page. See his two-volume *History and the Homeric Iliad,* a definitive study of the historical background of the Homeric poems, and *The Homeric Odyssey,* a series of lectures analyzing the *Odyssey.*

An excellent recent work is *The Ages of Homer,* edited by Jan B. Carter and Sarah P. Morris, a series of essays and papers on Homer and his time by leading Homeric authorities. There are two very good books on Homer's use of language, *Studies in the Language of Homer,* by George P. Shipp and *The Language of Homer,* by Richard P. Martin. See also Jasper Griffin's *Homer on Life and Death* and Howard Clarke's *Homer's Readers.*

There are several good books on the historical background and setting of the *Iliad* and the *Odyssey.* Two of the best are by the long-time Cambridge historian M. I. Finley, *Early Greece* and *The World of Odysseus.* There are three works specifically on the Mycenaean world: T. B. L. Webster, *From Mycenae to Homer;* Martin P. Nilsson, *The Mycenaean Origin of Greek Mythology;* and William Taylour, *The Mycenaeans.* (Titles with an asterisk are out of print.)

Bowra, C. M. *Homer.* London: Duckworth, 1972.

Camps, William A. *An Introduction to Homer.* Oxford: Clarendon Press, 1980.

Carter, Jan B., and Sarah P. Morris, eds. *The Ages of Homer, A Tribute to Emily Townsend Vermeule.* Austin: University of Texas Press, 1995.

Clarke, Howard. *Homer's Readers: A Historical Introduction to the "Iliad" and the "Odyssey."* Newark, N.J.: University of Delaware Press, 1981.

Edwards, Mark W. *Homer: The Poet of the Iliad.* Baltimore: Hopkins, 1987.

Finley, M. I. *Early Greece: The Bronze and Archaic Ages.* Rev. ed. 1981. London: Chatto and Windus, 1970.

———. *The World of Odysseus.* 2nd rev. ed. New York: Viking Press, 1978, reissued 1982.

Fitzgerald, Robert. *The Iliad.* Garden City, N.Y.: Anchor Books, 1974, reissued 1984.

Griffin, Jasper. *Homer on Life and Death*. Oxford: Clarendon Press, 1983.

Kirk, G. S. *Commentaries on the Iliad*. Cambridge and New York: Cambridge University Press, 1985–93.

———. *Homer and the Epic*. Cambridge: Cambridge University Press, 1965, reprinted 1974.

———. *Homer and the Oral Tradition*. Cambridge and New York: Cambridge University Press, 1976.

———. *The Songs of Homer*. Cambridge: Cambridge University Press, 1962, reprinted 1977.

———, ed. *The Language and Background of Homer: Some Recent Studies and Controversies*. Cambridge: W. Heffer, 1964, reissued 1967.

Lattimore, Richmond. *The Iliad of Homer*. Chicago: University of Chicago Press, 1951.

———. *The Odyssey of Homer*. New York: Harper & Row, 1967.

Lord, Albert B. *The Singer of Tales*. Cambridge, Mass.: Harvard University Press, 1960, reissued 1978 and 1981.

Martin, Richard P. *The Language of Homer: Speech and Performance in the "Iliad."* Ithaca, N.Y.: Cornell University Press, 1989.

Murray, Gilbert. *The Rise of the Greek Epic*. 2nd ed., revised and enlarged. Oxford: Clarendon Press, 1911.*

Nilsson, Martin P. *The Mycenaean Origin of Greek Mythology*. Berkeley: University of California Press, 1983.

Page, Denys L. *History and the Homeric Iliad*. Berkeley and Los Angeles: University of California Press, 1959.

———. *The Homeric Odyssey*. Oxford: Clarendon Press, 1966.

Parry, Milman. *The Making of Homeric Verse, The Collected Papers of Milman Parry*, ed. Adam Parry. Oxford: Clarendon Press, 1971.

Richardson, Scott. *The Homeric Narrator*. Nashville, Tenn.: Vanderbilt University Press, 1990.

Shewring, Walter. *The Odyssey*. New York: Oxford University Press, 1980.

Shipp, George P. *Studies in the Language of Homer*. 2nd ed. Cambridge: Cambridge University Press, 1972.

Simonsuuri, K. *Homer's Original Genius*. Cambridge: Cambridge University Press, 1979.

Taylour, William. *The Mycenaeans*. Rev. ed. London and New York: Thames and Hudson, 1983.

Von Dourn, William. *Of the Tribe of Homer*. 1932. Reprint, Darby, Pa.: Arden Library, 1980.

Webster, T. B. L. *From Mycenae to Homer*. New York: Norton, 1964, reprinted 1977.

THE IMAGE OF
SOCRATES:
MAN OR MYTH?

c. 470 B.C.	Born
c. 431–424 B.C.	Served in Peloponnesian War
423 B.C.	Satirized in Aristophanes' *The Clouds*
406–405 B.C.	Served as a member of Athenian executive council
c. 423–399 B.C.	Developed the "Socratic method"
399 B.C.	Trial and death

By the lifetime of Socrates, in the late fifth century B.C., Greek civilization was almost at an end. This historic civilization was centered in Socrates' own city of Athens, which Pericles proudly called "the school of Hellas." But that magnificent city, which has so captivated our imagination, was widely regarded by its fellow city-states as a threat to their own independence—and with more than a little justification.

This threat led to the great Peloponnesian War, so vividly recounted in the pages of Socrates' contemporary, the historian Thucydides. Athens and its subject states were set against its arch-rival Sparta and Sparta's allies, the Peloponnesian League. It was a long, costly, and enervating war of almost thirty years' duration, and Athens finally lost it. Athens was humiliated, forced to accept its enemies' terms, and stripped of its subject states, its wealth, its navy. The buoyant optimism that had earlier characterized the city was one of the prime casualties of the war, along with confidence in its institutions and even in many of the presuppositions of its public life and private morality. It is in the backwash of these events that we must seek the life, and the death, of Socrates.

Socrates was surely the most famous Athenian of his age. Yet despite that fame, the facts of his life remain stubbornly vague. He was not a public official; hence we do not have archival records to rely on. And though he is a famous figure in literature, he actually wrote nothing himself to which we can refer. There are scattered references to him in Aristotle; a substantial (though prosaic) account in the works of Xenophon, who knew him; and, of course, the principal source of our information about him, the dialogues of the great philosopher Plato, who was Socrates' adoring pupil and disciple and made him the main character in most of his dialogues. And there are references and anecdotes from a considerable number of near-contemporary accounts of Socrates that have been preserved, although the original sources are now lost.

What we know about Socrates is this. He was born an Athenian citizen about 470 B.C. His family belonged to the class of small artisans; his mother was a midwife and his father a stone mason. Socrates himself followed his father's trade. Rather late in life he married Xanthippe, and they had three sons, two of them still very young at the time of their father's death. Like most able-bodied Athenians of his time, Socrates was a veteran of the Peloponnesian War and even served with some distinction. On two occasions he seems to have held office on the large civic boards and commissions that carried on the business of the city. But generally he avoided public life. From a number of surviving descriptions and portrait busts we know what Socrates looked like—small and balding, anything but the lofty Greek ideal of physical beauty. We also know that he spent most of his time going about the city, trailed by a delighted and curious crowd of bright young aristocrats, asking often embarrassing questions of people who interested him, usually public officials and individuals of substance and position. This practice was to the detriment of his own family and his trade. Socrates was a poor man.

The Clouds

ARISTOPHANES

The preceding bare account of Socrates is supplemented—one must almost say contradicted—by a single additional source, The Clouds *of Aristophanes. This work is of considerable value in that it is the only really substantial account of Socrates by a mature contemporary. Even Plato, our principal source of information, was forty years younger than Socrates, knew him only as an old man, and wrote* The Dialogues *many years after Socrates' death.* The Clouds *is, of course, not a biography. It is a play, by the greatest of Greek comic dramatists, in which Socrates is not only one of its chief characters but also the object of its satire.*

Aristophanes was a conservative, and his plays are a catalog of his objections to the management of the war and public policy, the state of literature and philosophy, the subversion of the stern old virtues "of our forefathers," and the "new morality" that he saw about him. In The Clouds *he accused Socrates of being a professional teacher who received, nay extracted, money for his "lessons"—which was not true. He denounced him as a cynical, opportunistic atheist—which was also apparently not the case. He attributed to him an expert competence in natural philosophy—which was highly unlikely. And, in what was perhaps the most unfounded of all his charges, he portrayed Socrates as being the chief of the Sophists.*

The Sophists were a school of professional teachers, then very popular in Athens, who taught young men of wealth and position (usually for substantial fees) the techniques of public life, mostly logic and oratorical persuasion. The Sophists also tended to a flexible morality in which success was to be preferred to virtue, victory to either morality or philosophic consistency. It is a more than Socratic irony that Socrates should have been depicted as one of them, for it was squarely against the Sophists and their moral relativism that he had taken his stand. The whole point of his life, the reason he engaged other people in his famous questioning and endured their animosity, the entire "Socratic method" was an attempt to make people understand that there are moral absolutes, unchanging abstract principles of conduct to which they must ultimately resort.

Why Aristophanes portrayed Socrates in this fashion we do not know. Perhaps he genuinely believed that Socrates was a Sophist. Or perhaps he knew the truth but simply did not care, and made use of Socrates' notoriety in Athens to score his own point about the scandalous decline of education and what he regarded as philosophic quackery.

In any event, the play is cruel, mean, and malicious, but it is also outrageously funny. And it gives us a view, however hostile, of the historical Socrates.

The Clouds *opens in the house of Strepsiades, a foolish old farmer, whose son's extravagant passion for racehorses—his name is Pheidippides—has piled up so many debts that the old man is faced with ruin. One night, unable to sleep, Strepsiades decides to enroll the boy in the Sophist's school down the street. He calls*

41

it the "Thinkery." But Pheidippides will have nothing to do with "those filthy charlatans you mean—those frauds, those barefoot pedants with the look of death. Chairephon and that humbug, Sokrates."

The old man then decides to go to the school himself. He kicks on the door, and a student-doorman answers. As they stand at the door, the student extols the wisdom of his master Socrates, citing a number of examples, not the least of which is Socrates' resolution of the problem of how the gnat hums. "According to him, the intestinal tract of the gnat is of puny proportions, and through this diminutive duct the gastric gas of the gnat is forced under pressure down to the rump. At that point the compressed gases, as through a narrow valve, escape with a whoosh, thereby causing the characteristic tootle or cry of the flatulent gnat."

Strepsiades is suitably impressed. "Why, Thales himself was an amateur com-pared to this! Throw open the Thinkery! Unbolt the door and let me see this wizard Sokrates in person. Open up! I'm MAD for education!" And Strepsiades enters the school.

STREPSIADES

Look: who's that dangling up there in the basket?

STUDENT

Himself.

STREPSIADES

Who's Himself?

STUDENT

Sokrates.

STREPSIADES

SOKRATES!

Then call him down. Go on. Give a great big shout.

STUDENT

Hastily and apprehensively taking his leave.

Er . . . *you* call him. I'm a busy man.

Exit Student.

STREPSIADES

O Sokrates!

No answer from the basket.

Yoohoo. Sokrates!

SOKRATES

From a vast philosophical height.

            Well, creature of a day?

STREPSIADES

What in the world are you doing up there?

SOKRATES

                                   Ah, sir,
I walk upon the air and look down upon the sun
from a superior standpoint.

STREPSIADES

                      Well, I suppose it's better
that you sneer at the gods from a basket up in the air
than do it down here on the ground.

SOKRATES

                           Precisely. You see,
only by being suspended aloft, by dangling
my mind in the heavens and mingling my rare thought
with the ethereal air, could I ever achieve strict
scientific accuracy in my survey of the vast empyrean.
Had I pursued my inquiries from down there on the ground,
my data would be worthless. The earth, you see, pulls down
the delicate essence of thought to its own gross level.

As an afterthought.

Much the same thing happens with watercress.

STREPSIADES

Ecstatically bewildered.

                              You don't say?
Thought draws down . . . delicate essence . . . into
watercress. O dear little Sokrates, please come down.
Lower away, and teach me what I need to know!

Sokrates is slowly lowered earthwards.

SOKRATES

                             What subject?

STREPSIADES

Your course on public speaking and debating techniques.
You see, my creditors have become absolutely ferocious.

You should see how they're hounding me. What's more,
Sokrates, they're about to seize my belongings.

SOKRATES

                                        How in the
world could you fall so deeply in debt without realizing it?

STREPSIADES

How? A great, greedy horse-pox ate me up, that's how.
But that's why I want instruction in your second Logic,
you know the one—the get-away-without-paying argument.
I'll pay you *any* price you ask. I swear it.
By the gods.

SOKRATES

            By the gods? The gods, my dear simple fellow,
are a mere expression coined by vulgar superstition.
We frown upon such coinage here.

STREPSIADES

                                What do *you* swear by?
Bars of iron, like the Byzantines?

SOKRATES

                                Tell me, old man,
would you honestly like to learn the truth, the *real* truth,
about the gods?

STREPSIADES

            By Zeus, I sure would. The *real* truth. . . .

[*At this point the chorus of clouds enters, singing.*]

STREPSIADES

Holy Zeus, Sokrates, who were those ladies that sang
that solemn hymn? Were they heroines of mythology?

SOKRATES

                                No, old man.
Those were the Clouds of heaven, goddesses of men of
leisure and philosophers. To them we owe our repertoire of
verbal talents: our eloquence, intellect, fustian, casuistry,
force, wit, prodigious vocabulary, circumlocutory skill—

. . . .

[*The leader of the chorus greets them.*]

KORYPHAIOS

                    Hail, superannuated man!
Hail, old birddog of culture!

To Sokrates.

                    And hail to you, O Sokrates,
high priest of poppycock!
                    Inform us what your wishes are.
For of all the polymaths on earth, it's you we most prefer—
. . . .
sir, for your swivel-eyes, your barefoot swagger down the
street, because you're poor on our account and terribly
affected.

STREPSIADES

Name of Earth, what a voice! Solemn and holy and awful!

SOKRATES

These are the only gods there are. The rest are but figments.

STREPSIADES

Holy name of Earth! Olympian Zeus is a figment?

SOKRATES

Zeus?
        What Zeus?
                    Nonsense.
                    There is no Zeus.

STREPSIADES

                              No Zeus?
Then *who* makes it rain? Answer me that.

SOKRATES

                              Why, the Clouds,
of course.
            What's more, the proof is incontrovertible.
                              For instance,
have you ever yet seen rain when you didn't see a cloud?
But if your hypothesis were correct, Zeus could drizzle
from an empty sky
while the clouds were on vacation.

STREPSIADES

                By Apollo, you're right. A pretty
proof.
And to think I always used to believe the rain was just Zeus
pissing through a sieve.
          All right, *who* makes it thunder?
Brrr. I get goosebumps just saying it.

SOKRATES

              The Clouds again,
of course. A simple process of Convection.

STREPSIADES

                 I admire you,
but I don't follow you.

SOKRATES

    Listen. The Clouds are a saturate water-solution.
Tumescence in motion, of necessity, produces precipitation.
When these distended masses collide—*boom!*
              Fulmination.

STREPSIADES

But who makes them move before they collide? Isn't that
Zeus?

SOKRATES

Not Zeus, idiot. The Convection-principle!

STREPSIADES

               Convection? That's
a new one.
Just think. So Zeus is out and Convection-principle's in.
Tch, tch.
    But wait: you haven't told me who makes it thunder.

SOKRATES

But I just *finished* telling you! The Clouds are water-packed;
they collide with each other and explode because of the
pressure.

STREPSIADES

    Yeah?
And what's your proof for *that?*

SOKRATES

Why, take yourself as example.
You know that meat-stew the vendors sell at the Panathenaia?[1]
How it gives you the cramps and your stomach
starts to rumble?

STREPSIADES

Yes,
by Apollo! I remember. What an awful feeling! You feel
sick and your belly churns and the fart rips loose like
thunder. First just a gurgle, *pappapax;* then louder,
pappaPAPAXapaX, and finally like thunder,
PAPAPAPAXAPAXAPPAPAXapap!

SOKRATES

Precisely.
First think of the tiny fart that your intestines make.
Then consider the heavens: their infinite farting is thunder.
For thunder and farting are, in principle, one and the same.

[*Strepsiades is convinced and is initiated into Socrates' school. But, alas, he is incapable of learning the subtleties Socrates sets out to teach him and is contemptuously dismissed from the school. Then the leader of the chorus suggests that he fetch his son to study in his place. A splendid idea! As Strepsiades drags his son on to the scene, Pheidippides protests.*]

PHEIDIPPIDES

But Father,
what's the matter with you? Are you out of your head?
Almighty Zeus, you must be mad!

STREPSIADES

"Almighty Zeus!"
What musty rubbish! Imagine, a boy your age
still believing in Zeus!

PHEIDIPPIDES

What's so damn funny?

STREPSIADES

It tickles me when the heads of toddlers like you
are still stuffed with such outdated notions. Now then,

---

[1]The quadrennial festival of Athena, the patron goddess of Athens.

listen to me and I'll tell you a secret or two
that might make an intelligent man of you yet.
But remember: you mustn't breathe a word of this.

PHEIDIPPIDES
A word of what?

STREPSIADES
　　　　　Didn't you just swear by Zeus?

PHEIDIPPIDES
I did.

STREPSIADES
　　Now learn what Education can do for *you:*
Pheidippides, there is no Zeus.

PHEIDIPPIDES
　　　　　　　There is no Zeus?

STREPSIADES
No Zeus. Convection-principle's in power now.
Zeus has been banished.

PHEIDIPPIDES
　　　　　Drivel!

STREPSIADES
　　　　　　　　Take my word for it,
it's absolutely true.

PHEIDIPPIDES
　　　　Who says so?

STREPSIADES
　　　　　　Sokrates.
And Chairephon too. . . .

PHEIDIPPIDES
Are you so far gone on the road to complete insanity
you'd believe the word of those charlatans?

STREPSIADES

Hush, boy.
For shame. I won't hear you speaking disrespectfully
of such eminent scientists and geniuses. And, what's more,
men of such fantastic frugality and Spartan thrift,
they regard baths, haircuts, and personal cleanliness
generally as an utter waste of time and money—whereas
you, dear boy, have taken me to the cleaner's so many times,
I'm damn near washed up. Come on, for your father's sake,
go and learn.

[*Some time later*]
Enter Strepsiades from his house, counting on his fingers.

STREPSIADES

Five days, four days, three days, two days, and then
that one day of the days of the month
I dread the most that makes me fart with fear—
the last day of the month, Duedate for debts,
when every dun in town has solemnly sworn
to drag me into court and bankrupt me completely.
And when I plead with them to be more reasonable—
"But PLEASE, sir. Don't demand the whole sum now.
Take something on account. I'll pay you later."—
they snort they'll never see the day, curse me
for a filthy swindler and say they'll sue.
                                                Well,
let them. If Pheidippides has learned to talk,
I don't give a damn for them and their suits.
                                        Now then,
a little knock on the door and we'll have the answer.

He knocks on Sokrates' door and calls out.

Porter!
        Hey, porter!

Sokrates opens the door.

SOKRATES

Ah, Strepsiades. Salutations.

STREPSIADES

Same to you, Sokrates.

He hands Sokrates a bag of flour.

Here. A token of my esteem.
Call it an honorarium. Professors always get honorariums.

Snatching back the bag.

But wait: has Pheidippides learned his rhetoric yet—. . . .

SOKRATES

Taking the bag.

He has mastered it.

STREPSIADES

O great goddess Bamboozle!

SOKRATES

Now, sir, you can evade any legal action you wish to.

[*But instead of help with his creditors, Strepsiades gets a very different kind of treatment from his son.*]

With a bellow of pain and terror, Strepsiades plunges out of his house, hotly pursued by Pheidippides with a murderous stick.

STREPSIADES

OOOUUUCH!!!
          HALP!
                    For god's sake, help me!

Appealing to the Audience.

                                   Friends!
Fellow-countrymen! Aunts! Uncles! Fathers! Brothers!
To the rescue!
          He's beating me!
                    Help me!
                              Ouuch!
O my poor head!
          Ooh, my jaw!

To Pheidippides.

                    —You great big bully,
Hit your own father, would you?

PHEIDIPPIDES

                    Gladly, Daddy.

STREPSIADES

You hear that? The big brute *admits* it.

PHEIDIPPIDES

                    Admit it? Hell,
I *proclaim* it. . . .
         Would a logical demonstration
convince you?

STREPSIADES

      A logical demonstration? You mean to tell me
you can *prove* a shocking thing like that?

PHEIDIPPIDES

                  Elementary, really.
What's more, you can choose the logic. Take your pick.
Either one.

STREPSIADES

      Either *which?*

PHEIDIPPIDES

            Either *which?* Why,
Socratic logic or pre-Socratic logic. Either logic.
Take your pick.

STREPSIADES

      Take my pick, damn you? Look,
who do you think paid for your shyster education anyway?
And now you propose to convince *me* that there's nothing
wrong in whipping your own father?

PHEIDIPPIDES

             I not only propose it:
I propose to *prove* it. Irrefutably, in fact. Rebuttal
is utterly inconceivable. . . .

[*Pheidippides then "proves" that since his father beat him as a child "for your own damn good" "because I loved you," then it is only "a fortiori" logic that the father be beaten by the son, since "old men logically deserve to be beaten more, since at their age they have clearly less excuse for the mischief that they do."*]

There is a long tense silence as the full force of this crushing argument takes its effect upon Strepsiades.

STREPSIADES

What?

But how. . . ?

Hmm,

by god, you're right!

To the Audience.

—Speaking for the older generation,
gentlemen, I'm compelled to admit defeat. The kids have
proved their point: naughty fathers should be flogged. . . .

[*But this arrogance is too much, logic or no logic, for Strepsiades.*]

STREPSIADES

O Horse's Ass, Blithering Imbecile,
Brainless Booby, Bonehead that I was to ditch the gods
for Sokrates!

*He picks up Pheidippides' stick and savagely smashes the potbellied model
of the Universe in front of the Thinkery. He then rushes to his own house
and falls on his knees before the statue of Hermes.*

—Great Hermes, I implore you!

[*Strepsiades and his slave set fire to the Thinkery and he beats the choking,
sputtering Socrates and his pallid students off the stage.*]

The Apology

PLATO

In 399 B.C., twenty-five years after The Clouds, *Socrates stood before the great
popular court of Athens. He was accused of much the same charges that had been
leveled at him by Aristophanes, specifically "that Socrates is a doer of evil, who
corrupts the youth; and who does not believe in the gods of the state, but has other
new divinities of his own." The charges were brought by three fellow Athenians,
Meletus, Lycon, and Anytus. Although only one of the accusers, Anytus, was a
person of any importance, and he only a minor political figure, the charges carried
the death penalty if the court so decided. Indeed, this was the intent of the accusers.*

*Socrates, now seventy years old, rose to speak in his own defense; he was not the
pettifogging buffoon of* The Clouds. *Perhaps that man never really existed. By
the same token, did the speaker at the trial ever exist? The trial is Socrates', but the
account of it is Plato's.* The Apology, *from* The Dialogues of Plato, *is the
"defense" of Socrates at his trial.*

How you, O Athenians, have been affected by my accusers, I cannot tell; but I know that they almost made me forget who I was—so persuasively did they speak; and yet they have hardly uttered a word of truth. But . . . first, I have to reply to the older charges and to my first accusers, and then I will go on to the later ones. For of old I have had many accusers, who have accused me falsely to you during many years; and I am more afraid of them than of Anytus and his associates, who are dangerous, too, in their own way. But far more dangerous are the others, who began when you were children, and took possession of your minds with their falsehoods, telling of one Socrates, a wise man, who speculated about the heaven above, and searched into the earth beneath, and made the worse appear the better cause. The disseminators of this tale are the accusers whom I dread; for their hearers are apt to fancy that such enquirers do not believe in the existence of the gods. And they are many, and their charges against me are of ancient date, and they were made by them in the days when you were more impressible than you are now—in childhood, or it may have been in youth—and the cause when heard went by default, for there was none to answer. And hardest of all, I do not know and cannot tell the names of my accusers; unless in the chance case of a Comic poet. . . .

I dare say, Athenians, that some one among you will reply, 'Yes, Socrates, but what is the origin of these accusations which are brought against you; there must have been something strange which you have been doing? All these rumours and this talk about you would never have arisen if you had been like other men: tell us, then, what is the cause of them, for we should be sorry to judge hastily of you.' Now I regard this as a fair challenge, and I will endeavour to explain to you the reason why I am called wise and have such an evil fame. . . .

. . . I will refer you to a witness who is worthy of credit; that witness shall be the God of Delphi—he will tell you about my wisdom, if I have any, and of what sort it is. You must have known Chaerephon; he was early a friend of mine. . . .Well, Chaerephon, as you know, was very impetuous in all his doings, and he went to Delphi and boldly asked the oracle to tell him whether—as I was saying, I must beg you not to interrupt—he asked the oracle to tell him whether any one was wiser than I was, and the Pythian prophetess answered, that there was no man wiser. Chaerephon is dead himself; but his brother, who is in court, will confirm the truth of what I am saying.

Why do I mention this? Because I am going to explain to you why I have such an evil name. When I heard the answer, I said to myself, What can the god mean? and what is the interpretation of his riddle? for I know that I have no wisdom, small or great. What then can he mean when he says that I am the wisest of men? And yet he is a god, and cannot lie; that would be against his nature. After long consideration, I thought of a method of trying the question. I reflected that if I could only find a man wiser than myself, then I might go to the god with a refutation in my hand. I should say to him, 'Here is a man who is wiser than I am; but you said that I was the wisest.' Accordingly I went to one who had the reputation of wisdom, and observed him— his name I need not mention; he was a politician whom I selected for examination—and the result was as follows: When I began to talk with him, I could not help thinking that he was not really wise, although he was thought wise by many, and still wiser by himself; and thereupon I tried to explain to him that he thought himself wise, but was not really wise; and the consequence was that he hated me, and his enmity was shared by several who were present and heard me. So I left him, saying to myself, as I went away: Well, although I do not suppose that either of us knows anything really beautiful and good, I am better off than he is,—for he knows nothing, and thinks that he knows; I neither know nor think that I know. In this latter particular, then, I seem to have slightly the advantage of him. Then I went to another who had still higher pretensions to wisdom, and my conclusion was exactly the same. Whereupon I made another enemy of him, and of many others besides him. . . .

This inquisition has led to my having many enemies of the worst and most dangerous kind, and has given occasion also to many calumnies. And I am called wise, for my hearers always imagine that I myself possess the wisdom which I find wanting in others: but the truth is, O men of Athens, that God only is wise, and by his answer he intends to show that the wisdom of men is worth little or nothing; he is not speaking of Socrates, he is only using my name by way of illustration, as if he said, He, O men, is the wisest, who, like Socrates, knows that his wisdom is in truth worth nothing. And so I go about the world, obedient to the god, and search and make enquiry into the wisdom of any one, whether citizen or stranger, who appears to be wise; and if he is not wise, then in vindication of the oracle I show him that he is not wise, and my occupation quite absorbs me, and I have no time to give either to any public matter of interest or to any concern of my own, but I am in utter poverty by reason of my devotion to the god.

There is another thing:—young men of the richer classes, who have not much to do, come about me of their own accord; they like to hear the pretenders examined, and they often imitate me, and proceed to examine others; there are plenty of persons, as they quickly discover, who think they know something, but really know little or nothing; and then those who are examined by them instead of being angry with themselves are angry with me: This confounded Socrates, they say; this villainous misleader of youth—and then if somebody asks them, Why, what evil does he practise or teach? They do not know, and cannot tell; but in order that they may not appear to be at a loss, they repeat the ready-made charges which are used against all philosophers about teaching things up in the clouds and under the earth, and having no gods and making the worse appear the better cause. . . .

Turning to the formal charges against him, Socrates dismisses them almost contemptuously, returning to the main charges as he sees them and his lifelong "argument" with his city and its citizenry.

And now, Athenians, I am not going to argue for my own sake, as you may think, but for yours, that you may not sin against the God by condemning me, who am his gift to you. For if you kill me you will not easily find a successor to me, who, if I may use such a ludicrous figure of speech, am a sort of gadfly, given to the state by God; and the state is a great and noble steed who is tardy in his motions owing to his very size, and requires to be stirred into life. I am that gadfly which God has attached to the state, and all day long and in all places am always fastening upon you, arousing and persuading and reproaching you. You will not easily find another like me, and therefore I would advise you to spare me. I dare say that you may feel out of temper (like a person who is suddenly awakened from sleep), and you think that you might easily strike me dead as Anytus advises, and then you would sleep on for the remainder of your lives, unless God in his care of you sent you another gadfly. When I say I am given to you by God, the proof of my mission is this:—if I had been like other men, I should not have neglected all my own concerns or patiently seen the neglect of them during all these years, and have been doing yours, coming to you individually like a father or elder brother, exhorting you to regard virtue; such conduct, I say, would be unlike human nature. If I had gained anything, or if my exhortations had been paid, there would have been some sense in my doing so; but now, as you will perceive, not even the impudence of my accusers dares to say that I have ever exacted or sought pay of any one; of that they have no witness. And I have a sufficient witness to the truth of what I say—my poverty. . . .

The jury returns the verdict of guilty.

There are many reasons why I am not grieved, O men of Athens, at the vote of condemnation. I expected it, and am only surprised that the votes are so nearly equal; for I had thought that the majority against me would have been far larger; but now, had thirty votes gone over to the other side, I should have been acquitted. And I may say, I think, that I have escaped Meletus. I may say more; for without the assistance of Anytus and Lycon, any one may see that he would not have had a fifth part of the votes, as the law requires, in which case he would have incurred a fine of a thousand drachmae.

And so he proposes death as the penalty. . . .

Some one will say: Yes, Socrates, but cannot you hold your tongue, and then you may go into a foreign city, and no one will interfere with you? Now I have great difficulty in making you understand my answer to this. For if I tell you that to do as you say would be a disobedience to the God, and therefore that I cannot hold my tongue, you will not believe that I am serious; and if I say again that daily to discourse about virtue, and of those other things about which you hear me examining myself and others, is the greatest good of man, and that the unexamined life is not worth living, you are still less likely to believe me. Yet I say what is true, although a thing of which it is hard for me to persuade you. Also, I have never been accustomed to think that I deserve to suffer any harm. Had I money I might have estimated the offence at what I was able to pay, and not have been much the worse. But I have none, and therefore I must ask you to proportion the fine to my means. Well, perhaps I could afford a mina, and therefore I propose that penalty: Plato, Crito, Critobulus, and Apollodorus, my friends here, bid me say thirty minae, and they will be the sureties. Let thirty minae be the penalty; for which sum they will be ample security to you. . . .

Socrates is condemned to death.

And now, O men who have condemned me, I would fain prophesy to you; for I am about to die, and in the hour of death men are gifted with prophetic power. And I prophesy to you who are my murderers, that immediately after my departure punishment far heavier than you have inflicted on me will surely await you. Me you have killed because you wanted to escape the accuser, and not to give an account of your lives. But that will not be as you suppose: far otherwise. For I say that there will be more accusers of you than there are now; accusers whom hitherto I have restrained: and as they are younger they will be more inconsiderate with you, and you will be more offended at them. If you think that by killing men you can prevent some one from censuring your evil lives, you are mistaken; that is not a way of escape which is either possible or honourable; the easiest and the noblest way is not to be disabling others, but to be improving yourselves. This is the prophecy which I utter before my departure to the judges who have condemned me.

Friends, who would have acquitted me, I would like also to talk with you about the thing which has come to pass, while the magistrates are busy, and before I go to the place at which I must die. Stay then a little, for we may as well talk with one another while there is time. You are my friends, and I should like to show you the meaning of this event which has happened to me. O my judges—for you I may truly call judges—I should like to tell you of a wonderful circumstance. Hitherto the divine faculty of which the internal oracle[2] is the source has constantly been in the habit of opposing me even about trifles, if I was going to make a slip or error in any matter; and now as you see there has come upon me that which may be thought, and is generally believed to be, the last and worst evil. But the oracle made no sign of opposition, either when I was leaving my house in the morning, or when I was on my way to the court, or while I was speaking, at anything which I was going to say; and yet I have often been stopped in the middle of a speech, but now in nothing I either said or did touching the matter in hand has the oracle opposed me. What do I take to be the explanation of this silence? I will tell you. It is an intimation that what has happened to me is a good, and that those of us who think that death is an evil are in error. For the customary sign would surely have opposed me had I been going to evil and not to good. . . .

Wherefore, O judges, be of good cheer about death, and know of a certainty, that no evil can happen to a good man, either in life or after death. He and his are not neglected by the gods; nor has my own approaching end happened by mere chance. But I see clearly that the time had arrived when it was better for me to die and be released from trouble wherefore the oracle gave no sign. For which reason, also, I am not angry with my condemners, or with my accusers; they have done me no harm, although they did not mean to do me any good; and for this I may gently blame them.

Still I have a favour to ask them. When my sons are grown up, I would ask you, O my friends, to punish them; and I would have you trouble them, as I have troubled you, if they seem to care about riches, or anything, more than about virtue; or if they pretend to be something when they are really nothing,—then reprove them, as I have reproved you, for not caring about that for which they ought to care, and thinking that they are something when they are really nothing. And if you do this, both I and my sons will have received justice at your hands.

The hour of departure has arrived, and we go our ways—I to die, and you to live. Which is better God only knows.

---

[2]This was Socrates' famous "daimon," more than a conscience, less perhaps than a separate "in-dwelling" god, but, as he claimed, at least a guiding voice.

Socrates: A Modern Perspective

MOSES HADAS AND MORTON SMITH

Which Socrates are we to choose? Is it even possible to reconstruct the real man from either the idealized, "gospel"-like account of Plato or the malicious parody of Aristophanes, or from both together? Two distinguished American professors, Moses Hadas (d. 1966) and Morton Smith, do not think so. They state their case in the following selection from their book Heroes and Gods: Spiritual Biographies in Antiquity.

As surely as the figure of Achilles is the paradigm for heroic epic, so surely is Socrates the paradigm for aretalogy.[3] He is manifestly the point of departure for the development of the genre after his time, but he is also the culmination of antecedent development. It is likely that the historical Achilles (assuming there was one) was both more and less than Homer's image of him, but even if he was exactly as the image represents him, without it he could never have served posterity as a paradigm. Nor could Socrates have served posterity except through the image Plato fashioned. It is not, strictly speaking, a developed aretalogy that Plato presents; that is to say, he does not provide a single systematic account of a career that can be used as a sacred text. Indeed, Plato's treatment made it impossible for others to elaborate the image plausibly or to reduce it to a sacred text. But the whole image, full and consistent and unmistakable, is presupposed in every Platonic dialogue which contributes to it. Undoubtedly the historical Socrates was an extraordinarily gifted and devoted teacher, and his image does undoubtedly reflect the historical figure, but the image clearly transcends the man, and the image is the conscious product of Plato's art.

Because of Plato, and only Plato, Socrates' position in the tradition of western civilization is unique. Other fifth-century Greeks have won admiration bordering on adulation for high achievement in various fields, but only Socrates is completely without flaw; the perfect image leaves no opening for impugning his wisdom or temperance or courage or wholehearted devotion to his mission. We might expect that a dim figure out of the imperfectly recorded past, an Orpheus or Pythagoras or even Empedocles, might be idealized, but Socrates lived in the bright and merciless light of a century that could ostracize Aristides, deny prizes to Sophocles, throw Pericles out of office. Perhaps the nearest approach to Plato's idealization of Socrates is Thu-

---

[3]The worship of, or reverence for, nobility or virtue; from the Greek *areté*, "virtue."

cydides' idealization of Pericles; some critics have thought that Thucydides' main motive in writing his history was to glorify Pericles. But Thucydides never claimed for Pericles the kind of potency that Plato suggests for Socrates, and on the basis of Thucydides' own history the world has accepted Pericles as a farseeing but not preternaturally gifted or wholly successful statesman. Only in the case of Socrates has the idealized image effaced the reality.

What makes Plato's share in the idealization obvious is the existence of parallel accounts of Socrates that are less reverent. Plato's reports are indeed the fullest: the larger part of his extensive writings purports to be an exposition of Socrates' thought. But there are other witnesses. . . . In the *Clouds* of Aristophanes, Socrates is the central figure, and the boot is on a different foot, for it was produced in 423, when Socrates was not yet fifty and therefore in the prime of his career but not yet shielded by the extraordinary eminence later bestowed upon him. Nor was Aristophanes' comedy the only caricature of Socrates. Also in 423 a comic Socrates figures in a play of Amipsias and two years later in one of Eupolis. These poets, it must be remembered, were dealing with a personality that was familiar to them and also, perhaps more important, to their audiences.

The caricature, certainly Aristophanes' and presumably the others' also, is of course grossly unfair: Socrates did not meddle with natural science or receive pay for his teaching, as the *Clouds* alleges he did: the most carping critic could not question his probity. The very absurdity of the charges and the topsy-turvy carnival atmosphere of the festival eliminated the possibility of rancor; in the *Symposium*, of which the fictive date is a decade after the presentation of the *Clouds*, Plato represents Aristophanes and Socrates as consorting on the friendliest of terms. And yet it is plain that Aristophanes' large audience was not outraged by the frivolous treatment of a saint, and in the *Apology*, which Socrates is presumed to have pronounced at his defense twenty-five years later, the point is made that the caricature had seriously prejudiced the public against Socrates. To some degree, then, the caricature is a significant corrective to later idealization. . . .

Really to know where the truth lies, . . . we should have his actual words or a public record of his deeds, but Socrates wrote nothing and was not, like Pericles, a statesman. The image is therefore not subject to correction on the basis of his own works. Aristophanes also deals harshly with Euripides, but we have Euripides' own plays to read, so that the caricature tells us more of Aristophanes than it does of Euripides. Isocrates wrote an encomium of Evagoras and Xenophon of Agesilaus, but the praise of these statesmen carries its own corrective. Of Socrates we know, or think we know, much more than of those others—what he looked like, how he dressed and walked and talked, and most of all, what he thought and taught. . . .

Actually the only significant datum in the inventory which is beyond dispute is that Socrates was condemned to death in 399 B.C. and accepted his penalty when he might have evaded it. The magnanimity of this act no one can belittle; it is enough to purify and enhance even a questionable career, and it is certainly enough to sanctify a Socrates. For Plato it clearly marked a decisive turn, as he himself records in his autobiographical *Seventh Epistle*. For him it undoubtedly crystallized the image of Socrates that fills the early dialogues. . . . All of Plato's earlier dialogues, and the more plainly in the degree of their earliness, are as much concerned with the personality of Socrates as with his teachings. His pre-eminence in reason, his devotion to his mission, his selfless concern for the spiritual welfare of his fellow men, the purity of his life, even his social gifts, are made prominent. The *Apology,* quite possibly the earliest of the Socratic pieces, is concerned with the man and his personal program, not his doctrines. Here he is made to present, without coyness or swagger or unction, his own concept of his mission to sting men, like a gadfly, to self-examination and to serve as midwife to their travail with ideas. The *Apology* also illustrates the devotion of his disciples to Socrates and the surprisingly large proportion of his jurors who were willing to acquit him. Again, in the short early dialogues, which are mainly concerned with questioning common misconceptions of such abstract nouns as "piety" or "friendship," it is the man as defined by his program, not the abstract doctrine, that is being presented. In the great central group—*Protagoras, Gorgias, Symposium, Republic*—the proportion of doctrinal content is larger, but the doctrine requires the personality of Socrates to make it plausible. The moral significance of education may emerge from the rather piratical dialectic in the *Protagoras,* but the argument takes on special meaning from Socrates' wise and tender treatment of the eager and youthful disciple who is enamored of Protagoras' reputation. That it is a worse thing for a man to inflict than to receive an injury and that a good man is incapable of being injured is the kind of doctrine which absolutely requires that its promulgator be a saint, as Socrates is pictured in the *Gorgias;* on the lips of a lesser man it would be nothing more than a rhetorical paradox. A great weight of individual prestige must similarly be built up to enable a man to enunciate the grand scheme of the *Republic,* and the occasional playfulness of the tone only emphasizes the stature of the individual who enunciates it. People too earth-bound to recognize such stature, like Thrasymachus in Book I, can only find the whole proceeding absurd. And only from a man whose special stature was recognized could the vision of Er be accepted as other than an old wives' tale.

In the *Symposium* more than in other dialogues the individuality of Socrates is underscored. It is not a trivial matter, for establishing the character of Socrates, that he could be welcome at a party of the fashionable wits of Athens, could get himself respectably groomed for the occasion, and engage in banter with his fellow guests without compromising his spiritual ascendancy one whit. We hear incidentally of his absolute bravery in battle and his disregard of self in the service of a friend, of his extraordinary physical vitality that enabled him to stand all night pondering some thought while his fellow soldiers biv- ouacked around him to watch the spectacle, of how he could lose himself in some doorway in a trance and so make himself late for his appointment until he had thought through whatever was on his mind. The subject of the *Symposium* is love, and love had been con- ceived of, in the series of speeches praising it, in a range from gross homosexuality to romantic attachment, to a cosmic principle of attrac- tion and repulsion, to Socrates' own concept . . . of an ascent to union with the highest goodness and beauty. . . .

But it is in the *Phaedo* that Socrates comes nearest to being trans- lated to a higher order of being. In prison, during the hours preced- ing his death, Socrates discourses to his devoted followers on the most timely and timeless of all questions, the immortality of the soul. The *Phaedo* is the most spiritual and the most eloquent of all dialogues; the account of Socrates' last moments is surely the second most compel- ling passion in all literature. If Plato's object was to inculcate a belief in immortality, there are of course sound practical reasons for giving the spokesman of the doctrine extraordinary prestige. In such an issue it is the personality of the teacher rather than the cogency of his arguments that is most persuasive. . . .

But the saintliness with which Socrates is endowed in the *Phaedo* seems more than a mere device to promote belief in the immortality of the soul. If belief is being inculcated, it is belief in Socrates, not in immortality. Only an occasional reader of the *Phaedo* could rehearse its arguments for immortality years or months after he had laid the book down; the saintliness of Socrates he can never forget. It is his image of Socrates rather than any specific doctrine that Plato wished to crystallize and perpetuate. From the tenor of all his writing it is clear that Plato believed that the welfare of society depended upon leadership by specially endowed and dedicated men. Ordinary men following a prescribed code would not do. Indeed, Plato conceived of his own effectiveness as teacher in much the same way; in the autobio- graphical *Seventh Epistle* he tells us that no one could claim to have apprehended his teachings merely from study of his writings: long personal contact with a master spirit is essential.

In the centuries after Plato the images of certain saintly figures who, like Socrates, had selflessly devoted themselves to the spiritual improvement of the community and had accepted the suffering, sometimes the martyrdom, these efforts entailed, played a consider- able role in the development of religious ideas and practices. In some cases the image may have masked a character negligible or dishonest, and the men who created and exploited the image may have done so for selfish motives; but in some cases, surely, the man behind the image was a devoted teacher whose disciples embroidered his career in good faith into a kind of hagiology[4] that they then used for moral edification. Whatever the motivation, there can be little doubt that the prime model for the spiritual hero was Socrates. . . .

Questions for Review and Study

1. How did Socrates respond to the charges brought against him at his trial?
2. Considering his conduct at his trial, do you think Socrates was seeking martyrdom? Explain your answer.
3. Is there any historical validity in the image of Socrates presented by Aristophanes in *The Clouds*?
4. Do you consider Plato's image of Socrates in *The Apology* more historically valid than Aristophanes' image of him in *The Clouds*?
5. What part did the temper of the times play in the trial and execution of Socrates?
6. Was Socrates a "spiritual hero"? Give reasons for your answer.

Questions for Comparison

1. Compare Moses and Socrates as creators of distinctively Hebrew and Greek attitudes. Of whom do we know most, and by what means? What were their messages, for whom were they meant, and what were the sources of their truths? How did each define the virtuous life? To what extent did each represent a break from his culture's past? What problems do interpreters face when defining the "true" Moses and Socrates? Whose thought exerts a greater influence on (y)our culture? Explain.
2. Discuss Homer and Socrates as representatives of different moments in ancient Greek history. For what audience and purpose was Homer's poetry created: what kind of elite did it suppose, and what qualities did it celebrate? How do the social and cultural conditions of Greek society seem to have changed from Homer's to Socrates' day? What did Socrates most value, and why? How much does Socrates resemble those we now label "rationalists"? Does the term "heroic" apply as well to Socrates as to Homer's epic poetry? Whose achievement represents a finer expression of the human spirit?

---

[4]Veneration of a saint or saints.

Suggestions for Further Reading

Socrates is a maddeningly illusive historical figure: he exists only in the works of others. Luis E. Navia's *Socratic Testimonies* is a convenient outline of the sources of historical information we do have for Socrates and of the major critical problems in Socratic studies. Because of the lack of historical sources there is a nearly irresistible urge to create a "historical Socrates," which has produced a number of biographical or semibiographical works on him. The preeminent modern account is A. E. Taylor's *Socrates*, in which the great British Platonist argues that the striking figure of Socrates as derived from Plato's dialogues is essentially an accurate historical account. The book is clear and readable as well as authoritative. An almost equally good account is Jean Brun's *Socrates*, in which the author, writing for young people, simplifies and sorts out the leading elements in the traditional view of Socrates—that is, the Delphic dictum "Know thyself," Socrates' "in-dwelling daimon," and the Socratic irony. At the other extreme are Alban D. Winspear and Tom Silverberg, *Who Was Socrates?* and Norman Gulley, *The Philosophy of Socrates*. Winspear and Silverberg argue—not entirely convincingly—for a complete revision of the tradition and make Socrates evolve in the course of his career from a democratic liberal to an aristocratic conservative. Gulley argues for the rejection of Plato's view of Socrates as a skeptic and agnostic in favor of a more constructive role for Socrates in ancient philosophy. In *Socratic Humanism*, Laszlo Versényi, while not going as far as Gulley, does advocate a separation between the often paired Socrates and Plato in favor of tying Socrates more closely to the Sophists, especially Protagoras and Gorgias. Students should find especially interesting Alexander Eliot's *Socrates*. It is less a fresh appraisal than a popular and extremely readable review of Socrates' background, his life, and the evidence brought to his trial. The second part of the book is what the author calls "a free synthesis" of all the Platonic dialogues touching on the trial and death of Socrates—essentially a new, dramatic dialogue account in fresh, modern English. On the matter of "the case" of Socrates—that is, his trial and the evidence and testimony presented—two essays in *The Philosophy of Socrates*, edited by Gregory Vlastos, Kenneth J. Dover's "Socrates in the *Clouds*" and A. D. Woozley's "Socrates on Disobeying the Law," are of considerable interest. See also *Socratic Studies*, a collection of papers by Vlastos, an eminent authority on Greek philosophy.

On the two dialogues most pertinent to the trial and death of Socrates, *The Apology* and *The Crito*, two books are recommended. R. E. Allen's *Socrates and Legal Obligation* is a clear and penetrating analysis of the dialogues, as is Richard Kraut's *Socrates and the State*, which also makes the case for Socrates' conscious civil disobedience: Kraut's is the best modern treatment of Socrates before the law. The text by Thomas C. Brickhouse and Nicholas D. Smith, *Socrates on Trial*, judiciously surveys all the evidence for the trial. On the other hand, I. F. Stone's *The Trial of*

Socrates is a muckraking attempt to portray Socrates as an antidemocratic reactionary—an outrageous book, but an interesting one. Mario Montuori's *Socrates* is an account paralleling that of Hadas and Smith in the chapter, but more detailed. Also see James W. Hulse's *The Reputation of Socrates,* a series of modern essays in criticism.

Of somewhat larger scope is the important scholarly work of Victor Ehrenberg, *The People of Aristophanes,* a study not only of the characters in the plays but also of the audiences; see especially ch. 10, on religion and education, for Socrates. Of larger scope still is T. B. L. Webster's *Athenian Culture and Society,* a superb analysis of the linkage between the culture of Athens and its society—the background to an understanding of the place of Socrates in that society and culture. For this sort of analysis, students may prefer Rex Warner's book, *Men of Athens,* a brilliant popularization that sees Socrates as the end product as well as the victim of fifth-century Athenian culture. J. W. Roberts's *City of Sokrates,* however, is the best modern historical treatment of Socrates' Athens. The standard work on the system of Athenian government is A. H. M. Jones, *Athenian Democracy,* which should be updated by reference to W. R. Connor's *The New Politicians of Fifth Century Athens.*

Two additional books may be recommended for general historical background. Malcolm F. McGregor deals with the period immediately preceding the trial of Socrates in *The Athenians and Their Empire.* A more general but important work by an eminent ancient historian is *A History of the Ancient World* by Chester G. Starr. (Titles with an asterisk are out of print.)

Allen, R. E. *Socrates and Legal Obligation.* Minneapolis: University of Minnesota Press, 1980.

Brickhouse, Thomas C., and Nicholas D. Smith. *Socrates on Trial.* Princeton, N.J.: Princeton University Press, 1989.

Brun, Jean. *Socrates.* Trans. Douglas Scott. New York: Walker, 1962.

Connor, W. R. *The New Politicians of Fifth Century Athens.* Princeton, N.J.: Princeton University Press, 1971.

Dover, Kenneth J. "Socrates in the *Clouds.*" In *The Philosophy of Socrates: A Collection of Critical Essays,* ed. Gregory Vlastos. South Bend, Ind.: University of Notre Dame Press, 1971, 1980.

Ehrenberg, Victor. *The People of Aristophanes: A Sociology of Old Attic Comedy.* New York: Schocken, 1943, 1962.

Eliot, Alexander. *Socrates: A Fresh Appraisal of the Most Celebrated Case in History.* New York: Crown, 1967.*

Gulley, Norman. *The Philosophy of Socrates.* London: Macmillan, 1968; and New York: St. Martin's, 1968.*

Hulse, James W. *The Reputation of Socrates: The Afterlife of a Gadfly.* New York: Peer Lang, 1995.

Jones, A. H. M. *Athenian Democracy.* Oxford: Oxford University Press, 1957.

Kraut, Richard. *Socrates and the State.* Princeton, N.J.: Princeton University Press, 1984.

McGregor, Malcolm F. *The Athenians and Their Empire.* Vancouver: University of British Columbia Press, 1987.

Montuori, Mario. *Socrates: Physiology of a Myth.* Trans. J. M. P. and M. Langdale. Amsterdam: J. C. Gieben, 1981.

Navia, Luis E. *Socratic Testimonies.* Lanham, Md.: University Press of America, 1987.

Roberts, J. W. *City of Sokrates: A Social History of Classical Athens.* London: Routledge and Kegan Paul, 1984.

Starr, Chester G. *A History of the Ancient World.* 4th ed. New York: Oxford University Press, 1991.

Stone, I. F. *The Trial of Socrates.* Garden City, N.Y.: Anchor, 1989.

Taylor, A. E. *Socrates.* Garden City, N.Y.: Anchor, 1933, 1953.

Versényi, Laszlo. *Socratic Humanism.* New Haven, Conn.: Yale University Press, 1963.*

Vlastos, Gregory. *Socratic Studies.* Cambridge and New York: Cambridge University Press, 1994.

Warner, Rex. *Men of Athens.* New York: Viking, 1972.*

Webster, T. B. L. *Athenian Culture and Society.* Berkeley and Los Angeles: University of California Press, 1973.

Winspear, Alban D., and Tom Silverberg. *Who Was Socrates?* New York: Russell and Russell, 1939, 1960.*

Woozley, A. D. "Socrates on Disobeying the Law." In *The Philosophy of Socrates: A Collection of Critical Essays,* ed. Gregory Vlastos. South Bend, Ind.: University of Notre Dame Press, 1971, 1980.

THE "PROBLEM" OF ALEXANDER THE GREAT

356 B.C.	Born
336 B.C.	Became king of Macedonia
334 B.C.	Began conquest of Persia
333 B.C.	Battle of Issus
331 B.C.	Battle of Gaugamela and death of Darius, the Persian king
326 B.C.	Battle of Hydaspes in India
323 B.C.	Died

If Alexander had been simply a successful conqueror, no matter how stupefying his conquests, there would really be no "Alexander problem." But, from his own lifetime, there lingered about Alexander the sense that there was something more to him, that he was "up to something," that he had great, even revolutionary, plans. The conviction of manifest destiny that Alexander himself felt so strongly contributed to this, as did his instinct for the unusual, the cryptic, the dramatic in political and religious, as well as in strategic and military, decisions. But most of all, his death at age thirty-three, in the year 323 B.C.—his conquests barely completed and his schemes for the future only hinted at or imperfectly forecast—led the ancient writers to speculate about the questions "What if Alexander had lived on?" and "What plans would his imperial imagination have conceived?" and to sift and resift every scrap of information available—and invent a few that were not!

The problem of the ancient sources themselves has added greatly to the difficulty of interpretation. This is surely ironic, for Alexander's own sense of his destiny made him unusually sensitive to the need for keeping records of his deeds. A careful log or journal was maintained, but it exists today only in the most useless fragments, if indeed the "fragments" in question even came from that record. Alexander's staff included at least two scholar-secretaries to keep records. One was Callisthenes, the nephew of Alexander's old friend and tutor Aristotle. The other was the scientist-philosopher Aristobulus. Callisthenes subsequently fell out with Alexander and was executed for complicity in a plot in 327 B.C. But, while nothing of his work remains, it was clearly the basis for a strongly anti-Alexandrian tradition that flourished in Greece, especially in Athens. This hostile tradition is best represented in Cleitarchus, a Greek rhetorician of the generation following Alexander, who never knew him but who became "the most influential historian of Alexander."[1] The account of Aristobulus, who was apparently much closer and more favorable to Alexander than was Callisthenes or Cleitarchus, is also lost. Ptolemy, one of Alexander's most trusted generals and later founder of the Hellenistic monarchy in Egypt, wrote a detailed memoir based in part on Alexander's own *Journal,* but this did not survive either.

Later ancient writers such as Diodorus, Plutarch, Curtius, and Justin did know these sources and used them. But of the accounts of Alexander surviving from antiquity, the best one is that of the Greek writer Arrian, of the second century—thus over four hundred years removed from his sources! Furthermore, while Arrian's account is our fullest and most detailed and is based scrupulously on his sources, it is terribly prosaic: we miss precisely what we most want to have, some sense of the "why" of Alexander. Despite Arrian's devotion to his subject, he tends to tell the story—mainly the military side of it at that—without significant comment. And where we would like to have him analyze, he moralizes instead.

Modern scholars have continued to be fascinated by the puzzle of what Alexander was "up to," and none more than W. W. Tarn (d. 1957). Tarn was one of those brilliant English "amateurs" of independent means and equally independent views who have contributed so uniquely to scholarship in a score of fields. He was a lawyer by profession, but he devoted most of his scholarly life—more than half a century—to Greek history. Tarn practically invented Hellenistic scholarship, that is, the study of the post-Alexandrian period in the history of Greek civilization. He authored numerous books and studies, beginning with his "Notes on Hellenism in Bactria and India," which appeared in the *Journal of Hellenic Studies* for 1902, through his first important book, *Antigonos Gonatas* (1913), to *Hellenistic Civilization* (1928), *Hellenistic Military and Naval Developments* (1930), *The Greeks in Bactria and India* (1938), and chapters in the first edition of the *Cambridge Ancient History* (1924–1929).

Because the springboard of the Hellenistic Age was Alexander, Tarn devoted special attention to him. He adopted the stance of a scholar-lawyer, in a sense, taking Alexander as his "client" and setting out to make a case for the defense. And Alexander was badly in

---

[1]N. G. L. Hammond, *Alexander the Great: King, Commander and Statesman* (Park Ridge, N.J.: Noyes Press, 1980), p. 2.

need of such defense. The trend of modern scholarship before Tarn had been to view Alexander as an archtyrant, arbitrary and megalomaniac, a drunken murderer, and the oppressor of Greek political freedom and philosophic independence—a view derived ultimately from the Callisthenic-Cleitarchan tradition of antiquity.

Tarn was brilliantly successful in turning opinion around in his defense of Alexander, so much so that the "traditional" view of Alexander today is still essentially that created by Tarn. His authority has been so great that it has even affected the way in which we interpret the ancient sources themselves, whether they seem to be "for" or "against" Tarn's case.

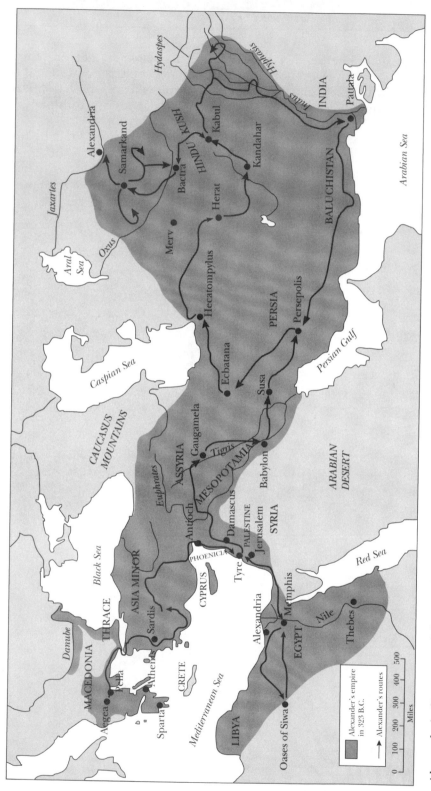

Alexander's Conquest of the Persian Empire, 334–323 B.C.

The Ancient Sources:
Arrian, Eratosthenes, and Plutarch

In the first selection of this chapter, we present the five "proof texts" on which Tarn built his defense of Alexander: one from Arrian, one from Eratosthenes (preserved in Strabo), and three from Plutarch.

This passage, from The Life of Alexander the Great *by Arrian, took place near the end of Alexander's incredible journey of conquest. In 324 B.C. Alexander assembled his Macedonian troops at Opis in Mesopotamia and announced that he proposed to discharge and send home, with lavish rewards, all those who were disabled or overage. But, instead of gratitude, a smoldering resentment surfaced, and the entire Macedonian force began to clamor to be sent home. Arrian attributes the resentment to Alexander's "orientalizing," his adoption of Persian dress and customs, and his attempt to incorporate Persians and other peoples into his army. This had offended the Macedonians' stubborn pride and sense of exclusiveness, and they now threatened a mutiny. Alexander was furious. After having the ringleaders arrested, he addressed the Macedonians in a passionate, blistering speech, reminding them of their own accomplishments, as well as his, and of what he had done for them. Alexander's speech had a profound effect upon the Macedonians, as did the plans, immediately put into effect, for reorganizing the army in the event that they defected. But, instead of deserting, the Macedonians repented.*

Alexander, the moment he heard of this change of heart, hastened out to meet them, and he was so touched by their grovelling repentance and their bitter lamentations that the tears came into his eyes. While they continued to beg for his pity, he stepped forward as if to speak, but was anticipated by one Callines, an officer of the mounted Hetaeri, distinguished both by age and rank. "My lord," he cried, "what hurts us is that you have made Persians your kinsmen— Persians are called 'Alexander's kinsmen'—Persians kiss you. But no Macedonian has yet had a taste of this honour."

"Every man of you," Alexander replied, "I regard as my kinsman, and from now on that is what I shall call you."

Thereupon Callines came up to him and kissed him, and all the others who wished to do so kissed him too. Then they picked up their weapons and returned to their quarters singing the song of victory at the top of their voices.

To mark the restoration of harmony, Alexander offered sacrifice to the gods he was accustomed to honour, and gave a public banquet which he himself attended, sitting among the Macedonians, all of whom were present. Next to them the Persians had their places, and next to the Persians distinguished foreigners of other nations; Alexander and his friends dipped their wine from the same bowl and poured the same libations, following the lead of the Greek seers and the Magi. The chief object of his prayers was that Persians and Macedonians might rule together in harmony as an imperial power. It is said that 9,000 people attended the banquet; they unanimously drank the same toast, and followed it by the paean of victory.

After this all Macedonians—about 10,000 all told—who were too old for service or in any way unfit, got their discharge at their own request.

Eratosthenes of Cyrene, who lived about 200 B.C., was head of the great Library of Alexandria and one of the most learned individuals of antiquity. But his works exist only in fragments and in citations in the writings of others, such as the following, from The Geography *by the Greek scientist Strabo, of the first century B.C.*

Now, towards the end of his treatise—after withholding praise from those who divide the whole multitude of mankind into two groups, namely, Greeks and Barbarians, and also from those who advised Alexander to treat the Greeks as friends but the Barbarians as enemies—Eratosthenes goes on to say that it would be better to make such divisions according to good qualities and bad qualities; for not only are many of the Greeks bad, but many of the Barbarians are refined—Indians and Arians, for example, and, further, Romans and Carthaginians, who carry on their governments so admirably. And this, he says, is the reason why Alexander, disregarding his advisers, welcomed as many as he could of the men of fair repute and did them favours—just as if those who have made such a division, placing some people in the category of censure, others in that of praise, did so for any other reason than that in some people there prevail the law-abiding and the political instinct, and the qualities associated with education and powers of speech, whereas in other people the opposite characteristics prevail! And so Alexander, not disregarding his advisers, but rather accepting their opinion, did what was consistent with, not contrary to, their advice; for he had regard to the real intent of those who gave him counsel.

Two of the Plutarch passages are from his essay "On the Fortune of Alexander," which is one of the pieces comprising the collection known as the Moralia.

Moreover, the much-admired *Republic* of Zeno, the founder of the Stoic sect, may be summed up in this one main principle: that all the inhabitants of this world of ours should not live differentiated by their respective rules of justice into separate cities and communities, but that we should consider all men to be of one community and one polity, and that we should have a common life and an order common to us all, even as a herd that feeds together and shares the pasturage of a common field. This Zeno wrote, giving shape to a dream or, as it were, shadowy picture of a well-ordered and philosophic commonwealth; but it was Alexander who gave effect to the idea. For Alexander did not follow Aristotle's advice to treat the Greeks as if he were their leader, and other peoples as if he were their master; to have regard for the Greeks as for friends and kindred, but to conduct himself toward other peoples as though they were plants or animals; for to do so would have been to cumber his leadership with numerous battles and banishments and festering seditions. But, as he believed that he came as a heaven-sent governor to all, and as a mediator for the whole world, those whom he could not persuade to unite with him, he conquered by force of arms, and he brought together into one body all men everywhere, uniting and mixing in one great loving-cup, as it were, men's lives, their characters, their marriages, their very habits of life. He bade them all consider as their fatherland the whole inhabited earth, as their stronghold and protection his camp, as akin to them all good men, and as foreigners only the wicked; they should not distinguish between Grecian and foreigner by Grecian cloak and targe, or scimitar and jacket; but the distinguishing mark of the Grecian should be seen in virtue, and that of the foreigner in iniquity; clothing and food, marriage and manner of life they should regard as common to all, being blended into one by ties of blood and children.

After dwelling on the wisdom of Alexander in affecting a mixed Graeco-Macedonian and Persian costume, Plutarch continues.

For he did not overrun Asia like a robber nor was he minded to tear and rend it, as if it were booty and plunder bestowed by unexpected good fortune. . . . But Alexander desired to render all upon earth subject to one law of reason and one form of government and to reveal all men as one people, and to this purpose he made himself conform. But if the deity that sent down Alexander's soul into this world of ours had not recalled him quickly, one law would govern all mankind, and they all would look toward one rule of justice as though toward a common source of light. But as it is, that part of the world which has not looked upon Alexander has remained without sunlight.

The passage from the famous "Life of Alexander" in Plutarch's Lives *deals with an incident early in Alexander's career, after his conquest of Egypt—his journey across the desert to the oracle of Ammon at Siwah.*

When Alexander had passed through the desert and was come to the place of the oracle, the prophet of Ammon gave him salutation from the god as from a father; whereupon Alexander asked him whether any of the murderers of his father had escaped him.[2] To this the prophet answered by bidding him be guarded in his speech, since his was not a mortal father. Alexander therefore changed the form of his question, and asked whether the murderers of Philip had all been punished; and then, regarding his own empire, he asked whether it was given to him to become lord and master of all mankind. The god gave answer that this was given to him, and that Philip was fully avenged. Then Alexander made splendid offerings to the god and gave his priests large gifts of money. . . . We are told, also, that he listened to the teachings of Psammon[3] the philosopher in Egypt, and accepted most readily this utterance of his, namely, that all mankind are under the kingship of God, since in every case that which gets the mastery and rules is divine. Still more philosophical, however, was his own opinion and utterance on this head, namely that although God was indeed a common father of all mankind, still, He made peculiarly His own the noblest and best of them.

Alexander the Great and the Unity of Mankind

W. W. TARN

We turn now to the thesis that W. W. Tarn built in defense of Alexander. He had begun to develop his characteristic view in a number of journal articles and anticipated it in fairly complete form in his contributions to the 1927 edition of the Cambridge Ancient History. *He was later to state it most completely in his*

---

[2]Alexander had come to the throne of Macedonia upon the murder of his father, Philip II, in 336 B.C.

[3]This is the only reference in antiquity to such a person.

monumental two-volume Alexander the Great *(Cambridge: Cambridge University Press, 1948). But the most succinct statement of the Tarn thesis is that contained in his Raleigh Lecture on History, read before the British Academy in 1933. It is entitled "Alexander the Great and the Unity of Mankind."*

What I am going to talk about is one of the great revolutions in human thought. Greeks of the classical period, speaking very roughly, divided mankind into two classes, Greeks and non-Greeks; the latter they called barbarians and usually regarded as inferior people, though occasionally some one, like Herodotus or Xenophon, might suggest that certain barbarians possessed qualities which deserved consideration, like the wisdom of the Egyptians or the courage of the Persians. But in the third century B.C. and later we meet with a body of opinion which may be called universalist; all mankind was one and all men were brothers, or anyhow ought to be. Who was the pioneer who brought about this tremendous revolution in some men's way of thinking? Most writers have had no doubt on that point; the man to whom the credit was due was Zeno, the founder of the Stoic philosophy. But there are several passages in Greek writers which, *if* they are to be believed, show that the first man actually to think of it was not Zeno but Alexander. This matter has never really been examined; some writers just pass it over, which means, I suppose, that they do not consider the passages in question historical; others have definitely said that it is merely a case of our secondary authorities attributing to Alexander ideas taken from Stoicism. I want to consider to-day whether the passages in question are or are not historical and worthy of credence; that is, whether Alexander was or was not the first to believe in, and to contemplate, the unity of mankind. This will entail, among other things, some examination of the concept which Greeks called Homonoia, a word which meant more than its Latin translation, Concord, means to us; it is more like Unity and Concord, a being of one mind together, or if we like the phrase, a union of hearts; ultimately it was to become almost a symbol of the world's longing for something better than constant war. For convenience of discussion I shall keep the Greek term Homonoia.

Before coming to the ideas attributed to Alexander, I must sketch very briefly the background against which the new thought arose, whoever was its author; and I ought to say that I am primarily talking throughout of theory, not of practice. It may be possible to find, in the fifth century, or earlier, an occasional phrase which looks like a groping after something better than the hard-and-fast division of Greeks and barbarians; but this comes to very little and had no importance for history, because anything of the sort was strangled by the idealist philosophies. Plato and Aristotle left no doubt about their views. Plato said that all barbarians were enemies by nature; it was proper to wage war upon them, even to the point of enslaving or extirpating them. Aristotle said that all barbarians were slaves by nature, especially those of Asia; they had not the qualities which entitled them to be free men, and it was proper to treat them as slaves. His model State cared for nothing but its own citizens; it was a small aristocracy of Greek citizens ruling over a barbarian peasantry who cultivated the land for their masters and had no share in the State—a thing he had seen in some cities of Asia Minor. Certainly neither Plato nor Aristotle was quite consistent; Plato might treat an Egyptian priest as the repository of wisdom, Aristotle might suggest that the constitution of Carthage was worth studying; but their main position was clear enough, as was the impression Alexander would get from his tutor Aristotle.

There were, of course, other voices. Xenophon, when he wanted to portray an ideal shepherd of the people, chose a Persian king as shepherd of the Persian people. And there were the early Cynics. But the Cynics had no thought of any union or fellowship between Greek and barbarian; they were not constructive thinkers, but merely embodied protests against the vices and follies of civilization. When Diogenes called himself a cosmopolite, a horrible word which he coined and which was not used again for centuries, what he meant was, not that he was a citizen of some imaginary world-state—a thing he never thought about—but that he was not a citizen of any Greek city; it was pure negation. And the one piece of Cynic construction, the ideal figure of Heracles, labouring to free Greece from monsters, was merely shepherd of a *Greek* herd till after Alexander, when it took colour and content from the Stoics and became the ideal benefactor of humanity. All that Xenophon or the Cynics could supply was the figure of an ideal shepherd, not of the human herd, but of some national herd.

More important was Aristotle's older contemporary Isocrates, because of his conception of Homonoia. The Greek world, whatever its practice, never doubted that in theory unity in a city was very desirable; but though the word Homonoia was already in common use among Greeks, it chiefly meant absence of faction-fights, and this rather negative meaning lasted in the cities throughout the Hellenistic period, as can be seen in the numerous decrees in honour of the judicial commissions sent from one city to another, which are praised because they tried to compose internal discord. There was hardly a trace as yet of the more positive sense which Homonoia was to acquire later—a mental attitude which should make war or faction impossible because the parties were at one; and Isocrates extended the application of the word without changing its meaning. He took up a suggestion of the sophist Gorgias and proposed to treat the whole Greek world as one and the futile wars between city and city as faction fights—to apply Homonoia to the Greek race. For this purpose he utilized Plato's idea that the barbarian was a natural enemy, and decided that the way to unite Greeks was to attack Persia; "I come," he said, "to advocate two things: war against the barbarian, Homonoia between ourselves." But somebody had to do the uniting; and Isocrates bethought him of the Cynic Heracles, benefactor of the Greek race, and urged King Philip of Macedonia, a descendant of Heracles, to play the part. But if Philip was to be Heracles and bring about the Homonoia of the Greek world, the way was being prepared for two important ideas of a later time; the essential quality of the king must be that love of man, φιλανθρωπία,[4] which had led Heracles to perform his labours, and the essential business of the king was to promote Homonoia; so far this only applied to Greeks, but if its meaning were to deepen it would still be the king's business. The actual result of all this, the League of Corinth[5] under Philip's presidency, was not quite what Isocrates had dreamt of.

This then was the background against which Alexander appeared. The business of a Macedonian king was to be a benefactor of Greeks to the extent of preventing inter-city warfare; he was to promote Homonoia among Greeks and utilize their enmity to barbarians as a bond of union; but barbarians themselves were still enemies and slaves by nature, a view which Aristotle emphasized when he advised his pupil to treat Greeks as free men, but barbarians as slaves.

I now come to the things Alexander is supposed to have said or thought; and the gulf between them and the background I have sketched is so deep that one cannot blame those who have refused to believe that he ever said or thought anything of the sort. There are five passages which need consideration: one in Arrian; one from Eratosthenes, preserved by Strabo; and three from Plutarch, one of which, from its resemblance to the Strabo passage, has been supposed by one of the acutest critics of our time to be taken in substance from Eratosthenes,[6] and as such I shall treat it. The passage in Arrian says that, after the mutiny of the Macedonians at Opis and their reconciliation to Alexander, he gave a banquet to Macedonians and Persians, at which he prayed for Homonoia and partnership in rule between these two peoples. What Eratosthenes says amounts to this. Aristotle told Alexander to treat Greeks as friends, but barbarians like animals; but Alexander knew better, and preferred to divide men into good and bad without regard to their race, and thus carried out Aristotle's real intention. For Alexander believed that he had a mission from the deity to harmonize men generally and be the reconciler of the world, mixing men's lives and customs as in a loving cup, and treating the

---

[4]Literally "philanthropy."

[5]The league Philip formed after defeating the Greek states at Chaeronea in 338 B.C.

[6]The reference is to the German scholar E. Schwarz.

good as his kin, the bad as strangers; for he thought that the good man was the real Greek and the bad man the real barbarian. Of the two Plutarch passages, the first says that his intention was to bring about, as between mankind generally, Homonoia and peace and fellowship and make them all one people; and the other, which for the moment I will quote without its context, makes him say that God is the common father of all men.

It is obvious that, wherever all this comes from, we are dealing with a great revolution in thought. It amounts to this, that there is a natural brotherhood of all men, though bad men do not share in it; that Homonoia is no longer to be confined to the relations between Greek and Greek, but is to unite Greek and barbarian; and that Alexander's aim was to substitute peace for war, and reconcile the enmities of mankind by bringing them all—all that is whom his arm could reach, the peoples of his empire—to be of one mind together: as men were one in blood, so they should become one in heart and spirit. That such a revolution in thought did happen is unquestioned; the question is, was Alexander really its author, or are the thoughts attributed to him those of Zeno or somebody else? . . .

"To try to answer that question," Tarn follows with a long and complex analysis of Homonoia and kingship in Graeco-Roman history, leading to the universalism of the late Roman empire.

The belief that it was the business of kings to promote Homonoia among their subjects without distinction of race thus travelled down the line of kingship for centuries; but the line, you will remember, had no beginning. . . . It must clearly have been connected with some particular king at the start, and that king has to be later than Isocrates and Philip and earlier than Diotogenes and Demetrius.[7] It would seem that only one king is possible; we should have to postulate Alexander at the beginning of the line, even if there were not a definite tradition that it *was* he. This means that Plutarch's statement, that Alexander's purpose was to bring about Homonoia between men generally—that is, those men whom his arm could reach—must be taken to be true, unless some explicit reason be found for disbelieving it; and I therefore now turn to the Stoics, in order to test the view that the ideas attributed to him were really taken from Stoicism. . . . We have seen that it was the business of kings to bring about Homonoia;

---

[7]Isocrates (436–338 B.C.), the Athenian orator; Philip II of Macedonia (382–336 B.C.); Diotogenes, an early Hellenistic author of uncertain date; Demetrius (336–283 B.C.), an early Hellenistic ruler.

but this was not the business of a Stoic, because to him Homonoia had already been brought about by the Deity, and it existed in all completeness; all that was necessary was that men should see it. . . .

This is the point I want to make, the irreconcilable opposition between Stoicism and the theory of kingship, between the belief that unity and concord existed and you must try and get men to see it, and the belief that unity and concord did not exist and that it was the business of the rulers of the earth to try and bring them to pass. . . . Consequently, when Eratosthenes says that Alexander aspired to be the harmonizer and reconciler of the world, and when Plutarch attributes to him the intention of bringing about fellowship and Homonoia between men generally—those men whom his arm reached— then, wherever these ideas came from, they were not Stoic; between them and Stoicism there was a gulf which nothing could bridge. This does not by itself prove that Alexander held these ideas; what it does do is to put out of court the only alternative which has ever been seriously proposed, and to leave the matter where I left it when considering the theory of kingship, that is, that there is a strong presumption that Alexander *was* their author. . . .

Before leaving Stoicism, I must return for a moment to Zeno's distinction of the worthy and the unworthy; for Alexander, as we saw, is said to have divided men into good and bad, and to have excluded the bad from the general kinship of mankind and called them the true barbarians. Might not *this* distinction, at any rate, have been taken from Stoicism and attributed to him? The reasons against this seem conclusive, apart from the difficulty of discarding a statement made by so sound and scientific a critic as Eratosthenes. First, no Stoic ever equated the unworthy class with barbarians; for to him there were no barbarians. . . . Secondly, while the unworthy in Zeno, as in Aristotle, are the majority of mankind, Alexander's "bad men" are not; they are, as Eratosthenes says, merely that small residue everywhere which cannot be civilized. One sees this clearly in a story never questioned, his [Alexander's] prayer at Opis, when he prayed that the Macedonian and Persian races (without exceptions made) might be united in Homonoia. And thirdly, we know where the idea comes from: Aristotle had criticized some who said that good men were really free and bad men were really slaves (whom he himself equated with barbarians), and Alexander is in turn criticizing Aristotle; as indeed Eratosthenes says, though he does not quote this passage of Aristotle. The matter is not important, except for the general question of the credibility of Eratosthenes, and may conceivably only represent that period in Alexander's thought when he was outgrowing Aristotle; it does not conflict, as does Zeno's conception of the unworthy, with a general belief in the unity of mankind. . . .

There is just one question still to be asked; whence did Zeno get his universalism? Plutarch says that behind Zeno's dream lay Alexander's reality; and no one doubts that Alexander was Zeno's inspiration, but the question is, in what form? Most writers have taken Plutarch to mean Alexander's *empire;* but to me this explains nothing at all. One man conquers a large number of races and brings them under one despotic rule; how can another man deduce from this that distinctions of race are immaterial and that the universe is a harmony in which men are brothers? It would be like the fight between the polar bear and the parallelepiped. The Persian kings had conquered and ruled as large an empire as Alexander, including many Greek cities; why did Darius never inspire any one with similar theories? It does seem to me that what Plutarch really means is not Alexander's empire but Alexander's ideas; after all, the frequent references in antiquity to Alexander as a philosopher, one at least of which is contemporary, must mean *something.* Zeno's inspiration, then, was Alexander's idea of the unity of mankind; and what Zeno himself did was to carry this idea to one of its two logical conclusions. Judging by his prayer at Opis for the Homonoia of Macedonians and Persians, Alexander, had he lived, would have worked through national groups, as was inevitable in an empire like his, which comprised many different states and subject peoples; Theophrastus,[8] who followed him, included national groups in his chain of progress towards world-relationship. But Zeno abolished all distinctions of race, all the apparatus of national groups and particular states, and made his world-state a theoretic whole. His scheme was an inspiration to many; but in historical fact it was, and remained, unrealizable. But Alexander's way, or what I think was his way, led to the Roman Empire being called one people. I am not going to bring in modern examples of these two different lines of approach to world-unity, but I want to say one thing about the Roman Empire. It has been said that Stoic ideas came near to realization in the empire of Hadrian and the Antonines, but it is quite clear, the moment it be considered, that this was not the case; that empire was a huge national state, which stood in the line of kingship and was a partial realization of the ideas of Alexander. When a Stoic *did* sit on the imperial throne, he was at once compelled to make terms with the national state; to Marcus Aurelius, the Stoic world-state was no theoretic unity, but was to comprise the various particular states as a city comprises houses. And there is still a living reality in what he said about himself: "As a man I am a citizen of the world-state, but as the particular man Marcus Aurelius I am a citizen of Rome."

I may now sum up. We have followed down the line of kingship the theory that it was the business of a king to promote Homonoia among his subjects—all his subjects without distinction of race; and we have seen that this theory ought to be connected at the start with some

---

[8]The philosopher-scientist who followed Aristotle as head of his school.

king, who must be later than Philip and earlier than Demetrius; and there is a definite tradition which connects the origin of the theory with Alexander. We have further seen that the intention to promote Homonoia among mankind, attributed in the tradition to Alexander, is certainly not a projection backwards from Stoicism, or apparently from anything else, while it is needed to explain certain things said by Theophrastus and done by Alexarchus.[9] Lastly, we have seen the idea of the kinship or brotherhood of mankind appearing suddenly in Theophrastus and Alexarchus; their common source can be no one but Alexander, and again tradition supports this. Only one conclusion from all this seems possible: the things which, in the tradition, Alexander is supposed to have thought and said are, in substance, true. He did say that all men were sons of God, that is brothers, but that God made the best ones peculiarly his own; he did aspire to be the harmonizer and reconciler of the world—that part of the world which his arm reached; he did have the intention of uniting the peoples of his empire in fellowship and concord and making them of one mind together; and when, as a beginning, he prayed at Opis for partnership in rule and Homonoia between Macedonians and Persians, he meant what he said—not partnership in rule only, but true unity between them. I am only talking of theory, not of actions; but what this means is that he was the pioneer of one of the supreme revolutions in the world's outlook, the first man known to us who contemplated the brotherhood of man or the unity of mankind, whichever phrase we like to use. I do not claim to have given you exact proof of this; it is one of those difficult borderlands of history where one does not get proofs which could be put to a jury. But there is a very strong presumption indeed that it is true. Alexander, for the things he *did*, was called The Great; but if what I have said to-day be right, I do not think we shall doubt that this idea of his—call it a purpose, call it a dream, call it what you will—was the greatest thing about him.

The New Alexander

N. G. L. HAMMOND

Despite Tarn's enormous scholarly reputation and his lordly dismissal of critics, his own interpretive view of Alexander was bound to be challenged, and it has been. Tarn massively overstated his case. As Mary Renault put it, "the defence was

---

[9]A minor Macedonian princeling, following Alexander, who set up his small state apparently on the model of Alexander's ideas.

pushed too far."[10] *And Ernst Badian, probably Tarn's most effective critic among this generation of scholars, has called the Alexander of Tarn's vision a "phantom" that "has haunted the pages of scholarship" for "a quarter of a century."*[11] *In reaction against Tarn's view of Alexander not only as a stunning conqueror but as a conqueror of stunning philosophic profundity as well, scholars have again depicted him "as a ruthless murderer, an autocratic megalomaniac, even a bisexual profligate."*[12] *Even more careful and moderate scholars like R. D. Milns hold that such an idea as the kinship of mankind was quite beyond Alexander and must be attributed to "later thinkers and philosophers."*[13]

Now the reaction seems to be moving back toward the Tarn view. The "new" Alexander is more anchored in his own times and mores, and none of the more recent authorities attributes to Alexander the "great revolution in thought" that Tarn did. But the Alexander we see today is considerably more cerebral and innovative both in thought and in action. This new image of Alexander is nowhere better represented than in the work of the distinguished Cambridge classicist N. G. L. Hammond, Alexander the Great: King, Commander and Statesman, *from which the following excerpt is taken.*

We have the advantage of hindsight. We can see that it was Alexander's leadership and training which made the Macedonians incomparable in war and in administration and enabled them as rulers of the so-called Hellenistic kingdoms to control the greater part of the civilised world for a century or more. In a reign of thirteen years he brought to Macedonia and Macedonians the immense wealth which maintained their strength for generations. All this was and is an unparalleled achievement. Moreover, as king of Macedonia he did not drain his country unduly in his lifetime, since Antipater had enough men to defeat the Greeks in 331 B.C. and 322 B.C. Yet the system he was creating—quite apart from any further conquests he had in mind in 323 B.C.—was certain to put an immense strain on present and future Macedonians. They were spread dangerously thin at the time of his death, and the prolonged absence of so many Macedonians abroad was bound to cause a drop in the birth rate in Macedonia itself. Of course Alexander expected his Macedonians to undertake almost superhuman dangers and labours, and it was their response to his challenge that made them great. But the dangers and labours were being demanded for the sake of a policy which was not Macedonian in a nationalistic sense, which the Macedonians did not wholly understand, and which they never fully implemented. Philip's sin-

---

[10]Mary Renault, *The Nature of Alexander* (New York: Pantheon, 1975), p. 23.
[11]Ernst Badian, "Alexander the Great and the Unity of Mankind," *Historia*, 7 (1958), 425.
[12]Hammond, *Alexander the Great*, p. 5.
[13]R. D. Milns, *Alexander the Great* (London: Robert Hale, 1968), p. 265.

glemindedness made him the greatest king of Macedonia. Alexander's wider vision made him at the same time something more and something less than the greatest king of Macedonia. . . .

As constitutionally elected king, Alexander had sole right of command and an inherited authority. From the age of twenty onwards he appointed his deputies without let or hindrance, issued all orders, and controlled all payments, promotions, and discharges. His authority as a commander was almost absolute, his discipline unquestioned, and his position unchallenged. As religious head of the state, he interceded for his men and was seen daily to sacrifice on their behalf.

Unique in his descent from Zeus and Heracles, he was acclaimed "son of Zeus" by the oracle at Didyma, the Sibyl at Erythrae, and the oracle of Ammon (the last at least in the opinion of his men), and he fostered the idea of divine protection by having the sacred shield of Athena carried into battle by his senior Bodyguard (it saved his life against the Malli; [Arrian 6.10.2]).[14] Before engaging at Gaugamela Alexander prayed in front of the army, raising his right hand towards the gods and saying, "If I am really descended from Zeus, protect and strengthen the Greeks." That prayer, apparently, was answered. In the eyes of most men—and most men then had faith in gods, oracles, and omens—Alexander was favoured by the supernatural powers. To those who were sceptical he had extraordinarily good luck.

The brilliance of Alexander's mind is seen most clearly in his major battles. . . . For example, he saw at once the advantages and disadvantages of Darius' position on the Pinarus river and he anticipated the effects of his own detailed dispositions and orders to a nicety. "He surpassed all others in the faculty of intuitively meeting an emergency," whether in besieging Tyre or facing Scythian tactics or storming an impregnable fortress. He excelled in speed and precision of thought, the calculation of risks, and the expectation of an enemy's reactions. Having himself engaged in every kind of action and having grappled with practical problems from a young age, he had a sure sense of the possible and extraordinary versatility in invention. Unlike many famous commanders, his mind was so flexible that at the time of his death he was creating an entirely new type of army.

A most remarkable quality of Alexander's was the concern for his men. No conqueror had so few casualties in battle, and the reason was that Alexander avoided "the battle of rats" by using his brains not just to win, but to win most economically. He made this his

---

[14]Arrian (c. 90–170) was a Greek historian, pupil, and friend of Epictetus. The Emperor Hadrian appointed him prefect of Cappadocia, and he defeated an invading band of Alani. In his later years, he retired from public life.

priority because he loved his Macedonians. He grew up among them and fought alongside them, both as a youth admiring his seniors and as a mature man competing with his companions. He honoured and rewarded courage and devotion to duty in them, paying a unique tribute to the first casualties by having bronze statues made by the leading sculptor, and he felt deeply with them in their sufferings and privations. He aroused in them an amazing response. He not only admired courage and devotion to duty in his own men but in his enemies, whom he treated with honour. In return he won the respect and loyalty of Asians of many races whom he had just defeated in battle. . . . Some commanders may have rivalled him in the handling of his own race. None have had such a capacity for leading a multiracial army. . . .

We have already touched upon his statesmanship in enhancing the prestige of the Macedonian monarchy and advancing the power of the Macedonian state. He reduced the harshness of customary law (for instance, he no longer required the execution of the male relatives of a convicted traitor), and he was concerned for the welfare and the birth rate of Macedonia. He provided tax reliefs for the dependants of casualties, brought up war orphans at his own expense, and sought to avoid conflicts between the European and Asian families of his Macedonians by maintaining the latter in Asia. He increased the number of young Macedonians when he legitimised the soldiers' children by Asian women, and he sent the 10,000 veterans home in the expectation of their begetting more children in Macedonia. . . .

While Philip invented and inaugurated the Greek League, it was Alexander who demonstrated its efficacy as a *modus operandi* for the Macedonians and the Greeks and used their joint forces to overthrow the Persian Empire. By opening Asia to Greek enterprise and culture Alexander relieved many of the social and economic pressures which had been causing distress and anarchy in the Greek states. At the same time he was personally concerned with affairs in Greece, as we see from the large number of embassies which came to him in Asia rather than to his deputy, Antipater, in Macedonia. . . .

Alexander's originality is seen most clearly in Asia. He set himself an unparalleled task when he decided in advance not to make the Macedonians and the Greeks the masters of the conquered peoples but to create a self-sustaining Kingdom of Asia. Within his kingdom he intended the settled peoples to conduct their internal affairs in accordance with their own laws and customs, whether in a Greek city or a native village, in a Lydian or a Carian state, in a Cyprian or a Phoenician kingdom, in Egypt, Babylonia, or Persis, in an Indian principality or republic. As his power extended, he did not introduce European administrators at a level which would inhibit native self-rule (as so-called colonial powers have so often done); instead he continued native administrators in office and raised the best of them to the highest level in civil affairs by appointing them as his immediate deputies in the post of satrap (e.g., Mazaeus at Babylon) or nomarch (e.g., Doloaspis in Egypt). . . .

What is important is the effectiveness of Alexander's system: native civilians and armed forces alike lodged complaints with Alexander, the accused were tried legally and openly, and those found guilty were executed forthwith, in order "to deter the other satraps, governors, and civil officers" and to make it known that the rulers were not permitted to wrong the ruled in Alexander's kingdom. In the opinion of Arrian, who lived at the zenith of the Roman Empire and had a standard of comparison, it was this system which "more than anything else kept to an orderly way of life the innumerable, widely diffused peoples who had been subjugated in war or had of their own will joined him" (6.27.5). In the same way rebels, sometimes in the form of native pretenders, were put on trial; and, if found guilty, they were executed, often in the manner native to the particular area (Arrian 6.30.2). Where the rights of his subjects were at stake, he showed no mercy or favouritism for any Macedonian, Greek, Thracian, Persian, Median, or Indian. . . .

What Alexander sought in his senior administrators was summed up in the word "excellence" (*arete*). He assessed it by performance in his own army and in that of his enemy; for he approved courage and loyalty, wherever he found it. But a particular kind of excellence was needed where conquerors had to accept the conquered as their equals in administering the kingdom of Asia. The Macedonians justifiably regarded themselves as a military élite, superior to Greeks and barbarians, and closer to their king than any foreigner; and the Greeks despised all Asians as barbarians, fitted by nature only to be slaves. Yet here was Alexander according equal status, regardless of race, not only to all his administrators but also to all who served in his army! Resentment at this was the chief factor in the mutiny of the Macedonians at Opis. On that occasion Alexander enforced his will. He celebrated the concept of equal status in an official banquet, at which the Macedonians sat by their king, with whom they were not reconciled; next were the Persians; and after them persons of "the other races." All the guests were men who ranked first in reputation or in some other form of excellence (*arete*). . . .

When Alexander encountered nomadic or marauding peoples, he forced them, often by drastic methods of warfare, to accept his rule and to adopt a settled way of life. Many of his new cities were founded among these peoples so that "they should cease to be nomads," and he encouraged the concentration of native villages to form new urban centres. For he intended to promote peace, prosperity, and culture within these parts of his kingdom too, and the cities and centres were means to that end. Strongly fortified and well manned, they were bastions of peace, and the young men in them were trained by Macedonian and Greek veterans to join Alexander's new army and maintain his peace. They were sited to become markets for agricultural produce and interregional exchange, and their citizens, especially in the new cities by the deltas of the Nile, the Euphrates, and the Indus, learnt the capitalistic form of economy, which had brought such prosperity to the Greek states in the fifth and fourth centuries.

The cultural model for the new cities was the Macedonian town, itself very strongly imbued with Greek ideas and practices. The ruling element from the outset was formed by Macedonian and Greek veterans; and the Asians, although free to practise their own religion and traditions, were encouraged to learn Greek and adopt some forms of Greco-Macedonian life. According to Plutarch (*Moralia* 328 E) Alexander founded 70 new cities, which started their life with 10,000 adult male citizens as the norm, and he must have envisaged a fusion of European and Asian cultures developing within and spreading out from these arteries into the body of the kingdom. . . .

The effects of a statesman's ideas, especially if he dies at the age of thirty-two, are rarely assessable within his lifetime. Yet before Alexander died his ideas bore fruit in the integration of Asians and Macedonians in cavalry and infantry units; the training of Asians in Macedonian weaponry; the association of Asians and Macedonians in each file of the army; the settling of Macedonians, Greeks, and Asians in the new cities; the spread of Greek as a common language in the army and in the new cities; the development of Babylon as the "metropolis" or capital of the kingdom of Asia; the honouring of interracial marriage; and the raising of Eurasian children to a privileged status.

Peace reigned in this kingdom of Asia, and its people now had little to fear from their neighbours. Urbanisation, trade, water-borne commerce, agriculture, flood-control, land-reclamation, and irrigation were developing fast, and exchange was stimulated by the liberation of hoarded treasure. The gold and silver coinage of Alexander, uniform in types and weights, was universally accepted because it was of real, bullion value. In the eastern satrapies especially the gold darics and silver shekels of the Persian treasuries continued to circulate, and in the western satrapies local currencies were provided by the Greek, Cyprian, and Phoenician cities. . . .

The skill with which Alexander changed the economy of Asia into that system of commercial exchange which the Greeks had invented and we call capitalism, and at that within so few years, is one of the most striking signs of his genius. . . .

The fulfilment of Alexander's plans was impaired by his early death and by the strife between the generals which ensued. Yet even so, within the span of thirteen years, he changed the face of the world more decisively and with more longlasting effects than any other statesman has ever done. He first introduced into Asia the Greco-Macedonian city within the framework of a monarchical or autocratic state, and this form of city was to be the centre of ancient and medieval civilisation in the southern Balkans, the Aegean, and the Near East. For the city provided that continuity of Greek language, literature, and culture which enriched the Roman world, fostered Christianity, and affected Western Europe so profoundly. The outlook and the achievements of Alexander created an ideal image, an apotheosis of kingship which was to inspire the Hellenistic kings, some Roman emperors, and the Byzantine rulers. And his creation of a state which rose above nationalism and brought liberators and liberated, victors and defeated into collaboration and parity of esteem puts most of the expedients of the modern world to shame. . . .

That Alexander should grow up with a sense of mission was certainly to be expected. For he was descended from Zeus and Heracles, he was born to be king, he had the career of Philip as an exemplar, and he was advised by Isocrates, Aristotle, and others to be a benefactor of Macedonians and Greeks alike. His sense of mission was inevitably steeped in religious associations, because from an early age he had been associated with the king, his father, in conducting religious ceremonies, and he was imbued with many ideas of orthodox religion and of ecstatic mysteries. Thus two observations by Plutarch (*Moralia* 342 A and F) have the ring of truth. "This desire (to bring all men into an orderly system under a single leadership and to accustom them to one way of life) was implanted in Alexander from childhood and grew up with him"; and on crossing the Hellespont to the Troad Alexander's first asset was "his reverence towards the gods." Already by then he planned to found a Kingdom of Asia, in which he would rule over the peoples, as Odysseus had done, "like a kindly father" (*Odyssey* 5.11). He promoted the fulfilment of that plan "by founding Greek cities among savage peoples and by teaching the principles of law and peace to lawless, ignorant tribes." When he had completed the conquest of "Asia" through the favour of the gods and especially that of Zeus Ammon, he went on to establish for all men in his kingdom "concord and peace and partnership with one another" (*Moralia* 329 F).

This was a practical development, springing from a religious concept and not from a philosophical theory (though it led later to the philosophical theory of the Cynics, who substituted for Asia the whole inhabited world and talked of the brotherhood of all men), and it came to fruition in the banquet at Opis, when he prayed in the presence of men of various races for "concord and partnership in the ruling" of his kingdom "between Macedonians and Persians."

What distinguishes Alexander from all other conquerors is this divine mission. He had grown up with it, and he had to a great extent fulfilled it, before he gave expression to it at the banquet at Opis in such words as those reported by Plutarch (*Moralia* 329 C). "Alexander considered," wrote Plutarch, "that he had come from the gods to be a general governor and reconciler of the world. Using force of arms when he did not bring men together by the light of reason, he harnessed all resources to one and the same end, mixing the lives, manners, marriages and customs of men, as it were in a loving-cup." This is his true claim to be called "Alexander the Great": that he did not crush or dismember his enemies, as the conquering Romans crushed Carthage and Molossia and dismembered Macedonia into four parts; nor exploit, enslave or destroy the native peoples, as "the white man" has so often done in America, Africa, and Australasia; but that he created, albeit for only a few years, a supranational community capable of living internally at peace and of developing the concord and partnership which are so sadly lacking in the modern world.

Questions for Review and Study

1. In your judgment, do the ancient sources excerpted in this chapter support the interpretation of W. W. Tarn? Explain.
2. Why do we have so few of the ancient sources for Alexander?
3. Is it credible, given the nature and temperament of Alexander, that he was responsible for such a sophisticated concept as "the natural brotherhood of all men"?
4. In what ways did Tarn overstate his case?
5. Is it justifiable to characterize Alexander as "the Great"? Give your reasons.

Questions for Comparison

1. Evaluate the conquerors Alexander the Great and Julius Caesar. Why have these men so often been compared? By what definition of greatness can these men be lionized? In what sense might each be judged a symptom of his civilization's corruption? Do you think the term "civilization" (whether Greek, Roman, or other) incompatible with tyrannical rule when referring to the ancient world, or was tyranny needed to combat "barbarism"? What interpretive problems arise from the sources concerning Alexander and Julius Caesar?

Suggestions for Further Reading

As is often the case, the classical sources for the biography of Alexander are among the liveliest and most entertaining works about him, especially

Plutarch and Arrian. Plutarch's "Life of Alexander" from his *Parallel Lives of Noble Greeks and Romans* (available in several editions) is, like the rest of the biographical sketches in this famous book, a gossipy and charming account, containing most of the familiar anecdotes associated with Alexander. Arrian's work, the most substantial of the ancient sources, despite a certain stuffiness and lack of analytical daring, is solidly based on more contemporary sources now long lost—particularly Ptolemy's journal and the work of Aristobulus. And it contains the best and most detailed account of Alexander's conquests. See the excellent modern translation by Aubrey de Sélincourt, *Arrian's Life of Alexander the Great.*

The views of W. W. Tarn summarized in the passage excerpted here from his Raleigh Lecture on History, "Alexander the Great and the Unity of Mankind," are spelled out in greater detail in the chapters he wrote on Alexander and his age in volume 6 of the *Cambridge Ancient History* and in his *Alexander the Great,* based on that account but expanded and updated.

Tarn's bitterest critic is Ernst Badian, who chose to challenge Tarn in particular for the views expressed in his Raleigh Lecture. See Badian's article of the same title, "Alexander the Great and the Unity of Mankind." This article is highly specialized and closely reasoned, and contains long passages in Greek; nevertheless, it is very important, and, despite the difficulties of the text, the argument can be clearly followed even by the nonspecialist. Peter Green's *Alexander of Macedon 356–323 B.C.* is a substantially revised edition of his *Alexander the Great,* a modern general account of Alexander's career in the same critical tradition as Badian. Three other modern works that deal more with the conquests than the conqueror are Peter Bamm's *Alexander the Great;* Sir Mortimer Wheeler's *Flames over Persepolis,* of particular interest because of Wheeler's expert knowledge of Near Eastern and Indian archaeology; and Richard A. Bellows's *Kings and Colonists,* a well-received book by an established Hellenistic scholar. A. B. Bosworth's *Conquest and Empire* is a substantially revisionist work, giving us, as one reviewer said, an "Alexander for our more cynical times," presented as a harsh opportunist and ruthless conqueror.

A book that stresses the continuing work in archaeology, including the dramatic finds at Vergina in Macedonia, is *The Search for Alexander,* by Robin Lane Fox. The most balanced and readable modern general account, however, may still be *Alexander the Great and the Hellenistic Empire,* by A. R. Burn, although R. D. Milns's *Alexander the Great* is also recommended.

Finally, Alexander is the subject of two first-rate historical novels by Mary Renault, *Fire from Heaven,* and *The Persian Boy,* the first carrying the story through Alexander's childhood to his accession to the throne of Macedonia, the second recounting his conquests as narrated by the Persian boy-eunuch Bagoas, Alexander's companion and lover. Renault has also produced a nonfiction account, fully as readable as her novels, and based on the meticulous research she prepared for them, *The Nature of Alexander.* (Titles with an asterisk are out of print.)

Badian, Ernst. "Alexander the Great and the Unity of Mankind." In *Alexander the Great: The Main Problems,* ed. G. T. Griffith. New York: Barnes and Noble, 1966.

Bamm, Peter. *Alexander the Great: Power as Destiny.* Trans. J. M. Brownjohn. New York: McGraw-Hill, 1968.

Bellows, Richard A. *Kings and Colonists: Aspects of Macedonian Imperialism.* Columbia Studies in the Classical Tradition. London and New York: E. J. Brill, 1994.

Bosworth, A. B. *Conquest and Empire: The Reign of Alexander the Great.* Cambridge: Cambridge University Press, 1988.

Burn, A. R. *Alexander the Great and the Hellenistic Empire.* London: The English Universities Press, 1947.

De Sélincourt, Aubrey. *Arrian's Life of Alexander the Great.* Harmondsworth, England: Penguin, 1958.

Fox, Robin Lane. *The Search for Alexander.* Boston: Little, Brown, 1980.

Green, Peter. *Alexander of Macedon 356–323 B.C.: A Historical Biography.* Berkeley and Los Angeles: University of California Press, 1991.

Milns, R. D. *Alexander the Great.* London: Robert Hale, 1968.*

Plutarch. "Life of Alexander." In *Parallel Lives of Noble Greeks and Romans.*

Renault, Mary. *Fire from Heaven.* New York: Pantheon, 1969.

———. *The Nature of Alexander.* New York: Pantheon, 1975.

———. *The Persian Boy.* New York: Pantheon, 1972.

Tarn, W. W. *Alexander the Great.* 2 vols. Cambridge: Cambridge University Press, 1948.

———. *Cambridge Ancient History,* vol. 6. Cambridge: Cambridge University Press, 1927, chs. 12–15.

Wheeler, Sir Mortimer. *Flames over Persepolis: Turning Point in History.* New York: Morrow, 1968.

JULIUS CAESAR: THE COLOSSUS THAT BESTRODE THE NARROW WORLD

C. 100 B.C.	Born
84 B.C.	Appointed a priest of Jupiter
c. 80 B.C.	Hostility of the dictator Sulla
69 or 68 B.C.	Elected quaestor
62 B.C.	Elected praetor
59 B.C.	Elected consul; first Triumvirate with Crassus and Pompey
58–50 B.C.	Conquest of Gaul
49–45 B.C.	Civil war
44 B.C.	Assassinated

Unlike Alexander, who conquered the world "as a boy" and was dead at thirty-three, Julius Caesar reached a mature age without achieving astonishing success. He did have considerable experience as a political faction leader, but in the judgment of most of his contemporaries he was not likely to be a world conqueror of Alexander's stamp. And yet, in 49 B.C., when Caesar was fifty years old, a series of events began to unfold that would make him one of the great conquerors of world history and set him alongside Alexander in the estimation of scholar and schoolboy alike.

For ten years, Caesar had been building a military reputation with his successful campaigns in Gaul and Britain and along the Rhine frontier, but always with an eye on events in the city of Rome and the Roman senate, where he had a personal interest in the fierce contest among cliques and factions that dominated senatorial politics in the last years of the Roman Republic. As the year 49 B.C. approached, Caesar's proconsular authority in Gaul was running out. He demanded that he be permitted to stand *in absentia* for the consulship for the following year—a neither unprecedented nor unreasonable demand. Caesar attempted to negotiate with his old ally, the great general Pompey, perhaps to prolong their alliance. But Pompey, his own military reputation threatened by Caesar's growing prestige, and relentlessly pressured by Caesar's enemies in the senate, refused him and joined with the senate in demanding that Caesar surrender his military command and return to Rome as a private citizen to stand for the consulship. But to do so would have meant his death or proscription. Thus, in January of 49 B.C., Caesar took the fateful step into open revolution, leading a token force across the Rubicon, the little stream that separated his Gallic province from peninsular Italy.

For nearly a century, the Roman constitution had been progressively subverted by a succession of extralegal expedients to legitimize the authority of one strong man after another, one faction after another—whether the prolonged consulships of Marius, the perpetual dictatorship of Sulla, or the triumviral authority that Caesar himself had held with Pompey and Crassus. Such practices, as well as a pervasive disenchantment with the self-serving senatorial oligarchy, had created broad support in Rome and in Italy for a policy of change, even revolutionary change. Caesar's popular reputation attracted that support as he marched south toward Rome. Even Pompey's legions in Spain declared for Caesar. Pompey and his remaining allies fled to Greece, where they were pursued by Caesar under vast emergency authority readily granted by an overawed senate, and were defeated at Pharsalus. In the next four years, Caesar moved through Asia Minor and Syria, Egypt, North Africa, and Spain and encircled the Mediterranean with his conquests, giving the final rough form to the greatest empire of antiquity.

It was at this point that the plot to assassinate Caesar was formed. It was carried out on the Ides of March of the year 44 B.C.

Caesar and Alexander beg for comparison, despite the many dissimilarities in their lives. Plutarch, the greatest of ancient biographers, paired them in his *Parallel Lives of Noble Greeks and Romans,* and almost every other ancient writer who speculates upon the meaning of Caesar's career suggests comparison with Alexander. The obvious basis for the comparison is, of course, the military parallel along with the fact that Caesar, like Alexander, seized his time and wrenched it so violently that the direction of world events was fundamentally changed. But, equally important, both men were cut off before their schemes for a civil order could be realized. There was about Caesar, as about Alexander, an aura of things to come, of unfulfilled dreams even more astounding than his conquests. Thus the question again intrigues us, "What would Caesar have accomplished had he lived on?"

In one important respect, Caesar differs radically from Alexander—in our sources of information about him. As we saw in the last chapter, all the contemporary works that dealt with the career of Alexander have been lost, and the best surviving account of him was written some four hundred years after he died. Not so with Caesar. He lived during the most heavily documented period in ancient history, a time when we know more about the people and events at the center of the world's stage than we will know again for more than a thousand years. We have Caesar's own considerable volume of writings. We have the works of his great senatorial contemporary Cicero. We have the writings of poets and essayists and narrative historians. But, despite the abundance of material and the wealth of detail about Julius Caesar, a clear and convincing picture of the man—what he was and what he might have become—eludes us, precisely because, as Shakespeare's Cassius says in *Julius Caesar,* ". . . he doth bestride the narrow world like a colossus," because his dominating personality, his overweening ambition, and his striking accomplishments made it nearly impossible for his contemporaries to be objective about him. His own writings are propagandistic, and the writings of Cicero, his often bitter and vindictive opponent, and Sallust, his partisan, are obviously biased. The accounts of both Pollio and Livy exist in epitomes or in traces in others' works. For our best account of Caesar, we must reach down into the imperial period that followed his own brilliant "golden age of Latin literature," to one of the writers of "the silver age," the biographer Suetonius.

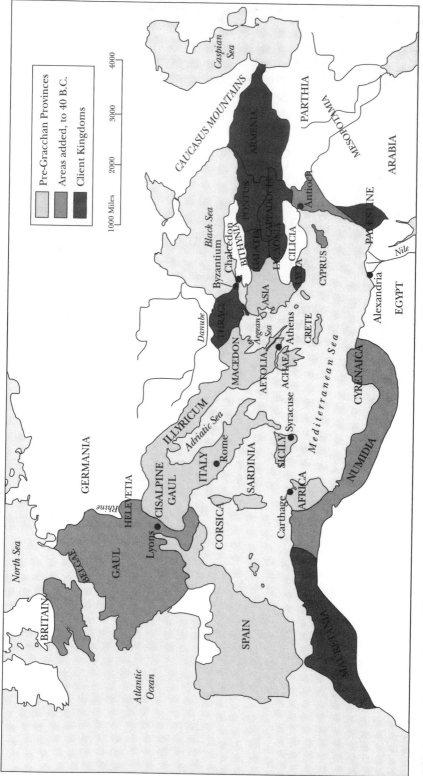

The Roman Republic's Holdings at the Death of Julius Caesar, 44 B.C.

The Life of Caesar

SUETONIUS

The choice of Suetonius is a good one on a number of counts. Although he has been charged with a journalistic style and mentality and with too great a fondness for scandal, rumor, and portent, the late imperial Historia Augusta, *for what it is worth, refers to him as having written* vere, *"truly," and a great modern Roman historian calls him "far and away the best authority" on Caesar.[1] Unlike his contemporary Plutarch, Suetonius was not a moralist using biography as a source of example. Nor was he a deliberate partisan: the factionalism of Caesar's age was long dead. Suetonius was interested only in writing a plain, straightforward account of the characters and events that were his subject. Like Arrian, he turned to archival sources for his information. The book in which his biography of Caesar appears,* The Lives of the Twelve Caesars, *was begun when Suetonius was still in the imperial civil service of the Emperor Hadrian. It is clear that he had access to archival records, now long lost, as well as to literary sources, and that he followed his sources carefully. His biography of Caesar was apparently a part of the book done before Suetonius left the imperial service in about* A.D. *120 and thus is especially well documented with records and sources.*

And yet, in an important sense, Suetonius was the captive of those very sources he followed so scrupulously. For even though he was more than a century removed from his sources, the hostility toward Caesar that these records expressed is clearly reflected in Suetonius's writing. Despite his fascination and admiration for Caesar, Suetonius's basic assessment is that Caesar's arrogance and his flaunting of the republican tradition led to his murder: "He abused his powers and was justly slain."

Even after the civil war and the furious activity of the years 48–44 B.C., *Suetonius tells us, Caesar was full of plans for beautifying the city of Rome, opening libraries, draining the Pomptine marshes, building new highways, constructing a canal through the Isthmus of Corinth, and waging war against both the Dacians and the Parthians.*

All these enterprises and plans were cut short by his death. But before I speak of that, it will not be amiss to describe briefly his personal appearance, his dress, his mode of life, and his character, as well as his conduct in civil and military life.

He is said to have been tall of stature, with a fair complexion, shapely limbs, a somewhat full face, and keen black eyes; sound of

---

[1]Sir Ronald Syme, in a review of Matthias Gelzer's *Caesar der Politiker und Staatsmann* in *Journal of Roman Studies*, 34 (1944), 95.

health, except that towards the end he was subject to sudden fainting fits and to nightmares as well. He was twice attacked by the falling sickness during his campaigns. He was somewhat overnice in the care of his person, not only keeping the hair of his head closely cut and his face smoothly shaved, but as some have charged, even having super-fluous hair plucked out. His baldness was a disfigurement which troubled him greatly, since he found that it was often the subject of the gibes of his detractors. Because of it he used to comb forward his scanty locks from the crown of his head, and of all the honors voted him by the Senate and people there was none which he received or made use of more gladly than the privilege of wearing a laurel wreath at all times. . . .

It is admitted by all that he was much addicted to women, as well as very extravagant in his intrigues with them, and that he seduced many illustrious women, among them Postumia, wife of Servius Sulpicius, Lollia, wife of Aulus Gabinius, Tertulla, wife of Marcus Crassus, and even Gnaeus Pompey's wife Mucia. . . .

He had love affairs with Queens, too, including Eunoe the Moor, wife of Bogudes, on whom, as well as on her husband, he bestowed many splendid presents, as Naso writes. But his greatest favorite was Cleopatra, with whom he often feasted until daybreak, and he would have gone through Egypt with her in her state-barge almost to Aethiopia, had not his soldiers refused to follow him. Finally he called her to Rome and did not let her leave until he had laden her with high honors and rich gifts, and he allowed her to give his name to the child which she bore. . . .

That he drank very little wine not even his enemies denied. There is a saying of Marcus Cato that Caesar was the only man who undertook to overthrow the state when sober. Even in the matter of food Gaius Oppius tells us that he was so indifferent, that once when his host served stale oil instead of fresh, and the other guests would have none of it, Caesar partook even more plentifully than usual, that he might not seem to charge his host with carelessness or lack of manners.

But his abstinence did not extend to pecuniary advantages, either when in command of armies or when in civil office. For we have the testimony of some writers that when he was Proconsul in Spain, he not only begged money from the allies, to help pay his debts, but also attacked and sacked some towns of the Lusitanians, although they did not refuse his terms and opened their gates to him on his arrival. In Gaul he pillaged shrines and temples of the Gods filled with offerings, and oftener sacked towns for the sake of plunder than for any fault. . . .

He was highly skilled in arms and horsemanship, and of incredible powers of endurance. On the march he headed his army, sometimes on horseback, but oftener on foot, bareheaded both in the heat of the sun and in rain. He covered great distances with incredible speed, making a hundred miles a day in a hired carriage and with little baggage, swimming the rivers which barred his path or crossing them on inflated skins, and very often arriving before the messengers sent to announce his coming. . . .

He joined battle, not only after planning his movements in advance but on a sudden opportunity, often immediately at the end of a march, and sometimes in the foulest weather, when one would least expect him to make a move. It was not until his later years that he became slower to engage, through a conviction that the oftener he had been victor, the less he ought to tempt fate, and that he could not possibly gain as much by success as he might lose by a defeat. He never put his enemy to flight without also driving him from his camp, thus giving him no respite in his panic. When the issue was doubtful, he used to send away the horses, and his own among the first, to impose upon his troops the greater necessity of standing their ground by taking away that aid to flight. . . .

When his army gave way, he often rallied it single-handed, planting himself in the way of the fleeing men, laying hold of them one by one, even seizing them by the throat and turning them to face the enemy; that, too, when they were in such a panic that an eagle-bearer made a pass at him with the point as he tried to stop him, while another left the standard in Caesar's hand when he would hold him back. . . .

At Alexandria, while assaulting a bridge, he was forced by a sudden sally of the enemy to take to a small skiff. When many others threw themselves into the same boat, he plunged into the sea, and after swimming for two hundred paces, got away to the nearest ship, holding up his left hand all the way, so as not to wet some papers which he was carrying, and dragging his cloak after him with his teeth, to keep the enemy from getting it as a trophy.

He valued his soldiers neither for their personal character nor their fortune, but solely for their prowess, and he treated them with equal strictness and indulgence. . . .

He certainly showed admirable self-restraint and mercy, both in his conduct of the civil war and in the hour of victory. While Pompey threatened to treat as enemies those who did not take up arms for the government, Caesar gave out that those who were neutral and of neither party should be numbered with his friends. He freely allowed all those whom he had made Centurions[2] on Pompey's recommendation to go over to his rival. . . . At the battle of Pharsalus he cried out, "Spare your fellow citizens," and afterwards allowed each of his men to save any one man he pleased of the opposite party. . . .

Yet after all, his other actions and words so far outweigh all his good qualities that it is thought he abused his power and was justly slain. For not only did he accept excessive honors, such as an uninter-

---

[2]Centurions were "company grade" officers in the Roman legion.

rupted consulship, the dictatorship for life, and the censorship of public morals, as well as the forename Imperator,[3] the surname of Father of his Country, a statue among those of the Kings,[4] and a raised couch in the orchestra of the theater. He also allowed honors to be bestowed on him which were too great for mortal man: a golden throne in the House and on the judgment seat; a chariot and litter in the procession at the circus; temples, altars, and statues beside those of the Gods; a special priest; an additional college of the Luperci; and the calling of one of the months by his name. In fact, there were no honors which he did not receive or confer at pleasure.

He held his third and fourth consulships in name only, content with the power of the dictatorship conferred on him at the same time as the consulships. Moreover, in both years he substituted two Consuls for himself for the last three months, in the meantime holding no elections except for Tribunes and plebeian Aediles, and appointing Praefects instead of the Praetors, to manage the affairs of the city during his absence. When one of the Consuls suddenly died the day before the Kalends of January, he gave the vacant office for a few hours to a man who asked for it. With the same disregard of law and precedent he named magistrates for several years to come, bestowed the emblems of consular rank on ten ex-Praetors, and admitted to the House men who had been given citizenship, and in some cases even half-civilized Gauls. He assigned the charge of the mint and of the public revenues to his own slaves, and gave the oversight and command of the three legions which he had left at Alexandria to a favorite boy of his called Rufio, son of one of his freedmen.

No less arrogant were his public utterances, which Titus Ampius records: that the Republic was a name only, without substance or reality; that Sulla did not know his A. B. C. when he laid down his dictatorship; that men ought now to be more circumspect in addressing him, and to regard his word as law. So far did he go in his presumption, that when a soothsayer once announced to him the direful omen that a victim offered for sacrifice was without a heart, he said: "The entrails will be more favorable when I please. It ought not to be taken as a miracle if a beast have no heart."

But it was the following action in particular that roused deadly hatred against him. When the Senate approached him in a body with many highly honorary decrees, he received them before the temple of

---

[3]The title *Imperator,* synonymous with conqueror, was that by which troops would hail a victorious commander. It first assumed a permanent and royal character through Caesar's use of it as a praenomen.

[4]Statues of each of the seven Kings of Rome were in the Capitol, to which an eighth was added in honor of Brutus, who expelled the last of the Kings. The statue of Julius was afterward raised near them.

Venus Genetrix without rising. Some think that when he attempted to get up, he was held back by Cornelius Balbus; others, that he made no such move at all, but on the contrary frowned angrily on Gaius Trebatius when he suggested that he should rise. This action of his seemed the more intolerable, because when he himself in one of his triumphal processions rode past the benches of the Tribunes, he was so incensed because one of their number, Pontius Aquila by name, did not rise, that he cried: "Come then, Aquila, mighty Tribune, and take from me the Republic," and for several days afterwards, he would promise a favor to no one without adding, "That is, if Pontius Aquila will give me leave."

To an insult which so plainly showed his contempt for the Senate he added an act of even greater insolence. After the sacred rites of the Latin Festival, as he was returning to the city, amid the extravagant and unprecedented demonstrations of the populace, some one in the press placed on his statue a laurel wreath with a white fillet tied to it. When Epidius Marullus and Caesetius Flavus, Tribunes of the Commons, gave orders that the ribbon be removed from the crown and the man taken off to prison, Caesar sharply rebuked and deposed them, either offended that the hint at regal power had been received with so little favor, or, as was said, that he had been robbed of the glory of refusing it. But from that time on he could not rid himself of the odium of having aspired to the title of monarch, although he replied to the Commons, when they hailed him as King, "I am Caesar and not King." At the Lupercalia, when the Consul Antony several times attempted to place a crown upon his head as he spoke from the rostra, he put it aside and at last sent it to the Capitol, to be offered to Jupiter Optimus Maximus. Nay, more, the report had spread in various quarters that he intended to move to Ilium or Alexandria, taking with him the resources of the state, draining Italy by levies, and leaving it and the charge of the city to his friends; also that at the next meeting of the Senate Lucius Cotta would announce as the decision of the Fifteen,[5] that inasmuch as it was written in the books of fate that the Parthians could be conquered only by a King, Caesar should be given that title. . . .

More than sixty joined the conspiracy against him, led by Gaius Cassius and Marcus and Decimus Brutus. At first they hesitated whether to form two divisions at the elections in the Campus Martius, so that while some hurled him from the bridge as he summoned the tribes to vote, the rest might wait below and slay him; or to set upon him in the Sacred Way or at the entrance to the theater. When, however, a meeting of the Senate was called for the Ides of March in the Hall of Pompey, they readily gave that time and place the preference.

---

[5]The college of fifteen priests who inspected and expounded the Sybilline books.

Now Caesar's approaching murder was foretold to him by unmistakable signs: . . . when he was offering sacrifice, the soothsayer Spurinna warned him to beware of danger, which would come not later than the Ides of March. . . .

Both for these reasons and because of poor health he hesitated for a long time whether to stay at home and put off what he had planned to do in the Senate. But at last, urged by Decimus Brutus not to disappoint the full meeting, which had for some time been waiting for him, he went forth almost at the end of the fifth hour. When a note revealing the plot was handed him by some one on the way, he put it with others which he held in his left hand, intending to read them presently. Then, after many victims had been slain, and he could not get favorable omens, he entered the House in defiance of portents, laughing at Spurinna and calling him a false prophet, because the Ides of March were come without bringing him harm. Spurinna replied that they had of a truth come, but they had not gone.

As he took his seat, the conspirators gathered about him as if to pay their respects, and straightway Tillius Cimber, who had assumed the lead, came nearer as though to ask something. When Caesar with a gesture put him off to another time, Cimber caught his toga by both shoulders. As Caesar cried, "Why, this is violence!" one of the Cascas stabbed him from one side just below the throat. Caesar caught Casca's arm and ran it through with his stylus, but as he tried to leap to his feet, he was stopped by another wound. When he saw that he was beset on every side by drawn daggers, he muffled his head in his robe, and at the same time drew down its lap to his feet with his left hand, in order to fall more decently, with the lower part of his body also covered. And in this wise he was stabbed with three and twenty wounds, uttering not a word, but merely a groan at the first stroke, though some have written that when Marcus Brutus rushed at him, he said in Greek, "You too, my child?" All the conspirators made off, and he lay there lifeless for some time, until finally three common slaves put him on a litter and carried him home, with one arm hanging down.

The Heroic Image of Caesar

THEODOR MOMMSEN

Theodor Mommsen (1817–1903) was awarded the Nobel Prize for Literature in 1902, largely for the literary achievement of his monumental, multivolume His-tory of Rome. The Nobel citation called him the "greatest . . . master of historical narrative" of his age—a considerable claim in an era that had produced Ranke and Burckhardt, Guizot, Grote, Carlyle, and Macaulay. Still, the assertion may be true. Mommsen, a prolific writer, had gained an immense and well-deserved authority, and his massive History of Rome *was profoundly influential. It was Mommsen who at last placed the study of ancient history on a scientific and critical foundation. He also began and directed the first great critical collection of ancient Latin inscriptions.*

Like W. W. Tarn, Theodor Mommsen was trained both in classics and in law. His first academic appointment was as professor of law at Leipzig. Then in 1858 he was appointed to the chair of ancient history at the University of Berlin. Throughout his long life, Mommsen was not only a professor but a passionate political activist. He was involved in the Revolution of 1848 and lost his academic post at Leipzig because of it. In the 1870s he was a prominent member of the Prussian Parliament, frequently clashing with Otto von Bismarck. Like many great historians, Mommsen read the past in terms of present politics. Thus his view of Caesar and the late Roman Republic was colored by his profound disillusionment with German political liberalism and an equally profound hatred for Junker conservatism. Julius Caesar became for Mommsen the archetypal strongman who had swept away the broken pieces of a ruined oligarchy and set the rule of the beneficent Roman Empire firmly on its base. While Mommsen has been rightly criticized for the extravagance of his opinions both on Caesar and on the late Roman Republic, his views, though never quite accepted as the "standard" interpretation, did exert a strong influence on modern scholarship until fairly recently.

Here, from The History of Rome, *is Mommsen's evaluation of Julius Caesar. The prose is old-fashioned and florid, and the judgments are dated, but there is still some power left in the sweep of Mommsen's portrayal of his "perfect man."*

The new monarch of Rome, the first ruler over the whole domain of Romano-Hellenic civilization, Gaius Julius Caesar, was in his fifty-sixth year . . . when the battle at Thapsus [46 B.C.], the last link in a long chain of momentous victories, placed the decision as to the future of the world in his hands. Few men have had their elasticity so thoroughly put to the proof as Caesar—the sole creative genius produced by Rome, and the last produced by the ancient world, which accordingly moved on in the path that he marked out for it until its sun went down. Sprung from one of the oldest noble families of Latium—which traced back its lineage to the heroes of the Iliad and the kings of Rome, and in fact to the Venus-Aphrodite common to both nations—he spent the years of his boyhood and early manhood as the genteel youth of that epoch were wont to spend them. He had tasted the sweetness as well as the bitterness of the cup of fashionable life, had recited and declaimed, had practised literature and made verses in his idle hours, had prosecuted love-intrigues of every sort, and got himself initiated into all the mysteries of shaving, curls, and ruffles pertaining to the toilette-wisdom of the day, as well as into the still more mysterious art of always borrowing and never paying. But the flexible steel of that nature was proof against even these dissipated and flighty courses; Caesar retained both his bodily vigour and his elasticity of mind and of heart unimpaired. In fencing and in riding he was a match for any of his soldiers, and his swimming saved his life at Alexandria; the incredible rapidity of his journeys, which usually for the sake of gaining time were performed by night—a thorough contrast to the procession-like slowness with which Pompeius moved from one place to another—was the astonishment of his contemporaries and not the least among the causes of his success. The mind was like the body. His remarkable power of intuition revealed itself in the precision and practicability of all his arrangements, even where he gave orders without having seen with his own eyes. His memory was matchless, and it was easy for him to carry on several occupations simultaneously with equal self-possession. . . .

Caesar was thoroughly a realist and a man of sense; and whatever he undertook and achieved was pervaded and guided by the cool sobriety which constitutes the most marked peculiarity of his genius. To this he owed the power of living energetically in the present, undisturbed either by recollection or by expectation; to this he owed the capacity of acting at any moment with collected vigour, and of applying his whole genius even to the smallest and most incidental enterprise; to this he owed the many-sided power with which he grasped and mastered whatever understanding can comprehend and will can compel; to this he owed the self-possessed ease with which he arranged his periods as well as projected his campaigns; to this he owed the "marvellous serenity" which remained steadily with him through good and evil days; to this he owed the complete independence, which admitted of no control by favourite or by mistress, or even by friend. It resulted, moreover, from this clearness of judgment that Caesar never formed to himself illusions regarding the power of fate and the ability of man; in his case the friendly veil was lifted up, which conceals from man the inadequacy of his working. Prudently as he laid his plans and considered all possibilities, the feeling was never absent from his breast that in all things fortune, that is to say accident, must bestow success; and with this may be connected the circumstance that he so often played a desperate game with destiny, and in particular again and again hazarded his person with daring indifference. As indeed occasionally men of predominant sagacity betake themselves to a pure game of hazard, so there was in Caesar's rationalism a point at which it came in some measure into contact with mysticism.

Gifts such as these could not fail to produce a statesman. From early youth, accordingly, Caesar was a statesman in the deepest sense of the term, and his aim was the highest which man is allowed to propose to himself—the political, military, intellectual, and moral regeneration of his own deeply decayed nation, and of the still more deeply decayed Hellenic nation intimately akin to his own. The hard school of thirty years' experience changed his views as to the means by which this aim was to be reached; his aim itself remained the same in the times of his hopeless humiliation and of his unlimited plenitude of power, in the times when as demagogue and conspirator he stole towards it by paths of darkness, and in those when, as joint possessor of the supreme power and then as monarch, he worked at his task in the full light of day before the eyes of the world. . . . According to his original plan he had purposed to reach his object, like Pericles and Gaius Gracchus, without force of arms, and throughout eighteen years he had as leader of the popular party moved exclusively amid political plans and intrigues—until, reluctantly convinced of the necessity for a military support, he, when already forty years of age, put himself at the head of an army [59 B.C.]. . . .

The most remarkable peculiarity of his action as a statesman was its perfect harmony. In reality all the conditions for this most difficult of all human functions were united in Caesar. A thorough realist, he never allowed the images of the past or venerable tradition to disturb him; for him nothing was of value in politics but the living present and the law of reason, just as in his character of grammarian he set aside historical and antiquarian research and recognized nothing but on the one hand the living *usus loquendi* and on the other hand the rule of symmetry. A born ruler, he governed the minds of men as the wind drives the clouds, and compelled the most heterogeneous natures to place themselves at his service—the plain citizen and the rough subaltern, the genteel matrons of Rome and the fair princesses of Egypt and Mauretania, the brilliant cavalry-officer and the calculating banker. His talent for organization was marvellous; no statesman has ever compelled alliances, no general has ever collected an army out of unyielding and refractory elements with such decision, and kept them together with such firmness, as Caesar displayed in constraining and upholding his coalitions and his legions; never did regent judge his instruments and assign each to the place appropriate for him with so acute an eye.

He was monarch; but he never played the king. Even when absolute lord of Rome, he retained the deportment of the party-leader; perfectly pliant and smooth, easy and charming in conversation, complaisant towards every one, it seemed as if he wished to be nothing but the first among his peers. Caesar entirely avoided the blunder into which so many men otherwise on an equality with him have fallen, of carrying into politics the military tone of command; however much occasion his disagreeable relations with the senate gave for it, he never resorted to outrages. . . . Caesar was monarch; but he was never seized with the giddiness of the tyrant. He is perhaps the only one among the mighty ones of the earth, who in great matters and little never acted according to inclination or caprice, but always without exception according to his duty as ruler, and who, when he looked back on his life, found doubtless erroneous calculations to deplore, but no false step of passion to regret. There is nothing in the history of Caesar's life, which even on a small scale can be compared with those poetico-sensual ebullitions—such as the murder of Kleitos or the burning of Persepolis—which the history of his great predecessor in the east records. He is, in fine, perhaps the only one of those mighty ones who has preserved to the end of his career the statesman's tact of discriminating between the possible and the impossible, and has not broken down in the task which for greatly gifted natures is the most difficult of all—the task of recognizing, when on the pinnacle of success, its natural limits. What was possible he performed, and never left the possible good undone for the sake of the impossible better, never disdained at least to mitigate by palliatives evils that were incurable. But where he recognized that fate had spoken, he always obeyed. . . .

Such was this unique man, whom it seems so easy and yet is so infinitely difficult to describe. His whole nature is transparent clearness; and tradition preserves more copious and more vivid information about him than about any of his peers in the ancient world. Of such a personage our conceptions may well vary in point of shallowness or depth, but they cannot be, strictly speaking, different; to every not utterly perverted inquirer the grand figure has exhibited the same essential features, and yet no one has succeeded in reproducing it to the life. The secret lies in its perfection. In his character as a man as well as in his place in history, Caesar occupies a position where the great contrasts of existence meet and balance each other. Of mighty creative power and yet at the same time of the most penetrating judgment; no longer a youth and not yet an old man; of the highest energy of will and the highest capacity of execution; filled with republican ideals and at the same time born to be a king; a Roman in the deepest essence of his nature, and yet called to reconcile and combine in himself as well as in the outer world the Roman and the Hellenic types of culture—Caesar was the entire and perfect man.

Caesar the Politician

RONALD SYME

The longtime Oxford professor Sir Ronald Syme is probably our leading ancient historian today. His most important book, and possibly the outstanding work in Roman history in this century,[6] is The Roman Revolution. *Syme worked on*

---

[6]Cf. the review, for example, of Michael Ginsburg in *American Historical Review*, 46 (1940), 108.

this book through the late 1930s, against the backdrop of events taking place in Mommsen's Germany, but the vision of one-person rule was not quite as alluring to him as it had been to Mommsen. Syme's view of Caesar, however, was not only affected by the rise of Hitler and the political drift toward World War II. He had before him an impressive accumulation of scholarly research on the darker side of the Caesarian monarchy. Eduard Meyer's Caesars Monarchie und das Principat des Pompejus *(1919) argues that Caesar aspired to the establishment of a Hellenistic monarchy in Rome. The second volume of Jerome Carcopino's* Histoire Romaine *(1936) deals with Caesar and maintains that, since his youth, Caesar's ambition was directed toward monarchy.*

*Syme also read the important work of Matthias Gelzer—*Die Nobilität der Römischen Republik *(1912) and* Caesar der Politiker und Staatsmann *(1921)—which prompted him to examine some of the same ground, the social and political setting in which Caesar lived and died. Syme, like Gelzer, was especially interested in the senatorial oligarchy. The "Roman Revolution" of his title, he argues, occurred when this oligarchy lost its power to a new social group composed of people from all parts of Italy, even the provinces. And he saw Caesar as the political genius who began the revolution that he could not then control.*

Syme insists that Caesar be judged—as he was murdered—"for what he was, not for what he might become," be that an oriental despot or a Hellenistic monarch. What Caesar was was a Roman aristocrat whose brilliance and luck enabled him to surpass his fellow aristocrats. The key factor leading to his assassination was not his arrogance, which was common to his class and station, or even his high-handedness in subverting the republic; it was the Caesarian dictatorship, prolonged first for ten years and then, in January of 44 B.C., for life, that was intolerable to the senatorial nobility and led to his murder.

The following, from The Roman Revolution, *is Syme's analysis of Caesar.*

The conquest of Gaul, the war against Pompeius and the establishment of the Dictatorship of Caesar are events that move in a harmony so swift and sure as to appear pre-ordained; and history has sometimes been written as though Caesar set the tune from the beginning, in the knowledge that monarchy was the panacea for the world's ills, and with the design to achieve it by armed force. Such a view is too simple to be historical.

Caesar strove to avert any resort to open war. Both before and after the outbreak of hostilities he sought to negotiate with Pompeius. Had Pompeius listened and consented to an interview, their old *amicitia* might have been repaired. With the nominal primacy of Pompeius recognized, Caesar and his adherents would capture the government—and perhaps reform the State. Caesar's enemies were afraid of that—and so was Pompeius. After long wavering Pompeius chose at last to save the oligarchy. Further, the proconsul's proposals as conveyed to the State were moderate and may not be dismissed as mere manoeuvres for position or for time to bring up his armies.

Caesar knew how small was the party willing to provoke a war. As the artful motion of a Caesarian tribune had revealed, an overwhelming majority in the Senate, nearly four hundred against twenty-two, wished both dynasts to lay down their extraordinary commands. A rash and factious minority prevailed.

The precise legal points at issue in Caesar's claim to stand for the consulate in absence and retain his province until the end of the year 49 B.C. are still matters of controversy. If they were ever clear, debate and misrepresentation soon clouded truth and equity. The nature of the political crisis is less obscure. Caesar and his associates in power had thwarted or suspended the constitution for their own ends many times in the past. Exceptions had been made before in favour of other dynasts; and Caesar asserted both legal and moral rights to preferential treatment. In the last resort his rank, prestige and honour, summed up in the Latin word *dignitas*, were all at stake: to Caesar, as he claimed, "his *dignitas* had ever been dearer than life itself." Sooner than surrender it, Caesar appealed to arms. A constitutional pretext was provided by the violence of his adversaries: Caesar stood in defence of the rights of the tribunes and the liberties of the Roman People. But that was not the plea which Caesar himself valued most— it was his personal honour.

His enemies appeared to have triumphed. They had driven a wedge between the two dynasts, winning over to their side the power and prestige of Pompeius. They would be able to deal with Pompeius later. It might not come to open war; and Pompeius was still in their control so long as he was not at the head of an army in the field. Upon Caesar they had thrust the choice between civil war and political extinction. . . .

Caesar was constrained to appeal to his army for protection. At last the enemies of Caesar had succeeded in ensnaring Pompeius and in working the constitution against the craftiest politican of the day: he was declared a public enemy if he did not lay down his command before a certain day. By invoking constitutional sanctions against Caesar, a small faction misrepresented the true wishes of a vast majority in the Senate, in Rome, and in Italy. They pretended that the issue lay between a rebellious proconsul and legitimate authority. Such venturesome expedients are commonly the work of hot blood and muddled heads. The error was double and damning. Disillusion followed swiftly. Even Cato was dismayed. It had confidently been expected that the solid and respectable classes in the towns of Italy would rally in defence of the authority of the Senate and the liberties of the Roman People, that all the land would rise as one man against the invader. Nothing of the kind happened. Italy was apathetic to the war-cry of the Republic in danger, sceptical about its champions. . . .

Caesar, it is true, had only a legion to hand: the bulk of his army was still far away. But he swept down the eastern coast of Italy, gathering troops, momentum and confidence as he went. Within two months of the crossing of the Rubicon he was master of Italy. Pompeius made his escape across the Adriatic carrying with him several legions and a large number of senators, a grievous burden of revenge and recrimination. The enemies of Caesar had counted upon capitulation or a short and easy war.

They had lost the first round. Then a second blow, quite beyond calculation: before the summer was out the generals of Pompeius in Spain were outmanoeuvred and overcome. Yet even so, until the legions joined battle on the plain of Pharsalus, the odds lay heavily against Caesar. Fortune, the devotion of his veteran legionaries and the divided counsels of his adversaries secured the crowning victory. But three years more of fighting were needed to stamp out the last and bitter resistance of the Pompeian cause in Africa and in Spain.

"They would have it thus," said Caesar as he gazed upon the Roman dead at Pharsalus, half in patriot grief for the havoc of civil war, half in impatience and resentment. They had cheated Caesar of the true glory of a Roman aristocrat—to contend with his peers for primacy, not to destroy them. His enemies had the laugh of him in death. Even Pharsalus was not the end. His former ally, the great Pompeius, glorious from victories in all quarters of the world, lay unburied on an Egyptian beach, slain by a renegade Roman, the hireling of a foreign king. Dead, too, and killed by Romans, were Caesar's rivals and enemies, many illustrious consulars. Ahenobarbus fought and fell at Pharsalus, and Q. Metellus Scipio ended worthy of his ancestors; while Cato chose to fall by his own hand rather than witness the domination of Caesar and the destruction of the Free State.

That was the nemesis of ambition and glory, to be thwarted in the end. After such wreckage, the task of rebuilding confronted him, stern and thankless. Without the sincere and patriotic co-operation of the governing class, the attempt would be all in vain, the mere creation of arbitrary power, doomed to perish in violence. . . .

Under these unfavourable auspices, a Sulla but for *clementia,* a Gracchus but lacking a revolutionary programme, Caesar established his Dictatorship. His rule began as the triumph of a faction in civil war: he made it his task to transcend faction, and in so doing wrought his own destruction. A champion of the People, he had to curb the People's rights, as Sulla had done. To rule, he needed the support of the *nobiles,* yet he had to curtail their privileges and repress their dangerous ambitions.

In name and function Caesar's office was to set the State in order again (*rei publicae constituendae*). Despite odious memories of Sulla, the choice of the Dictatorship was recommended by its comprehensive powers and freedom from the tribunician veto. Caesar knew that secret enemies would soon direct that deadly weapon against one who had used it with such dexterity in the past and who more recently claimed to be asserting the rights of the tribunes, the liberty of the Roman People. He was not mistaken. Yet he required special powers: after a civil war the need was patent. The Dictator's task might well demand several years. In 46 B.C. his powers were prolonged to a tenure of ten years, an ominous sign. A gleam of hope that the emergency period would be quite short flickered up for a moment, to wane at once and perish utterly. In January 44 B.C. Caesar was voted the Dictatorship for life. About the same time decrees of the Senate ordained that an oath of allegiance should be taken in his name. Was this the measure of his ordering of the Roman State? Was this a *res publica constituta?*

It was disquieting. Little had been done to repair the ravages of civil war and promote social regeneration. For that there was sore need, as both his adherents and his former adversaries pointed out. From Pompeius, from Cato, and from the oligarchy, no hope of reform. But Caesar seemed different: he had consistently advocated the cause of the oppressed, whether Roman, Italian, or provincial. He had shown that he was not afraid of vested interests. But Caesar was not a revolutionary. . . .

[He] postponed decision about the permanent ordering of the State. It was too difficult. Instead, he would set out for the wars again, to Macedonia and to the eastern frontier of the Empire. At Rome he was hampered: abroad he might enjoy his conscious mastery of men and events, as before in Gaul. Easy victories—but not the urgent needs of the Roman People.

About Caesar's ultimate designs there can be opinion, but no certainty. The acts and projects of his Dictatorship do not reveal them. For the rest, the evidence is partisan—or posthumous. No statement of unrealized intentions is a safe guide to history, for it is unverifiable and therefore the most attractive form of misrepresentation. The enemies of Caesar spread rumours to discredit the living Dictator: Caesar dead became a god and a myth, passing from the realm of history into literature and legend, declamation and propaganda. . . .

Yet speculation cannot be debarred from playing round the high and momentous theme of the last designs of Caesar the Dictator. It has been supposed and contended that Caesar either desired to establish or had actually inaugurated an institution unheard of in Rome and unimagined there—monarchic rule, despotic and absolute, based upon worship of the ruler, after the pattern of the monarchies of the Hellenistic East. Thus may Caesar be represented as the heir in all things of Alexander the Macedonian and as the anticipator of Caracalla, a king and a god incarnate, levelling class and nation, ruling a subject, united and uniform world by right divine.

This extreme simplification of long and diverse ages of history seems to suggest that Caesar alone of contemporary Roman statesmen possessed either a wide vision of the future or a singular and elementary blindness to the present. But this is only a Caesar of myth or rational construction. . . .

If Caesar must be judged, it is by facts and not by alleged intentions. As his acts and his writings reveal him, Caesar stands out as a realist and an opportunist. In the short time at his disposal he can hardly have made plans for a long future or laid the foundation of a consistent government. Whatever it might be, it would owe more to the needs of the moment than to alien or theoretical models. More important the business in hand; it was expedited in swift and arbitrary fashion. Caesar made plans and decisions in the company of his intimates and secretaries: the Senate voted but did not deliberate. As the Dictator was on the point of departing in the spring of 44 B.C. for several years of campaigning in the Balkans and the East, he tied up magistracies and provincial commands in advance by placing them, according to the traditional Roman way, in the hands of loyal partisans, or of reconciled Pompeians whose good sense should guarantee peace. For that period, at least, a salutary pause from political activity: with the lapse of time the situation might become clearer in one way or another. . . .

At the moment it was intolerable: the autocrat became impatient, annoyed by covert opposition, petty criticism, and laudations of dead Cato. That he was unpopular he well knew. "For all his genius, Caesar could not see a way out," as one of his friends was subsequently to remark. And there was no going back. To Caesar's clear mind and love of rapid decision, this brought a tragic sense of impotence and frustration—he had been all things and it was no good. He had surpassed the good fortune of Sulla Felix and the glory of Pompeius Magnus. In vain—reckless ambition had ruined the Roman State and baffled itself in the end. Of the melancholy that descended upon Caesar there stands the best of testimony—"my life has been long enough, whether reckoned in years or in renown." The words were remembered. The most eloquent of his contemporaries did not disdain to plagiarize them.

The question of ultimate intentions becomes irrelevant. Caesar was slain for what he was, not for what he might become. . . .

It is not necessary to believe that Caesar planned to establish at Rome a "Hellenistic Monarchy," whatever meaning may attach to that phrase. The Dictatorship was enough. The rule of the *nobiles,* he could see, was an anachronism in a world-empire; and so was the power of the Roman plebs when all Italy enjoyed the franchise. Caesar in truth was more conservative and Roman than many have fancied; and no Roman conceived of government save through an oligarchy. But Caesar was being forced into an autocratic position. It meant the lasting domination of one man instead of the rule of the law, the constitution, and the Senate; it announced the triumph soon or late of new forces and new ideas, the elevation of the army and the provinces, the depression of the traditional governing class. Caesar's autocracy appeared to be much more than a temporary expedient to liquidate the heritage of the civil war and reinvigorate the organs of the Roman State. It was going to last—and the Roman aristocracy was not to be permitted to govern and exploit the Empire in its own fashion. The tragedies of history do not arise from the conflict of conventional right and wrong. They are more august and more complex. Caesar and Brutus each had right on his side. . . .

Without a party a statesman is nothing. He sometimes forgets that awkward fact. If the leader or principal agent of a faction goes beyond the wishes of his allies and emancipates himself from control, he may have to be dropped or suppressed. . . .

When Caesar took the Dictatorship for life and the sworn allegiance of senators, it seemed clear that he had escaped from the shackles of party to supreme and personal rule. For this reason, certain of the most prominent of his adherents combined with Republicans and Pompeians to remove their leader. The Caesarian party thus split by the assassination of the Dictator none the less survived, joined for a few months with Republicans in a new and precarious front of security and vested interests led by the Dictator's political deputy until a new leader, emerging unexpected, at first tore it in pieces again, but ultimately, after conquering the last of his rivals, converted the old Caesarian party into a national government in a transformed State. The composition and vicissitudes of that party, though less dramatic in unity of theme than the careers and exploits of the successive leaders, will yet help to recall the ineffable complexities of authentic history.

Questions for Review and Study

1. Compare Julius Caesar with Alexander the Great.
2. Why was Caesar assassinated?
3. How did Caesar interpret the nature of his rule over the Roman Empire?
4. Caesar has been viewed as the assassin of the Roman Republic. Do you agree? Why, or why not?
5. What role do you think Caesar played in the history of the Roman Republic?

Questions for Comparison

1. Evaluate the conquerors Alexander the Great and Julius Caesar. Why have these men so often been compared? By what definition of great-

ness can these men be lionized? In what sense might each be judged a symptom of his civilization's corruption? Do you think the term "civilization" (whether Greek, Roman, or other) incompatible with tyrannical rule when referring to the ancient world, or was tyranny needed to combat "barbarism"? What interpretive problems arise from the sources concerning Alexander and Julius Caesar?

Suggestions for Further Reading

As in the case of Alexander, the ancient sources for the life of Julius Caesar are among the liveliest and most entertaining accounts of him. Students are encouraged to read the rest of Suetonius's sketch beyond what is excerpted in this chapter. They are also encouraged to read Plutarch's "Life of Caesar," which, as we have noted, he wrote to be compared with his "Life of Alexander." Plutarch and Suetonius between them give us most of the anecdotal matter commonly associated with Caesar. We have in addition the considerable volume of Caesar's own writings in several attractive modern editions of *The Gallic War* and *The Civil War*. We also have references to Caesar scattered throughout the works of such contemporaries as Cicero and Sallust.

Caesar has always been a fascinating figure, and there are an impossibly large number of biographies of him. Two can be especially recommended to students. Probably the best brief biography is J. P. V. D. Balsdon's *Julius Caesar and Rome*, an authoritative work by an established authority, another in the excellent "Teach Yourself History Library" series. Students may prefer the somewhat larger and more lavish *Caesar* by Michael Grant, in the "Great Lives" series; it is interesting and readable as well as authoritative, another book by one of the best modern popularizers of ancient history. In *Julius Caesar and His Public Image*, Zwi Yavetz attempts to assess the various answers to the question of why Caesar was assassinated. Students will find the last chapter, "Public Opinion and the Ides of March," particularly useful as a summary and review of the problem.

There are also many books dealing with Caesar's era and the late Roman Republic. One of the best of these, and one that combines the account of the man and the era, is Matthias Gelzer's *Caesar*. Despite its relentlessly prosaic quality, it is an important interpretive work by a great German scholar, stressing Caesar as a political figure of genius and paralleling the views of Sir Ronald Syme, which are represented in this chapter. A somewhat broader account, still considered a standard work by many authorities, is that of F. E. Adcock in volume 9 of *Cambridge Ancient History*. Also recommended are R. E. Smith's *The Failure of the Roman Republic;* the somewhat more detailed work by Erich S. Gruen, *The Last Generation of the Roman Republic;* and the now famous small study by Lily Ross Taylor, *Party Politics in the Age of Caesar*.

A number of special studies are also recommended: the attractive small book by F. E. Adcock, *Caesar as Man of Letters;* General John F. C. Fuller's *Julius Caesar,* a lively, opinionated, and somewhat debunking book by a great military historian about Caesar as a less-than-brilliant general; *Caesar's Army,* by H. P. Judson; *Caesar's Invasion of Britain,* by Peter B. Ellis; and *A History of the Art of War among the Romans down to the End of the Roman Empire,* by Theodore A. Dodge. (Titles with an asterisk are out of print.)

Adcock, F. E. *Caesar as Man of Letters.* Cambridge: Cambridge University Press, 1956.*

————. *Cambridge Ancient History,* vol. 9. Cambridge: Cambridge University Press, 1932, chs. 15–17.

Balsdon, J. P. V. D. *Julius Caesar and Rome.* Teach Yourself History Library. London: The English Universities Press, 1967.*

Caesar, Julius. *The Civil War.* Ed. and tr. Jane F. Mitchell. Baltimore: Penguin, 1967.

————. *The Gallic War.* Trans. and ed. Moses Hadas. New York: Modern Library, 1957.

————. *The Gallic War.* Trans. S. A. Handford. Baltimore: Penguin, 1965.

————. *The Gallic War.* Trans. J. Warrington. New York: Heritage, 1955.

Dodge, Theodore A. *A History of the Art of War among the Romans down to the End of the Roman Empire, with a Detailed Account of the Campaigns of Caius Julius Caesar.* London: Greenhill Books, 1995; and Mechanicsburg, Pa.: Stackpole Books, 1995.

Ellis, Peter B. *Caesar's Invasion of Britain.* London: Constable, 1994.

Fuller, Gen. John F. C. *Julius Caesar: Man, Soldier, and Tyrant.* New Brunswick, N.J.: Rutgers University Press, 1965.

Gelzer, Matthias. *Caesar: Politician and Statesman.* Trans. Peter Needham. Cambridge, Mass.: Harvard University Press, 1968.

Grant, Michael. *Caesar.* London: Weidenfeld and Nicolson, 1974.

Gruen, Erich S. *The Last Generation of the Roman Republic.* Berkeley and Los Angeles: University of California Press, 1974.*

Judson, H. P. *Caesar's Army: A Study of the Military Art of the Romans in the Last Days of the Republic.* Chicago: Ares, 1993.

Plutarch. "Life of Caesar."

Smith, R. E. *The Failure of the Roman Republic.* Cambridge: Cambridge University Press, 1955.

Taylor, Lily Ross. *Party Politics in the Age of Caesar.* Berkeley and Los Angeles: University of California Press, 1949, 1975.

Yavetz, Zwi. *Julius Caesar and His Public Image.* Ithaca, N.Y.: Cornell University Press, 1983.

THE CONVERSION OF CONSTANTINE

c. 283	Born
306	Hailed as Augustus (emperor) by his father's army in Gaul
312	Battle of Milvian Bridge; victory over Maxentius
313	Edict of Milan; toleration for Christians
330	Dedication of Constantinople
337	Died

As Julius Caesar stood at the beginning of the Roman empire, Constantine stood at its end. For more than a century before his rise to power, the civil structure of the empire had been undermined by an increasing militarization of the monarchy that had finally degenerated into a bloody scramble among rival contenders for the imperial throne. Under the stress of nearly constant civil war, the economic system of the empire broke down. Coinage was hopelessly corrupt, trade was replaced by barter and payment in kind, and the empire was pillaged to support the forces of one general after another, one emperor after another. With the empire preoccupied by civil war, hordes of barbarians moved across its undefended frontiers to ravage some of its richest lands. The military system was barbarized, with the greater number of its soldiers recruited from the most remote and backward parts of the empire, from the frontier army camps, even with the direct cooptation of entire barbarian units. Civil law and civil order were almost nonexistent. Classical civilization itself seemed threatened not only by these ruinous assaults upon its economic and political system but by the bankruptcy of paganism as a system of thought and belief, resulting in the influx and chaotic growth of literally hundreds of eastern religious cults to which people of every class and station swarmed in the hope of personal immortality and release from the burdens of their earthly existence. Among these cults was Christianity.

In 305 Constantine joined his father in Gaul and crossed with him to Britain for a campaign against the Picts. Within months Constantius died in his camp at York in northern England, and his soldiers promptly hailed his son Augustus. Constantine's political career had begun; he was in his early twenties. In the late summer of 312 Constantine took the initiative. Leaving the bulk of his army to protect the Rhine frontier, he took the rest of it south to Italy. Quickly disposing of the armies and overwhelming the fortifications of Maxentius in northern Italy, he pressed on toward Rome. At some point about this time there occurred for Constantine a profound conversion experience, and he became a Christian. It was under the sign and favor of his new Christian God that he defeated Maxentius at the ensuing battle of the Milvian Bridge over the Tiber. Maxentius was routed, and most of his troops perished in the river. On the following day, Maxentius's body was washed up on the shore. His head was cut off and carried into the city on a spear.

Constantine was the master of Rome and Italy. He pushed forward with what now had become a general civil war in the empire. Within two more years, he had eliminated his last remaining rivals and stood forth as sole emperor. But neither Constantine nor the empire was ever to be quite the same again. The emperor's conversion had changed both the man and his state. In 313 he proclaimed the Edict of Milan, which for the first time recognized the legality of the Christian religion throughout the empire. He ordered restitution for wrongs done to Christians under the recent persecutions. And for the rest of his long reign, he favored Christianity in every possible way. By 324 he had decided to establish a new imperial capital at the site of Byzantium in the Greek east. This New Rome was called Constantinople—the city of Constantine. It was dedicated in 330 to the Trinity and the Virgin Mary. Constantine was in the process of creating not only an eastern Roman empire but an empire that, from this time on, for more than a thousand years, would be fundamentally Christian. Thus the conversion of Constantine becomes one of the most important events in the history of Western civilization—and one of the most mysterious. Intriguing questions remain about what inspired Constantine's religious conversion. What really happened on the way to the Milvian Bridge? Why did it happen? And what did it mean?

The Life of Constantine

EUSEBIUS OF CAESAREA

The only contemporary account of Constantine's conversion is from The Life of Constantine *by the Christian ecclesiastic, bishop, theologian, and historian Eusebius of Caesarea (c. 260–c. 340). He claims to have seen Constantine while still a boy, a member of Diocletian's court when that emperor visited Caesarea. But it was many years later when Eusebius came to know Constantine as emperor himself. Eusebius had been active during the Arian controversy of the 320s and at some point became a court figure and personal friend of the emperor. He was a voluminous writer. His* Ecclesiastical History *is the best source we have for the early history of the Christian church. After Constantine's death in 337, Eusebius wrote his* Life of Constantine.

Eusebius belongs to the group known in early Christian tradition as the apologists—those who undertook specifically to defend Christianity against the claims of classical paganism. It was in this tradition that he wrote his Ecclesiastical History *and his* Life of Constantine. *His intention in both was to prove that historic events moved in such a way as to be "pleasing to God, the Sovereign of all." Thus, in his* Life of Constantine, *he says he intends "to pass over the greater part of the royal deeds of this thrice-blessed prince"—his battles, victories, triumphs, his legislative enactments and other imperial labors. Rather, he says, he will treat "of those circumstances only which have reference to his religious character" (1:484). Like the apologist he was, Eusebius sought—and found—every scrap of information that would presage the eventual Christian conversion of Constantine. He comes as close as possible to claiming that his father Constantius was a Christian, saying that he "entered into the friendship of the Supreme God" (1:485), and goes on to extol his clemency toward the Christians under his rule. Later on in his narrative he attributes the knowledge of "the God of his father" to Constantine (1:489). He attributes Constantine's own elevation to the will of God, declaring that of all his fellow rulers, "he is the only one to whose elevation no mortal may boast of having contributed" (ibid.).*

Clearly, the conversion of Constantine must be the central incident in a career so auspiciously begun. Eusebius tells us what happened on the occasion of the conversion.

As soon then as he was established on the throne, he began to care for the interests of his paternal inheritance, and visited with much considerate kindness all those provinces which had previously been under his father's government. . . .

While, therefore, he regarded the entire world as one immense body, and perceived that the head of it all, the royal city of the Roman empire, was bowed down by the weight of a tyrannous oppression; at first he had left the task of liberation to those who governed the other divisions of the empire, as being his superiors in point of age. But when none of these proved able to afford relief, and those who had attempted it had experienced a disastrous termination of their enterprise, he said that life was without enjoyment to him as long as he saw the imperial city thus afflicted, and prepared himself for the overthrowal of the tyranny.

Being convinced, however, that he needed some more powerful aid than his military forces could afford him, on account of the wicked and magical enchantments which were so diligently practiced by the tyrant, he sought Divine assistance, deeming the possession of arms and a numerous soldiery of secondary importance, but believing the cooperating power of Deity invincible and not to be shaken. He considered, therefore, on what God he might rely for protection and assistance. While engaged in this enquiry, the thought occurred to him, that, of the many emperors who had preceded him, those who had rested their hopes in a multitude of gods, and served them with sacrifices and offerings, had in the first place been deceived by flattering predictions, and oracles which promised them all prosperity, and at last had met with an unhappy end, while not one of their gods had stood by to warn them of the impending wrath of heaven; while one alone who had pursued an entirely opposite course, who had condemned their error, and honored the one Supreme God during his whole life, had found him to be the Saviour and Protector of his empire, and the Giver of every good thing. Reflecting on this, and well weighing the fact that they who had trusted in many gods had also fallen by manifold forms of death, without leaving behind them either family or offspring, stock, name, or memorial among men: while the God of his father had given to him, on the other hand, manifestations of his power and very many tokens: and considering farther that those who had already taken arms against the tyrant, and had marched to the battle-field under the protection of a multitude of gods, had met with a dishonorable end. . . .

. . . Reviewing, I say, all these considerations, he judged it to be folly indeed to join in the idle worship of those who were no gods, and, after such convincing evidence, to err from the truth; and therefore felt it incumbent on him to honor his father's God alone.

Accordingly he called on him with earnest prayer and supplications that he would reveal to him who he was, and stretch forth his right hand to help him in his present difficulties. And while he was thus praying with fervent entreaty, a most marvelous sign appeared to him from heaven, the account of which it might have been hard to believe had it been related by any other person. But since the victorious emperor himself long afterwards declared it to the writer of this history, when he was honored with his acquaintance and society, and confirmed his statement by an oath, who could hesitate to accredit the relation, especially since the testimony of after-time has established its truth? He said that about noon, when the day was already beginning to decline, he saw with his own eyes the trophy of a cross of light in the heavens, above the sun, and bearing the inscription, Conquer by This. At this sight he himself was struck with amazement, and his whole army also, which followed him on this expedition, and witnessed the miracle. . . .

He said, moreover, that he doubted within himself what the import of this apparition could be. And while he continued to ponder and reason on its meaning, night suddenly came on; then in his sleep the Christ of God appeared to him with the same sign which he had seen in the heavens, and commanded him to make a likeness of that sign which he had seen in the heavens and to use it as a safeguard in all engagements with his enemies. . . .

At dawn of day he arose, and communicated the marvel to his friends: and then, calling together the workers in gold and precious stones, he sat in the midst of them, and described to them the figure of the sign he had seen, bidding them represent it in gold and precious stones. And this representation I myself have had an opportunity of seeing. . . .

Now it was made in the following manner: a long spear, overlaid with gold, formed the figure of the cross by means of a transverse bar laid over it. On the top of the whole was fixed a wreath of gold and precious stones; and within this, the symbol of the Saviour's name, two letters indicating the name of Christ by means of its initial characters, the letter P being intersected by X in its centre: and these letters the emperor was in the habit of wearing on his helmet at a later period. From the cross-bar of the spear was suspended a cloth, a royal piece, covered with a profuse embroidery of most brilliant precious stones; and which, being also richly interlaced with gold, presented an indescribable degree of beauty to the beholder. This banner was of a square form, and the upright staff, whose lower section was of great length, bore a golden half-length portrait of the pious emperor and his children on its upper part, beneath the trophy of the cross, and immediately above the embroidered banner.

The emperor constantly made use of this sign of salvation as a safeguard against every adverse and hostile power, and commanded that others similar to it should be carried at the head of all his armies.

These things were done shortly afterwards. But at the time above specified, being struck with amazement at the extraordinary vision, and resolving to worship no other God save Him who had appeared to him, he sent for those who were acquainted with the mysteries of His doctrines, and enquired who that God was, and what was intended by the sign of the vision he had seen.

They affirmed that He was God, the only begotten Son of the one and only God: that the sign which had appeared was the symbol of immortality, and the trophy of that victory over death which He had gained in time past when sojourning on earth. They taught him also the causes of His advent, and explained to him the true account of His incarnation. Thus he was instructed in these matters, and was impressed with wonder at the divine manifestation which had been presented to his sight. Comparing, therefore, the heavenly vision with the interpretation given, he found his judgment confirmed; and, in the persuasion that the knowledge of these things had been imparted to him by Divine teaching, he determined thenceforth to devote himself to the reading of the Inspired writings.

Moreover, he made the priests of God his counselors, and deemed it incumbent on him to honor the God who had appeared to him with all devotion. And after this, being fortified by well-grounded hopes in Him, he hastened to quench the threatening fire of tyranny. . . .

Constantine, however, filled with compassion on account of all these miseries, began to arm himself with all warlike preparation against the tyranny. Assuming therefore the Supreme God as his patron, and invoking His Christ to be his preserver and aid, and setting the victorious trophy, the salutary symbol, in front of his soldiers and body-guard, he marched with his whole forces, trying to obtain again for the Romans the freedom they had inherited from their ancestors.

And whereas, Maxentius, trusting more in his magic arts than in the affection of his subjects, dared not even advance outside the city gates, but had guarded every place and district and city subject to his tyranny, with large bodies of soldiers, the emperor, confiding in the help of God, advanced against the first and second and third divisions of the tyrant's forces, defeated them all with ease at the first assault, and made his way into the very interior of Italy. . . .

And already he was approaching very near Rome itself, when, to save him from the necessity of fighting with all the Romans for the tyrant's sake, God himself drew the tyrant, as it were by secret cords, a long way outside the gates. And now those miracles recorded in Holy Writ, which God of old wrought against the ungodly (discredited by most as fables, yet believed by the faithful), did he in every deed confirm to all alike, believers and unbelievers, who were eye-witnesses of the wonders. For as once in the days of Moses and the Hebrew nation, who were worshipers of God, "Pharaoh's chariots and his host hath he cast into the sea, and his chosen chariot-captains are drowned in the Red Sea,"—so at this time Maxentius, and the soldiers and guards with him, "went down into the depths like stone," when, in his flight before the divinely-aided forces of Constantine, he essayed to cross the river which lay in his way, over which, making a strong bridge of boats, he had framed an engine of destruction, really against himself, but in the hope of ensnaring thereby him who was beloved by God. For his God stood by the one to protect him, while the other, godless,[1] proved to be the miserable contriver of these secret devices to his own ruin. So that one might well say, "He hath made a pit, and digged it, and is fallen into the ditch which he made. His mischief shall return upon his own head, and his violence shall come down upon his own pate." Thus, in the present instance, under divine direction, the machine erected on the bridge, with the ambuscade concealed therein, giving way unexpectedly before the appointed time, the bridge began to sink, and the boats with the men in them went bodily to the bottom. And first the wretch himself, then his armed attendants and guards, even as the sacred oracles had before described, "sank as lead in the mighty waters." So that they who thus obtained victory from God might well, if not in the same words, yet in fact in the same spirit as the people of his great servant Moses, sing and speak as they did concerning the impious tyrant of old: "Let us sing unto the Lord, for he hath been glorified exceedingly: the horse and his rider hath he thrown into the sea. He is become my helper and my shield unto salvation." And again, "Who is like unto thee, O Lord, among the gods? who is like thee, glorious in holiness, marvelous in praises, doing wonders?" . . .

Having then at this time sung these and suchlike praises to God, the Ruler of all and the Author of victory, after the example of his great servant Moses, Constantine entered the imperial city in triumph.

The Christian Fable

EDWARD GIBBON

The matter of Constantine's conversion lay essentially where Eusebius had left it until Edward Gibbon (1737–1794) decided to write The History of the Decline and Fall of the Roman Empire, *which must still be considered the greatest of all histories of Rome. For some time Gibbon had been looking in vain for a suitable subject for a major literary work. He was traveling on the continent and had gone to Italy in the spring of the year 1764. By the autumn he and his party had arrived in Rome. To quote a famous passage in his* Memoirs, *"It was on the fifteenth of October in the gloom of evening, as I sat musing on the Capitol, while the barefooted fryars were chanting their litanies in the temple of Jupiter, that I conceived the first thought of my history."[2] But, as Gibbon continues, "Several*

---

[1]What this engine of destruction might have been is unknown. There is no other reference to it, not even in the parallel passage in Eusebius's *Ecclesiastical History,* pp. 363–64

[2]There are several versions of this incident in Gibbon's papers. This is the one preferred by his editor John Murray in *Autobiography of Edward Gibbon* (London: John Murray, 1896), p. 405.

years elapsed, and several avocations intervened" before the first volume of his famous book appeared in 1776. It was an immediate sensation and something of a scandal, mainly because of Gibbon's treatment of the history of early Christianity. The scandal, however, was more apparent than real. Unlike Voltaire, Gibbon was not a thoroughgoing skeptic in matters of religion. While it is true that his most famous dictum on the decline of Rome was, "I have described the triumph of barbarism and religion," his more circumspect judgment is contained in another: "If the decline of the Roman empire was hastened by the conversion of Constantine, his victorious religion broke the violence of the fall" (4:163).

If Gibbon was not a skeptic in matters of religion, he was still a figure of the Enlightenment and, as such, he introduced into historical writing and thinking the concept of natural causation, the idea that in the case of the decline of the Roman empire, that great and complex phenomenon ought to be explained in natural and rational terms arising out of the events themselves and not as a matter of prophecy or portent, predetermined destiny or the intervention of supernatural forces.

The conversion of Constantine is as central to Gibbon's history as it was to that of Eusebius. And Gibbon had, of course, to treat Eusebius as his primary source. But he does so with the greatest caution. He accepts Eusebius's judgment—now discredited—that Constantine may have had some earlier disposition to Christianity. But he questions Eusebius's readiness to turn to the supernatural for the explanation of events, even the strangest ones. He questions the methodology and the judgment of Eusebius, who was willing to rely only upon the single unsupported statement of Constantine himself about the fiery sign in the sky rather than confirming it by resort to the many others still living who must have seen it. But while he admits that many, especially of Protestant or philosophic disposition, might "arraign the truth of the first Christian emperor," he does not do so. He sees the conversion of Constantine rather as a matter of enlightened self-interest and a willingness to be flattered that he had been chosen by heaven for this singular favor. This, Gibbon tells us, is why the conversion happened. And he concludes that even if the piety of Constantine was a specious piety at the time of his conversion, it matured into a "serious faith and fervent devotion."

We turn now to Gibbon's analysis, beginning with his assessment of Eusebius.

He affirms, with the most perfect confidence, that, in the night which preceded the last battle against Maxentius, Constantine was admonished in a dream to inscribe the shields of his soldiers with the *celestial sign of God,* the sacred monogram of the name of Christ; that he executed the commands of heaven; and that his valour and obedience were rewarded by the decisive victory of the Milvian Bridge. Some considerations might perhaps incline a sceptical mind to suspect the judgment or the veracity of the rhetorician, whose pen, either from zeal or interest, was devoted to the cause of the prevailing faction. . . .

In favor of Licinius, who still dissembled his animosity to the Christians, the same author has provided a similar vision, of a form of prayer, which was communicated by an angel, and repeated by the whole army before they engaged the legions of the tyrant Maximin. The frequent repetition of miracles serves to provoke, where it does not subdue, the reason of mankind; but, if the dream of Constantine is separately considered, it may be naturally explained either by the policy or the enthusiasm of the emperor. Whilst his anxiety for the approaching day, which must decide the fate of the empire, was suspended by a short and interrupted slumber, the venerable form of Christ, and the well-known symbol of his religion, might forcibly offer themselves to the active fancy of a prince who reverenced the name, and had perhaps secretly implored the power, of the God of the Christians. . . .

The praeternatural origin of dreams was universally admitted by the nations of antiquity, and a considerable part of the Gallic army was already prepared to place their confidence in the salutary sign of the Christian religion. The secret vision of Constantine could be disproved only by the event; and the intrepid hero who had passed the Alps and the Apennine might view with careless despair the consequences of a defeat under the walls of Rome. . . .

The philosopher, who with calm suspicion examines the dreams and omens, the miracles and prodigies, of profane or even of ecclesiastical history, will probably conclude that, if the eyes of the spectators have sometimes been deceived by fraud, the understanding of the readers has much more frequently been insulted by fiction. Every event, or appearance, or accident, which seems to deviate from the ordinary course of nature, has been rashly ascribed to the immediate action of the Deity; and the astonished fancy of the multitude has sometimes given shape and colour, language and motion, to the fleeting but uncommon meteors of the air. . . .

The Christian fable of Eusebius, which in the space of twenty-six years might arise from the original dream, is cast in a much more correct and elegant mould. In one of the marches of Constantine, he is reported to have seen with his own eyes the luminous trophy of the cross, placed above the meridian sun, and inscribed with the following words: By This Conquer. This amazing object in the sky astonished the whole army, as well as the emperor himself, who was yet undetermined in the choice of a religion; but his astonishment was converted into faith by the vision of the ensuing night. Christ appeared before his eyes, and, displaying the same celestial sign of the cross, he directed Constantine to frame a similar standard, and to march, with an assurance of victory, against Maxentius and all his enemies. The learned bishop of Caesarea appears to be sensible that the recent discovery of this marvellous anecdote would excite some surprise and distrust among the most pious of his readers. Yet instead of ascertaining the precise circumstances of time and place, which always serve to detect falsehood or establish truth; instead of collecting and recording the evidence of so many living witnesses, who must have been spectators of this stupendous miracle; Eusebius contents himself with alleging a very singular testimony; that of the deceased Constantine, who, many years after the event, in the freedom of conversation, had related to him this extraordinary incident of his own life, and had attested the truth of it by a solemn oath. The prudence and gratitude of the learned prelate forbade him to suspect the veracity of his victorious master; but he plainly intimates that in a fact of such a nature, he should have refused his assent to any meaner authority. . . .

The vision of Constantine maintained an honourable place in the legend of superstition, till the bold and sagacious spirit of criticism presumed to depreciate the triumph and to arraign the truth of the first Christian emperor.

The protestant and philosophic readers of the present age will incline to believe that, in the account of his own conversion, Constantine attested a wilful falsehood by a solemn and deliberate perjury. They may not hesitate to pronounce that, in the choice of a religion, his mind was determined only by a sense of interest; and that . . . he used the altars of the church as a convenient footstool to the throne of the empire. A conclusion so harsh and so absolute is not, however, warranted by our knowledge of human nature, of Constantine, or of Christianity. In an age of religious fervour, the most artful statesmen are observed to feel some part of the enthusiasm which they inspire; and the most orthodox saints assume the dangerous privilege of defending the cause of truth by the arms of deceit and falsehood. Personal interest is often the standard of our belief, as well as of our practice; and the same motives of temporal advantage which might influence the public conduct and professions of Constantine would insensibly dispose his mind to embrace a religion so propitious to his fame and fortunes. His vanity was gratified by the flattering assurance that *he* had been chosen by Heaven to reign over the earth; success had justified his divine title to the throne, and that title was founded on the truth of the Christian revelation. As real virtue is sometimes excited by undeserved applause, the specious piety of Constantine, if at first it was only specious, might gradually, by the influence of praise, of habit, and of example, be matured into serious faith and fervent devotion.

Constantine
and the "Great Thaw"

PETER BROWN

The preponderance of more modern scholars have tended to follow the cautious rationalism of Gibbon in the matter of the conversion of Constantine and what it meant. Some, it is true, have followed the lead of the great nineteenth-century historian Jakob Burckhardt, who regarded Constantine as "essentially unreligious" and "driven without surcease by ambition and lust for power" and who characterized Eusebius as "guilty of so many distortions, dissimulations, and inventions that he has forfeited all claim to figure as a decisive source."³

More typically, A. H. M. Jones regards Constantine as "an impulsive man of violent temper" and "above all things ambitious for power"; but that he was in some sense converted to Christianity in the year 312 "there is no manner of doubt."⁴ He rejects out of hand the possibility that his conversion was an act of political expediency.

This is the position as well of Peter Brown, the Oxford historian of late Roman antiquity from whose provocative The World of Late Antiquity *the following selection is taken. In this selection, while accepting the genuineness of Constantine's conversion experience, Brown turns it around and looks at it from the point of view of the Christian cult rather than the soldier-emperor who became a member of that cult in 312. And he sees it as the event that decisively affected the shape of the Christian Roman empire that Constantine founded. This, Brown argues, is what the conversion of Constantine meant.*

With the return of peace after the accession of Diocletian, the wound began to close between the new, military governing class and the urban civilization of the Mediterranean. But there were now two groups who claimed to represent this civilization: the traditional pagan governing class, whose resilience and high standards had been shown in the revival and spread of Platonic philosophy in the late third century, were in danger of being outbid by the new, "middle-brow" culture of the Christian bishops, whose organizing power and adaptability had been proved conclusively in the previous generation.

At first, organization for survival was more important to the emper-

---

³Jakob Burckhardt, *The Age of Constantine the Great*, trans. Moses Hadas (New York: Pantheon, 1949 [1852]), pp. 292–93.

⁴A. H. M. Jones, *The Later Roman Empire, 284–602* (Norman: University of Oklahoma Press, 1964), 1:78; Jones, *Constantine and the Conversion of Europe* (London: English Universities Press, 1949), p. 79.

ors than culture. Diocletian was a sincere, Roman traditionalist; yet he ruled for nineteen years without giving a thought to the Christians. The "Great Persecution," which began in 302 and continued spasmodically for a decade, came as a brutal shock to respectable Christians. They found themselves officially outcastes in the society with which they had so strenuously identified themselves. It was a terrifying and, on the whole, a deeply demoralizing experience. They were saved by an obscure event. In 312, a usurping emperor, Constantine, won a battle over his rival at the Milvian Bridge, outside Rome. He ascribed this victory to the protection of the Christian God, vouchsafed in a vision.

If God helps those who help themselves, then no group better deserved the miracle of the "conversion" of Constantine in 312 than did the Christians. For the Christian leaders seized their opportunity with astonishing pertinacity and intelligence. They besieged Constantine in his new mood: provincial bishops, notably Hosius of Cordova (c. 257–357), attached themselves to his court; other bishops, from Africa, swept him into their local affairs as a judge; Lactantius emerged as tutor to his son; and, when Constantine finally conquered the eastern provinces in 324, he was greeted by Eusebius of Caesarea, who placed his pen at the emperor's disposal with a skill and enthusiasm such as no traditional Greek rhetor had seemed able to summon up for Constantine's grim and old-fashioned predecessors—Diocletian and Galerius.

This prolonged exposure to Christian propaganda was the true "conversion" of Constantine. It began on a modest scale when he controlled only the under-Christianized western provinces; but it reached its peak after 324, when the densely Christianized territories of Asia Minor were united to his empire. Its results were decisive. Constantine could easily have been merely a "god-fearing" emperor, who, for reasons of his own, was prepared to tolerate the Christians: there had been many such in the third century (one of whom, Philip (244–249), was even regarded as a crypto-Christian). Given the religious climate of the age, there was no reason, either, why his decision to tolerate the Church might not have been ascribed to intimations from the Christian God. Constantine rejected this easy and obvious solution. He came to be the emperor we know from his speeches and edicts: a crowned Christian Apologist. He viewed himself and his mission as a Christian emperor in the light of the interpretation of Christianity that had beeen presented to the average educated layman by the Christian Apologists of his age. In becoming a Christian, Constantine publicly claimed to be saving the Roman empire: even more—in mixing with bishops, this middle-aged Latin soldier sincerely believed that he had entered the charmed circle of "true" civilization, and had turned his back on the Philistinism of the raw men who had recently attacked the Church.

One suspects that Constantine was converted to many more aspects of Mediterranean life than to Christianity alone. The son of a soldier, he threw in his lot with a civilian way of life that had been largely ignored by the grey administrators of the age of Diocletian. From 311 onwards, Constantine put the landed aristocracy on its feet again: he is the "restorer of the Senate," to whom the aristocracy of the West owed so much. In 332, he gave these landowners extensive powers over their tenants. After 324, he grouped a new civilian governing class round himself in the Greek East. He gave the provincial gentry of Asia Minor what they had long wanted: Constantinople, a "new" Rome, placed within convenient range of the imperial court as it moved along the routes connecting the Danube to Asia Minor. For the Greek senator and bureaucrat, roads that had long ceased to lead to Rome converged quite naturally at this new capital.

Constantine, very wisely, seldom said "no." The first Christian emperor accepted pagan honours from the citizens of Athens. He ransacked the Aegean for pagan classical statuary to adorn Constantinople. He treated a pagan philosopher as a colleague. He paid the travelling expenses of a pagan priest who visited the pagan monuments of Egypt. After a generation of "austerity" for everyone, and of "terror" for the Christians, Constantine, with calculated flamboyance, instituted the "Great Thaw" of the early fourth century: it was a whole restored civilian world, pagan as well as Christian, that was pressing in round the emperor.

In this restored world, the Christians had the advantage of being the most flexible and open group. The bishops could accept an uncultivated emperor. They were used to autodidacts, to men of genuine eccentric talent who—so they claimed—were taught by God alone. Constantine, one should remember, was the younger contemporary of the first Christian hermit, St. Anthony. Neither the Latin-speaking soldier nor the Coptic-speaking farmer's son would have been regarded as acceptable human material for a classical schoolmaster: yet Eusebius of Caesarea wrote the life of Constantine the soldier, and Athanasius of Alexandria—an equally sophisticated Greek—the life of Anthony the Egyptian. It was over the wide bridge of a "middlebrow" identification of Christianity with a lowest common denominator of classical culture, and not through the narrow gate of a pagan aristocracy of letters, that Constantine and his successors entered the civilian civilization of the Mediterranean.

Questions for Review and Study

1. Why is the conversion of Constantine an important topic in the history of Western civilization?
2. Why do you suppose Eusebius made no effort to verify Constantine's

account of the heavenly vision apparently seen by so many other people?

3. Given the enlightened skepticism that characterized Gibbon's historical writings, do you detect any of it in his account of the conversion of Constantine?

4. How does Peter Brown deal with the problem of Constantine's conversion?

Questions for Comparison

1. Compare and contrast the conversions of Constantine and Martin Luther. What were the social, political, and personal catalysts of their conversions? How helpful is psychology in understanding their motives? In what personal changes did their transformations result? What were the historical effects of their choices? How had the church changed from Constantine to Luther's day, and what were the two men's relations to it? Were the two men's Christian faiths essentially similar?

Suggestions for Further Reading

There are a number of good modern biographical studies of Constantine. Probably the best is Ramsey MacMullen's *Constantine*, but also recommended are *Constantine and the Conversion of Europe*, by A. H. M. Jones; and the biographies by John Holland Smith, Hermann Dörries, Frieda Upson, Nancy Z. Walworth, and Michael Grant.

A greater number of good modern works treat Constantine and his reign as part of the history of late Roman antiquity. The most important and magisterial of these is *The Later Roman Empire, 284–602*, by A. H. M. Jones. Three excellent shorter surveys are by Diana Bowder's *The Age of Constantine and Julian;* Stewart Perowne's *The End of the Roman World;* and Joseph Vogt's *The Decline of Rome*, especially good on the Germanic peoples. Ramsey MacMullen's book *Paganism in the Roman Empire* is the best work on this topic.

There are two books of essays, *The Awful Revolution*, by F. W. Walbank, and *The Making of Late Antiquity*, by Peter Brown. See also *The World of Late Antiquity*, by Peter Brown. A specialized work of considerable interest is *Helena Augusta*, by Jan W. Drijvers, subtitled *The Mother of Constantine the Great and the Legend of Her Finding the True Cross.*

Bowder, Diana. *The Age of Constantine and Julian.* New York: Barnes and Noble, 1978.

Brown, Peter. *The Making of Late Antiquity.* Cambridge, Mass., and London: Harvard University Press, 1978.

————. *The World of Late Antiquity.* New York: Harcourt, 1971.

Dörries, Hermann. *Constantine the Great.* Trans. R. H. Bainton. New York: Harper, 1972.

Drijvers, Jan W. *Helena Augusta: The Mother of Constantine the Great and the Legend of Her Finding the True Cross.* Studies in Intellectual History No. 17. New York and Leiden: Brill, 1994.

Grant, Michael. *Constantine the Great: The Man and His Times.* New York: Scribner's, 1994; and Toronto: Macmillan, 1994.

Jones, A. H. M. *Constantine and the Conversion of Europe.* London: English Universities Press, 1949.

————. *The Later Roman Empire, 284–602: A Social, Economic and Administrative Survey,* 2 vols. Norman: University of Oklahoma Press, 1964.

MacMullen, Ramsey. *Constantine.* New York: Dial, 1969.

————. *Paganism in the Roman Empire.* New Haven, Conn., and London: Yale University Press, 1981.

Perowne, Stewart. *The End of the Roman World.* New York: Crowell, 1967.

Smith, John Holland. *Constantine the Great.* New York: Scribner's, 1971.

Upson, Frieda. *Constantine the Great.* Brookline, Mass.: Holy Cross Orthodox, 1987.

Vogt, Joseph. *The Decline of Rome: The Metamorphosis of Ancient Civilisation.* Trans. Janet Sonheimer. London: Weidenfeld and Nicolson, 1967.

Walbank, F. W. *The Awful Revolution: The Decline of the Roman Empire in the West.* Toronto and London: Toronto University Press, 1969.

Walworth, Nancy Z. *Constantine.* World Leaders Past and Present. New York: Chelsea House, 1990.

CHARLEMAGNE
AND THE FIRST EUROPE

742 or 743	Born
768	Joint succession to Frankish throne with his brother Carloman
771	Death of Carloman; beginning of sole rule
772–787	Saxon wars
774	Conquered Lombard kingdom
800	Imperial coronation
814	Died

In the lifetime of St. Augustine (A.D. 354–430), the Roman Empire in the West had collapsed. Roman political order was being replaced by regional barbarian kingdoms under their German tribal chiefs, and the West had entered irretrievably upon what an earlier generation of historians was fond of calling the Dark Ages.

Though the darkness was by no means as pervasive as scholars once thought, the early Middle Ages were a time of great dislocation, surely one of the two or three most important periods of transition in the history of Western civilization—for the product of the transition was nothing less than what some historians have called "the first Europe."

It was a Europe no longer classical and imperial, no longer a vast free-trade network of cities governed by a centralized system and ruled by a common law. It was a Europe from which long-distance trade had disappeared, to be replaced by an economic localism. It was a Europe of equally localized culture, in which the common classical tradition was maintained by an ever dwindling minority of educated people, with an ever decreasing sophistication. Most, virtually all, of those educated were professional churchmen, for, perhaps most important of all, the first Europe was a Christian Europe.

The great Frankish king Charlemagne (r. 768–814) was, by all accounts and from whatever interpretive viewpoint we choose to see him, the pivotal figure in this first Europe. The Franks were one of the barbarian Germanic tribes that succeeded to the broken pieces of the western empire. By a combination of luck, talent, and timing, they had come to be the leading power among their fellow barbarians. Their position was enhanced by Charlemagne's immediate predecessors, his grandfather Charles Martel and his father Pepin, who established the claim of his house to the Frankish throne. Frankish supremacy was assured by Charlemagne's dramatic conquests, which brought most of continental western Europe—save only Moslem Spain south of the Ebro River, southern Italy, and the barbarian fringes of the Scandinavian north—under his rule.

Charlemagne's imperial rule was epitomized in his resumption of the ancient imperial title. On Christmas day of the year 800, in the church of St. Peter in Rome, Pope Leo III crowned Charlemagne as "Emperor of the Romans." No one had claimed this exalted title in more than three hundred-years, and no barbarian king had ever before presumed to such a dignity. Charlemagne continued to bear his other titles, so we are not sure precisely how he himself saw his imperial role—whether it was an "umbrella" title over his many different dominions, a Christian symbol for "the temporal sword," or simply "a feather in his cap." We do know that it involved him in a delicate and complex negotiation with the other "Emperor of the Romans" in Byzantium, whose rights, however remotely exercised, Charlemagne's act had encroached upon. The assumption of the title, moreover, by virtue of the part played by the pope, was inextricably bound up with the larger role of the church in the secular affairs of the West.

Charlemagne made important contributions to the culture of his Europe. He carried out extensive educational as well as clerical reforms and preached to his clergy on learning, discipline, and piety. His court was the principal center of what has been called the Carolingian Renaissance. The king himself encouraged this rejuvenation of learning. In connection with it he established the famous palace school at Aachen under the direction of the learned English scholar Alcuin (735–804), which attracted learned men from all over Europe. Classical as well as Christian texts were systematically collected and preserved. Alcuin introduced a new scholar's "hand," called Carolingian *minuscule*.

We cannot be sure what Charlemagne's plans for his empire were, although he saw to the imperial succession of his son Louis the Pious. We cannot even be certain of the extent to which Charles was able to realize the plans he did have, for the records of the time simply do not tell us.

But, however many unanswered questions remain, the records do contain a precious contemporary account of King Charles, written by his devoted friend, the Frankish noble Einhard.

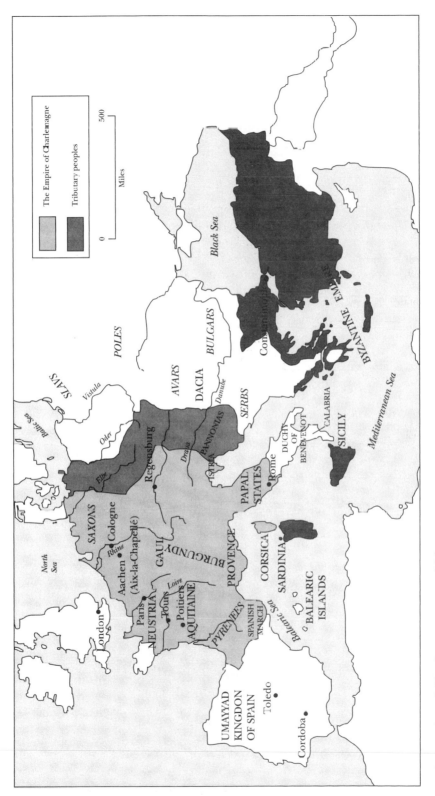

The Empire of Charlemagne, A.D. 814

The Emperor Charlemagne

EINHARD

One of the most obvious signs of the barbarism of early medieval Europe is the scarcity of records. Even scarcer than documentary records are the literary accounts—the biographies, the memoirs, the formal histories—that can give flesh and substance to historical figures. Most, even the greatest, personages of the early Middle Ages remain simply names, with only a handful of facts (and often doubtful "facts" at that) attached to them. Fortunately, this is not the case for Charlemagne. We might wish that Einhard's account had been longer and more detailed, or that he had included more information about Charles's public policy, his political motives, his plans for the empire, and the structure of his reign. But we are lucky to have what we do. Einhard was sensitive about his modest literary gifts. Indeed, he could not even conceive of a formal framework for his account; he simply took Suetonius's biography of Augustus and substituted his own material in the model. But so indebted was Einhard to Charles, his "lord and foster father," and so important were his lord's deeds that he chose to record them rather "than to suffer the most glorious life of this most excellent king, the greatest of all the princes of his day, and his illustrious deeds, hard for men of later times to imitate, to be wrapped in the darkness of oblivion."[1]

Despite its limitations, Einhard's Life of Charlemagne *is an extraordinarily valuable document. It would have been so under any circumstances. Its value is enhanced because Einhard was an intimate of the king and his family; he had been raised at Charles's court and later was one of his most trusted councillors. No one was in a better position than Einhard to write on Charles the Great.*

After sketching the background of Charles's dynasty and how the Carolingians (for this is the name historians have given to the house of Carolus Magnus) succeeded to the Frankish throne, how Charles's father, Pepin, set aside the last of the weak Merovingians with their "vain title of king," Einhard describes in some detail the wars of conquest that earned for Charles the title "Charles the Great"— his pacification of Aquitaine, his conquest of the Lombards and his assumption of the Lombard crown, his long wars with the pagan Saxons along the eastern frontier, his unsuccessful attempt to invade Moslem Spain, his successful quelling of the revolt of Bavaria, and his wars against the Avars along the Danube, the Danes, and other border peoples. Then Einhard continues:

Such are the wars, most skilfully planned and successfully fought, which this most powerful king waged during the forty-seven years of

---

[1] *The Life of Charlemagne by Einhard* (Ann Arbor: University of Michigan Press, 1960), Preface, p. 16. Translated from the *Monumenta Germaniae* by Samuel Epes Turner.

his reign. He so largely increased the Frank kingdom, which was already great and strong when he received it at his father's hands, that more than double its former territory was added to it. The authority of the Franks was formerly confined to that part of Gaul included between the Rhine and the Loire, the Ocean and the Balearic Sea; to that part of Germany which is inhabited by the so-called Eastern Franks, and is bounded by Saxony and the Danube, the Rhine and the Saale—this stream separates the Thuringians from the Sorabians; and to the country of the Alemanni and Bavarians. By the wars above mentioned he first made tributary Aquitania, Gascony, and the whole of the region of the Pyrenees as far as the River Ebro, which rises in the land of the Navarrese, flows through the most fertile districts of Spain, and empties into the Balearic Sea, beneath the walls of the city of Tortosa. He next reduced and made tributary all Italy from Aosta to Lower Calabria, where the boundary line runs between the Beneventans and the Greeks, a territory more than a thousand miles long; then Saxony, which constitutes no small part of Germany, and is reckoned to be twice as wide as the country inhabited by the Franks, while about equal to it in length; in addition, both Pannonias, Dacia beyond the Danube, and Istria, Liburnia, and Dalmatia, except the cities on the coast, which he left to the Greek Emperor for friendship's sake, and because of the treaty that he had made with him. In fine, he vanquished and made tributary all the wild and barbarous tribes dwelling in Germany between the Rhine and the Vistula, the Ocean and the Danube, all of which speak very much the same language, but differ widely from one another in customs and dress. The chief among them are the Welatabians, the Sorabians, the Abodriti, and the Bohemians, and he had to make war upon these; but the rest, by far the larger number, submitted to him of their own accord.

He added to the glory of his reign by gaining the good will of several kings and nations. . . . His relations with Aaron, King of the Persians,[2] who ruled over almost the whole of the East, India excepted, were so friendly that this prince preferred his favor to that of all the kings and potentates of the earth, and considered that to him alone marks of honor and munificence were due. Accordingly, when the ambassadors sent by Charles to visit the most holy sepulchre and place of resurrection of our Lord and Savior presented themselves before him with gifts, and made known their master's wishes, he not only granted what was asked, but gave possession of that holy and blessed spot. When they returned, he dispatched his ambassadors

---

[2]This was the famous Harun al-Raschid (786–809), not "King of the Persians" but the Abbasid Caliph of Baghdad, with whom Charles did indeed enjoy good diplomatic relations. Harun was most likely interested in a possible alliance against the Byzantine Empire.

with them, and sent magnificent gifts, besides stuffs, perfumes, and other rich products of the Eastern lands. A few years before this, Charles had asked him for an elephant, and he sent the only one that he had. The Emperors of Constantinople, Nicephorus, Michael, and Leo, made advances to Charles, and sought friendship and alliance with him by several embassies; and even when the Greeks suspected him of designing to wrest the empire from them, because of his assumption of the title Emperor, they made a close alliance with him, that he might have no cause of offense. In fact, the power of the Franks was always viewed by the Greeks and Romans with a jealous eye, whence the Greek proverb "Have the Frank for your friend, but not for your neighbor." . . .

He liked foreigners, and was at great pains to take them under his protection. There were often so many of them, both in the palace and the kingdom, that they might reasonably have been considered a nuisance; but he, with his broad humanity, was very little disturbed by such annoyances, because he felt himself compensated for these great inconveniences by the praises of his generosity and the reward of high renown.

Charles was large and strong, and of lofty stature, though not disproportionately tall (his height is well known to have been seven times the length of his foot); the upper part of his head was round, his eyes very large and animated, nose a little long, hair fair, and face laughing and merry. Thus his appearance was always stately and dignified, whether he was standing or sitting; although his neck was thick and somewhat short, and his belly rather prominent; but the symmetry of the rest of his body concealed these defects. His gait was firm, his whole carriage manly, and his voice clear, but not so strong as his size led one to expect. His health was excellent, except during the four years preceding his death, when he was subject to frequent fevers; at the last he even limped a little with one foot. Even in those years he consulted rather his own inclinations than the advice of physicians, who were almost hateful to him, because they wanted him to give up roasts, to which he was accustomed, and to eat boiled meat instead. In accordance with the national custom, he took frequent exercise on horseback and in the chase, accomplishments in which scarcely any people in the world can equal the Franks. He enjoyed the exhalations from natural warm springs, and often practiced swimming, in which he was such an adept that none could surpass him; and hence it was that he built his palace at Aix-la-Chapelle, and lived there constantly during his latter years until his death. He used not only to invite his sons to his bath, but his nobles and friends, and now and then a troop of his retinue or bodyguard, so that a hundred or more persons sometimes bathed with him.

He used to wear the national, that is to say, the Frank, dress—next his skin a linen shirt and linen breeches, and above these a tunic fringed with silk; while hose fastened by bands covered his lower limbs, and shoes his feet, and he protected his shoulders and chest in winter by a close-fitting coat of otter or marten skins. Over all he flung a blue cloak, and he always had a sword girt about him, usually one with a gold or silver hilt and belt; he sometimes carried a jeweled sword, but only on great feastdays or at the reception of ambassadors from foreign nations. He despised foreign costumes, however handsome, and never allowed himself to be robed in them, except twice in Rome, when he donned the Roman tunic, chlamys, and shoes; the first time at the request of Pope Hadrian, the second to gratify Leo, Hadrian's successor. On great feastdays he made use of embroidered clothes and shoes bedecked with precious stones, his cloak was fastened by a golden buckle, and he appeared crowned with a diadem of gold and gems, but on other days his dress varied little from the common dress of the people.

Charles was temperate in eating, and particularly so in drinking, for he abominated drunkenness in anybody, much more in himself and those of his household. . . . Charles had the gift of ready and fluent speech, and could express whatever he had to say with the utmost clearness. He was not satisfied with command of his native language merely, but gave attention to the study of foreign ones, and in particular was such a master of Latin that he could speak it as well as his native tongue; but he could understand Greek better than he could speak it. He was so eloquent, indeed, that he might have passed for a teacher of eloquence. He most zealously cultivated the liberal arts, held those who taught them in great esteem, and conferred great honors upon them. He took lessons in grammar of the deacon Peter of Pisa, at that time an aged man. Another deacon, Albin of Britain, surnamed Alcuin, a man of Saxon extraction, who was the greatest scholar of the day, was his teacher in other branches of learning. The King spent much time and labor with him studying rhetoric, dialectics, and especially astronomy; he learned to reckon, and used to investigate the motions of the heavenly bodies most curiously, with an intelligent scrutiny. He also tried to write, and used to keep tablets and blanks in bed under his pillow, that at leisure hours he might accustom his hand to form the letters; however, as he did not begin his efforts in due season, but late in life, they met with ill success.[3]

He cherished with the greatest fervor and devotion the principles of the Christian religion, which had been instilled into him from infancy. Hence it was that he built the beautiful basilica at Aix-la-Chapelle, which he adorned with gold and silver and lamps, and with

---

[3]What is probably meant here is not that Charles literally could not write but that he could not master the precise and beautiful "book hand," the Carolingian Minuscule, developed by Alcuin for the use of the court copyists.

rails and doors of solid brass. He had the columns and marbles for this structure brought from Rome and Ravenna, for he could not find such as were suitable elsewhere. . . .

He was very forward in succoring the poor, and in the gratuitous generosity which the Greeks call alms, so much so that he not only made a point of giving in his own country and his own kingdom, but when he discovered that there were Christians living in poverty in Syria, Egypt, and Africa, at Jerusalem, Alexandria, and Carthage, he had compassion on their wants, and used to send money over the seas to them. The reason that he zealously strove to make friends with the kings beyond seas was that he might get help and relief to the Christians living under their rule. He cherished the Church of St. Peter the Apostle at Rome above all other holy and sacred places, and heaped its treasury with a vast wealth of gold, silver, and precious stones. He sent great and countless gifts to the popes, and throughout his whole reign the wish that he had nearest at heart was to re-establish the ancient authority of the city of Rome under his care and by his influence, and to defend and protect the Church of St. Peter, and to beautify and enrich it out of his own store above all other churches. Although he held it in such veneration, he only repaired to Rome to pay his vows and make his supplications four times during the whole forty-seven years that he reigned.

When he made his last journey thither, he had also other ends in view. The Romans had inflicted many injuries upon the Pontiff Leo, tearing out his eyes and cutting out his tongue, so that he had been compelled to call upon the King for help. Charles accordingly went to Rome, to set in order the affairs of the Church, which were in great confusion, and passed the whole winter there. It was then that he received the titles of Emperor and Augustus, to which he at first had such an aversion that he declared that he would not have set foot in the Church the day that they were conferred, although it was a great feastday, if he could have foreseen the design of the Pope. He bore very patiently with the jealousy which the Roman emperors showed upon his assuming these titles, for they took this step very ill; and by dint of frequent embassies and letters, in which he addressed them as brothers, he made their haughtiness yield to his magnanimity, a quality in which he was unquestionably much their superior.

It was after he had received the imperial name that, finding the laws of his people very defective (the Franks have two sets of laws, very different in many particulars[4]), he determined to add what was wanting, to reconcile the discrepancies, and to correct what was vicious and wrongly cited in them. However, he went no further in this

---

[4]The codes of the two Frankish tribes, the Salian and Ripuarian, that had combined to form the nation.

matter than to supplement the laws by a few capitularies, and those imperfect ones; but he caused the unwritten laws of all the tribes that came under his rule to be compiled and reduced to writing. He also had the old rude songs that celebrate the deeds and wars of the ancient kings written out for transmission to posterity. He began a grammar of his native language. He gave the months names in his own tongue, in place of the Latin and barbarous names by which they were formerly known among the Franks. . . .

Toward the close of his life, when he was broken by ill-health and old age, he summoned Louis, King of Aquitania, his only surviving son by Hildegard, and gathered together all the chief men of the whole kingdom of the Franks in a solemn assembly. He appointed Louis, with their unanimous consent, to rule with himself over the whole kingdom, and constituted him heir to the imperial name; then, placing the diadem upon his son's head, he bade him be proclaimed Emperor and Augustus. This step was hailed by all present with great favor, for it really seemed as if God had prompted him to it for the kingdom's good; it increased the King's dignity, and struck no little terror into foreign nations. After sending his son back to Aquitania, although weak from age he set out to hunt, as usual, near his palace at Aix-la-Chapelle, and passed the rest of the autumn in the chase, returning thither about the first of November. While wintering there, he was seized, in the month of January, with a high fever, and took to his bed. As soon as he was taken sick, he prescribed for himself abstinence from food, as he always used to do in case of fever, thinking that the disease could be driven off, or at least mitigated, by fasting. Besides the fever, he suffered from a pain in the side, which the Greeks call pleurisy; but he still persisted in fasting, and in keeping up his strength only by draughts taken at very long intervals. He died January twenty-eighth, the seventh day from the time that he took to his bed, at nine o'clock in the morning, after partaking of the holy communion, in the seventy-second year of his age and the forty-seventh of his reign.

A New Portrait of the Emperor

HEINRICH FICHTENAU

We turn now from Einhard's contemporary account of Charlemagne to the description by the modern Austrian medievalist Heinrich Fichtenau. It is rather more a reconstruction than a description, for in The Carolingian Empire: The Age of

Charlemagne, *Fichtenau goes beyond Einhard's account to the other fragmentary records of Charles's age, as well as to the best of modern Carolingian scholarship. Fichtenau's work is a careful, even conservative, attempt to set Charlemagne
securely in his age. The result is a distinguished new portrait of the emperor to set
beside that of his adoring friend and subject.*

———————

No man's stature is increased by the accumulation of myths, and
nothing is detracted from genuine historical greatness by the consideration of a man's purely human side. In order to analyse an epoch
it is necessary to analyse the man who was its centre, who determined its character and who was, at the same time, shaped and
determined by it. It is therefore not mere curiosity but an endeavour
to fulfil the historian's task if we strive to pierce and get behind the
myth that has surrounded the figure of Charles. That myth has
been built up over a period of centuries and has tended to conjure
up in place of a tangible personality, full of vitality, the figure of a
timeless hero.

In the case of Charles—and that alone would justify our beginning
with him—we can even form a picture of his bodily physique. The
bodily appearance of his contemporaries, although we know their
names and their works, remains shadow-like for us to-day. But as far
as Charles the Great is concerned, we are not only in possession of his
bodily remains but also have an exact description of his appearance.
It is true that Charles's biographer Einhard borrowed the terms of his
description from Suetonius. Nevertheless it was possible for him to
choose from among the numerous biographies of the ancient emperors which he found in Suetonius those expressions which were most
applicable to his master. Einhard and his contemporaries were especially struck by Charles's bodily size. Ever since the opening of
Charles's tomb in 1861 we have known that his actual height was a
full 6 feet 3½ inches. It was therefore not poetic licence when one of
the court-poets, describing the royal hunt, remarked: "The king, with
his broad shoulders, towers above everybody else." . . .

It is a pity that Einhard fails us when he describes Charles's personality, for his description is entirely conventional. It had to be conventional, for, although emperors may differ in physical build, they must
all have the same virtues, namely the imperial virtues without which
nobody can be a real emperor. Thus his description of Charles is
couched in Aristotelian and Stoic terms, such as *temperantia, patientia,*
and *constantia animi*. And in so far as Einhard attributed *magnanimitas*
and *liberalitas* to Charles, we can discern a mingling of ancient and
Germanic princely ideals. When the hospitality shown to foreign
guests resulted in neglect of considerations of public economy, Stoic
magnanimitas was imperceptibly transformed into Germanic "loftiness
of spirit." For Charles "found in the reputation of generosity and in

the good fame that followed generous actions a compensation even for grave inconveniences."

The Stoic traits in Einhard's picture of Charles are, however, by no means insignificant. Many of Charles's counsellors must have drawn his attention to the fact that these traits were ideals that had been appropriate to his imperial predecessors and therefore appropriate for him. People must have appealed again and again to his *clementia*, a Stoic concept subsumed under *temperantia*, when it was a question of preventing the execution of conspirators, of liberating hostages, or of returning property that had been confiscated in punishment for an offence. Stoicism was, after all, allied with Christianity. A Christian ruler had to exercise self-control. If he indulged in *crudelitas* and raged against his enemies he was not far from the very opposite of a good king, the *rex iniquus* or tyrant.

Charles endeavoured in more than one sense to live up to the model of Stoic and Christian self-discipline. He could not tolerate drunkards in his palace. Banquets were held only on important feast days. Fasting, however, he deeply loathed. He often complained that it impaired his health. When he was an old man he conducted a long battle with his physicians who never succeeded in making him eat boiled meat in place of the roast to which he was accustomed. The fact that Einhard incorporated such stories in his biography and that a large number of almost humourous anecdotes, such as were collected later by Notker,[5] were recounted by his own contemporaries, shows that there was a very real difference between the late Roman, and especially the Byzantine, conception of the ruler, on one hand, and the Frankish conception, on the other. Charles did not observe in his court the stiff dignity and the ceremonious distance that became an emperor. In this respect he never modelled himself on anyone; he behaved naturally and revealed his true self.

There is no evidence that Charles ever withdrew from the people around him in order to ponder and work out his plans. He always needed the company of people, of his daughters, of his friends, and even of his menial retinue. He not only invited to his banquets everybody who happened to be about; he also gathered people for the hunt and even insisted that his magnates, his learned friends, and his bodyguard were to be present when he was having a bath. The author of a poetical description of palace life at Aix-la-Chapelle refers repeatedly to the noisy bustle in the baths. It seems that Charles was happiest among the din of the hunt or in the midst of the building going on at Aix-la-Chapelle.

Charles was the centre of the whole kingdom—not only because it became him as ruler to be the centre, but also because it suited his

---

[5] A late Carolingian monastic chronicler.

temperament. Generally receptive, and approaching both science and scholarship with an open mind, he wanted to feel that he was at the centre of everything. It must have been an easy matter for court scholars, like Theodulf of Orléans, to persuade the king that his intellectual faculties were broader than the Nile, larger than the Danube and the Euphrates, and no less powerful than the Ganges. . . . As a rule the courtiers, and Alcuin among them, vied with each other in hiding from the king that there was any difference of quality between the achievements of ancient Christian civilization and their own. A new Rome or Athens was expected to arise in Aix-la-Chapelle, and they were anxious to emphasize their superiority over Byzantium, where government was in the hands of females and theology was riddled with errors. Charles required all the fresh naturalness of his temperament in order to prevent himself from sliding from the realm of practical possibilities into the world of fantastic dreams and illusions in which so many Roman emperors had foundered. . . .

At times Charles's affability, so much praised by Einhard, gave way to surprising explosions of temper. . . . Without a reference to such explosions, however, the portrait of Charles's impulsive and impetuous nature would be incomplete. The king's ire, which made his contemporaries tremble, was quite a different matter. It was part of the Germanic, just as it was of the oriental, conception of a ruler and was contrary to the Stoic ideal. At the beginning of the legend of Charlemagne there stands the figure of the "iron Charles" as his enemies saw him approaching—clad from top to toe in iron, and with an iron soul as well. In confusion they shouted: "Oh, the iron! Woe, the iron!" Not only the king's enemies, however, but also his faithful followers stood in fear of him. Charles's grandson Nithard wrote with approval that Charles had governed the nations with "tempered severity." Charles was able to control the warring men and the centrifugal tendencies of his dominions because the fear of his personal severity made evil men as gentle as lambs. He had the power to make the "hearts of both Franks and barbarians" sink. No amount of official propaganda could produce the same effect as the hardness of Charles's determination. The lack of such determination in Louis, his successor, was among the factors that led to the decay of the empire.

This side of Charles's character, although necessary for the preservation of the kingdom, was well beyond the boundaries laid down by the precepts of Stoicism and of Christianity. Charles himself was probably not aware of this. But Einhard, his biographer, who had much sympathy with both these ideas, felt it deeply. . . . Charles thought of himself as a Christian through and through, but he never managed to transcend the limits of the popular piety of the Franks. . . . He supported needy Christians, even outside the borders of the empire. He sent money to Rome and made four pilgrimages to the papal city. Such were the religious works of Charles as related by his biographer, Einhard.

The inner life of the Christian, the regeneration of the soul and the new religious attitude which, at the very time when Einhard was writing, Charles's son, Louis the Pious, was labouring to acquire, are not so much as mentioned. The reason why Einhard is silent about such things is scarcely that he could not find the words to describe them in his model, Suetonius. Charles organized the salvation of his soul as he was wont to organize his Empire. It would have been contrary to his nature, and the most difficult task of all, for him to seek the highest levels of spiritual experience in his own heart. His task as a ruler, as he saw it, was to act upon the world.

We must remember, however, that the world upon which he acted bore little resemblance to the sober and dry reality created by modern commerce and technology. Such modern conceptions were shaped much later, mostly under the impression of Calvinism. They were unknown to Charles, who, for instance, first learnt of the pope's mutilation in distant Rome through a dream. He took it to be one of his duties as a ruler to observe the course of the stars with the greatest of attention, for the approach of misfortune for his kingdom could be foretold from the stars more accurately than from anything else. For this reason the emperor devoted more time and labour to the study of astronomy than to any other of the "liberal arts." If the observation of the stars had been a mere hobby, he would surely have interrupted it while he was devastating the Saxon country with his army. . . .

Charles the Great was not one of those men who have to fight against their times and who, misunderstood by their contemporaries, are appreciated only after their death. He embodied all the tendencies of his own age; he was carried forward by them and, at the same time, moved them forward. It is impossible to describe him except in close conjunction with his friends and the magnates of his land. But for the picture to be complete he must also be shown in the midst of his family. He was surrounded by his children, his wives and the retinue of females, whose numbers and conduct seemed so unbecoming to the puritanism of his successor when he first entered the palace. Such conditions were not peculiar to Charles. It was all part and parcel of Frankish tradition. Charles lived as the head of a clan. The servants were, at least for the purposes of everyday life, included in the clan. As part of the family they enjoyed peace and protection and were, together with their master's blood relations, subject to his authority. Within the framework of the old tribal law, the master ruled his household unconditionally. . . .

In the king's palace there was a constant going and coming. Emigrés from England and from Byzantium rubbed shoulders with foreign ambassadors and all manner of public officials. There must have been, nevertheless, a few fixed key positions in the organization. There was little love lost among the occupants of these positions. For the most part, our sources remain silent on this matter. But now and again we catch a glimpse of the situation. The office of the chamberlain was one of these key positions. It was he who received the people who had come to demand an audience. He decided whether and in what order they were to appear before the king. He also received the annual "donations" of the magnates to the royal treasure which was in his custody. Alcuin considered himself happy to count this man among his friends and emphasized again and again how many envious people and evil counsellors were busy in other places trying to ruin the king.

Alcuin wrote repeatedly that, though the king tried to enforce justice, he was surrounded by predatory men. His judgment was probably no less partisan than that of his opponents who maintained that he himself was ruining the king. . . . Charles's own open and generous nature had never been inclined to inquire too closely into the intrigues and corruptions of his trusted friends and servants.

All things considered, there is little difference between the picture we form of Charles's surroundings and the one we have of his ancestors and of other princes of the period. The only difference was that the imperial household, as in fact the empire itself, was greater, more splendid, and therefore also more exposed to danger. As long as its power and splendour were increasing, the cracks in the structure remained concealed. It was the achievement of Charles's own powerful personality to have brought about this rise which, without him, might have taken generations to reach its zenith. His efforts were crowned with success because his whole personality was in tune with the progressive forces active among his people. If this had not been the case, no amount of power concentrated in the hands of the king would have suffered to stamp his countenance upon the age. If this is remembered much of the illusion of well-nigh superhuman achievement, that has inspired both the mediaeval legend of Charlemagne and many modern narratives, is dispelled. What remains is quite enough justification for calling Charles historically great.

A More Somber Light

F. L. GANSHOF

Just as Heinrich Fichtenau represents the tradition of Austrian-German scholarship in modern Carolingian studies, the other great tradition, the Belgian-French, is represented by the Belgian scholar François Louis Ganshof, who has been justly called the dean of Carolingian studies. The passage excerpted below is from an address presented to the Mediaeval Academy of America in 1948. It is in the nature of a summary judgment drawn from a lifetime of patient study and reflec-

tion, and has not been materially altered by his continued work of the last thirty years. Ganshof does not really dissent from the portrait created by Fichtenau, but he has always had a penchant for analysis rather than interpretation. He therefore strives to go beyond the limitations of Einhard's biography and other contemporary biographical fragments to describe not so much Charlemagne the man as Charle-magne the statesman. The result is a somewhat somber judgment, dwelling more upon his limitations than his accomplishments. For Ganshof is sharply aware that if Fichtenau sees Charlemagne as the universal father figure of the first Europe,[6] it is of a Europe hardly yet born and due for many turns and reverses before it can realize the promise anticipated in the age of Charlemagne.

We begin just before what Ganshof calls the fifth and last period of Charle-magne's reign.

It would seem that by 792, when Charles was fifty years old, he had acquired experience and wisdom; perhaps, also, the advice of certain counsellors had brought him to understand that moderation is neces-sary to consolidate the results of victory. One of the deep causes of the Saxon revolt of 792–793 had been the reign of terror of 785, caused especially by the *Capitulatio de partibus Saxoniæ,*[7] to secure the Frankish domination and the authority of the Christian religion. One must men-tion, also, the ruthlessness shown by the clergy in exacting payment of the tithe. In 797 a more gentle rule was introduced in Saxony by the *Capitulare Saxonicum,* and the results of this new policy were favorable. In the Danube countries the methods used were less rigorous than formerly in Saxony.

A feature which at this period seems to have developed strongly was Charles' special care concerning the interests of the church and their close association with the interests of the state. In the capitulary, where dispositions made by the Synod of Frankfurt in 794 were pro-mulgated, regulations of purely political or administrative character are next to those concerning the life of the church, e.g., the measures taken to extend the right of exclusive jurisdiction of the church over the clerics, and those aiming to render the discipline of the higher clergy more strict by reestablishing over the bishops, chiefs of the dioceses, the superior hierarchical office of the metropolitan.

In matters of dogma the Synod of Frankfurt, under the presidency of Charlemagne, had agreed with Pope Hadrian to condemn adop-tianism, a christological heresy. Contrary to the advice of the pope, the synod had condemned the worship of images, which had been

---

[6]D. A. Bullough, "*Europae Pater:* Charlemagne and His Achievement in the Light of Recent Scholarship," *English Historical Review,* 85 (1970), 59–105.

[7]"The Capitulary on the Saxon Regions." Capitularies were edicts of the crown that had the effect of law and are among the best evidence we have of Charlemagne's paternalistic style of government.

restored to honor by the decision of a so called œcumenical council of
the Eastern Church. Charlemagne had already got his theologians to
criticize this worship in the *Libri Carolini*. In spite of his reverence for
the Holy See, Charlemagne appears to be, far more than the pope,
the real head of the church in the West. When Leo III ascended the
pontifical throne in 795, on the death of Hadrian, Charles stated
precisely their respective positions in a letter which leaves no doubt
on the subject. The pope became more or less the first of his bishops.

Alcuin and a few other clerics had developed an idea linked with
ancient traditions. To protect the church against many corrupt practices and dangers, the realization of the will of God on earth required
the reestablishment in the West of an imperial power that would
protect faith and church. Charlemagne, in their eyes, fulfilled the
necessary conditions to be that Roman Christian emperor; to be,
indeed, an emperor quite different in their minds from the historical
Constantine and Theodosius. Favorable circumstances occurred. A
revolution in Rome overthrew Pope Leo III in 799 and created an
extremely difficult situation which remained confused even after
Charles had had the pope reestablished on his throne. Charlemagne
not only admired in Alcuin the theologian and the scholar to whom
he had entrusted the task of revising the Latin text of the Bible, but
he also had confidence in his judgment and was strongly under his
influence. It was, I believe, owing to Alcuin that he went to Rome
with the idea of putting order into the affairs of the church; it was
under the same influence that he accepted there the imperial dignity.
Pope Leo III crowned him emperor on 25 December 800.

To give even a short account of the immediate and later effects of
this great event would be irrelevant here. I shall merely mention the
fifth and last period of the reign of Charlemagne, which began on the
day following the coronation. It is a rather incoherent stage of his
career. One notices this when trying to distinguish what changes in
Charlemagne's conduct could be attributed to the influence of his
newly acquired dignity.

He certainly appreciated his new position. He intended to make
the most of it towards Byzantium and he exercised a political and
military pressure on the eastern emperor until the Byzantine prince
recognized his imperial title in 812. However, in matters of government Charles's attitude was not constant. In 802, shortly after his
return from Italy, he appeared to be fully aware of the eminent character of his imperial power. He stated that it was his duty to see that all
western Christians should act according to the will of God; he ordered all his subjects to take a new oath of allegiance, this time in his
quality of emperor, and he extended the notion of allegiance. He
started legislating in the field of private law; he stipulated that the
clergy must obey strictly canonical legislation or the Rule of St. Benedict; he reformed the institution of his enquiring and reforming com-

missioners, the *missi dominici,* to make it more efficient. In spite of all this, when (806) he settled his succession, the imperial dignity appeared to have lost, in his eyes, much of its importance. Unless it were to lose its meaning entirely, the empire was indivisible. Yet Charles foresaw the partition of his states between his three sons, according to the ancient Frankish custom, and took no dispositions concerning the *imperialis potestas.* Doubtless those things that had influenced him a few years earlier were no longer effective and the Roman tradition and Alcuin's influence no longer dominated him. Everything was as if the imperial dignity had been for Charles a very high distinction but a strictly personal one. In the very last years of his reign, however, he seemed again to attach more importance to this dignity and most likely some new influences had altered his mind. His two older sons, Charles and Pepin, being dead, he himself conferred the title of emperor on his son Louis in 813.

During the end of the reign, with the one exception of the Spanish "march," which was enlarged and reinforced (Barcelona was taken in 801), no new territorial acquisition was made, in spite of military efforts often of considerable importance. The campaigns against the Northern Slavs, against Bohemia, against the Bretons of Armorica, and against the duke of Benevento only resulted in the recognition of a theoretical supremacy. Actually, fearful dangers became apparent. The Danes threatened the boundary of Saxony and their fleets devastated Frisia; the Saracen fleets threatened the Mediterranean coasts. The general impression left by the relation of these events is the weakening of the Carolingian monarchy. This impression increases when one examines internal conditions of the empire. In the state as in the church abuses increased; insecurity grew worse; the authority of the emperor was less and less respected. The capitularies, more and more numerous, constantly renewed warnings, orders, and interdictions which were less and less obeyed. Charles had grown old. Until then, his personal interferences and those which he directly provoked, had made up for the deficiencies of a quite inadequate administrative organization in an empire of extraordinary size. The physical and intellectual capacities of Charles were declining; he stayed almost continuously at Aachen, his favorite residence after 794, and he hardly ever left the place after 808. The strong antidote present before was now missing; all the political and social defects revealing a bad government appeared. When Charlemagne died in Aachen on 28 January 814, at the age of seventy-two, the Frankish state was on the verge of decay.

I have tried to describe and characterize briefly the successive phases of Charlemagne's reign. Is it possible to grasp his personality as a statesman? Perhaps. A primary fact that must be emphasized is that—even compared with others of his time—Charlemagne was not a cultivated man. In spite of his thirst for knowledge and his admiration of culture, he was ignorant of all that is connected with intellectual life and he had little gift for abstraction.

But he had a sense for realities, and especially those of power. He knew how one gains power, how one remains in power, and how one reaches the highest degrees of superior and supreme power. His attitude towards the imperial dignity revealed this. The conception of the clerics, and especially of Alcuin, for whom that dignity was an ideal magistrature infinitely above the royal power, was quite inaccessible to him. He knew or rather he felt, that the real basis of his power was solely his double royal authority[8] and he refused to omit evidence of this from his titles after the imperial coronation. For him the imperial dignity magnified and glorified the royal authority; it neither absorbed nor replaced it.

Charles had also the sense of what was practicable. Save for the campaign in Spain in 778, he undertook no tasks out of proportion to his means.

Einhard praises the equanimity of Charlemagne, his *constantia*. This was, indeed, a remarkable aspect of his personality. In the two periods of crisis which shook his reign—in 778 and in 792/793—no danger, no catastrophe, could make him give up the tasks he had undertaken or alter his methods of government. The moderation with which he happened to treat his vanquished enemies at certain times was not in contradiction with the constancy of his character. On the contrary. Equanimity implies a clear view of one's plans and one can therefore understand the variations of Charlemagne's attitude towards the imperial dignity, the full significance of which he never really understood.

To have a clear line of conduct and keep to it is one thing, but it is quite another to follow out a complete and detailed program. Charlemagne had, indeed, certain lines of conduct that he followed persistently. The facts presented are sufficient to show this as regards his foreign policy. It is also true as regards political, administrative, and juridical institutions. Charlemagne wanted to improve their efficiency so as to bring about a more complete fulfillment of his wishes and to achieve greater security for his subjects. But one cannot make out a real program in his actions. He resorted to shifts; he adopted and improved what was already existing. This is true of the institution of the *missi*, true also of the royal court of justice, of the royal vassality and of the "immunity." Occasionally he created something new, but without troubling about a general scheme. His reforms were empiric and at times went through several stages of development: as in the

---

[8]As king of the Franks and of the Lombards.

case of the organization of the *placita generalia*,[9] which was roughly outlined at the beginning of the reign but did not assume a definite shape until about the year 802, and also the use of writing in recording administrative and juridical matters, prescribed by a series of distinct decisions relating to particular cases.

One must avoid any attempt to credit Charlemagne with preoccupations proper to other times. Because of his efforts to protect *pauperes liberi homines*,[10] for instance, one cannot attribute to him the inauguration of a social policy; nor because he promulgated the *Capitulare de villis*[11] can one speak of an economic policy. In both cases he acted on the spur of urgent interests then on hand; free men of modest condition supplied soldiers and the royal manors had to be fit to maintain the court. . . .

This sketch of Charles as a statesman would be distorted if stress was not laid upon his religious concerns. It is indeed hard to draw a line between his religious and his political ideas. His will to govern and to extend his power was inseparable from his purpose to spread the Christian religion and let his subjects live according to the will of God. If something of the "clerical" conception of the empire struck him deeply, it was the feeling that he was personally responsible for the progress of God's Kingdom on earth. But always it was he who was concerned. His piousness, his zeal for the Christian religion were no obstacles to his will to power; in religious matters as in others the pope was nothing more than his collaborator.

One is often tempted to turn Charlemagne into a superman, a farseeing politician with broad and general views, ruling everything from above; one is tempted to see his reign as a whole, with more or less the same characteristics prevailing from beginning to end. This is so true that most of the works concerning him, save for the beginning and the end of his reign, use the geographical or systematic order rather than a chronological one. The distinctions that I have tried to make between the different phases of his reign may, perhaps, help to explain more exactly the development and effect of Charlemagne's power; they may help us to appreciate these more clearly. Perhaps, also, the features that I have noted bring out the human personality in the statesman and lead to the same results. The account I have given and the portrait I have drawn certainly justify the words which the poet ascribed to Charles in the last verse but one of the *Chanson de Roland:* "Deus" dist li Reis, "si penuse est ma vie." ("O Lord," said the king, "how arduous is my life.")

---

[9]The General Assembly.
[10]Impoverished free men.
[11]The Capitulary on Manors.

Questions for Review and Study

1. Who was Einhard and why is he important in the history of Charlemagne?
2. What kind of picture do you gain of Charlemagne from the readings in this chapter?
3. How do the accounts of Heinrich Fichtenau and F. L. Ganshof differ in their assessments of Charlemagne and his age?
4. Describe Charlemagne's court.
5. How would you characterize the programs and government of Charlemagne?

Questions for Comparison

1. Compare and contrast the reigns of Charlemagne and Elizabeth I of England. What were the ideological and spiritual bases of the power each inherited? What were its social and economic sources? What obstacles to kingdom or empire-building did each ruler face? Whose task was harder? Who proved more successful? How much had the geopolitical realities of Europe and the tasks of statecraft changed from Charlemagne to Elizabeth's time? On whom did government more squarely rest?

Suggestions for Further Reading

The almost unique value of Einhard's biography of Charlemagne is dramatized by the scarcity and poor quality of other contemporary sources. Students can become aware of this contrast by looking even briefly at some of these other materials. There is a life of Charlemagne nearly contemporary with Einhard's, authored by a monk of St. Gall—possibly Notker the Stammerer. But, unlike the solid and straightforward narrative of Einhard, the monk's account is disjointed and rambling, filled with legendary matter and scraps of the history of his monastery, and almost totally unreliable. It is available in a good modern edition, *Early Lives of Charlemagne by Einhard and the Monk of St. Gall,* translated and edited by A. J. Grant. Of the same sort are two somewhat later biographies of the brothers Adalard and Wala, abbots of Corbie, by the monk Radbertus of Corbie, although they contain only a few casual bits of information about Charlemagne, despite the fact that the two abbots were Charlemagne's cousins and both had played prominent roles at court: *Charlemagne's Cousins,* translated and edited by Allen Cabaniss. The only other narrative source of any value for the reign of Charlemagne is the Royal Frankish Annals, but they are thin and uncommunicative. They can be read as part of *Carolingian Chronicles: Royal Frankish Annals and Nithard's*

Histories, translated by Bernhard W. Scholz with Barbara Rogers. Several of these accounts and other sorts of documentary materials relating to Charlemagne's reign have been collected in a convenient and well-edited series of selections, *The Reign of Charlemagne,* edited by H. R. Lyons and John Percival.

Because of the stature and importance of Charlemagne and despite the problem of the sources, scholars continue to write about him. Many of their works are specialized scholarly studies. Some can be read profitably by beginning students, such as the several essays in Heinrich Fichtenau, *The Carolingian Empire,* excerpted in this chapter, or some of the articles of F. L. Ganshof collected in *The Carolingians and the Frankish Monarchy.* Pierre Riché's *Daily Life in the World of Charlemagne* is a fresh and useful work of social history by a great French authority. See also his book *The Carolingians.* For a recent and authoritative overview of all Carolingian history, including Charlemagne, see Rosamond McKitterick, *The Frankish Kingdoms under the Carolingians.* See also her *Carolingian Culture,* a new and innovative collection of essays by eminent Carolingian scholars, but somewhat marred by faulty citations.

There are three excellent modern works, all brief and readable, that treat interesting aspects of Charles's reign: Richard E. Sullivan in *Aix-la-Chapelle in the Age of Charlemagne,* focuses on the cultural achievements at Charles's capital; Jacques Boussard, in *The Civilization of Charlemagne,* presents a favorable revisionist interpretation of the Carolingian culture; and Robert Folz's *The Coronation of Charlemagne* is a close study of this important event, its background and context. One of the most important and most readable of the works on this period is *The Age of Charlemagne,* by Donald Bullough; another is a book by Eleanor S. Duckett, *Carolingian Portraits.*

Of the several biographies of Charlemagne, the best, as well as the most exciting and readable, is by Richard Winston's *Charlemagne.* A somewhat briefer and less colorful biography but by an established authority is the *Charlemagne* by James A. Cabaniss.

Henri Pirenne's *Mohammed and Charlemagne* is the masterwork of a great medieval historian and the chief entry in an important medieval scholarly controversy that continues to be of some interest to students of Charlemagne's reign. It has to do with the question of when and how the Middle Ages actually began. Pirenne says they did not begin until Charlemagne. The controversy and its chief figures are re-presented in *The Pirenne Thesis,* edited by Alfred F. Havighurst. Students are also referred to two more recent works that indicate that the Pirenne controversy is still alive, *The Origins of the Middle Ages,* by Bryce Lyon, and *The Birth of Europe,* Robert S. Lopez. (Titles with an asterisk are out of print.)

Boussard, Jacques. *The Civilization of Charlemagne.* Trans. Francis Partridge. New York: McGraw-Hill, 1968.

Bullough, Donald. *The Age of Charlemagne.* New York: Putnam, 1965.

Cabaniss, Allen, trans. and ed. *Charlemagne's Cousins: Contemporary Lives of Adalard and Wala.* Syracuse, N.Y.: Syracuse University Press, 1967.

Cabaniss, James A. *Charlemagne.* Rulers and Statesmen of the World. Boston: Twayne, 1972.*

Duckett, Eleanor S. *Carolingian Portraits: A Study in the Ninth Century.* Ann Arbor: University of Michigan Press, 1988.

Folz, Robert. *The Coronation of Charlemagne: 25 December 800.* Trans. J. E. Anderson. London: Routledge and Kegan Paul, 1974.

Ganshof, F. L. *The Carolingians and the Frankish Monarchy: Studies in Carolingian History.* Trans. Janet Sondheimer. Ithaca, N.Y.: Cornell University Press, 1971.*

Grant, A. J., trans. and ed. *Early Lives of Charlemagne by Einhard and the Monk of St. Gall.* New York: Cooper Square, 1966.*

Havighurst, Alfred F., ed. *The Pirenne Thesis: Analysis, Criticism, and Revision.* Boston: Heath, 1958.

Lopez, Robert S. *The Birth of Europe.* New York: Lippincott, 1967.

Lyon, Bryce. *The Origins of the Middle Ages: Pirenne's Challenge to Gibbon.* New York: Norton, 1972.

Lyon, H. R., and John, Percival, eds. *The Reign of Charlemagne: Documents on Carolingian Government and Administration.* New York: St. Martin's Press, 1975.*

McKitterick, Rosamond. *The Frankish Kingdoms under the Carolingians, 751–987.* London and New York: Longman, 1983.

———, ed. *Carolingian Culture: Emulation and Innovation.* Cambridge and New York: Cambridge University Press, 1994.

Pirenne, Henri. *Mohammed and Charlemagne.* Trans. Bernard Miall. New York: Barnes and Noble, 1958 [1939].*

Riché, Pierre. *The Carolingians: A Family who Forged Europe.* Trans. M. I. Allen. Philadelphia: University of Pennsylvania Press, 1993.

———. *Daily Life in the World of Charlemagne.* Trans. Jo Ann McNamara. Philadelphia: University of Pennsylvania Press, 1978.

Scholz, Bernhard W., and Barbara Rogers, trans. *Carolingian Chronicles: Royal Frankish Annals and Nithard's Histories.* Ann Arbor: University of Michigan Press, 1970.

Sullivan, Richard E. *Aix-la-Chapelle in the Age of Charlemagne.* Centers of Civilization Series. Norman: University of Oklahoma Press, 1963.

Winston, Richard. *Charlemagne: From the Hammer to the Cross.* New York: Vintage, 1954.*

ELEANOR OF AQUITAINE AND THE WRATH OF GOD

c. 1122	Born
1137	Married the future Louis VII of France
1147–1149	Second crusade
1152	Divorced from Louis VII and married to the future Henry II of England
1192–1194	Regency during captivity of Richard I
1204	Died

Eleanor of Aquitaine was one of the most remarkable and important figures in medieval history. In her own right, she was duchess of the vast domain of Aquitaine and Countess of Poitou, the wife first of Louis VII of France and then of Henry II of England, the mother of "good King Richard" and "bad King John," patroness of poets and minstrels. Tradition remembers her as beautiful and passionate, headstrong and willful. But beyond that intriguing traditional reputation, she is a figure only imperfectly seen and, ironically enough, seen at all largely through the accounts of her enemies.

The sources of medieval history are scanty at best and tend, moreover, to record men's doings in a preponderantly man's world. Even the greatest of medieval women appear in the records of their time as conveyors of properties and channels for noble blood lines, and we know of them only that they were "good and faithful wives"—or that they were not. So it is with Eleanor. We do not even have a contemporary description of her. Troubadour poets sang rapturously of her "crystal cheeks," her "locks like threads of gold," her eyes "like Orient pearls." One even proclaims:

> Were the world all mine,
> From the sea to the Rhine,
> I'd give it all

> If so be the Queen of England
> Lay in my arms.

In sober fact, we do not know what color her eyes were, nor her hair, whether it was indeed "like threads of gold" or raven black. Even the few pictorial representations we have of her—including her tomb effigy at the Abbey of Fontevrault—are purely conventional.

But Eleanor's part in the great events of her time was real enough. It began with her marriage, at the age of fifteen, to Louis the young king, son of Louis VI (Louis the Fat) of France. Her father, the turbulent Duke William X of Aquitaine, had died suddenly and unexpectedly on pilgrimage to Spain, leaving Eleanor his heir. And, in feudal law, the disposition of both Eleanor and her fiefs was a matter to be decided by her father's overlord, Louis VI of France. Duke William had been Louis's most intractable vassal, and his death was a priceless opportunity not only to put an end to the contumaciousness of Aquitaine but to tie that large and wealthy duchy to the French realm. Louis decided that the interests of his house were best served by the marriage of Eleanor to his son. And so, it was done. There is no record of how either the young bride or the young groom responded, only an account of the brilliant assemblage that gathered to witness the ceremony in Bordeaux and to accompany the couple back by weary stages to Paris. In the course of this journey, the aged King Louis died. His son was now Louis VII, the Duchess Eleanor now Queen of France. The year was 1137.

Then, less than a decade, word reached Paris of the fall of Edessa in the distant Latin Kingdom of Jerusalem, one of those fortress principalities to secure the Holy Land dating from the first crusade almost half a century before. The resurgence of Moslem power was clearly seen to threaten the Holy Land, and the call for a second crusade went out. The pious King Louis took the cross—to the consternation of his more realistic advisers—and Eleanor insisted upon accompanying him. Whatever Louis and his fellow crusaders may have thought about this matter, Eleanor's position as a great vassal who could summon a substantial host of warriors from her own lands made her support crucial: and her support was contingent upon her going in person. There is a persistent legend that the queen and her ladies decked themselves out as Amazons in anticipation of their role in the coming military adventure.

But the military adventure itself turned into a military disaster. The second crusade was a dismal failure. In this atmosphere, what had apparently been a growing estrangement between King Louis and Queen Eleanor became an open break. Their troubles were aggravated by what was then considered the boldness and outspokenness of the queen and in particular by her attentions to her handsome uncle, only eight years older than she, Raymond of Poitiers, Prince of

Antioch. It may have been no more than an innocent flirtation. But Louis thought otherwise. He brooded not only on his queen's conduct but on what he perceived as her failure to produce a son for him, and his mind turned to divorce, the grounds for which were to be found in consanguinity, a marriage within the prohibited degree of blood relationship, which was the usual legal pretext for the dissolution of feudal marriages no longer bearable or profitable.

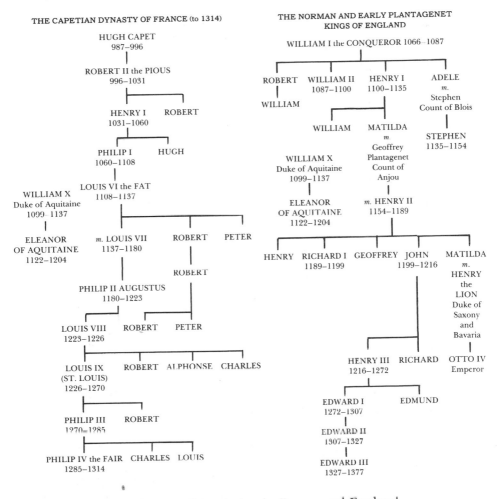

The Legacy of Eleanor of Aquitaine in France and England

Eleanor and the Chroniclers

WILLIAM OF TYRE
AND JOHN OF SALISBURY

*Eleanor's role in the second crusade is scarcely mentioned by the chroniclers who recorded the deeds of its other leading figures. Odo of Deuil, a monk of the French royal monastery of St. Denis and the chaplain of Louis VII, wrote the most detailed account of Louis's part in the crusade—*De profectione Ludovici VII in orientem*—but he makes only four passing references to the queen in the entire narrative. Odo clearly had reason to favor the cause of the king, his master. And, for one reason or another, so did the few other chroniclers who give any account at all of the estrangement between Louis and Eleanor. The most detailed is that of William Archbishop of Tyre. William is generally regarded as the best of all the chroniclers of the crusades, but he was not present at the time of this crisis, and we do not know what source he used. In any event, he regarded the behavior of the queen and the resulting breach with her husband as part of a cynical attempt by Raymond of Antioch to turn the crusade to his own advantage. Here is the account of William of Tyre.*

For many days Raymond, prince of Antioch, had eagerly awaited the arrival of the king of the Franks. When he learned that the king had landed in his domains, he summoned all the nobles of the land and the chief leaders of the people and went out to meet him with a chosen escort. He greeted the king with much reverence and conducted him with great pomp into the city of Antioch, where he was met by the clergy and the people. Long before this time—in fact, as soon as he heard that Louis was coming—Raymond had conceived the idea that by his aid he might be able to enlarge the principality of Antioch. With this in mind, therefore, even before the king started on the pilgrimage, the prince had sent to him in France a large store of noble gifts and treasures of great price in the hope of winning his favor. He also counted greatly on the interest of the queen with the lord king, for she had been his inseparable companion on his pilgrimage. She was Raymond's niece, and eldest daughter of Count William of Poitou, his brother.

As we have said, therefore, Raymond showed the king every attention on his arrival. He likewise displayed a similar care for the nobles and chief men in the royal retinue and gave them many proofs of his great liberality. In short, he outdid all in showing honor to each one according to his rank and handled everything with the greatest magnificence. He felt a lively hope that with the assistance of the king and his troops he would be able to subjugate the neighboring cities, namely, Aleppo, Shayzar, and several others. Nor would this hope have been futile, could he have induced the king and his chief men to undertake the work. For the arrival of King Louis had brought such fear to our enemies that now they not only distrusted their own strength but even despaired of life itself.

Raymond had already more than once approached the king privately in regard to the plans which he had in mind. Now he came before the members of the king's suite and his own nobles and explained with due formality how his request could be accomplished without difficulty and at the same time be of advantage and renown to themselves. The king, however, ardently desired to go to Jerusalem to fulfil his vows, and his determination was irrevocable. When Raymond found that he could not induce the king to join him, his attitude changed. Frustrated in his ambitious designs, he began to hate the king's ways; he openly plotted against him and took means to do him injury. He resolved also to deprive him of his wife, either by force or by secret intrigue. The queen readily assented to this design, for she was a foolish woman. Her conduct before and after this time showed her to be, as we have said, far from circumspect. Contrary to her royal dignity, she disregarded her marriage vows and was unfaithful to her husband.

As soon as the king discovered these plots, he took means to provide for his life and safety by anticipating the designs of the prince. By the advice of his chief nobles, he hastened his departure and secretly left Antioch with his people. Thus the splendid aspect of his affairs was completely changed, and the end was quite unlike the beginning. His coming had been attended with pomp and glory; but fortune is fickle, and his departure was ignominious.

The only other substantial account of the events leading to the divorce of Louis and Eleanor is that of the great twelfth-century ecclesiastic and intellectual John of Salisbury, in his Historia Pontificalis. *In one respect, John was even further removed from the events than was William of Tyre. He had no direct knowledge of the East at all and was, at this time, in Rome on a mission from the see of Canterbury and attached to the papal court. We do not know what source he used for the events in Antioch. It is likely that he is simply repeating the story as he heard it from members of Louis's retinue, for the hostility against Eleanor that already animated Louis's close supporters is clearly present in John's account. It is also possible that the hostility of the account and its strong pro-French bias is related to the later time at which John's work was actually written, about 1163. At this time, John was involved in the growing bitterness between Thomas Becket, whom he supported, and Henry II of England, who had just sent John into exile for his support of Becket. John found refuge in France.*

But in any event, the account in the Historia Pontificalis *is strongly favorable to Louis, even to the extent of ascribing to Eleanor the initiative in the proposal for the divorce.*

In the year of grace 1149 the most Christian king of the Franks reached Antioch, after the destruction of his armies in the east, and was nobly entertained there by Prince Raymond, brother of the late William, count of Poitiers. He was as it happened the queen's uncle, and owed the king loyalty, affection, and respect for many reasons. But whilst they remained there to console, heal, and revive the survivors from the wreck of the army, the attentions paid by the prince to the queen, and his constant, indeed almost continuous, conversation with her, aroused the king's suspicions. These were greatly strengthened when the queen wished to remain behind, although the king was preparing to leave, and the prince made every effort to keep her, if the king would give his consent. And when the king made haste to tear her away, she mentioned their kinship, saying it was not lawful for them to remain together as man and wife, since they were related in the fourth and fifth degrees. Even before their departure a rumour to that effect had been heard in France, where the late Bartholomew, bishop of Laon, had calculated the degrees of kinship; but it was not certain whether the reckoning was true or false. At this the king was deeply moved; and although he loved the queen almost beyond reason he consented to divorce her if his counsellors and the French nobility would allow it. There was one knight amongst the king's secretaries, called Terricus Gualerancius, a eunuch whom the queen had always hated and mocked, but who was faithful and had the king's ear like his father's before him. He boldly persuaded the king not to suffer her to dally longer at Antioch, both because "guilt under kinship's guise could lie concealed," and because it would be a lasting shame to the kingdom of the Franks if in addition to all the other disasters it was reported that the king had been deserted by his wife, or robbed of her. So he argued, either because he hated the queen or because he really believed it, moved perchance by widespread rumour. In consequence, she was torn away and forced to leave for Jerusalem with the king; and, their mutual anger growing greater, the wound remained, hide it as best they might.

In the next passage, John is on more familiar ground since he was in Rome, a familiar of the curia and of Pope Eugenius III, and perhaps even a witness to some of the events he describes.

In the year of grace eleven hundred and fifty the king of the Franks returned home. But the galleys of the Emperor of Constantinople lay in wait for him on his return, capturing the queen and all who were journeying in her ship. The king was appealed to to return to his Byzantine brother and friend, and force was being brought to bear on him when the galleys of the king of Sicily came to the rescue. Freeing the queen and releasing the king, they escorted them back to Sicily rejoicing, with honour and triumph. This was done by order of the king of Sicily, who feared the wiles of the Greeks and desired an opportunity of showing his devotion to the king and queen of the Franks. Now therefore he hastened to meet him with an ample retinue, and escorted him most honourably to Palermo, heaping gifts both on him and on all his followers; thereafter he travelled with him right across his territory to Ceprano, supplying all his needs on the way. This is the last point on the frontier between the principality of Capua and Campania, which is papal territory.

At Ceprano the cardinals and officials of the church met the king and, providing him with all that he desired, escorted him to Tusculum to the lord pope, who received him with such tenderness and reverence that one would have said he was welcoming an angel of the Lord rather than a mortal man. He reconciled the king and queen, after hearing severally the accounts each gave of the estrangement begun at Antioch, and forbade any future mention of their consanguinity: confirming their marriage, both orally and in writing, he commanded under pain of anathema that no word should be spoken against it and that it should not be dissolved under any pretext whatever. This ruling plainly delighted the king, for he loved the queen passionately, in an almost childish way. The pope made them sleep in the same bed, which he had had decked with priceless hangings of his own; and daily during their brief visit he strove by friendly converse to restore love between them. He heaped gifts upon them; and when the moment for departure came, though he was a stern man, he could not hold back his tears, but sent them on their way blessing them and the kingdom of the Franks, which was higher in his esteem than all the kingdoms of the world.

Eleanor, the Queen of Hearts

AMY KELLY

Despite "the lord pope's" good offices, his tears and his blessing, even his threat of anathema, the estrangement between Louis and Eleanor continued. Louis was adamant, and finally, in the spring of 1152 at a solemn synod in Beaugency on the Loire, Louis's representatives argued the case of the consanguinity of their lord and his queen, and the Archbishop of Sens proclaimed their marriage invalid. The Archbishop of Bordeaux, the queen's surrogate, sought only the assurance that her lands be restored. But this had already been arranged, as had all the other details of this elaborate royal charade. Eleanor was not even present. She had already returned to Poitou.

But Eleanor was not destined to reign as a dowager duchess in her own domains. Within two months, she married Henry, Duke of Normandy. He was not only the Norman duke but also the heir to the fiefs of his father, Geoffrey Plantagenet, Count of Maine and Anjou. These already substantial lands, when joined to those of his new bride, made Henry lord of a nearly solid block of territories that stretched from the English Channel to the Mediterranean and from Bordeaux to the Vexin, hardly a day's ride from Paris. At one stroke, Henry of Anjou had become the greatest feudatory of France, with lands and resources many times the size of those held by his nominal overlord, King Louis VII. Two years later, another piece of Henry's inheritance came into his hands. His mother, Matilda, was the daughter of the English King Henry I and had never ceased to press the claim of her son to the English throne. The reign of King Stephen was coming to an end, and he had no surviving heirs. At his death in 1154, Henry of Anjou claimed his crown, and there was none to deny him. Eleanor was a queen once more.

But this time, she had a very different king. Henry II was as godless as Louis had been pious, as flamboyant as Louis had been humble. Where Louis was stubborn and persistent, Henry was furiously energetic and decisive. The setting was at hand for one of the classic confrontations of medieval history that was to stretch into the following generation of the kings of both France and England.

As for Eleanor, the sources are once more almost silent. We do know that she and Henry produced a large family. The eldest son, William, born before the succession to England, died in childhood. But in 1155 came Henry; in 1156, their first daughter, Matilda; in 1157 came Richard, to be called the Lion Hearted; in 1158 came Geoffrey; in 1161, Eleanor; in 1165, Johanna; and in 1166, John. We know that through the early years of her marriage to Henry, Eleanor was often with him at court and sometimes presided in his absence, a fact attested by writs and seals. But her marriage was by no means serene. There were long periods of separation during which the king was known to be unfaithful. The incidents of his infidelity grew more flagrant with the passing years. At about the time of Prince John's birth in 1166, Henry was involved with a paramour of spectacular beauty, Rosamond Clifford. Their affair was the object of such celebration by poets, balladeers, and wags alike that Eleanor may have decided that her bed and her dignity could no longer endure such an affront. But there may have been other matters at issue. The queen may have become alarmed at her husband's efforts to substitute his rule for hers in her dower lands.

In any case, about 1170 she returned to Poitou with her favorite son, Richard, whom she installed as her heir for the lands of Poitou and Aquitaine. For the next three or four years she lived in her old capital of Poitiers, separated from her husband. In these years of self-imposed exile, Eleanor not only reasserted her rights to her own lands, but created a center in Poitiers for the practice of the troubadour culture and l'amour courtois that had long been associated with her family.

The following passage, from Amy Kelly's Eleanor of Aquitaine and the

Four Kings—the book that has come to be regarded as the standard work on Eleanor—is a brilliant reconstruction of this period of Eleanor's life.

When the countess of Poitou settled down to rule her own heritage, she took her residence in Poitiers, which offered a wide eye-sweep on the world of still operative kings. In the recent Plantagenet building program her ancestral city, the seat and necropolis of her forebears, had been magnificently enlarged and rebuilt, and it stood at her coming thoroughly renewed, a gleaming exemplar of urban elegance. The site rose superbly amidst encircling rivers. Its narrow Merovingian area had lately been extended to include with new and ampler walls parishes that had previously straggled over its outer slopes; ancient quarters had been cleared of immemorial decay; new churches and collegials had sprung up; the cathedral of Saint Pierre was enriched; markets and shops of tradesmen and artisans bore witness to renewed life among the *bourgeoisie;* bridges fanned out to suburbs and monastic establishments lying beyond the streams that moated the city. Brimming with sunshine, the valleys ebbed far away below—hamlet and croft, mill and vineyard—to a haze as blue as the vintage. . . .

When Eleanor came in about 1170 to take full possession of her newly restored city of Poitiers and to install her favorite son there as ruling count and duke in her own patrimony, she was no mere game piece as were most feudal women, to be moved like a queen in chess. She had learned her role as *domina* in Paris, Byzantium, Antioch, London, and Rouen, and knew her value in the feudal world. She was prepared of her own unguided wisdom to reject the imperfect destinies to which she had been, as it were, assigned. In this, her third important role in history, she was the pawn of neither prince nor prelate, the victim of no dynastic scheme. She came as her own mistress, the most sophisticated of women, equipped with plans to establish her own assize, to inaugurate a regime dedicated neither to Mars nor to the Pope, nor to any king, but to Minerva, Venus, and the Virgin. She was resolved to escape from secondary roles, to assert her independent sovereignty in her own citadel, to dispense her own justice, her own patronage, and when at leisure, to survey, like the Empress of Byzantium, a vast decorum in her precincts. . . .

The heirs of Poitou and Aquitaine who came to the queen's high place for their vassals' homage, their squires' training, and their courtiers' service, were truculent youths, boisterous young men from the baronial strongholds of the south without the Norman or Frankish sense of nationality, bred on feuds and violence, some of them with rich fiefs and proud lineage, but with little solidarity and no business but local warfare and daredevil escapade. The custom of lateral rather than vertical inheritance of fiefs in vogue in some parts of Poitou and

Aquitaine—the system by which lands passed through a whole generation before descending to the next generation—produced a vast number of landless but expectant younger men, foot-loose, unemployed,
ambitious, yet dependent upon the reluctant bounty of uncles and
brothers, or their own violent exploits. These wild young men were a
deep anxiety not only to the heads of their houses, but to the Kings of
France and England and to the Pope in Rome. They were the stuff of
which rebellion and schism are made. For two generations the church
had done what it could with the problem of their unemployment,
marching hordes out of Europe on crusade and rounding other hordes
into the cloister.

It was with this spirited world of princes and princesses, of apprentice knights and chatelaines, at once the school and the court of
young Richard, that the duchess, busy as she was with the multifarious
business of a feudal suzerain, had to deal in her palace in Poitiers. . . .

---

*Eleanor found a willing and helpful deputy to assist her in the person of Marie,
Countess of Champagne, her daughter by Louis of France. Marie, now entrusted
to Eleanor's tutelage, was a well-educated young woman and apparently well
disposed to her mother's plans.*

. . . The character of the milieu which Marie appears to have set up in
Poitiers suggests a genuine sympathy between the queen and her
daughter who had so long been sundered by the bleak fortuities of
life. Old relationships were knit up. Something native blossomed in
the countess, who shone with a special luster in her mother's court.
The young Count of Poitou learned to love particularly his half sister
Marie and forever to regard the Poitiers of her dispensation as the
world's citadel of valor, the seat of courtesy, and the fountainhead of
poetic inspiration. Long after, in his darkest hours, it was to her good
graces he appealed. The countess, having carte blanche to proceed
with the very necessary business of getting control of her academy,
must have striven first for order. Since the miscellaneous and high-
spirited young persons in her charge had not learned order from the
liturgy nor yet from hagiography, the countess bethought her, like
many an astute pedagogue, to deduce her principles from something
more germane to their interests. She did not precisely invent her
regime; rather she appropriated it from the abundant resources at
her hand.

The liberal court of Eleanor had again drawn a company of those
gifted persons who thrive by talent or by art. Poets, *conteurs* purveying
romance, ecclesiastics with Latin literature at their tongues' end and
mere clerks with smatterings of Ovid learned from quotation books,
chroniclers engaged upon the sober epic of the Plantagenets, came to

their haven in Poitiers. The queen and the countess, with their native poetic tradition, were the natural patrons of the troubadours. It will be seen that the Countess Marie's resources were rich and abundant, but not so formalized as to afford the disciplines for a royal academy nor give substance to a social ritual. The great hall was ready for her grand assize; the expectant court already thronged to gape at its suggestive splendors. . . .

At least one other important source Marie employed. She levied upon the social traditions of her Poitevin forebears. Nostredame relates that in Provence chatelaines were accustomed to entertain their seasonal assemblies with so-called "courts of love," in which, just as feudal vassals brought their grievances to the assizes of their overlords for regulation, litigants in love's thrall brought their problems for the judgment of the ladies. André in his famous work[1] makes reference to antecedent decisions in questions of an amatory nature by "les dames de Gascogne," and the poetry of the troubadours presupposes a milieu in which their doctrines of homage and deference could be exploited. Thus we have in André's *Tractatus* the framework of Ovid with the central emphasis reversed, the Arthurian code of manners, the southern ritual of the "courts of love," all burnished with a golden wash of troubadour poetry learned by the queen's forebears and their vassals in the deep Midi, probably beyond the barrier of the Pyrenees. Marie made these familiar materials the vehicle for her woman's doctrine of civility, and in so doing, she transformed the gross and cynical pagan doctrines of Ovid into something more ideal, the woman's canon, the chivalric code of manners. Manners, she plainly saw, were after all the fine residuum of philosophies, the very flower of ethics. . . .

With this anatomy of the whole corpus of love in hand, Marie organized the rabble of soldiers, fighting cocks, jousters, springers, riding masters, troubadours, Poitevin nobles and debutantes, young chatelaines, adolescent princes, and infant princesses in the great hall of Poitiers. Of this pandemonium the countess fashioned a seemly and elegant society, the fame of which spread to the world. Here was a woman's assize to draw men from the excitements of the tilt and the hunt, from dice and games to feminine society, an assize to outlaw boorishness and compel the tribute of adulation to female majesty. . . .

While the ladies, well-accoutered, sit above upon the dais, the sterner portion of society purged, according to the code, from the odors of the kennels and the highway and free for a time from spurs

---

[1]André, simply known as the Chaplain, a scholar of this court whose work *Tractatus de Amore*, referred to here, is one of the basic works on medieval chivalry and the courts of love.

and falcons, range themselves about the stone benches that line the walls, stirring the fragrant rushes with neatly pointed shoe. There are doubtless preludes of music luring the last reluctant knight from the gaming table, *tensons* or *pastourelles,* the plucking of rotes, the "voicing of a fair song and sweet," perhaps even some of the more complicated musical harmonies so ill-received by the clerical critics in London; a Breton *lai* adding an episode to Arthurian romance, or a chapter in the tale of "sad-man" Tristram, bringing a gush of tears from the tender audience clustered about the queen and the Countess of Champagne.

After the romance of the evening in the queen's court, the jury comes to attention upon petition of a young knight in the hall. He bespeaks the judgment of the queen and her ladies upon a point of conduct, through an advocate, of course, so he may remain anonymous. A certain knight, the advocate deposes, has sworn to his lady, as the hard condition of obtaining her love, that he will upon no provocation boast of her merits in company. But one day he overhears detractors heaping his mistress with calumnies. Forgetting his vow in the heat of his passion, he warms to eloquence in defense of his lady. This coming to her ears, she repudiates her champion. Does the lover, who admits he has broken his pledge to his mistress, deserve in this instance to be driven from her presence?

The Countess of Champagne, subduing suggestions from the floor and the buzz of conference upon the dais, renders the judgment of the areopagus. The lady in the case, anonymous of course, is at fault, declares the Countess Marie. She has laid upon her lover a vow too impossibly difficult. The lover has been remiss, no doubt, in breaking his vow to his mistress, no matter what cruel hardship it involves; but he deserves leniency for the merit of his ardor and his constancy. The jury recommends that the stern lady reinstate the plaintiff. The court takes down the judgment. It constitutes a precedent. Does anyone guess the identity of the young pair whose estrangement is thus delicately knit up by the countess? As a bit of suspense it is delicious. As a theme for talk, how loosening to the tongue!

A disappointed petitioner brings forward a case, through an advocate, involving the question whether love survives marriage. The countess, applying her mind to the code, which says that marriage is no proper obstacle to lovers (*Causa coniugii ab amore non est excusatio recta*), and after grave deliberation with her ladies, creates a sensation in the court by expressing doubt whether love in the ideal sense can exist between spouses. This is so arresting a proposition that the observations of the countess are referred to the queen for corroboration, and all wait upon the opinion of this deeply experienced judge. The queen with dignity affirms that she cannot gainsay the Countess of Champagne, though she finds it admirable that a wife should find love and marriage consonant. Eleanor, Queen of France and then of

England, had learned at fifty-two that, as another medieval lady put it, "Mortal love is but the licking of honey from thorns."

Eleanor the Regent

MARION MEADE

During the years of Eleanor's dalliance at Poitiers, her husband's larger world had been turned upside down by his quarrel with Thomas Becket. It had not ended even with the martyrdom of that troublesome prelate at the altar of Canterbury in 1170. The question of whether Henry ordered Becket's murder or not—and he probably did not—is quite immaterial. For he bore its consequences. And its principal consequence was to give to the French king a priceless justification to move against Henry and his fiefs. What is more, Henry's own sons were as often as not in league with the French king. With some of them, Henry had been too hard, with others too soft. And when he favored one, the others feared and plotted against the favorite of the moment. Even Henry's proposed disposition of his estates and titles served only to further their quarrels with each other and with him. These quarrels reached their first climax in the great rebellion of 1173, in which Henry the young king, Richard, and Geoffrey were in open alliance with Louis of France against their father. To the alliance flocked rebellious barons from Scotland to Aquitaine. Henry charged Eleanor with sedition and with embittering their sons against him. As the rebellion faltered and then was quelled, Henry was reconciled, however fitfully, with his sons but not their mother. With Eleanor, Henry was unyielding. She was imprisoned, first at Salisbury Castle, later at Winchester and other places, for the next sixteen years. One must imagine that the captivity was genteel, but it was nonetheless real. From time to time, she was released for a holiday visit to court or to participate in some stormy family council.

In the last years of Eleanor's imprisonment, two of her sons, Henry and Geoffrey, died, but the surviving sons, Richard and John, could still intrigue against their father. They did so in league with a new and more dangerous Capetian enemy, Philip II Augustus, the able and energetic son of Louis VII, who had followed him to the throne in 1180. Henry II's final years were filled with his sons' rebellion, and he died in 1189 shamed by defeat at their hands. It was only after Henry's death and the succession of Richard that Eleanor was released from her captivity.

With none of her ardor dimmed, the queen, now almost seventy, set about to serve her favored son, now king at last. While Richard was still on the Continent, Eleanor assumed the regency and on her own authority convoked a court at Westminster to demand the oaths of loyalty from the English feudality to their new king. She then traveled to other centers to take similar obeisances and to set the affairs of the kingdom in order. Her son arrived for an undisputed coronation in the summer of 1189.

But Richard's thoughts in that triumphal summer season were not upon the affairs of England or any of his other lands. He had already taken the cross almost two years before, and the third crusade was about to begin. The Lion Hearted was to be its greatest hero.

The third crusade, despite Richard's heroics, was as unsuccessful as the second. And, after three years, during which most of his fellow crusaders had declared their vows discharged and returned to their own lands—including his Capetian rival, Philip Augustus—Richard started for home.

We pick up the story of his return—with its delays and betrayals—and of Eleanor's role in it from her recent biography, by Marion Meade, Eleanor of Aquitaine: A Biography. *Meade's book is broadly revisionist, and the basis of her revisionism is her feminism. Meade observes that "the historical record, written to accommodate men" has judged Eleanor "a bitch, harlot, adultress, and monster" and that this is not surprising "for she was one of those rare women who altogether refused to be bound by the rules of proper behavior for her sex; she did as she pleased, although not without agonizing personal struggle" (p. ix). In Meade's account, as in any other account of Eleanor, there is much latitude for interpretation, given the pervasive silence of contemporary chronicles. Meade further argues that even these are "riddled with lies since monks and historians—in the twelfth century one and the same—have always abhorred emancipated women" (p. xi). Meade intends to redress the balance. And she does so, in no part of her account more forcefully than in the following passage.*

In England, Eleanor was expecting her son home for Christmas. All through November and early December companies of Crusaders had begun arriving in the kingdom; in the ports and marketplaces there were firsthand reports of the king's deeds in Palestine and plans for celebrations once he arrived. But the days passed without news, and newly arrived contingents of soldiers expressed astonishment that they had beaten the king home although they had left Acre after Richard. Along the coast, lookouts peered into the foggy Channel in hope of sighting the royal vessel, and messengers waited to race over the frozen roads toward London with the news of the king's landing. Eleanor learned that Berengaria and Joanna[2] had safely reached Rome, but of her son, weeks overdue, there was an alarming lack of information. She held a cheerless Christmas court at Westminster, her apprehension mounting with each day, her silent fears being expressed openly in the ale houses along the Thames: The king had encountered some calamity, a storm along the Adriatic coast no doubt, and now he would never return.

Three days after Christmas, the whereabouts of the tardy Richard

---

[2]Berengaria was Richard's wife—a Spanish princess he had married, at Eleanor's urging, on his way to the crusade. Joanna was Richard's sister, the widowed Queen of Sicily, whom he had taken under his protection to Palestine.

Plantagenet became known, not at Westminster but at the Cité Palace in Paris. On December 28, Philip Augustus received an astounding letter from his good friend Henry Hohenstaufen, the Holy Roman emperor:[3]

> We have thought it proper to inform your nobleness that while the enemy of our empire and the disturber of your kingdom, Richard, King of England, was crossing the sea to his dominions, it chanced that the winds caused him to be shipwrecked in the region of Istria, at a place which lies between Aquila and Venice. . . . The roads being duly watched and the entire area well-guarded, our dearly beloved cousin Leopold, Duke of Austria, captured the king in a humble house in a village near Vienna. Inasmuch as he is now in our power, and has always done his utmost for your annoyance and disturbance, we have thought it proper to relay this information to your nobleness.

Shortly after the first of the new year, 1193, the archbishop of Rouen was able to send Eleanor a copy of the letter, accompanied by a covering note in which he cited whatever comforting quotations he could recall from Scripture to cover an outrage of this magnitude.

Eleanor's most imperative problem—finding the location where Richard was being held prisoner—she tackled with her usual energy and resourcefulness. From all points, emissaries were dispatched to find the king: Eleanor herself sent the abbots of Boxley and Pontrobert to roam the villages of Bavaria and Swabia, following every lead and rumor; Hubert Walter, bishop of Salisbury, stopping in Italy on his way home from the Crusade, changed course and hastened to Germany; even William Longchamp, the exiled chancellor, set out at once from Paris to trace his master. It was not until March, however, that Richard's chaplain, Anselm, who had shared many of the king's misadventures, arrived in England, and Eleanor was able to obtain authentic details [including the fact that Richard was being held in a remote castle of Durrenstein in Austria].

Treachery was rife not only in Germany but in Paris and Rouen; it even percolated rapidly in the queen's own family. Before Eleanor could take steps to secure Coeur de Lion's release, she was faced with more immediate catastrophes in the form of Philip Augustus and his newest ally, her son John. These two proceeded on the assumption that Richard, king of England, was dead. Or as good as dead. But before Eleanor could take her youngest son in hand, he fled to Normandy, where he declared himself the king's heir, an announcement the Norman barons greeted with disdain. John did not wait to con-

---

[3]The Plantagenet kings were related by marriage to the great German feudal family, the Welfs, who were the most dangerous rivals to the imperial house of Hohenstaufen. The Angevins, including Richard, had frequently supported the Welfs, hence the emperor's hostility.

vince them, proceeding instead to Paris, where he did homage to Philip for the Plantagenet Continental domains and furthermore agreeing to confirm Philip's right to the Vexin.[4] . . . In the meantime, Eleanor, "who then ruled England," had taken the precaution of closing the Channel ports and ordering the defense of the eastern coast against a possible invasion, her hastily mustered home guard being instructed to wield any weapon that came to hand, including their plowing tools.

At this point, Eleanor's dilemma in regard to her sons would have taxed the most patient of mothers. John, returning to England, swaggered about the countryside proclaiming himself the next king of England—perhaps he sincerely believed that Richard would never be released alive—and, never known for his sensitivity, constantly regaled Eleanor with the latest rumors concerning the fate of her favorite son. Her actions during this period indicate clearly that she failed to take John seriously. Although he was twenty-seven, she thought of him as the baby of the family, always a child showing off and trying to attract attention. Her attitude was probably close to that of Richard's when, a few months later, he was informed of John's machinations: "My brother John is not the man to subjugate a country if there is a person able to make the slightest resistance to his attempts." With one hand, Eleanor deftly managed to anticipate John's plots and render him harmless; with the other, she worked for Richard's release. After Easter, the king had been removed from Durrenstein Castle and the hands of Duke Leopold and, after some haggling, had been taken into custody by Leopold's suzerain, the Holy Roman emperor. As the emperor's prisoner, Richard found himself the object of high-level decisions. His death, it was decided, would achieve no useful purpose; rather the arrogant Plantagenets, or what remained of them, should be made to redeem their kin, but at a price that would bring their provinces to their knees: 100,000 silver marks with two hundred hostages as surety for payment. The hostages, it was specified, were to be chosen from among the leading barons of England and Normandy or from their children.

Relieved as Eleanor must have felt to learn that her son could be purchased, she could only have been appalled at the size of the ransom. The prospect of collecting such an enormous sum, thirty-five tons of pure silver, seemed impossible after Henry's Saladin tithe[5] and Richard's great sale before the Crusade.[6] Where was the money to be

---

[4]The Vexin was an area at the juncture of Normandy, Anjou, and the Ile de France, long disputed by the English and French kings.

[5]A tax that Henry had levied for a crusade, hence called after the great Moslem leader Saladin.

[6]A sale of movable property not only of the crown but of such protected folk as foreign and Jewish merchants, and of what could be extracted from the nobility.

found? Where were two hundred noble hostages to be located? At a council convened at Saint Albans on June 1, 1193, she appointed five officers to assist with the dreaded task. During the summer and fall, England became a marketplace to raise the greatest tax in its history. The kingdom was stripped of its wealth. "No subject, lay or clerk, rich or poor, was overlooked. No one could say, 'Behold I am only So-and-So or Such-and-Such, pray let me be excused.'" Barons were taxed one-quarter of a year's income. Churches and abbeys were relieved of their movable wealth, including the crosses on their altars. The Cistercians, who possessed no riches, sheared their flocks and donated a year's crop of wool. Before long, the bars of silver and gold began slowly to pile up in the crypt of Saint Paul's Cathedral under Eleanor's watchful eyes. But not quickly enough to comfort her. Even more painful was the job of recruiting hostages from the great families, their lamentations and pleadings rising like a sulphurous mist all over the kingdom and providing constant agony for the queen.

From Haguenau, where Richard was incarcerated, came a flood of letters to his subjects and most especially to his "much loved mother." He had been received with honor by the emperor and his court, he is well, he hopes to be home soon. He realizes that the ransom will be difficult to raise but he feels sure that his subjects will not shirk their duty; all sums collected should be entrusted to the queen. . . .

It is said that in her anguish she addressed three letters to Pope Celestine III imploring his assistance in securing Richard's release and in her salutation addressed the pontiff as "Eleanor, by the wrath of God, Queen of England." . . . Why, she demands, does the sword of Saint Peter slumber in its scabbard when her son, a "most delicate youth," the anointed of the Lord, lies in chains? Why does the pope, a "negligent," "cruel" prevaricator and sluggard, do nothing?

These letters, supposedly written for her by Peter of Blois, are so improbable that it is surprising that many modern historians have accepted them as authentic. While preserved among the letters of Peter of Blois, who is undoubtedly their author—they are characteristic of his style and use his favorite expressions—there is no evidence that they were written for Eleanor or that they were ever sent. Most likely they were rhetorical exercises. No contemporary of Eleanor's mentioned that she wrote to the pope, and not until the seventeenth century were the letters attributed to her. From a diplomatic point of view, they are too fanciful to be genuine; Eleanor, clearheaded and statesmanlike, was never a querulous old woman complaining of age, infirmities, and weariness of life. On the contrary, her contemporaries unanimously credit her with the utmost courage, industry, and political skill. A second point to notice is that the details of the letters misrepresent the facts of Richard's imprisonment. He was never "detained in bonds," and as both she and the pope knew, Celestine had instantly, upon receiving news of Richard's capture, excommunicated

Duke Leopold for laying violent hands on a brother Crusader; he had threatened Philip Augustus with an interdict if he trespassed upon Plantagenet territories; and he had menaced the English with interdict should they fail to collect the ransom. Under the circumstances, Celestine had done all he could. In the last analysis, the letters must be viewed as Peter of Blois's perception of Eleanor's feelings, a view that may or may not be accurate.

In December 1193, Eleanor set sail with an imposing retinue of clerks, chaplains, earls, bishops, hostages, and chests containing the ransom. By January 17, 1194, the day scheduled for Richard's release, she had presented herself and the money at Speyer, but no sooner had they arrived than, to her amazement, Henry Hohenstaufen announced a further delay. He had received letters that placed an entirely new light on the matter of the king's liberation. As the gist of the problem emerged, it seemed Philip Augustus and John Plantagenet had offered the emperor an equivalent amount of silver if he could hold Coeur de Lion in custody another nine months, or deliver him up to them. These disclosures, and Henry's serious consideration of the counteroffer, provoked horror from the emperor's own vassals, and after two days of argument, Henry relented. He would liberate Richard as promised if the king of England would do homage to him for all his possessions, including the kingdom of England. This request, a calculated humiliation, would have made Richard a vassal of the Holy Roman emperor, a degradation that the Plantagenets were hard put to accept. Quick to realize the meaninglessness, as well as the illegality, of the required act, Eleanor made an on-the-spot decision. According to Roger of Hovedon, Richard, "by advice of his mother Eleanor, abdicated the throne of the kingdom of England and delivered it to the emperor as the lord of all." On February 4, the king was released "into the hands of his mother" after a captivity of one year six weeks and three days.

Seven weeks later, on March 12, the king's party landed at Sandwich and proceeded directly to Canterbury, where they gave thanks at the tomb of Saint Thomas. By the time they reached London, the city had been decorated, the bells were clanging furiously, and the Londoners ready to give a rapturous welcome to their hero and champion. Her eldest son "hailed with joy upon the Strand," Eleanor looked in vain for the remaining male member of her family, but the youngest Plantagenet was nowhere to be found. Once Richard's release had been confirmed, he had fled to Paris upon Philip Augustus's warning that "beware, the devil is loose." . . .

According to the chronicles, "the king and John became reconciled through the mediation of Queen Eleanor, their mother." In the circumstances, it seemed the safest course as well as the wisest. There was no doubt in Eleanor's mind that the boy, now twenty-eight, could not be held responsible for his actions, that he was, as Richard of

Devizes termed him, "light-minded." But at that moment, he was the last of the Plantagenets. With luck, Richard might reign another twenty-five years or more. Who was to say that he would not produce an heir of his own? Thus the queen must have reasoned in the spring of 1194 when her son, after so many adversities, had come home to her.

Questions for Review and Study

1. What role did Eleanor play in the evolution of medieval chivalric culture?
2. What role did Eleanor play in European political affairs?
3. To what extent should Eleanor be considered a feminist heroine?

Suggestions for Further Reading

As we have seen, despite her importance and inherent interest, there are virtually no contemporary source materials for Eleanor. Thus, whether hostile or sympathetic, the treatments of Eleanor have tried to be not so much biographies as life-and-times books. This is true even of the best modern works. Two of them—*Eleanor of Aquitaine and the Four Kings,* by Amy Kelly, and *Eleanor of Aquitaine,* by Marion Meade—are excerpted in this chapter, and students are encouraged to read further in them. Two additional works are also recommended, by Curtis H. Walker and by Regine Pernould, both titled *Eleanor of Aquitaine* and both well written, lively, and fast moving. The *Eleanor of Aquitaine* edited by William W. Kibler is a series of specialized papers on aspects of Eleanor's life and reign. D. D. R. Owen's book of the same title is not very satisfactory.

Of Eleanor's contemporaries, the best and most comprehensive work on Henry II is by W. L. Warren. Somewhat less intimidating are the smaller but entirely competent texts by Richard Barber, *Henry Plantagenet,* and John Schlight, *Henry II Plantagenet.* Probably the best biography of Richard I is by Philip Henderson, *Richard Coeur de Lion,* but students are also encouraged to read James A. Brundage's *Richard Lion Heart,* largely a study of Richard as soldier and crusader, and a tough, realistic work. The standard work on John is Sidney Painter, *The Reign of King John.* W. L. Warren's *King John* is a somewhat revisionist treatment of John showing him as a hard-working monarch and more the victim than the cause of his troubles—but he still is a far from attractive figure. For Eleanor's French royal contemporaries, see *The Capetian Kings of France,* by R. Fawtier. Studies of important nonroyal figures whose lives intertwined with Eleanor's include *William Marshall,* by Sidney Painter, and *Hubert Walter,* by Charles R. Young. Of the number of books on the durable subject of Henry and Becket, the best are Richard Winston's

Thomas Becket, a tough, skeptical, but solidly source-based work; Dom David Knowles's *Thomas Becket,* a scrupulously objective account by a great ecclesiastical historian, but, naturally, most occupied with the arguments of Thomas and the church; and *My Life for My Sheep,* by Alfred L. Duggan, a lively novelized account by an experienced historical novelist.

Two special topics relate to Eleanor throughout her life—chivalry and courtly love and the crusades. Both have been much studied and written about. On chivalry and courtly love, see three excellent and well-written background works: John C. Moore, *Love in Twelfth-Century France;* Jack Lindsay, *The Troubadours and Their World of the Twelfth and Thirteenth Centuries;* and C. Stephen Jaeger, *The Origins of Courtliness;* and two equally interesting ones dealing with the actual operation of knightly chivalry as well as its romanticized literary aspects—Sidney Painter's *French Chivalry,* and the more comprehensive *The Knight and Chivalry,* by Richard Barber. But the definitive work in all its aspects is *Chivalry,* by Maurice Keen. The standard work on the crusades is now *The History of the Crusades,* a great multiauthored work under the general editorship of Kenneth M. Setton. Steven Runciman's three-volume *History of the Crusades* may, however, still be the best account. Students may prefer *The Crusades* by Zoë Oldenbourg, somewhat less successful than her famous historical novels but still excellent and exciting. For the warfare of the period, students should look at the recent and comprehensive Philippe Contamine text, *War in the Middle Ages,* especially the sections on the feudal ages and medieval society at its prime. (Titles with an asterisk are out of print.)

Baldwin, M. W., ed. *The First Hundred Years* Vol. 1 of *The History of the Crusades,* ed. Kenneth M. Setton. Philadelphia: University of Pennsylvania Press, 1955.

Barber, Richard. *Henry Plantagenet.* Totowa, N.J.: Rowman and Littlefield, 1964.*

———. *The Knight and Chivalry.* New York: Scribner's, 1970.

Brundage, James A. *Richard Lion Heart.* New York: Scribner's, 1974.

Contamine, Philippe. *War in the Middle Ages.* Trans. Michael Jones. Oxford: Blackwell, 1984.

Duggan, Alfred L. *My Life for My Sheep.* New York: Coward-McCann, 1955.*

Fawtier, R. *The Capetian Kings of France.* Trans. Lionel Butler and R. J. Adam. London: Macmillan, 1960.

Henderson, Philip. *Richard Coeur de Lion: A Biography.* New York: Norton, 1959.

Jaeger, C. Stephen. *The Origins of Courtliness: Civilizing Trends and the Formation of Courtly Ideals, 939–1210.* Philadelphia: University of Pennsylvania Press, 1985.

Keen, Maurice. *Chivalry.* New Haven, Conn.: Yale University Press, 1984.

Kelly, Amy. *Eleanor of Aquitaine and the Four Kings.* Cambridge, Mass.: Harvard University Press, 1950.

Kibler, Wm. W., ed. *Eleanor of Aquitaine: Patron and Politician.* Austin: University of Texas Press, 1976.*

Knowles, Dom David. *Thomas Becket.* London: A. and C. Black, 1970.

Lindsay, Jack. *The Troubadours and Their World of the Twelfth and Thirteenth Centuries.* London: Frederick Muller, 1976.

Meade, Marion. *Eleanor of Aquitaine: A Biography.* New York: Hawthorn, 1977.

Moore, John C. *Love in Twelfth-Century France.* Philadelphia: University of Pennsylvania Press, 1972.

Oldenbourg, Zoë. *The Crusades.* Trans. Anne Carter. New York: Pantheon, 1966.

Owen, D. D. R. *Eleanor of Aquitaine: Queen and Legend.* Oxford and Cambridge, Mass.: Blackwell, 1993.

Painter, Sidney. *French Chivalry: Chivalric Ideas and Practices in Medieval France.* Baltimore: Johns Hopkins University Press, 1940.

———. *The Reign of King John.* Baltimore: Johns Hopkins University Press, 1949.

———. *William Marshall: Knight Errant, Baron, and Regent of England.* Baltimore: Johns Hopkins University Press, 1933.

Pernoud, Regine. *Eleanor of Aquitaine.* Trans. P. Wiles. New York: Coward-McCann, 1967.*

Runciman, Steven. *A History of the Crusades,* 3 vols. Cambridge: Cambridge University Press, 1951–1954.

Schlight, John. *Henry II Plantagenet.* Rulers and Statesman of the World. New York: Twayne, 1973.*

Setton, Kenneth M., ed. *The History of the Crusades.* Philadelphia: University of Pennsylvania Press, 1955–1962.

Walker, Curtis H. *Eleanor of Aquitaine.* Chapel Hill: University of North Carolina Press, 1950.*

Warren, W. L. *Henry II.* London: Eyre Methuen, 1973.

———. *King John.* Berkeley: University of California Press, 1978.

Winston, Richard. *Thomas Becket.* New York: Knopf, 1967.

Wolff, R. L., ed. *The Later Crusades, 1189–1311.* Vol. 2 in *The History of the Crusades,* ed. Kenneth M. Setton. Philadelphia: University of Pennsylvania Press, 1962.

Young, Charles R. *Hubert Walter: Lord of Canterbury and Lord of England.* Durham, N.C.: Duke University Press, 1968.

DANTE ALIGHIERI

THE MEANING OF DANTE

1265	Born
c. 1293	Wrote *Vita Nuova*, his first major literary work
1301	Exiled from Florence
1313	Death of Emperor Henry VII in Italy
1307–1320	Wrote *Divine Comedy*
1321	Died

The ambitious title of this chapter does not announce a new break-through in Dante scholarship. It refers instead to the sampling of views presented here from the incredible volume of writing that has been done in an attempt to determine what Dante means—as historical figure, as historical symbol, or as a symbol of eternal truths. The need to "interpret" Dante in order to discover his meaning arises in part from the great complexity and range of his work and its seeming obscurity to many modern readers and in part from the contradictory rather than conforming nature of Dante himself.

In his youth Dante fought for the cause of the Guelfs against the Ghibellines, the two political factions of medieval Italy, and was a functionary of Guelf Florence. The Guelfs opposed the cause of the German emperors; the Ghibellines supported them. As a mature exile Dante reviled his city—"ingrato popolo maligno"—revived classical Ghibellinism, made an unlikely hero of the Emperor Henry VII, and in his *Divine Comedy* lodged Pope Boniface VIII in hell! Although he remained a layman, Dante was as learned in theology as any clerical theologian of his time. He wrote a book defending the use of the vernacular, but he wrote it in Latin, *De Vulgari Eloquentia*, and then chose to write his greatest work, *The Divine Comedy*, in the vernacular Italian.

The problem of interpreting Dante is further complicated by the nature of our information about him. Dante was reticent and prickly, stiff, aloof, and secretive about himself, and, as a result, few of the routine facts of his life were recorded. We have, of course, the great corpus of his work, which even contains, in the *Vita Nuova*, what one scholar has called "one of the great spiritual autobiographies of all time." But Dante himself leaves many important questions unanswered, and his contemporaries are not much more helpful. In spite of the fact that Dante was the most famous poet of his time, with an international reputation and following, he had no contemporary biographer. The earliest life of Dante appeared some half century after his death, written by his fellow Florentine, Giovanni Boccaccio.

The Life of Dante

BOCCACCIO

Boccaccio (1313–1375), like Dante earlier, was one of the most celebrated literary figures of his own generation. Yet his Vita di Dante *is, in many respects, an unsatisfactory biography. The humanist Leonardo Bruni, who wrote a short sketch of Dante still another generation later, found it so. He took Boccaccio to task for his failure to collect the physical evidence about Dante's life and the recollections of contemporaries while they were still available. He criticized him for dwelling on the poet rather than the man. But Boccaccio, a poet himself, was much more interested in this aspect of his subject. We owe to Boccaccio the first body of serious, systematic Dante criticism, as well as the earliest biography. Indeed, Boccaccio was drawn to Dante in many ways and for many reasons, not the least of which was that Boccaccio was a master of the Italian language second only to Dante among its early literary users.*

But the generation gap between Dante and Boccaccio was also an important factor. For, unlike Dante, Boccaccio clearly lived across whatever line we may use to separate the Middle Ages from the Renaissance. Moreover, he was not only "in" but "of " the early Renaissance. He was a friend and disciple of Petrarch, "the Father of Humanism," and, while he did not share his master's snobbish disdain for the vernacular, he adopted a great many of his other notions and prejudices. One of these was a propensity to see the age in which he lived as a new age— "novous ordo saeculorum"—rather sharply set off from the barbaric period of the recent past, which later humanists would contemptuously dub "the Middle Ages," "the Dark Ages," or "the Gothic Age." And in his enthusiasm for Dante, Boccaccio tended to carry him across into his own new age, to view him as the first "modern" poet who had rescued literary art from the darkness, obscurity, and ignorance in which it had languished since antiquity.

We turn now to Boccaccio's account from The Life of Dante.

. . . I am going to record the banishment of that most illustrious man, Dante Alighieri, an ancient citizen and born of no mean parents, who merited as much through his virtue, learning, and good services as is adequately shown and will be shown by the deeds he wrought. If such deeds had been done in a just republic, we believe they would have earned for him the highest rewards.

O iniquitous design! O shameless deed! O wretched example, clear proof of ruin to come! Instead of these rewards there was meted to him an unjust and bitter condemnation, perpetual banishment with alienation of his paternal goods, and, could it have been effected, the profanation of his glorious renown by false charges. The recent traces of his flight, his bones buried in an alien land, and his children scattered in the houses of others, still in part bear witness to these things.

181

If all the other iniquities of Florence could be hidden from the all-seeing eyes of God, should not this one suffice to provoke his wrath upon her? Yea, in truth. . . .

But inasmuch as we should not only flee evil deeds, albeit they seem to go unpunished, but also by right action should strive to amend them, I, although not fitted for so great a task, will try to do according to my little talent what the city should have done with magnificence, but has not. For I recognize that I am a part, though a small one, of that same city whereof Dante Alighieri, if his merits, his nobleness, and his virtue be considered, was a very great part, and that for this reason I, like every other citizen, am personally responsible for the honors due him. Not with a statue shall I honor him, nor with splendid obsequies—which customs no longer hold among us, nor would my powers suffice therefor—but with words I shall honor him, feeble though they be for so great an undertaking. Of these I have, and of these will I give, that other nations may not say that his native land, both as a whole and in part, has been equally ungrateful to so great a poet. . . .

This special glory of Italy was born in our city in the year of the saving incarnation of the King of the universe 1265, when the Roman Empire was without a ruler owing to the death of the [Emperor] Frederick, and Pope Urban the Fourth was sitting in the chair of Saint Peter. The family into which he was born was of a smiling fortune—smiling, I mean, if we consider the condition of the world that then obtained. I will omit all consideration of his infancy—whatever it may have been—wherein appeared many signs of the coming glory of his genius. But I will note that from his earliest boyhood, having already learned the rudiments of letters, he gave himself and all his time, not to youthful lust and indolence, after the fashion of the nobles of to-day, lolling at ease in the lap of his mother, but to continued study, in his native city, of the liberal arts, so that he became exceedingly expert therein. And as his mind and genius ripened with his years, he devoted himself, not to lucrative pursuits, whereto every one in general now hastens, but, with a laudable desire for perpetual fame, scorning transitory riches, he freely dedicated himself to the acquisition of a complete knowledge of poetic creations and of their exposition by rules of art. In this exercise he became closely intimate with Virgil, Horace, Ovid, Statius, and with every other famous poet. And not only did he delight to know them, but he strove to imitate them in lofty song, even as his works demonstrate, whereof we shall speak at the proper time. . . .

. . . And to the end that no region of philosophy should remain unvisited by him, he penetrated with acute genius into the profoundest depths of theology. Nor was the result far distant from the aim. Unmindful of heat and cold, vigils and fasts, and every other physical hardship, by assiduous study he grew to such knowledge of the Divine Essence and of the other Separate Intelligences as can be compassed here by the human intellect. And as by application various sciences were learned by him at various periods, so he mastered them in various studies under various teachers. . . .

Studies in general, and speculative studies in particular—to which, as has been shown, our Dante wholly applied himself—usually demand solitude, remoteness from care, and tranquility of mind. Instead of this retirement and quiet, Dante had, almost from the beginning of his life down to the day of his death, a violent and insufferable passion of love, a wife, domestic and public cares, exile, and poverty, not to mention those more particular cares which these necessarily involve. The former I deem it fitting to explain in detail, in order that their burden may appear the greater.

In that season wherein the sweetness of heaven reclothes the earth with all its adornments, and makes her all smiling with varied flowers scattered among green leaves, the custom obtained in our city that men and women should keep festival in different gatherings, each person in his neighborhood. And so it chanced that among others Folco Portinari, a man held in great esteem among his fellow-citizens, on the first day of May gathered his neighbors in his house for a feast. Now among these came the aforementioned Alighieri, followed by Dante, who was still in his ninth year; for little children are wont to follow their fathers, especially to places of festival. And mingling here in the house of the feast-giver with others of his own age, of whom there were many, both boys and girls, when the first tables had been served he boyishly entered with the others into the games, so far as his tender age permitted.

Now amid the throng of children was a little daughter of the aforesaid Folco, whose name was Bice, though he always called her by her full name, Beatrice. She was, it may be, eight years old, very graceful for her age, full gentle and pleasing in her actions, and much more serious and modest in her words and ways than her few years required. Her features were most delicate and perfectly proportioned, and, in addition to their beauty, full of such pure loveliness that many thought her almost a little angel. She, then, such as I picture her, or it may be far more beautiful, appeared at this feast to the eyes of our Dante; not, I suppose, for the first time, but for the first time with power to inspire him with love. And he, though still a child, received the lovely image of her into his heart with so great affection that it never left him from that day forward so long as he lived.

Now just what this affection was no one knows, but certainly it is true that Dante at an early age became a most ardent servitor of love. . . . Forsaking, therefore, all other matters, with the utmost solicitude he went wherever he thought he might see her, as if he were to attain from her face and her eyes all his happiness and complete consolation.

O insensate judgment of lovers! who but they would think to check the flames by adding to the fuel? Dante himself in his *Vita Nuova* in part makes known how many and of what nature were the thoughts, the sighs, the tears, and the other grievous passions that he later suffered by reason of this love, wherefore I do not care to rehearse them more in detail. This much alone I do not wish to pass over without mention, namely, that according as he himself writes, and as others to whom his passion was known bear witness, this love was most virtuous, nor did there ever appear by look or word or sign any sensual appetite either in the lover or in the thing beloved; no little marvel to the present world, from which all innocent pleasure has so fled, and which is so accustomed to have the thing that pleases it conform to its lust before it has concluded to love it, that he who loves otherwise has become a miracle, even as a thing most rare.

If such love for so long season could interrupt his eating, his sleep, and every quietness, how great an enemy must we think it to have been to his sacred studies and to his genius? Certainly no mean one, although many maintain that it urged his genius on, and argue for proof from his graceful rimed compositions in the Florentine idiom, written in praise of his beloved and for the expression of his ardors and amorous conceits. But truly I should not agree with this, unless I first admitted that ornate writing is the most essential part of every science—which is not true.

As every one may plainly perceive, there is nothing stable in this world, and, if anything is subject to change, it is our life. A trifle too much cold or heat within us, not to mention countless other accidents and possibilities, easily leads us from existence to non-existence. Nor is gentle birth privileged against this, nor riches, nor youth, nor any other worldly dignity. Dante must needs experience the force of this general law by another's death before he did by his own. The most beautiful Beatrice was near the end of her twenty-fourth year when, as it pleased Him who governs all things, she left the sufferings of this world, and passed to the glory that her virtues had prepared for her.

. . . By her departure Dante was thrown into such sorrow, such grief and tears, that many of those nearest him, both relatives and friends, believed that death alone would end them. They expected that this would shortly come to pass, seeing that he gave no ear to the comfort and consolation offered him. The days were like the nights, and the nights like the days. Not an hour of them passed without groans, and sighs, and an abundant quantity of tears. His eyes seemed two copious springs of welling water, so that most men wondered whence he received moisture enough for his weeping. . . .

In Dante's time the citizens of Florence were perversely divided into two factions, and by the operations of astute and prudent leaders each party was very powerful, so that sometimes one ruled and sometimes the other, to the displeasure of its defeated rival. . . .

Dante decided, then, to pursue the fleeting honor and false glory of public office. Perceiving that he could not support by himself a third party, which, in itself just, should overthrow the injustice of the two others and reduce them to unity, he allied himself with that faction which seemed to him to possess most of justice and reason—working always for that which he recognized as salutary to his country and her citizens. But human counsels are commonly defeated by the powers of heaven. Hatred and enmities arose, though without just cause, and waxed greater day by day; so that many times the citizens rushed to arms, to their utmost confusion. They purposed to end the struggle by fire and sword, and were so blinded by wrath that they did not see that they themselves would perish miserably thereby.

After each of the fractions had given many proofs of their strength to their mutual loss, the time came when the secret counsels of threatening Fortune were to be disclosed. Rumor, who reports both the true and the false, announced that the foes of Dante's faction were strengthened by wise and wonderful designs and by an immense multitude of armed men, and by this means so terrified the leaders of his party that she banished from their minds all consideration, all forethought, all reason, save how to flee in safety. Together with them Dante, instantly precipitated from the chief rule of his city, beheld himself not only brought low to the earth, but banished from his country. Not many days after this expulsion, when the populace had already rushed to the houses of the exiles, and had furiously pillaged and gutted them, the victors reorganized the city after their pleasure, condemning all the leaders of their adversaries to perpetual exile as capital enemies of the republic, and with them Dante, not as one of the lesser leaders, but as it were the chief one. Their real property was meanwhile confiscated or alienated to the victors.

This reward Dante gained for the tender love which he had borne his country! . . .

In such wise, then, Dante left that city whereof not only he was a citizen, but of which his ancestors had been the rebuilders. . . .

Boccaccio recounts Dante's exile and his wandering from court to court, city to city, and his hopes for a restoration of order in Italy dashed by the death of the Emperor Henry VII.

Since all hope, though not the desire, of ever returning to Florence was gone, Dante continued in Ravenna several years, under the protection of its gracious lord. And here he taught and trained many scholars in poetry, and especially in the vernacular, which he first, in my opinion, exalted and made esteemed among us Italians, even as Homer did his tongue among the Greeks, and Virgil his among the

Latins. Although the vulgar tongue is supposed to have originated some time before him, none thought or dared to make the language an instrument of any artistic matter, save in the numbering of syllables, and in the consonance of its endings. They employed it, rather, in the light things of love. Dante showed in effect that every lofty subject could be treated of in this medium, and made our vulgar tongue above all others glorious.

But even as the appointed hour comes for every man, so Dante also, at or near the middle of his fifty-sixth year, fell ill. And having humbly and devoutly received the sacraments of the Church according to the Christian religion, and having reconciled himself to God in contrition for all that he, as a mortal, had committed against His pleasure, in the month of September in the year of Christ 1321, on the day whereon the Exaltation of the Holy Cross is celebrated by the Church, not without great sorrow on the part of the aforesaid Guido and in general of all the other citizens of Ravenna, he rendered to his Creator his weary spirit. . . .

Our poet was of moderate height, and, after reaching maturity, was accustomed to walk somewhat bowed, with a slow and gentle pace, clad always in such sober dress as befitted his ripe years. His face was long, his nose aquiline, and his eyes rather large than small. His jaws were large, and the lower lip protruded beyond the upper. His complexion was dark, his hair and beard thick, black, and curled, and his expression ever melancholy and thoughtful.

Our poet, in addition . . . was of a lofty and disdainful spirit. On one occasion a friend, moved by entreaties, labored that Dante might return to Florence—which thing the poet desired above all else—but he found no way thereto with those who then held the government in their hands save that Dante should remain in prison for a certain time, and after that be presented as a subject for mercy at some public solemnity in our principal church, whereby he should be free and exempt from all sentences previously passed upon him. But this seemed to Dante a fitting procedure for abject, if not infamous, men and for no others. Therefore, notwithstanding his great desire, he chose to remain in exile rather than return home by such a road. O laudable and magnanimous scorn, how manfully hast thou acted in repressing the ardent desire to return, when it was only possible by a way unworthy of a man nourished in the bosom of philosophy! . . .

This glorious poet composed many works during his lifetime, an orderly arrangement of which would, I think, be fitting, in order that his works may not be attributed to some one else, and that the works of another may not be ascribed to him.

In the first place, while his tears still flowed for the death of Beatrice, in his twenty-six year or thereabouts, he brought together in a little volume, entitled *Vita Nuova,* certain marvelously beautiful pieces in rime, like sonnets and canzoni, which he had previously written at various times. Before each one he wrote in order the causes that had led him to compose it, and after each one he placed its divisions. Although in his maturer years he was greatly ashamed of this little book, nevertheless, if his age be considered, it is very beautiful and pleasing, especially to the common people.

. . . Having long premeditated what was to be done, in his thirty-fifth year he began to put into effect what he had before deliberated upon, namely, to censure and reward the lives of men according to the diversity of their merits. And inasmuch as he saw that life was of three sorts—the vicious life, the life of departing from vice and advancing toward virtue, and the virtuous life—he admirably divided his work, which he entitled *Commedia,* into three books, in the first of which he censured the wicked and in the last rewarded the good. The three books he again divided into cantos, and the cantos into rhythms (*ritmi*), as may be plainly seen. He composed it in rime and in the vernacular with such art, and in so wonderful and beautiful an order, that there has yet been none who could justly find any fault therewith.

The Historical Dante

HENRY OSBORN TAYLOR

Although at the present time Dante is usually considered to be at least a transitional figure between the Middle Ages and the Renaissance, historians have traditionally viewed him as the summation of all the trends and tendencies of the Middle Ages. No one exemplifies this interpretive approach better than the American medievalist Henry Osborn Taylor (d. 1941). Taylor's most important book was his massive, brilliant, and original The Mediaeval Mind, *still one of the standard works in medieval intellectual history. The following selection is from the chapter on Dante, subtitled "The Mediaeval Synthesis," in which Dante is seen as bringing together all the strands of medieval thought and temperament.*

[Dante] is not merely mediaeval; he is the end of the mediaeval development and the proper issue of the mediaeval genius.

Yes, there is unity throughout the diversity of mediaeval life; and Dante is the proof. For the elements of mediaeval growth combine in him, demonstrating their congruity by working together in the stature of the full-grown mediaeval man. When the contents of patristic Christianity and the surviving antique culture had been conceived anew, and had been felt as well, and novel forms of sentiment evolved, at last comes Dante to possess the whole, to think it, feel it, visualize its sum, and make of it a poem. He had mastered the field of mediaeval knowledge, diligently cultivating parts of it, like the Graeco-Arabian astronomy; he thought and reasoned in the terms and assumptions of scholastic (chiefly Thomist-Aristotelian) philosophy; his intellectual interests were mediaeval; he felt the mediaeval reverence for the past, being impassioned with the ancient greatness of Rome and the lineage of virtue and authority moving from it to him and thirteenth-century Italy and the already shattered Holy Roman Empire. He took earnest joy in the Latin Classics, approaching them from mediaeval points of view, accepting their contents uncritically. He was affected with the preciosity of courtly or chivalric love, which Italy had made her own along with the songs of the Troubadours and the poetry of northern France. His emotions flowed in channels of current convention, save that they overfilled them; this was true as to his early love, and true as to his final range of religious and poetic feeling. His was the emotion and the cruelty of mediaeval religious conviction; while in his mind (so worked the genius of symbolism) every fact's apparent meaning was clothed with the significance of other modes of truth.

Dante was also an Italian of the period in which he lived; and he was a marvellous poet. One may note in him what was mediaeval, what was specifically Italian, and what, apparently, was personal. This scholar could not but draw his education, his views of life and death, his dominant inclinations and the large currents of his purpose, from the antecedent mediaeval period and the still greater past which had worked upon it so mightily. His Italian nature and environment gave point and piquancy and very concrete life to these mediaeval elements; and his personal genius produced from it all a supreme poetic creation.

The Italian part of Dante comes between the mediaeval and the personal, as species comes between the genus and the individual. The tremendous feeling which he discloses for the Roman past seems, in him, specifically Italian: child of Italy, he holds himself a Latin and a direct heir of the Republic. Yet often his attitude toward the antique will be that of mediaeval men in general, as in his disposition to accept ancient myth for fact; while his own genius appears in his beautifully apt appropriation of the Virgilian incident or image; wherein he excels his "Mantuan" master, whose borrowings from Homer were not always felicitous. Frequently the specifically Italian in Dante, his yearning hate of Florence, for example, may scarcely be distinguished from his personal temper; but its civic bitterness is different from the feudal animosities or promiscuous rages which were more generically mediaeval. . . .

Again, Dante's arguments in the *De monarchia* seem to be those of an Italian Ghibelline. Yet beyond his intense realization of Italy's direct succession to the Roman past, his reasoning is scholastic and mediaeval, or springs occasionally from his own reflections. The Italian contribution to the book tends to coalesce either with the general or the personal elements. . . .

The *De vulgari eloquentia* illustrates the difference between Dante accepting and reproducing mediaeval views, and Dante thinking for himself. . . . And in the *De Vulgari Eloquentia*, as in the *Convivio*, Dante is deeply conscious of the worth of the Romance vernacular. . . .

Certainly the *Convivio* gives evidence touching the writer's mental processes and the interests of his mind. Except for its lofty advocacy of the *volgare* and its personal apologetic references, it contains little that is not blankly mediaeval. . . . [A] significant phrase may be drawn from it: "Philosophy is a loving use of wisdom (*uno amoroso uso di sapienza*) which chiefly is in God, since in Him is utmost wisdom, utmost love, and utmost actuality." A loving use of wisdom—with Dante the pursuit of knowledge was no mere intellectual search, but a pilgrimage of the whole nature, loving heart as well as knowing mind, and the working virtues too. This pilgrimage is set forth in the *Commedia*, perhaps the supreme creation of the Middle Ages, and a work that by reason of the beautiful affinity of its speech with Latin, exquisitely expressed the matters which in Latin had been coming to formulation through the mediaeval centuries.

The *Commedia* (*Inferno, Purgatorio, Paradiso*) is a *Summa*, a *Summa salvationis*, a sum of saving knowledge. It is such just as surely as the final work of Aquinas is a *Summa theologiae*. But Aquinas was the supreme mediaeval theologian-philosopher, while Dante was the supreme theologian-poet; and with both Aquinas and Dante, theology includes the knowledge of all things, but chiefly of man in relation to God. Such was the matter of the *divina scientia* of Thomas, and such was the subject of the *Commedia*, which was soon recognized as the *Divina Commedia* in the very sense in which Theology was the divine science. The *Summa* of Thomas was *scientia* not only in substance, but in form; the *Commedia* was *scientia*, or *sapientia*, in substance, while in form it was a poem, the epic of man the pilgrim of salvation. . . . The *Commedia* rested upon the entire evolution of the Middle Ages. Therein had lain its spiritual preparation. To be sure it had its casual forerunners (*precursori*): narratives, real or feigned, of men faring to the regions of the dead. But these signified little; for everywhere thoughts of the other life pressed upon men's mind: fear of it blanched their hearts; its heavenly or hellish messengers had been seen, and not a few men dreamed that they had walked within those gates and witnessed clanging horrors or purgatorial pain. Heaven had been more rarely visited.

Dante gave little attention to any so-called "forerunners," save only two, Paul and Virgil. The former was a warrant for the poet's reticence as to the manner of his ascent to Heaven; the latter supplied much of his scheme of Hell. . . .

One observes mediaeval characteristics in the *Commedia* raised to a higher power. The mediaeval period was marked by contrasts of quality and of conduct such as cannot be found in the antique or the modern age. And what other poem can vie with the *Commedia* in contrasts of the beautiful and the loathsome, the heavenly and the hellish, exquisite refinement of expression and lapses into the reverse, love and hate, pity and cruelty, reverence and disdain? These contrasts not only are presented by the story; they evince themselves in the character of the author. Many scenes of the *Inferno* are loathsome: Dante's own words and conduct there may be cruel and hateful or show tender pity; and every reader knows the poetic beauty which glorifies the *Paradiso,* renders lovely the *Purgatorio,* and ever and anon breaks through the gloom of Hell.

Another mediaeval quality, sublimated in Dante's poem, is that of elaborate plan, intended symmetry of composition, the balance of one incident or subject against another. And finally one observes the mediaeval inclusiveness which belongs to the scope and purpose of the *Commedia* as a *Summa* of salvation. Dante brings in everything that can illuminate and fill out his theme. Even as the *Summa* of St. Thomas, so the *Commedia* must present a whole doctrinal scheme of salvation, and leave no loopholes, loose ends, broken links of argument or explanation.

The substance of the *Commedia,* practically its whole content of thought, opinion, sentiment, had source in the mediaeval store of antique culture and the partly affiliated, if not partly derivative, Latin Christianity. The mediaeval appreciation of the Classics, and of the contents of ancient philosophy, is not to be so very sharply distinguished from the attitude of the fifteenth or sixteenth, nay, if one will, the eighteenth, century, when the *Federalist* in the young inchoately united States, and many an orator in the revolutionary assemblies of France, quoted Cicero and Plutarch as arbiters of civic expediency. Nevertheless, if we choose to recognize deference to ancient opinion, acceptance of antique myth and poetry as fact, unbounded admiration for a shadowy and much distorted ancient world, as characterizing the mediaeval attitude toward whatever once belonged to Rome and Greece, then we must say that such also is Dante's attitude, scholar as he was; and that in his use of the Classics he differed from other mediaeval men only in so far as above them all he was a poet. . . .

Yet however universally Dante's mind was solicited by the antique matter and his poet's nature charmed, he was profoundly and mediaevally Christian. The *Commedia* is a mediaeval Christian poem. Its fabric, springing from the life of earth, enfolds the threefold quasi-other world of damned, of purging, and of finally purified, spirits. It is dramatic and doctrinal. Its drama of action and suffering, like the narratives of Scripture, offers literal fact, moral teaching, and allegorical or spiritual significance. The doctrinal contents are held partly within the poem's dramatic action and partly in expositions which are not fused in the drama. Thus, whatever else it is, the poem is a *Summa* of saving doctrine, which is driven home by illustrations of the sovereign good and abysmal ill coming to man under the providence of God. One may perhaps discern a twofold purpose in it, since the poet works out his own salvation and gives precepts and examples to aid others and help truth and rightcousness on earth. The subject is man as rewarded or punished eternally by God—says Dante in the letter to Can Grande.[1] This subject could hardly be conceived as veritable, and still less could it be executed, by a poet who had no care for the effect of his poem upon men. Dante had such care. But whether he, who was first and always a poet, wrote the *Commedia* in order to lift others out of error to salvation, or even in order to work out his own salvation,—let him say who knows the mind of Dante. No divination, however, is required to trace the course of the saving teaching, which, whether dramatically exemplified or expounded in doctrinal statement, is embodied in the great poem; nor is it hard to note how Dante drew its substance from the mediaeval past.

Dante's Relevance Today

PHILIP McNAIR

In our truncated search for "the meaning of Dante" we have examined that meaning as seen by the fourteenth-century Florentine poet and littérateur Boccaccio and the early twentieth-century American historian Henry Osborn Taylor. Boccaccio expressed the view that Dante was (or should be) the great preceptor of his ungrateful mother city, Taylor that he is the exemplification of the medieval mind. We turn now to a third view, in an essay by the Cambridge Italian scholar Philip McNair—"Dante's Relevance Today," one of the many works on Dante published in 1965 to commemorate the seven hundredth anniversary of the poet's birth. McNair finds the relevance of Dante today (and every day) in the fact that Dante, more than any other poet or most philosophers, deals "with the things which affect us most—and these things do not alter from one millennium to another"— things such as God, grace, sin, love, justice, and human nature.

---

[1]Can Grande della Scala, the Lord of Verona, to whom Dante dedicated part of the *Commedia*. Dante wrote a letter to Can Grande explaining the meaning of the poem.

"Poeta nascitur non fit"[2] is a well-worn tag, and a true one; that is why the birth of a supreme poet is supremely worth celebrating. Last year it was Shakespeare; this year it is Dante: and the conjunction of these two great names could hardly be happier, for in the words of the late T. S. Eliot: "Dante and Shakespeare divide the modern world between them; there is no third" (Weimar's objection overruled).[3]

"The modern world"—Eliot said—and at first blush "modern" may seem quite the wrong word to use when talking about Dante. Shakespeare, after all, stands closer to us by three centuries and half-a-dozen revolutions in taste and outlook, such as the Renaissance and the Reformation. But a cursory glance at *The Divine Comedy* discovers a medieval world reflected in a medieval mind. We are back in a pre-Copernican cosmology with God at the circumference and Satan at the centre, exploring a three-storeyed universe crammed with scholastic bric-à-brac and Christian myths. . . .

But dip deeper into Dante and we find how curiously relevant he is today—far more so than Virgil, for instance, or Homer, or practically any other poet who wrote before Shakespeare. Perhaps "perennial" is a better word than "modern," for, like the *philosophia perennis*[4] which it reflects, his poem just goes on applying to the human situation year after year and from age to age. Dante is seven hundred years old this summer, yet he is still the most topical poet for a cosmonaut floating in space to read; and seven centuries from now, when the science-fiction of his *Comedy* has come true, the men who contemplate this world from the stars will not have outsoared the shadow of his genius or exhausted the meaning of his poem.

Dante's relevance today stems from the fact that he is one of the most engaged writers of all time, as well as one of the most engaging. In commemorating him it is all too easy to slip into superlatives, and say that he is the poet "with the mostest" (most understanding, most insight, most vision, and so on); but surely we may make the modest claim that in the *Comedy,* despite its medieval structure, Dante is dealing with the things which affect us most—and these things do not alter from one millennium to another. God, grace, sin, love, justice, and human nature have not changed since Moses knew them. Dante's total involvement in them is best explained in terms of his purpose in writing the poem at all.

Apart from the basic urge which every poet feels to express himself, Dante's particular poetic reason for projecting the *Comedy* seems to have been his desire to measure up to an exacting challenge, to stretch his technique to the breaking-point in doing what no other

---

[2]"Poets are born, not made."

[3]A reference to the claim for similar stature for the German author Goethe.

[4]Eternal philosophy.

poet had ever done before—to pioneer in the vernacular, indeed in language itself. . . .

But Dante is more than a poet and his *Comedy* more than a poem. His prime purpose in writing is missionary and prophetic, and concerns the state of the world, the redemption of mankind. You do not have to read very far to know that he is not out simply to entertain—"A funny thing happened to me in the dark wood"—although reading him *is* tremendous fun. His aim, says that problematic letter to Can Grande della Scala, "is to rescue those living in this life from a state of misery and bring them to a state of bliss." It is, of course, the same end proposed by the Christian Gospel, and springs from the same realism about sin and damnation: in fact this led one nineteenth-century Pope to dub the *Divine Comedy* the "Fifth Gospel." But Dante is less an evangelist than a prophet.

If poets are born and not made, prophets are called by God and fitted by experience. Dante is robustly conscious of his call, but that is his own private affair and inscrutable. What falls under our survey is his experience as a man among men, and the most important thing that happened to him—apart from being born a poet in 1265—was banishment from his native Florence in January 1302, unjustly charged with injustice in the form of political corruption. Important, because it made him brood on justice: not only in his own life, but also in the history of the world. His exile from Florence is due to Man's injustice, but Man's exile from paradise is due to the justice of God. What then is this Divine Justice? How does it operate? And how does it square with God's love?

Here we have one of the *Comedy*'s central themes which must be seen against the dark background of human injustice. God's in His heaven, but all is *not* right with the world. Fallen Man is unjust because sin in him has disturbed the balance between reason and desire and warped his will. When we reach the poem's end we find Dante's *disio* and his *velle*[5] harmonized by the Divine Love which keeps the solar system in equilibrium. But the first note he strikes is the reality of sin. He begins with his own predicament—astray in a dark wood, having left the right road—and little by little reveals that this is the predicament of Man, of human nature, of every human institution. Florence is astray, Italy is astray, the papacy is astray, and so is the empire; the entire world is astray through sin, and therefore Dante is called to write "*in pro del mondo che mal vive.*"[6] Karl Vossler described the *Comedy* as the whole course of a religious conversion, but it is more than that: it is the whole programme of the world's redemption to God from sin. Dante sees himself not only as a sinner being saved,

---

[5]"Desire" and "ambition."
[6]"On behalf of the world that lives in evil."

but in some sense as an agent of the salvation of others. This accounts
for the fact that at times his tone is positively Messianic, for we have
no evidence that he underrated his mission.

For Dante, as for all prophets, *hora novissima, tempora pessima sunt.*[7]
The end of the world is at hand, the number of the Elect is almost
complete, nearly all the seats in heaven are already taken. But his
prophetic burden is not Bunyanesque; he does not suggest fleeing
from the wrath to come, or abandoning the world to its doom. He
does not even "look for new heavens and a new earth, wherein
dwelleth righteousness"; he looks rather for a regeneration of this
earth, for the coming of the Kingdom of God. The point of his
allegory of hell, purgatory, and heaven is not so much pie-in-the-sky
as the reorganization of this world in love and justice. . . .

It seems to me that Dante might have pictured hell in one of two
ways: either like a concentration camp, with Satan as its commandant,
in which sinners are at the mercy of a power more evil than themselves; or like a penitentiary, in which a just government exacts re-
tributive punishment for sin. Following Christ and the Church, he
has chosen the second way in his *Inferno,* where Divine Justice is seen
as Vengeance. This is never stressed more starkly than in the Third
Ring of the Seventh Circle, where the violent against God suffer the
inexorable rain which falls in broad flakes of fire upon them in a slow
downward drift "as Alpine snows in windless weather fall."

But God's justice is not only punitive. In purgatory, the "Mount
where Justice probes us," it sets the desire of the repentant toward
their purging pains as once that desire was set on sin. In heaven it
rewards the blessed with the vision of God. But it is also active in the
history of the world for Man's good and salvation. Here Dante's most
distinctive idea is that Divine Justice master-minded the rise and rule
of the Roman Empire *"che 'l buon mondo feo."*[8] In fact, this is one of his
key concepts, discussed in detail in the *Monarchia,* and informing the
Comedy from beginning to end. . . .

Of course Dante, like all political thinkers, starts out from the
existing situation in his own day, dominated by the two great institutions of the empire and the papacy, yet menaced by the rising power
of French nationalism and the emergence of city-states like Florence.
But with a prophet's mind he argues back to God's purpose behind
Rome's two suns—her *due soli*—and with a prophet's eye he sees their
destiny in God's salvation, when Man has attained his *duo ultima*—his
two supreme ends of temporal and eternal happiness. For God's plan
of salvation is one and indivisible, and Dante's study of history has
taught him how dovetailed that immense operation of love and jus-

---

[7]The most recent times are the worst.
[8]"that the good world might come about."

tice is: David contemporary with Aeneas; Christ, the Son of David, contemporary with Augustus, the son of Aeneas; the Roman Pope, Christ's Vicar, the complement of the Roman Emperor, Augustus Caesar's successor. And not only is there a developed parallelism in Dante's mind, which condemns Judas to the same fate as Brutus and Cassius, but also an ingenious interaction which provides the legal basis of his soteriology.[9]

For the Roman Emperor is the fount of Roman law, and is declared *de jure* the governing power in the world by God Himself in two great acts of Divine Vengeance. God willed that His Son should be born under the *Pax Romana* and suffer under Pontius Pilate, Caesar's Procurator. Thereby He willed that the Roman Emperor should perform a crucial function in the Atonement; for it was by the authority of Tiberius Caesar that God avenged the sin of Adam in the crucifixion of Christ, in whom the whole human race was vicariously punished to satisfy Divine Justice. But having avenged Man's sin in Christ's death under Tiberius, Justice avenged Christ's death upon the Jews by the destruction of Jerusalem under Titus. This devious doctrine is propounded to Dante in the Heaven of Mercury by no less an authority than the Emperor Justinian, who, inspired by *il primo amore* and *la viva giustizia*,[10] traces the course of Rome's rise to world dominion in a panoramic unfolding of history from the divine standpoint. But the sweep and scope of his review is capped by Beatrice, who takes his cryptic words on divine vengeance and explains them to Dante in one of the most impressive expositions of the Atonement to be found in non-canonical literature.

Echoing the Anselmian[11] doctrine of satisfaction, Beatrice proves how the justice and the love of God meet in the cross, where divine vengeance is exhausted and divine compassion expressed. Ruined by his fall, Adam's helpless race lay sick for many a century until it pleased the Word of God to descend and unite Man's estranged nature to Himself "with the sole act of His eternal love." The love that is the life of the Trinity, that binds the leaves of the volume of the universe together, the love that moves the sun and the other stars, that moved Beatrice to seek out Virgil on Dante's behalf—it is this primal eternal love that was kindled in the Virgin's womb and bore our nature to judicial execution on the cross.

In that Man was punished, the penalty was just; in that God suffered, it was outrageously *unjust*. Why God should take this way to redeem His creature "is buried from the eyes of all whose wit is not matured within Love's flame." But—Beatrice explains—if Man were

---

[9]Doctrine of salvation.
[10]"The first love" and "the living justice."
[11]St. Anselm of Canterbury, medieval theologian (d. 1109).

to be saved at all, one of two fords must be passed: either God of His sole courtesy must remit the debt, or Man of himself must make satisfaction for his sin. . . .

What the love and justice of God mean to the sinner saved by grace is witnessed throughout the *Purgatorio* and *Paradiso* as Dante's mind and heart are conformed to the pleasure of God. To take one instance, it is seen in Manfred,[12] whom we meet at the mountain's foot. He repented at the point of death, but died excommunicate. His dead body was cast out of the kingdom of Naples, but his undying soul was received into the Kingdom of God. Why? Because weeping he gave himself up to Him Who willingly pardons. Horrible though he confessed his sins to be, "Infinite Goodness has such wide arms that she accepts all who turn to her." The bishop and the pope who banned his corpse had read only the one face of God, His inexorable justice; but Manfred saw the face of everlasting love. God receives him because Christ has borne the penalty of his sins; but the laws of the kingdom still operate even though Manfred is forgiven, and Justice excludes him from purgatory until thirty times the period of his presumption is fulfilled.

Although Dante can write movingly about the wide arms of Infinite Goodness and the two faces of God, His justice and His love, it is disappointing to find that to the end of the *Comedy* his God remains strangely impersonal. Consummate poet though he is, Dante's greatest omission is his failure to portray Christ, the very personification of the justice and the love of God. Only three times do we glimpse Him in heaven, but although He is the Incarnate Word on no occasion does He speak. . . .

In the *Divine Comedy* we see the unveiled mystery and the radiant hosts, the uncreated light and the vision of God; but we do not see the Lamb, without Whose sacrifice we could not see heaven at all.

Questions for Review and Study

1. Why do you think Boccaccio was led to write a biographical account of Dante?
2. Sketch the life of Dante as presented by Boccaccio.
3. Do you think Dante belongs to the Middle Ages or the early Renaissance?
4. What were the Guelf and Ghibelline parties and how do they apply to Dante?
5. What was Dante's intention in writing the *Divine Comedy*?

---

[12]The son and successor of Emperor Frederick II.

Suggestions for Further Reading

Dante is, first and foremost, a poet—one of the two or three greatest of all time—and students ought to sample his poetry, no matter how difficult, abstruse, or philosophical it may seem. Dante's greatest work, *The Divine Comedy*, is available in many translations, but students will probably be most pleased with the three-volume contemporary verse translation, *The Inferno, The Purgatorio*, and *The Paradiso*, by the popular poet-critic John Ciardi. It is not entirely faithful to the letter (more so to the spirit) of the original, but is is a lively, often earthy, and always entertaining effort. Somewhat less successful is Dorothy L. Sayers's translation *The Comedy of Dante Alighieri, the Florentine*, which attempts the almost impossible task of duplicating Dante's interlocking three-line rhyme scheme. The translation suffers from it in places, but it is generally readable; the long introduction and critical notes are, however, first class and an enormous help. For a sampling of Dante's other writings, the most convenient work is *The Portable Dante*, edited by Paolo Milano, with the complete text of the *Divine Comedy* and *Vita Nuova* and excerpts from his other verse and Latin prose works. Two conventional guides to the *Divine Comedy* are *Companion to the Divine Comedy*, edited by C. S. Singleton, and *A Concordance to the Divine Comedy of Dante Alighieri*, edited by Ernest Hatch Wilkins and Thomas G. Bergin. See also *The Cambridge Companion to Dante*, edited by Rachel Jacoff.

There is an enormous literature of Dante criticism, much of it as difficult and obscure as the poet himself. A handful of works, however, can be recommended for beginning readers. The most readable and among the most sensible are two collections of essays by Dorothy L. Sayers, *Introductory Papers on Dante*, and *Further Papers on Dante*. Thomas G. Bergin is one of the world's great authorities on Dante, and three of his books are so clear and readable that they can be recommended even to those with little or no prior exposure to Dante: *Dante, Perspectives on the Divine Comedy*, and *A Diversity of Dante*. Two older famous books of Dante criticism are recommended: Erich Auerbach's *Dante, Poet of the Secular World*, and Etienne Gilson's *Dante and Philosophy*. See also Charles Williams, *The Figure of Beatrice*; J. F. Took, *Dante, Lyric Poet and Philosopher*; Teodolinda Bartolini, *Dante's Poets*; Joan M. Ferrante, *The Political Vision of the Divine Comedy*; James D. Collins, *Pilgrim in Love*; Marianne Shapiro, *De Vulgari Eloquentia*; Robert P. Harrison, *The Body of Beatrice*, and another work by Teodolinda Bartolini, *The Undivine "Comedy."*

Two brief books on Dante as a literary figure are well worth reading: *Dante Alighieri*, by Ricardo Quinones, and *Dante* by George Holmes. See also Michael Caesar's *Dante*, James J. Collins's *Dante*, and *Dante Now*, edited by Theodore J. Cachey, Jr.

Most of the foregoing books deal not only with Dante the poet but also with his life and times. The following works deal more explicitly with the man and his age. The most authoritative modern biography of Dante is by the great Italian Dante scholar Michele Barbi, *Life of Dante*.

The bulkier and more comprehensive *Mediaeval Culture,* by Karl Vossler, is also a standard work. Highly recommended is a book by Domenico Vittorini, *The Age of Dante,* which can serve as a corrective to the views of Vossler and Henry Osborn Taylor (excerpted in this chapter), in that Vittorini ties Dante into newer scholarly views on the early Renaissance. See also *Dante's Italy and Other Essays,* by Charles T. Davis, and *Dante and the Empire,* by Donna Mancusi-Ungaro.

Auerbach, Erich. *Dante, Poet of the Secular World.* Trans. Ralph Manheim. Chicago: University of Chicago Press, 1929, 1961.

Barbi, Michele. *Life of Dante.* Trans. and ed. Paul G. Ruggiers. Berkeley and Los Angeles: University of California Press, 1933, 1954.

Bartolini, Teodolinda. *Dante's Poets: Textuality and Truth in the Comedy.* Princeton, N.J.: Princeton University Press, 1984.

———. *The Undivine "Comedy" Detheologizing Dante.* Princeton, N.J.: Princeton University Press, 1993.

Bergin, Thomas G. *Dante.* Boston: Houghton Mifflin, 1965.

———. *Dante, Perspectives on the Divine Comedy.* New Brunswick, N.J.: Rutgers University Press, 1967.

———. *A Diversity of Dante.* New Brunswick, N.J.: Rutgers University Press, 1969.

Cachey, Theodore J., Jr., ed. *Dante Now: Current Trends in Dante Studies.* South Bend: University of Notre Dame Press, 1995.

Caesar, Michael. *Dante.* London: Routledge, 1989.

Ciardi, John, trans. *The Inferno.* New Brunswick, N.J.: Rutgers University Press, 1954.

———, trans. *The Paradiso.* New York: New American Library, 1970.

———, trans. *The Purgatorio.* New York: New American Library, 1961.

Collins, James D. *Pilgrim in Love: An Introduction to Dante and His Spirituality.* Chicago: Loyola University Press, 1984.

Collins, James J. *Dante: Layman, Prophet, Mystic.* Staten Island, N.Y.: Alba House, 1989.

Davis, Charles T. *Dante's Italy and Other Essays.* Philadelphia: University of Pennsylvania Press, 1984.

Ferrante, Joan M. *The Political Vision of the Divine Comedy.* Princeton, N.J.: Princeton University Press, 1994.

Gilson, Etienne. *Dante and Philosophy.* Trans. David Moore. New York: Harper, 1949, 1963.

Harrison, Robert P. *The Body of Beatrice.* Baltimore: Johns Hopkins University Press, 1988.

Holmes, George. *Dante.* New York: Hill and Wang, 1980.

Jacoff, Rachel, ed. *The Cambridge Companion to Dante.* Cambridge: Cambridge University Press, 1993.

Mancusi-Ungaro, Donna. *Dante and the Empire.* New York: Peter Lang, 1987.

Milano, Paolo, ed. *The Portable Dante*. New York: Viking, 1968.

Quinones, Ricardo. *Dante Alighieri*. New York: Twayne, 1979.

Sayers, Dorothy L. *The Comedy of Dante Alighieri, the Florentine*, 3 vols. Harmondsworth, England: Penguin, 1955–1973.

———. *Further Papers on Dante*. New York: Harper, 1957.

———. *Introductory Papers on Dante*. New York: Barnes and Noble, 1969.

Shapiro, Marianne. *De Vulgari Eloquentia: Dante's Book of Exile*. Lincoln: University of Nebraska Press, 1990.

Singleton, C. S., ed. *Companion to the Divine Comedy*. Cambridge, Mass.: Harvard University Press, 1975.

Took, J. F. *Dante, Lyric Poet and Philosopher: An Introduction to the Minor Works*. Oxford and New York: Oxford University Press, 1990.

Vittorini, Domenico. *The Age of Dante*. Westport, Conn.: Greenwood Press, 1957, 1975.

Vossler, Karl. *Mediaeval Culture: An Introduction to Dante and His Times*. Trans. William C. Lawton. New York: Harcourt, Brace, 1929.

Wilkins, Ernest Hatch, and Thomas G. Bergin, eds. *A Concordance to the Divine Comedy of Dante Alighieri*. Cambridge, Mass.: Harvard University Press, 1965.

Williams, Charles. *The Figure of Beatrice: A Study in Dante*. Suffolk: Boydell and Brewer, 1994.

LEONARDO DA VINCI: UNIVERSAL MAN OF THE RENAISSANCE

1452	Born
1472	Admitted to Florentine painters' guild
1482–1499	In service of Ludovico Sforza of Milan
1516	Entered service of Francis I of France
1519	Died

More than any other figure, Leonardo da Vinci is commonly regarded as the exemplar of that uniquely Renaissance ideal *uomo universale*, the universal man.

Leonardo, the spoiled, loved, and pampered illegitimate son of a well-to-do Florentine notary, was born in 1452 at the very midpoint of Florence's magnificent Renaissance century, the Quattrocento. The boy grew up at his father's country home in the village of Vinci. His precocious genius and his talent for drawing led his father to apprentice Leonardo to the artist Verrocchio in Florence. While Verrocchio is best remembered as a sculptor, it should be noted that he was, like most Florentine artists of his time, a versatile master of other artistic crafts, and that his *bottega*—like Ghiberti's earlier or Michelangelo's later—was not only a lively school of craftsmanship and technique but a place where people gathered to gossip and talk over a wide range of subjects. Here the young Leonardo's multiple talents bloomed.

At the age of twenty, Leonardo was admitted to the painters' guild and soon after set up his own shop and household. He was well enough received, and commissions came his way. But, for reasons that are not entirely clear, he seems not to have been marked for the lavish patronage of the Medici family—as were so many of his fellow artists—or of any other great Florentine houses. The fashion of the moment preferred those artists like Alberti and Botticelli who mingled learned humanism with their art and could converse in Latin with the humanists, poets, and philosophers who dominated the intel-

lectual scene in Florence. But Leonardo knew no Latin. His education consisted only of apprenticeship training and beyond that a
hodgepodge of self-instruction directed to his own wide-ranging interests, in some areas profound and original, in others hopelessly limited
and naive. It is also possible that Leonardo may simply have set himself apart from the circle of his fellow artists and their patrons. There
are hints of alienation and jealousy and even a vaguely worded reference to a homosexual charge against him that was brought before a
magistrate and then dropped. But it is most likely that Leonardo's
own restless curiosity was already carrying him beyond the practice of
his art.

In 1482 Leonardo left Florence for Milan and the court of its lord,
Ludovico Sforza, one of the most powerful princes of Italy. In the
letter Leonardo wrote commending himself to Ludovico, which has
been preserved, he described himself as a military architect, siege and
hydraulic engineer, ordnance and demolition expert, architect, sculptor, and painter; he ended the letter, "And if any one of the above-
named things seems to anyone to be impossible or not feasible, I am
most ready to make the experiment in your park, or in whatever place
may please your Excellency, to whom I commend myself with the
utmost humility."[1] Humility indeed! The universal man had declared
himself.

Leonardo spent the next seventeen years—the most vigorous and
productive of his life—at the court of Milan. He painted *The Last
Supper* (1495–1497) for the Dominican Convent of Santa Maria delle
Grazie. He conceived and created the model for what might well have
been the world's greatest equestrian statue; but the statue, memorializ-
ing Ludovico Sforza's father, the old soldier-duke Francesco, was
never cast, and the model was destroyed. In addition, Leonardo created gimcrackery for court balls and fêtes—costumes, jewelry, scen-
ery, engines, floats, spectacles. But increasingly he was occupied with
studies of a bewildering variety of subjects. The notebooks he kept
reveal drawings and notes on the flight of birds and the possibility of
human flight; military engineering, tanks, submarines, exploding
shells, rapid-firing artillery pieces, and fortifications; bold schemes
for city planning and hydraulic engineering; plans for machinery of
every sort, pulleys, gears, self-propelled vehicles, a mechanical clock,
and a file cutter; detailed studies of plant, animal, and human anatomy that go well beyond the needs of an artist; a complete treatise on
painting and another on the comparison of the arts. Despite the fact
that much of this body of work—including a treatise on perspective
that was reputed to be far in advance of other such works—was scat-

---

[1]Quoted in E. G. Holt (ed.), *A Documentary History of Art* (New York: Doubleday,
1957), vol. I, pp. 273–75.

tered and lost, some seven thousand pages have survived, all written in a code-like, left-handed mirror script.

Leonardo's handwriting is of particular interest, for it is indicative of a special side of his nature—almost obsessively secretive, aloof, touchy, and suspicious of others. These qualities are part of the traditional image of Leonardo that has been passed down to us, beginning with his earliest biography, by his younger contemporary Vasari.

In Praise of Leonardo

GIORGIO VASARI

Giorgio Vasari (1511–1574) was himself something of a universal man. He was an artist of more than middling ability who worked all over Italy. He was also a respected functionary, the familiar of popes, princes, and dignitaries, as well as artists and scholars. But his most important achievement was his book Lives of the Most Eminent Painters, Sculptors and Architects from Cimabue until Our Own Time, *the first edition published in Florence in 1550. Wallace K. Ferguson has called it "a masterpiece of art history."[2] In fact, the book is more than a masterpiece of art history, for it virtually created the concept of art history itself.*

Vasari introduces "our present age" with his treatment of Leonardo. But this biography, despite its extravagant praise of Leonardo's genius, is seriously limited. Vasari had access to many of Leonardo's notes, even some that we no longer have, but he was more familiar with the art and artists of Tuscany. It is clear that he had not actually seen several of Leonardo's most important works, in Milan and elsewhere. And much of the information he provided on Leonardo's life was nothing more than current rumor or gossip about him. Vasari, furthermore, was himself a pupil and lifelong admirer of Leonardo's great contemporary Michelangelo (1475–1564), and it was Vasari's thesis that the whole tradition of Italian art reached its fulfillment in Michelangelo. It might be recalled also that Michelangelo despised Leonardo; they had at least one nasty quarrel. And Michelangelo was fond of saying that Leonardo was a technically incompetent craftsman who could not complete the projects he began. Whether by design or not, this charge became the main line of criticism in Vasari's biography of Leonardo, and it has persisted alongside Leonardo's reputation as an enigmatic genius.

We look now at Vasari's account from Lives of the Most Eminent Painters, Sculptors and Architects.

The greatest gifts are often seen, in the course of nature, rained by celestial influences on human creatures; and sometimes, in supernatural fashion, beauty, grace, and talent are united beyond measure in one single person, in a manner that to whatever such an one turns his attention, his every action is so divine, that, surpassing all other men, it makes itself clearly known as a thing bestowed by God (as it is), and not acquired by human art. This was seen by all mankind in Leonardo da Vinci, in whom, besides a beauty of body never sufficiently extolled, there was an infinite grace in all his actions; and so great was his genius, and such its growth, that to whatever difficulties he turned

---

[2]In *The Renaissance in Historical Thought: Five Centuries of Interpretation* (Boston: Houghton Mifflin, 1948), p. 60.

his mind, he solved them with ease. In him was great bodily strength, joined to dexterity, with a spirit and courage ever royal and magnanimous; and the fame of his name so increased, that not only in his lifetime was he held in esteem, but his reputation became even greater among posterity after his death.

Truly marvellous and celestial was Leonardo, the son of Ser Piero da Vinci; and in learning and in the rudiments of letters he would have made great proficience, if he had not been so variable and unstable, for he set himself to learn many things, and then, after having begun them, abandoned them. Thus, in arithmetic, during the few months that he studied it, he made so much progress, that, by continually suggesting doubts and difficulties to the master who was teaching him, he would very often bewilder him. He gave some little attention to music, and quickly resolved to learn to play the lyre, as one who had by nature a spirit most lofty and full of refinement; wherefore he sang divinely to that instrument, improvising upon it. Nevertheless, although he occupied himself with such a variety of things, he never ceased drawing and working in relief, pursuits which suited his fancy more than any other. Ser Piero, having observed this, and having considered the loftiness of his intellect, one day took some of his drawings and carried them to Andrea del Verrocchio, who was much his friend, and besought him straitly to tell him whether Leonardo, by devoting himself to drawing, would make any proficience. Andrea was astonished to see the extraordinary beginnings of Leonardo, and urged Ser Piero that he should make him study it; wherefore he arranged with Leonardo that he should enter the workshop of Andrea, which Leonardo did with the greatest willingness in the world. And he practised not one branch of art only, but all those in which drawing played a part; and having an intellect so divine and marvellous that he was also an excellent geometrician, he not only worked in sculpture, making in his youth, in clay, some heads of women that are smiling, of which plaster casts are still taken, and likewise some heads of boys which appeared to have issued from the hand of a master; but in architecture, also, he made many drawings both of ground-plans and of other designs of buildings; and he was the first, although but a youth, who suggested the plan of reducing the river Arno to a navigable canal from Pisa to Florence. He made designs of flour-mills, fulling-mills, and engines, which might be driven by the force of water: and since he wished that his profession should be painting, he studied much in drawing after nature. . . . He was continually making models and designs to show men how to remove mountains with ease, and how to bore them in order to pass from one level to another; and by means of levers, windlasses, and screws, he showed the way to raise and draw great weights, together with methods for emptying harbours, and pumps for removing water from low places, things which his brain never ceased from devising;

and of these ideas and labours many drawings may be seen, scattered abroad among our craftsmen; and I myself have seen not a few. . . .

He was so pleasing in conversation, that he attracted to himself the hearts of men. And although he possessed, one might say, nothing, and worked little, he always kept servants and horses, in which latter he took much delight, and particularly in all other animals, which he managed with the greatest love and patience; and this he showed when often passing by the places where birds were sold, for, taking them with his own hand out of their cages, and having paid to those who sold them the price that was asked, he let them fly away into the air, restoring to them their lost liberty. For which reason nature was pleased so to favour him, that, wherever he turned his thought, brain, and mind, he displayed such divine power in his works, that, in giving them their perfection, no one was ever his peer in readiness, vivacity, excellence, beauty, and grace.

It is clear that Leonardo, through his comprehension of art, began many things and never finished one of them, since it seemed to him that the hand was not able to attain to the perfection of art in carrying out the things which he imagined; for the reason that he conceived in idea difficulties so subtle and so marvellous, that they could never be expressed by the hands, be they ever so excellent. And so many were his caprices, that, philosophizing of natural things, he set himself to seek out the properties of herbs, going on even to observe the motions of the heavens, the path of the moon, and the courses of the sun. . . .

He began a panel-picture of the Adoration of the Magi, containing many beautiful things, particularly the heads, which was in the house of Amerigo Benci, opposite the Loggia de' Peruzzi; and this, also, remained unfinished, like his other works.

It came to pass that Giovan Galeazzo, Duke of Milan, being dead, and Lodovico Sforza raised to the same rank, in the year 1494,[3] Leonardo was summoned to Milan in great repute to the Duke, who took much delight in the sound of the lyre, to the end that he might play it: and Leonardo took with him that instrument which he had made with his own hands, in great part of silver, in the form of a horse's skull—a thing bizarre and new—in order that the harmony might be of greater volume and more sonorous in tone; with which he surpassed all the musicians who had come together there to play. Besides this, he was the best improviser in verse of his day. The Duke, hearing the marvellous discourse of Leonardo, became so enamoured of his genius, that it was something incredible: and he prevailed upon him by entreaties to paint an altar-panel containing a Nativity, which was sent by the Duke to the Emperor.

---

[3]The date was actually 1482.

He also painted in Milan, for the Friars of S. Dominic, at S. Maria delle Grazie, a Last Supper, a most beautiful and marvellous thing; and to the heads of the Apostles he gave such majesty and beauty, that he left the head of Christ unfinished, not believing that he was able to give it that divine air which is essential to the image of Christ.[4] This work, remaining thus all but finished, has ever been held by the Milanese in the greatest veneration, and also by strangers as well; for Leonardo imagined and succeeded in expressing that anxiety which had seized the Apostles in wishing to know who should betray their Master. . . .

While he was engaged on this work, he proposed to the Duke to make a horse in bronze, of a marvellous greatness, in order to place upon it, as a memorial, the image of the Duke.[5] And on so vast a scale did he begin it and continue it, that it could never be completed. And there are those who have been of the opinion (so various and so often malign out of envy are the judgments of men) that he began it with no intention of finishing it, because, being of so great a size, an incredible difficulty was encountered in seeking to cast it in one piece; and it might also be believed that, from the result, many may have formed such a judgment, since many of his works have remained unfinished. But, in truth, one can believe that his vast and most excellent mind was hampered through being too full of desire, and that his wish ever to seek out excellence upon excellence, and perfection upon perfection, was the reason of it. "Tal che l'opera fosse ritardata dal desio,"[6] as our Petrarca has said. And, indeed, those who saw the great model that Leonardo made in clay vow that they have never seen a more beautiful thing, or a more superb; and it was preserved until the French came to Milan with King Louis of France, and broke it all to pieces.[7] Lost, also, is a little model of it in wax, which was held to be perfect, together with a book on the anatomy of the horse made by him by way of study.

He then applied himself, but with greater care, to the anatomy of man, assisted by and in turn assisting, in this research, Messer Marc' Antonio della Torre, an excellent philosopher, who was then lecturing at Pavia, and who wrote of this matter; and he was one of the first (as I have heard tell) that began to illustrate the problems of medicine with the doctrine of Galen, and to throw true light on anatomy, which up to that time had been wrapped in the thick and gross darkness of ignorance. And in this he found marvellous aid in the brain, work, and hand of Leonardo, who made a book drawn in red chalk, and

---

[4] The head of Christ was finished, along with the rest of the painting. Vasari was repeating gossip and had not seen the work.

[5] Rather of the Duke's father, Francesco, the founder of the Sforza dynasty.

[6] "So that the work was hindered by the very desire of it."

[7] Louis XII of France. The incident of the model's destruction took place during the French occupation of Milan in 1499.

annotated with the pen, of the bodies that he dissected with his own hand, and drew with the greatest diligence; wherein he showed all the frame of the bones; and then added to them, in order, all the nerves, and covered them with muscles; the first attached to the bone, the second that hold the body firm, and the third that move it; and beside them, part by part, he wrote in letters of an ill-shaped character, which he made with the left hand, backwards; and whoever is not practised in reading them cannot understand them, since they are not to be read save with a mirror. . . .

With the fall of Ludovico Sforza and the French occupation of Milan in 1499, the artist returned to Florence.

Leonardo undertook to execute, for Francesco del Giocondo, the portrait of Mona Lisa, his wife; and after toiling over it for four years, he left it unfinished; and the work is now in the collection of King Francis of France, at Fontainebleau. In this head, whoever wished to see how closely art could imitate nature, was able to comprehend it with ease; for in it were counterfeited all the minutenesses that with subtlety are able to be painted. . . .

By reason, then, of the excellence of the works of this divine craftsman, his fame had so increased that all persons who took delight in art—nay, the whole city of Florence—desired that he should leave them some memorial, and it was being proposed everywhere that he should be commissioned to execute some great and notable work, whereby the commonwealth might be honoured and adorned by the great genius, grace, and judgment that were seen in the works of Leonardo. And it was decided between the Gonfalonier[8] and the chief citizens, the Great Council Chamber having been newly built . . . and having been finished in great haste, it was ordained by public decree that Leonardo should be given some beautiful work to paint; and so the said hall was allotted to him by Piero Soderini, then Gonfalonier of Justice. Whereupon Leonardo, determining to execute this work, began a cartoon in the Sala del Papa, an apartment in S. Maria Novella, representing the story of Niccolò Piccinino,[9] Captain of Duke Filippo of Milan; wherein he designed a group of horsemen who were fighting for a standard, a work that was held to be very excellent and of great mastery, by reason of the marvellous ideas that he had in composing that battle. . . . It is said that, in order to draw that cartoon, he made a most ingenious stage, which was raised by contracting it and lowered

---

[8]The title of the chief magistrate of Florence.
[9]A mercenary commander who had worked for Florence.

by expanding. And conceiving the wish to colour on the wall in oils, he made a composition of so gross an admixture, to act as a binder on the wall, that, going on to paint in the said hall, it began to peel off in such a manner that in a short time he abandoned it, seeing it spoiling.[10] . . .

He went to Rome with Duke Giuliano de' Medici, at the election of Pope Leo,[11] who spent much of his time on philosophical studies, and particularly on alchemy; where, forming a paste of a certain kind of wax, as he walked he shaped animals very thin and full of wind, and, by blowing into them, made them fly through the air, but when the wind ceased they fell to the ground. . . .

He made an infinite number of such follies, and gave his attention to mirrors; and he tried the strangest methods in seeking out oils for painting, and varnish for preserving works when painted. . . . It is related that, a work having been allotted to him by the Pope, he straight-way began to distil oils and herbs, in order to make the varnish; at which Pope Leo said: "Alas! this man will never do anything, for he begins by thinking of the end of the work, before the beginning."

There was very great disdain between Michelagnolo Buonarroti and him, on account of which Michelagnolo departed from Florence, with the excuse of Duke Giuliano, having been summoned by the Pope to the competition for the façade of S. Lorenzo. Leonardo, understanding this, departed and went into France, where the King, having had works by his hand, bore him great affection; and he desired that he should colour the cartoon of S. Anne, but Leonardo, according to his custom, put him off for a long time with words.

Finally, having grown old, he remained ill many months, and, feeling himself near to death, asked to have himself diligently informed of the teaching of the Catholic faith. . . . [He] expired in the arms of the King, in the seventy-fifth year of his age.[12]

Leonardo the Scientist

JOHN HERMAN RANDALL JR.

From Vasari's time to the present, there has clung to the image of Leonardo da Vinci a kind of Faustian quality, linking him to the origins of modern science. Throughout his life, and increasingly from middle age on, Leonardo was preoccu-

---

[10]Michelangelo was assigned a companion panel and also abandoned his work on it before it was completed.

[11]Pope Leo X, the former Giovanni Cardinal de' Medici.

[12]Vasari is inaccurate. In the year Leonardo died, 1519, he actually was sixty-seven.

pied with technical studies and scientific experiments, often to the detriment of his art. But the judgments of modern scholars on "Leonardo the scientist" are much more varied and more circumspect than those upon "Leonardo the artist."

We turn first to the views of a distinguished philosopher and historian of science, especially medieval and Renaissance science, the longtime Columbia University professor of philosophy John Herman Randall Jr. This selection is from his article "The Place of Leonardo da Vinci in the Emergence of Modern Science."

Leonardo was not himself a scientist. "Science" is not the hundred-odd aphorisms or "pensieri" that have been pulled out of his Codici and collected, by Richter, Solmi, and others. "Science" is not oracular utterances, however well phrased; it is not bright ideas jotted down in a notebook. "Science" is systematic and methodical thought. . . .

"Science" is not just the appeal to experience, though it involves such an appeal, as Leonardo stated in answering those critics who had censured him as a mere empiric: "If I could not indeed like them cite authors and books, it is a much greater and worthier thing to profess to cite experience, the mistress of their masters." "Science" is not the mere rejection of authority, the case for which is well put by Leonardo: "He who argues by citing an authority is not employing intelligence but rather memory." . . .

It is true that during Leonardo's youth—the second half of the Quattrocento—the intellectual influence of the non-scientific humanists had been making for a kind of St. Martin's summer of the "authority" of the ancients, and that his life coincides with this rebirth of an authoritarian attitude toward the past. Leonardo's protests were magnificent, and doubtless pertinent. But they are not enough to constitute "science." "Science" is not merely fresh, first-hand observation, however detailed and accurate.

Above all, "science" is not the intuitions of a single genius, solitary and alone, however suggestive. It is cooperative inquiry, such as had prevailed in the Italian schools from the time of Pietro d'Abano (d.1315; his *Conciliator* appeared earlier)—and such as was to continue till the time of Galileo—the cumulative cooperative inquiry which actually played so large a part in the emergence of modern science. . . .

In practice, Leonardo always becomes fascinated by some particular problem—he has no interest in working out any systematic body of knowledge. His artist's interest in the particular and the concrete, which inspires his careful, precise and accurate observation, is carried further by his inordinate curiosity into a detailed analytic study of the factors involved. His thought seems always to be moving from the particularity of the painter's experience to the universality of intellect and science, without ever quite getting there. . . .

No evidence has ever been offered that anybody in the sixteenth century capable of appreciating scientific ideas ever saw the Codici of Leonardo. . . . But since the scientific ideas expressed therein were all well-known in the universities of Leonardo's day, and were accessible in much more elaborated form in the books the scientists were reading, there seems to be no "problem" of tracing any presumed "influence" of Leonardo on the development of sixteenth-century scientific thought in Italy.

The *Trattato de la Pittura,* or *Paragone,* was not printed until 1651, but its existence in manuscript form suggests that it had been read much earlier by the Urbino circle. It was put together from various manuscripts of Leonardo by an editor whose identity is not known, but who seems to have been responsible for its systematic organization—an organization which later editors have uniformly tried to improve upon.

With Leonardo's anatomical studies, the story is somewhat different. There is no evidence that Vesalius[13] ever actually saw his drawings; but in view of the marked similarities between them and his own much more systematically planned and organized series of drawings, it is difficult to think that he did not. . . .

Turning now from the things that Leonardo, despite all the adulations of his genius, was clearly not, let us try to state what seems to have been his real genius in scientific matters. During the Renaissance, as a result of the surprising dissolution of the rigid boundaries which had previously kept different intellectual traditions, as it were, in watertight compartments, the many different currents of thought which had long been preparing and strengthening themselves during the Middle Ages managed to come together, and to strike fire. The explanation of this phenomenon can ultimately be only sociological— the breaking down of the fairly rigid boundaries that had hitherto shut off one discipline and one intellectual tradition from another. Whatever its cause, the confluence of many different intellectual traditions in the fertile, all-too-fertile mind of Leonardo renders his views an unusually happy illustration of the way in which very diverse intellectual traditions managed during the Renaissance to unite together to create what we now call "modern science."

There is first the "scientific tradition," the careful, intelligent, co-operative and cumulative criticism of Aristotelian physics, which began with William of Ockham.[14] . . . In his reading Leonardo was in touch with this scientific tradition, as Duhem[15] has shown.

There is secondly Leonardo's enthusiasm for mathematics, which

---

[13]The Flemish anatomist at the University of Padua who in 1543 published the first modern, scientific descriptive treatise on human anatomy.

[14]The important nominalist philosopher of the early fourteenth century.

[15]The nineteenth-century French physicist and philosopher.

goes far beyond its obvious instrumental use. It is very hard to assay the precise sense in which Leonardo thought of mathematics as the alphabet of nature: in this area much work remains to be done. There seems to be in Leonardo no trace of the popular contemporary Pythagoreanism or Platonism. If we examine Leonardo's conception of mathematics as depicted in his drawings, not as inadequately stated in his prose, we find that it differs markedly from the static and very geometrical notion of Dürer.[16] It is movement, not geometrical relations, that Leonardo is trying to capture. There is much in his drawings that suggests a world envisaged in terms of the calculus—like the world of Leibniz[17]—rather than in terms of the purely geometrical vision of the Greek tradition. In his mathematical vision of the world, Leonardo seems to belong to the realm of "dynamic" and "Faustian" attitudes, rather than to the static geometrical perfection of Greek thought.

There is thirdly the tradition of what Edgar Zilsel has called the "superior craftsman"—the man who is not afraid to take an idea and try it out, to experiment with it. . . . As a pupil of Verrocchio [Leonardo] had no fastidious objections to sullying his hands with "experiment." This habit of Leonardo's of descending from the academic cathedra and actually trying out the ideas of which he read had broad repercussions: it is one of the activities of Leonardo that seems to have become generally known, and to have awakened emulation. The consequences of Leonardo's willingness to experiment are to be found in the "practical geometry" of Tartaglia, the greatest of the sixteenth-century Italian mathematicians. Galileo, of course, was in this tradition of the "practical geometers"; he too was an indefatigable inventor. Indeed, Leonardo can fairly claim to belong not to the line of scientists but to the noble tradition of the inventors. . . .

Many of Leonardo's aphorisms treat the matter of the proper intellectual method. He has much to say on the relation between "reason" and "experience," and what he says used to lead commentators to impute to him the anticipation of Francis Bacon's "inductive method"—God save the mark, as though that had anything to do with the method employed by the pioneering scientists of the seventeenth century!

Neither experience alone nor reason alone will suffice. "Those who are enamored of practice without science are like the pilot who boards his ship without helm or compass, and who is never certain where he is going." On the other hand, pure reasoning is without avail: "Should you say that the sciences which begin and end in the mind have achieved truth, that I will not concede, but rather deny for many

---

[16]The great German artist, a contemporary of Leonardo.
[17]The great German philosopher and mathematician of the seventeenth century who shares with Newton the discovery of the calculus.

reasons; and first, because in such mental discourse there occurs no experience, without which there is no certainty to be found."

But Leonardo does not bother to give any precise definition of what he means by his key terms, "experience," "reason," "certainty," or "truth." Certainty depends on "experience," but "there is no certainty where one of the mathematical sciences cannot apply, or where the subject is not united with mathematics." And—maxim for all inventors!—"Mechanics is the paradise of the mathematical sciences, because in it they come to bear their mathematical fruits." . . .

These aphorisms as to the relation between reason and experience are no doubt rhetorically effective. But we have only to compare such vague utterances with the very detailed analyses of precisely the same methodological relation which were being carried out at this very time in the Aristotelian schools of the Italian universities to realize the difference between an artist's insights and the scientist's analysis.

Leonardo was above all else the anatomist of nature. He could see, and with his draughtsmanship depict clearly, the bony skeleton of the world—the geological strata and their indicated past. He could also see everywhere nature's simple machines in operation—in man and in the non-human world alike. . . .

As a genuine contributor, then, to the descriptive sciences, Leonardo reported with his pencil fundamental aspects of nature the great machine—in anatomy, geology, and hydrostatics. As a writer rather than as a graphic reporter, Leonardo shows himself an extremely intelligent reader. But he was clearly never so much the scientist as when he had his pencil in hand, and was penetrating to the mechanical structure of what he was observing.

Leonardo the Technologist

LADISLAO RETI

A substantial group of modern scholars agrees with Randall. Some, however, do not. In the following selection, we will sample the views of one of them, Ladislao Reti, a historian of science and medicine and an authority on Leonardo's scientific and technical manuscripts. Reti not only attaches more importance to Leonardo's scientific work than does Randall; he vigorously denies Randall's charges that Leonardo failed to exhibit a sustained, systematic body of scientific thought; that he stood alone outside the tradition of science; that he failed to develop a methodological terminology; and that he failed to influence the evolution of science beyond his own time. But most of all, Reti disputes Randall's view that science is abstract conception. Rather, he takes the position that science must be the accumulation of particular observations and applications. Reti views "Leonardo the scientist" as "Leonardo the technologist," and he insists that a technologist of such brilliance and inventiveness as Leonardo cannot be so readily dismissed. "The greatest engineer of all times" surely deserves a place in the history of science.

Varied as Leonardo's interests were, statistical analysis of his writings points to technology as the main subject. As was acutely pointed out by Bertrand Gille in a recent book, judging by the surviving original documents, Leonardo's métier was rather an engineer's than an artist's.

However we may feel about this opinion, it is disturbing to take an inventory of Leonardo's paintings, of which no more than half a dozen are unanimously authenticated by the world's leading experts.

Contrast this evident disinclination to paint with the incredible toil and patience Leonardo lavished on scientific and technical studies, particularly in the fields of geometry, mechanics, and engineering. Here his very indulgence elicited curious reactions from his contemporaries and in the minds of his late biographers. They regretted that a man endowed with such divine artistic genius should waste the precious hours of his life in such vain pursuits. And, of course, as the well-known episodes of his artistic career testify, this exposed him not only to criticism but also to serious inconveniences.

But were Leonardo's nonartistic activities truly marginal?

Documentary evidence proves that every official appointment refers to him not only as an artist but as an engineer as well.

At the court of Ludovico il Moro he was *Ingeniarius et pinctor.*[18] Cesare Borgia called him his most beloved *Architecto et Engegnero Generale.*[19] When he returned to Florence he was immediately consulted as military engineer. . . . Louis XII called him *nostre chier et bien amé Léonard da Vincy, nostre paintre et ingenieur ordinaire.*[20] Even in Rome, despite the pope's famous remark on hearing of Leonardo's experiments with varnishes preparatory to beginning an artistic commission, Leonardo's duties clearly included technical work, as is documented by three rough copies of a letter to his patron Giuliano de' Medici. Nor was his position different when he went to France at the invitation of Francis I. The official burial document calls him *Lionard de Vincy, noble millanois, premier peinctre et ingenieur et architecte du Roy, mescanichien d'Estat, et anchien directeur du peincture du Duc de Milan.*[21]

We can thus see that Leonardo had a lively interest in the me-

---

[18]Engineer and painter.
[19]Architect and Engineer-General.
[20]Our dear and well-loved Leonardo da Vinci, our painter and engineer ordinary.
[21]Leonardo da Vinci, Milanese nobleman, first painter and engineer and architect of the King, state technician, and former director of painting of the Duke of Milan.

chanical arts and engineering from his earliest youth, as evidenced by the oldest drawing in the Codex Atlanticus, to the end of his industrious life. Thousands of his drawings witness to it, from fleeting sketches (though always executed with the most uncanny bravura) to presentation projects finished in chiaroscuro wash. Often these sketches and drawings are accompanied by a descriptive text, comments, and discussion.

The drawings and writings of Leonardo on technical matters, though scattered throughout the notebooks and especially in the Codex Atlanticus (a true order probably never existed nor did the author attempt to make one), represent an important and unique source for the history of technology. . . .

It is far from my intention and beyond my possibilities to discuss Leonardo's technology as a whole on this occasion. Enough is said when we remember that there is hardly a field of applied mechanics where Leonardo's searching mind has left no trace in the pages of his notebooks. To illustrate Leonardo's methods I shall limit myself to discussing some little-known aspects of how he dealt with the main problem of technology, the harnessing of energy to perform useful work.

At the time of Leonardo the waterwheel had been improved and in some favored places wind was used to grind corn or pump water. But the main burden of human industry still rested on the muscle power of man or animal. Little thought was given to how this should be used. Animals were attached to carts or traction devices; fortunately collar harness was already in use, multiplying by five the pulling strength of the horse. Men worked tools by hand, turned cranks, or operated treadmills. Of course, power could be gained, sacrificing time, with the help of levers, screws, gears, and pulleys. Little attention was given to the problems of friction, strength of materials, and to the rational development of power transmission. At least this is the picture suggested by studying the few manuscripts that precede Leonardo, devoted to technological matters.

Leonardo's approach was fundamentally different. He firmly believed that technological problems must be dealt with not by blindly following traditional solutions but according to scientific rules deduced from observation and experiment.

When Leonardo searched for the most efficient ways of using the human motor, the force of every limb, of every muscle, was analyzed and measured. Leonardo was the first engineer who tried to find a quantitative equivalent for the forms of energy available.

In MS H (written c. 1494) on folios 43v and 44r (Figs. 1 and 2) there are two beautiful sketches showing the estimation of human muscular effort with the help of a dynamometer. The force is measured in pounds which represent the lifting capacity of the group of muscles under scrutiny. In figure 1 no less than six different cases covering the whole body are examined, while in figure 2 Leonardo

Figure 1

MS H, fol. 43*v*.

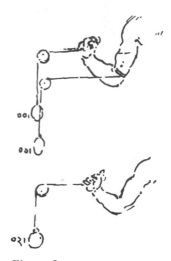

Figure 2

MS H, fol. 44*r*.

tries to compare the force of the arm in different positions and points of attachment. Between the last two drawings a diagram shows the arm as a compound lever. In many other instances Leonardo compares the human body with a mechanical system, anticipating Borelli. We shall see one of them on folio 164*r, a* of the Codex Atlanticus. . . .

The interest of Leonardo in the maximum efficiency of muscle power is understandable. It was the only motor he could have used in a flying machine; a project that aroused his ambition as early as the year 1488 and in which he remained interested till the end of his life.

The efficiency of the human motor depends not only on its intrinsic strength but also on the ways the force is applied. Indeed, what is the greatest strength a man can generate, without the help of mechanical devices like levers, gears, or pulleys? In a very interesting passage of MS A, folio 30*v* (Fig. 3), Leonardo answers the question:

> A man pulling a weight balanced against himself (as in lifting a weight with the help of a single block) cannot pull more than his own weight. And if he has to raise it, he will raise as much more than his weight, as his strength may be more than that of another man. The greatest force a man can apply, with equal velocity and impetus, will be when he sets his feet on one end of the balance and then leans his shoulders against some stable support. This will raise, at the other end of the balance, a weight equal to his own, and added to that, as much weight as he can carry on his shoulders.

Masterly executed marginal sketches illustrate the three different cases. The problem has been already touched on folio 90*v* of MS B,

Figure 3

MS A, fol. 30v.

Figure 4

Belidor, *Architecture Hydraulique*, pt. 2, p. 128, pl. 8.

where the following suggestion is made beside a similar sketch: "See at the mill how much is your weight, stepping on the balance and pressing with your shoulders against something."

But Leonardo was always anxious to integrate theory with application. His own advice was: "When you put together the science of the motions of water, remember to include under each proposition its application and use, in order that this science may not be useless" (MS F, fol. 2v).

I should like to select, among many, a few cases in which Leonardo demonstrates the usefulness of his rules. One of them is pile driving for foundation work or the regulation of river banks. The simplest pile-driving machine consists of a movable frame, provided with a drop hammer raised by men pulling at a rope provided with hand lines. After being raised, the hammer is released by a trigger. The operation is repeated until the pile has been sunk to the necessary depth. In Belidor's classic treatise we may see the figure of this age-old device (Fig. 4).

Leonardo, often engaged in architectural and hydraulic projects, obviously had a more than theoretical interest in the operation. . . .

As for the practical improvements, I should like to present a group of notes on this subject, from the Leicester Codex, folio 28*v*, which so far as I know have never been reproduced, commented upon, or translated. Marginal drawings (Figs. 5 and 6) illustrate the text.

The very best way to drive piles (*ficcare i pali a castello*) is when the man lifts so much of the weight of the hammer as is his own weight. And this shall be done in as much time as the man, without burden, is able to climb a ladder quickly. Now, this man shall put his foot immediately in the stirrup and he will descend with so much weight as his weight exceeds that of the hammer. If you want to check it thoroughly, you can have him carry a stone weighing a pound. He will lift so much weight as is his own on descending from the top of the ladder and the hammer will raise and remain on top, locked by itself, until the man dismounts the stirrup and again climbs the ladder. When you unlock the hammer with a string, it will descend furiously on top of the pile you want to drive in. And with the same speed the stirrup will rise again to the feet of

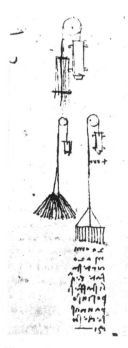

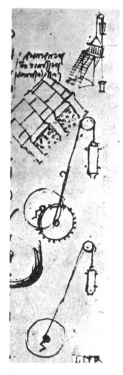

Figure 5
MS Leicester, fol. 28*v*.

Figure 6
MS Leicester, fol. 28*v*.

the man. And this shall be done again and again. And if you want to have more men, take several ropes that end in one rope and several ladders to allow the men to reach the top of the ladders at the same time. Now, at a signal from the foreman, they shall put their feet in the stirrups and climb the ladder again. They will rest while descending and there is not much fatigue in climbing the ladders because it is done with feet and hands, and all the weight of the man that is charged on the hands will not burden the feet. But one man shall always give the signal.

Pile driving by raising the hammer by hand is not very useful, because a man cannot raise his own weight if he does not sustain it with his arms. This cannot be done unless the rope he is using is perpendicular to the center of his gravity. And this happens only to one of the men in a crowd who is pulling on the hammer.

We can further observe in the sketches of the Leicester Codex that Belidor's first two improvements had already been considered by Leonardo: the substitution of a large wheel for the block and use of a capstan or a winch. . . .

But arts and techniques can be easily lost when genius is not understood and assimilated. The technology of the sixteenth and seventeenth centuries was much inferior to the standards set by Leonardo; only at the end of the seventeenth century was there a renewal that led to the beginning of modern engineering. A thorough study of Leonardo's technical activities and ideas, even if presented in the disorderly state of the mutilated and plundered heritage, points to him, as Feldhaus has correctly remarked, as the greatest engineer of all times.

Questions for Review and Study

1. How does Vasari both praise and criticize Leonardo in his biographical sketch?
2. How do you imagine Leonardo saw himself, as an artist or as a scientist? Explain.
3. Why do you think Leonardo left so many of his projects uncompleted?
4. To what extent can Leonardo be regarded as a scientist? Comment.
5. Can Leonardo really be considered "the greatest engineer of all times"? Give your reasons.

Questions for Comparison

1. Compare Cortés (see p. 225) and Da Vinci as expressions of the Renaissance spirit. How far removed were these men from the medieval

concern for a unified Christian order? In what ways did each man still belong to the Middle Ages? To what degree did Christianity inspire their work? How did each display a "Faustian" exertion of the human will? What explicit or implied notions of progress are evident in their respective projects? Whose feats shed a more favorable light on Western culture?

Suggestions for Further Reading

The two standard editions of Leonardo's notebooks are *Notebooks*, translated and edited by Edward McCurdy, and *The Notebooks of Leonardo da Vinci*, edited by Jean Paul Richter, as well as a small collection of excerpts, titled *Philosophical Diary*, translated and edited by Wade Baskin. There is also the recent *Leonardo on Painting*, edited by Martin Kemp. Of the many collections of his artistic works, one of the best is *Leonardo da Vinci*, the catalogue of the comprehensive Milan Leonardo Exposition of 1938. Another, relevant to the emphasis of this chapter, is *Leonardo da Vinci: Engineer and Architect*, the catalogue of a major exhibit in 1987. A. E. Popham's *The Drawings of Leonardo da Vinci* is the most complete collection of the drawings, with a comprehensive introduction. Several general works on Leonardo can be recommended: *Leonardo da Vinci*, edited by Morris Philipson, a well-selected set of articles and special studies, and *Leonardo*, by Cecil H. M. Gould. Both these books recognize the two aspects of Leonardo's life and work that are generally dealt with, the scientific and the artistic. Of the works on Leonardo the artist, the best is Kenneth M. Clark's *Leonardo da Vinci;* it may well be the best work on him of any sort. See also *The Artist and the Man*, by Serge Bramly, and *Leonardo da Vinci*, edited by E. H. Gombrich, a collection of essays on Leonardo and a partial catalogue of paintings and drawings. For Leonard's mechanical engineering interests, the pioneer studies are by Ivor B. Hart, *The Mechanical Investigations of Leonardo da Vinci*, and a later work by Hart updating the research, *The World of Leonardo*. In this regard, see also Giancarlo Maiorino's *Leonardo da Vinci*. For Leonardo's anatomical studies, see Elmer Belt, *Leonardo the Anatomist;* Kenneth D. Keele, *Leonardo da Vinci's "Elements of the Science of Man";* and Martin Clayton, *Leonardo da Vinci*.

A special interest in Leonardo was stirred by two works of Sigmund Freud, *Leonardo da Vinci: A Study in Psychosexuality* and *Leonardo da Vinci and a Memory of His Childhood*, in which Freud treated Leonardo as the subject of his most extensive attempt at psychohistory. The works are full of errors and not solidly based on research, but they thrust into the forefront of controversy about Leonardo the questions of his homosexuality and the paralyzing duality of his interests in science and art. Two later books in this controversy are *Leonardo da Vinci*, by Kurt R. Sissler, and *The Sublimation of Leonardo da Vinci,* by Raymond S. Stites, the latter a large, detailed, and difficult book but an important revisionist study of Freud's tentative conclusions.

Although its assertions and research are now dated, students may still enjoy a famous historical novel by Dmitrii Merezhkovskii, *The Romance of Leonardo da Vinci.*

For the background to Leonardo's biography and the Renaissance, see Wallace K. Ferguson's *Europe in Transition, 1300–1520,* and Ernst Breisach's *Renaissance Europe, 1300–1517.* And for an attractive and readable book on the Italy that formed Leonardo, see *Power and Imagination,* by Lauro Martines. (Titles with an asterisk are out of print.)

Belt, Elmer. *Leonardo the Anatomist.* New York: Greenwood, 1955.

Bramly, Serge. *The Artist and the Man.* New York: Penguin, 1995.

Breisach, Ernst. *Renaissance Europe, 1300–1517.* New York: Macmillan, 1973.

Clark, Kenneth M. *Leonardo da Vinci: An Account of His Development as an Artist.* Rev. ed. Baltimore: Penguin, 1958.

Clayton, Martin. *Leonardo da Vinci: The Anatomy of Man: Drawings from the Collection of Her Majesty Queen Elizabeth II.* Houston and Boston: Museum of Fine Arts and Bulfinch Press, 1992.

Da Vinci, Leonardo. *Leonardo on Painting: An Anthology of Writings by Leonardo da Vinci, with a selection of documents relating to his career as an artist.* Ed. Martin Kemp. New Haven, Conn.: Yale University Press, 1989.

———. *Notebooks.* 2 vols. Trans. and ed. Edward McCurdy. London: Cape, 1956.

———. *The Notebooks of Leonardo da Vinci,* 2 vols. Ed. Jean Paul Richter, New York: Dover, 1970.

———. *Philosophical Diary.* Trans. and ed. Wade Baskin. New York: Philosophical Library, 1959.

Ferguson, Wallace K. *Europe in Transition, 1300–1520.* Boston: Houghton Mifflin, 1962.

Freud, Sigmund. *Leonardo da Vinci: A Study in Psychosexuality.* Trans. A. A. Brill. New York: Random House, 1947.

———. *Leonardo da Vinci and a Memory of His Childhood.* Trans. Alan Tyson. New York: Norton, 1964.

Gombrich, E. H. et al, eds. *Leonardo da Vinci.* New Haven, Conn.: Yale University Press, 1989.

Gould, Cecil H. M. *Leonardo: The Artist and the Non-artist.* Boston: New York Graphic Society, 1975.*

Hart, Ivor B. *The Mechanical Investigations of Leonardo da Vinci.* 2nd ed. Berkeley: University of California Press, 1925, 1963.

———. *The World of Leonardo: Man of Science, Engineer, and Dreamer of Flight.* New York: Viking, 1961.*

Keele, Kenneth D. *Leonardo da Vinci's "Elements of the Science of Man."* New York: Academic Press, 1983.

Leonardo da Vinci. New York: Reynal, 1956.

Leonardo da Vinci: Engineer and Architect. Montreal: Museum of Fine Arts, 1987.

Maiorino, Giancarlo. *Leonardo da Vinci: The Daedalian Mythmaker.* University Park: Pennsylvania State University Press, 1992.

Martines, Lauro. *Power and Imagination: City-States in Renaissance Italy.* New York: Knopf, 1979.

Merezhkovskii, Dmitrii. *The Romance of Leonardo da Vinci.* Trans. B. G. Guerney. New York: Heritage, 1938.*

Philipson, Morris, ed. *Leonardo da Vinci: Aspects of the Renaissance Genius.* New York: Braziller, 1966.*

Popham, A. E., ed. *The Drawings of Leonardo da Vinci.* London: Cape, 1964.

Sissler, Kurt R. *Leonardo da Vinci: Psychoanalytic Notes on an Enigma.* New York: International Universities Press, 1961.

Stites, Raymond S. *The Sublimation of Leonardo da Vinci, with a Translation of the Codex Trivulzianus.* Washington, D.C.: Smithsonian, 1970.*

ET FORTITUDO EIVS CORROBORAVIT BRACHIVM MEVM

CORTÉS AND THE CONQUEST OF MEXICO

1485	Born
1504	Arrived in New World
1511	Accompanied expedition for the conquest of Cuba
1518	Named captain of the expedition for the conquest of Mexico
1519	Arrived at Tenochtitlan (Mexico City)
1521	Fall of Tenochtitlan
1540	Return to Spain
1547	Came again to Mexico
1547	Died

The Spaniards who flocked to the New World in the wake of Columbus's discoveries were after not only land but the gold that was persistently rumored to be had there in such abundance. Among the seekers was an impoverished *hidalgo*[1] named Hernán Cortés. He made himself useful to Don Diego Velásquez, the Deputy Admiral of the Islands and Governor of Cuba, and was entrusted with an expedition to the mainland of Mexico. With only a bare handful of men and horses and a few cannon and shotguns, this man, who would shortly become the greatest of the *conquistadores*, set out on an incredible journey of conquest. He won the support of native people near the coast, including an invaluable woman, Doña Marina, who became his interpreter and mistress. And he began to hear of the great and wealthy empire of the Aztecs, the Mexica. He allied himself with the Tlaxcalans, another native people, who were bitter enemies of the Aztecs, and with some Tlaxcalan support and his own small force Cortés pressed inland toward the Aztec capital of Tenochtitlan, the later site of Mexico City, entering the city on November 8, 1519. He was met by a large delegation of high officials sent out by the Emperor Moctezuma—or Montezuma, as he was more commonly called by the Spaniards—and at last by the emperor himself.

His state comprised the Aztec Empire, which had been put to-

---

[1] A *hidalgo* was a Spanish nobleman of secondary rank, below that of a grandee.

gether over the past two centuries by the conquests of his aggressive, warlike people. The Aztecs had subjugated the many indigenous peoples of central Mexico in a closely controlled imperial state that claimed between a million and a million and a half people, ruled from the capital city of Tenochtitlan. Tenochtitlan itself had some 400,000 people and spread out from its central temple, with its towering twin pyramids and spacious temple compound, to cover more than five square miles. It included religious structures, government buildings, and residences of the nobility, all built of stone and coated in glistening white and painted stucco, and the more modest homes of craftsmen and artisans. It had an enormous market where all the products of Meso-America were available for purchase. It was supplied with fresh water by aqueducts from Chapultapec and surrounded by the waters of Lake Texcoco, entered by an elaborate system of elevated causeways that also acted as dikes and breakwaters.

But the Aztec state was also a religious community. The Aztecs worshipped many gods, but the all-powerful "Lord of the World" was the sun god Huitzilopochtli, the Blue Hummingbird. It was mainly this god whose worship accounted for the most arresting feature of Aztec religion—mass human sacrifice and cannibalism. The practice of human sacrifice had grown over recent years until by the time of Montezuma thousands of persons were sacrificed every year—their chests slashed open by priests in ceremonies that took place atop the temple pyramids, their blood and still-beating hearts consecrated to the god, and their flesh cooked and eaten by the priests and the people. One of the main motives of Aztec wars was to capture prisoners to serve as sacrifices; they were called, ironically, "flower wars." Montezuma, as Great Speaker, was the chief priest of Huitzilopochtli, the servant of the god on behalf of his subjects.

But conquest tradition claimed that Montezuma was also devoted to Quetzalcoatl, the Feathered Serpent, the special deity of an earlier warrior people, the Toltecs, to whom the Aztec nobility traced their own ancestry. This tradition also recounted how Quetzalcoatl had returned to find his people so contented with their way of life and so intermingled with the native inhabitants that they refused to follow him. So he returned to the East once more, whence he had come. But the Aztecs were convinced that he would come again to reclaim their loyalty or that he would send someone in his stead.

On that November day of 1519 the stage was set for the most important confrontation in the entire story of the Spanish conquest of the New World.

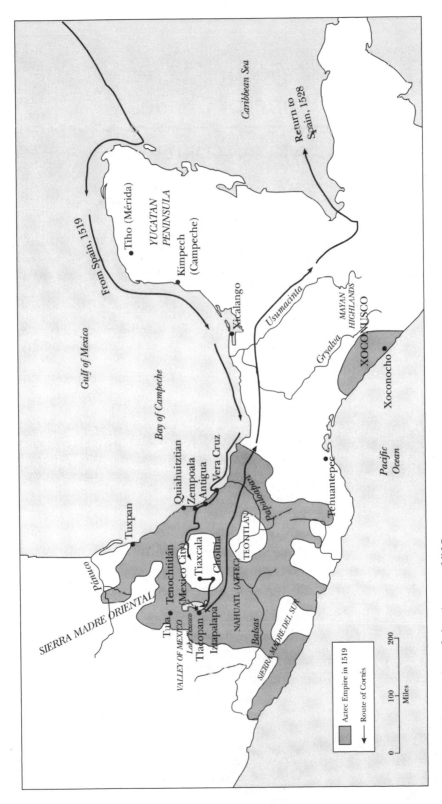

Cortés in the Empire of the Aztecs, 1519

The Second Letter
to Emperor Charles V

HERNÁN CORTÉS

There are several contemporary Spanish accounts of the first meeting and subsequent relations between Cortés and Montezuma. The most interesting and authoritative is that of Cortés himself, in the form of one of several detailed dispatch letters that he sent to Spain, to the Emperor Charles V, in whose name he claimed his conquests. The Second Letter, describing his dealings with Montezuma, was written less than a year after the events, and was dated October 30, 1520.

When we had passed this bridge Muteczuma himself came out to meet us with some two hundred nobles, all barefoot and dressed in some kind of uniform also very rich, in fact more so than the others. They came forward in two long lines keeping close to the walls of the street, which is very broad and fine and so straight that one can see from one end of it to the other, though it is some two-thirds of a league in length and lined on both sides with very beautiful, large houses, both private dwellings and temples. Muteczuma himself was borne along in the middle of the street with two lords one on his right hand and one on his left, being respectively the chief whom I described as coming out to meet me in a litter and the other, Muteczuma's brother, ruler of Iztapalapa, from which only that day we had set out. All three were dressed in similar fashion except that Muteczuma wore shoes whereas the others were barefoot. The two lords bore him along each by an arm, and as he drew near I dismounted and advanced alone to embrace, but the two lords prevented me from touching him, and they themselves made me the same obeisance as did their comrades, kissing the earth: which done, he commanded his brother who accompanied him to stay with me and take me by the arm, while he with the other lord went on a little way in front. After he had spoken to me all the other lords who were in the two long lines came up likewise in order one after the other, and then re-formed in line again. And while speaking to Muteczuma I took off a necklace of pearls and crystals which I was wearing and threw it round his neck; whereupon having proceeded some little way up the street a servant of his came back to me with two necklaces wrapped up in a napkin, made from the shells of sea snails, which are much prized by them; and from each necklace hung eight prawns fashioned very beautifully in gold some six inches in length. The messenger who brought them put them round my neck and we then continued up the street in the manner described until we came to a large and very handsome house which Muteczuma had prepared for our lodging. There he took me by the hand and led me to a large room opposite the patio by which we had entered, and seating me on a daïs very richly worked, for it was intended for royal use, he bade me await him there, and took his departure. After a short time, when all my company had found lodging, he returned with many various ornaments of gold, silver, and featherwork, and some five or six thousand cotton clothes, richly dyed and embroidered in various ways, and having made me a present of them he seated himself on another low bench which was placed next to mine, and addressed me in this manner:

"Long time have we been informed by the writings of our ancestors that neither myself nor any of those who inhabit this land are natives of it, but rather strangers who have come to it from foreign parts. We likewise know that from those parts our nation was led by a certain lord (to whom all were subject), and who then went back to his native land, where he remained so long delaying his return that at his coming those whom he had left had married the women of the land and had many children by them and had built themselves cities in which they lived, so that they would in no wise return to their own land nor acknowledge him as lord; upon which he left them. And we have always believed that among his descendants one would surely come to subject this land and us as rightful vassals. Now seeing the regions from which you say you come, which is from where the sun rises, and the news you tell of this great king and ruler who sent you hither, we believe and hold it certain that he is our natural lord: especially in that you say he has long had knowledge of us.[2] Wherefore be certain that we will obey you and hold you as lord in place of that great lord of whom you speak, in which service there shall be neither slackness nor deceit: and throughout all the land, that is to say all that I rule, you may command anything you desire, and it shall be obeyed and done, and all that we have is at your will and pleasure. And since you are in your own land and house, rejoice and take your leisure from the fatigues of your journey and the battles you have fought; for I am well informed of all those that you have been forced to engage in on your way here from Potonchan, as also that the natives of Cempoal and Tlascala have told you many evil things of me; but believe no more than what you see with your own eyes, and especially not words from the lips of those who are my enemies, who were formerly my vassals and on your coming rebelled

---

[2]This "knowledge" on the part of the Spanish emperor was, of course, simply made up by Cortés.

against me and said these things in order to find favour with you: I am aware, moreover, that they have told you that the walls of my houses were of gold as was the matting on my floors and other household articles, even that I was a god and claimed to be so, and other like matters. As for the houses, you see that they are of wood, stones and earth." Upon this he lifted his clothes showing me his body, and said: "and you see that I am of flesh and blood like yourself and everyone else, mortal and tangible."

Grasping with his hands his arms and other parts of his body, he continued: "You see plainly how they have lied. True I have a few articles of gold which have remained to me from my forefathers, and all that I have is yours at any time that you may desire it. I am now going to my palace where I live. Here you will be provided with all things necessary for you and your men, and let nothing be done amiss seeing that you are in your own house and land."

I replied to all that he said, satisfying him in those things which seemed expedient, especially in having him believe that your Majesty was he whom they had long expected, and with that he bade farewell. On his departure we were very well regaled with great store of chickens, bread, fruit, and other necessities, particularly household ones. And in this wise I continued six days very well provided with all that was necessary and visited by many of the principal men of the city. . . .

Having passed six days, then, in the great city of Tenochtitlan, invincible Prince, and having seen something of its marvels, though little in comparison with what there was to be seen and examined, I considered it essential both from my observation of the city and the rest of the land that its ruler should be in my power and no longer entirely free; to the end that he might in nowise change his will and intent to serve your Majesty, more especially as we Spaniards are somewhat intolerant and stiff-necked, and should he get across with us he would be powerful enough to do us great damage, even to blot out all memory of us in the land; and in the second place, could I once get him in my power all the other provinces subject to him would come more promptly to the knowledge and service of your Majesty, as indeed afterwards happened. I decided to capture him and place him in the lodging where I was, which was extremely strong. . . .

Cortés's stratagem was to accuse Montezuma of an attack on his men that had occurred earlier, along the way, at the hands of some of his subject chiefs. Montezuma immediately summoned those chiefs to account for themselves, but in the meantime, Cortés insisted that Montezuma accompany him to the quarters provided for him, under house arrest. Amazingly, Montezuma agreed! A few days later the guilty chiefs were taken and executed.

Muteczuma proclaimed an assembly of all the chiefs of the neighbouring towns and districts; and on their coming together he sent for me to mount to the platform where he already was and proceeded to address them in this manner: "Brothers and friends, you know well that for many years you, your fathers and your grandfathers have been subjects and vassals to me and to my forefathers, and have ever been well treated and held in due esteem both by them and me, as likewise you yourselves have done what it behooves good and loyal vassals to do for their lords; moreover I believe you will recollect hearing from your ancestors that we are not natives of this land, but that they came to it from another land far off, being led hither by a powerful lord whose vassals they all were; after many years he returned to find our forefathers already settled in the land married to native wives and with many children by them in such wise that they never wished to go back with him nor acknowledge him as lord of the land, and upon this he returned saying that he would come again himself or send another with such power as to force them to re-enter his service. And you know well that we have always looked to this and from what the captain has told us of the king and lord who sent him hither, and the direction from which he came I hold it certain as ye also must hold it, that he is the lord whom we have looked to, especially in that he declares he already had knowledge of us in his own land. Therefore while our ancestors did not that which was due to their lord, let us not so offend now, but rather give praise to the gods that in our times that which was long expected is come to pass. And I earnestly beg of you, since all that I have said is notorious to everyone of you, that as you have up till now obeyed and held me as your sovereign lord, so from henceforth you will obey and hold this great king as your natural lord, for such he is, and in particular this captain in his place: and all those tributes and services which up to this time you have paid to me, do you now pay to him, for I also hold myself bound to do him service in all that he shall require me: and over and above doing that which is right and necessary you will be doing me great pleasure."

All this he spoke to them weeping, with such sighs and tears as no man ever wept more, and likewise all those chieftains who heard him wept so that for a long space of time they could make no reply. And I can assure your Majesty that there was not one among the Spaniards who on hearing this speech was not filled with compassion. After some time when their tears were somewhat dried they replied that they held him as their lord and had promised to do whatever he should bid them, and hence that for that reason and the one he had given them they were content to do what he said, and from that time offered themselves as vassals to your royal Majesty, promising severally and collectively to carry out whatever should be required of them in your Majesty's royal name as loyal and obedient vassals, and duly to render him all such tributes and services as were formerly rendered to Muteczuma, with all other things whatsoever that may be commanded them in your Majesty's name. All this took place in the presence of the public notary and was duly drawn up by him in legal form and witnessed in the presence of many Spaniards. . . .

From this point, however, the situation began to deteriorate. The Spaniards had discovered vast treasuries of gold in the city. There was an incident in which they attacked the Aztecs during a religious festival and killed a large number of priests and nobles. The Aztec nobility, now led by Montezuma's brother, turned against the Spaniards and besieged them in their quarters.

Muteczuma, who was still a prisoner together with his son and many other nobles who had been taken on our first entering the city, requested to be taken out on to the flat roof of the fortress, where he would speak to the leader of the people and make them stop fighting. I ordered him to be brought forth and as he mounted a breastwork that extended beyond the fortress, wishing to speak to the people who were fighting there, a stone from one of their slings struck him on the head so severely that he died three days later: when this happened I ordered two of the other Indian prisoners to take out his dead body on their shields to the people, and I know not what became of it; save only this that the fighting did not cease but rather increased in intensity every day.

Cortés and his men at this point were forced to withdraw from the city with many casualties, but he recovered and, against impossible odds, defeated the Aztec army sent after him. After enlisting more Tlaxcalan allies, he returned and besieged the city of Tenochtitlan, which finally surrendered on August 13, 1521. There was never again to be serious native resistance to Spanish rule.

An Heroic Cortés

WILLIAM H. PRESCOTT

The first modern scholar to deal with Cortés's epic achievement was the American historian William H. Prescott in his monumental History of the Conquest of Mexico *in 1843. In spite of the daunting handicap of nearly total blindness, Prescott worked tirelessly at his research and writing. Fortunately he was a man of considerable means who could afford not only the enormous volume of research materials he required but the secretaries necessary to read to him and assist in his research.*

Cortés was the hero of Prescott's account. He saw Cortés as the embodiment of the age of chivalry. "Of all the band of adventurous cavaliers," he wrote, "whom Spain, in the sixteenth century, sent forth on the career of discovery and conquest, there was none more deeply filled with the spirit of romantic enterprise than Hernando Cortés."[3]

Thus pressed by enemies without and by factions within, that leader was found, as usual, true to himself. Circumstances so appalling as would have paralysed a common mind, only stimulated his to higher action, and drew forth all its resources. He combined what is most rare, singular coolness and constancy of purpose, with a spirit of enterprise that might well be called romantic. His presence of mind did not now desert him. He calmly surveyed his condition, and weighed the difficulties which surrounded him, before coming to a decision. Independently of the hazard of a retreat in the face of a watchful and desperate foe, it was a deep mortification to surrender up the city, where he had so long lorded it as a master; to abandon the rich treasures which he had secured to himself and his followers; to forgo the very means by which he had hoped to propitiate the favour of his sovereign, and secure an amnesty for his irregular proceedings. This, he well knew, must, after all, be dependent on success. To fly now was to acknowledge himself further removed from the conquest than ever. What a close was this to a career so auspiciously begun! What a contrast to his magnificent vaunts! What a triumph would it afford to his enemies! The governor of Cuba would be amply revenged.

But, if such humiliating reflections crowded on his mind, the alternative of remaining, in his present crippled condition, seemed yet more desperate. With his men daily diminishing in strength and numbers, their provisions reduced so low that a small daily ration of bread was all the sustenance afforded to the soldier under his extraordinary fatigues, with the breaches every day widening in his feeble fortifications, with his ammunition, in fine, nearly expended, it would be impossible to maintain the place much longer—and none but men of iron constitutions and tempers, like the Spaniards, could have held it out so long—against the enemy. The chief embarrassment was as to the time and manner in which it would be expedient to evacuate the city. The best route seemed to be that of Tlacopan (Tacuba). For the causeway, the most dangerous part of the road, was but two miles long in that direction, and would therefore place the fugitives much

---

[3]William H. Prescott, *History of the Conquest of Mexico* (Philadelphia: McKay, 1894), vol. III, p. 297.

sooner than either of the other great avenues on terra firma. Before his final departure, however, he proposed to make another sally in that direction, in order to reconnoitre the ground, and, at the same time, divert the enemy's attention from his real purpose by a show of active operations.

For some days his workmen had been employed in constructing a military machine of his own invention. It was called a *manta,* and was contrived somewhat on the principle of the mantelets used in the wars of the Middle Ages. It was, however, more complicated, consisting of a tower made of light beams and planks, having two chambers, one over the other. These were to be filled with musketeers, and the sides were provided with loop-holes, through which a fire could be kept up on the enemy. The great advantage proposed by this contrivance was, to afford a defence to the troops against the missiles hurled from the terraces. These machines, three of which were made, rested on rollers, and were provided with strong ropes, by which they were to be dragged along the streets by the Tlascalan auxiliaries.

The Mexicans gazed with astonishment on this warlike machinery, and, as the rolling fortresses advanced, belching forth fire and smoke from their entrails, the enemy, incapable of making an impression on those within, fell back in dismay. By bringing the *mantas* under the walls of the houses, the Spaniards were enabled to fire with effect on the mischievous tenants of the *azoteas,* and when this did not silence them, by letting a ladder, or light drawbridge, fall on the roof from the top of the *manta,* they opened a passage to the terrace, and closed with the combatants hand to hand. They could not, however, thus approach the higher buildings, from which the Indian warriors threw down such heavy masses of stone and timber as dislodged the planks that covered the machines, or, thundering against their sides, shook the frail edifices to their foundations, threatening all within with indiscriminate ruin. Indeed, the success of the experiment was doubtful, when the intervention of a canal put a stop to their further progress.

The Spaniards now found the assertion of their enemies to well confirmed. The bridge which traversed the opening had been demolished; and, although the canals which intersected the city were in general of no great width or depth, the removal of the bridges not only impeded the movements of the general's clumsy machines, but effectually disconcerted those of his cavalry. Resolving to abandon the *mantas,* he gave orders to fill up the chasm with stone, timber, and other rubbish drawn from the ruined buildings, and to make a new passage-way for the army. While this labour was going on, the Aztec slingers and archers on the other side of the opening kept up a galling discharge on the Christians, the more defenceless from the nature of their occupation. When the work was completed, and a safe passage secured, the Spanish cavaliers rode briskly against the enemy, who, unable to resist the shock of the steel-clad column, fell back with

precipitation to where another canal afforded a similar strong position for defence.

There were no less than seven of these canals, intersecting the
great street of Tlacopan, and at every one the same scene was renewed, the Mexicans making a gallant stand, and inflicting some loss,
at each, on their persevering antagonists. These operations consumed two days, when, after incredible toil, the Spanish general had
the satisfaction to find the line of communication completely reestablished through the whole length of the avenue, and the principal
bridges placed under strong detachments of infantry. At this juncture, when he had driven the foe before him to the furthest extremity
of the street, where it touches on the causeway, he was informed that
the Mexicans, disheartened by their reverses, desired to open a parley
with him respecting the terms of an accommodation, and that their
chiefs awaited his return for that purpose at the fortress. Overjoyed
at the intelligence, he instantly rode back, attended by Alvarado,
Sandoval, and about sixty of the cavaliers, to his quarters.

The Mexicans proposed that he should release the two priests
captured in the temple, who might be the bearers of his terms, and
serve as agents for conducting the negotiation. They were accordingly sent with the requisite instructions to their countrymen. But
they did not return. The whole was an artifice of the enemy, anxious
to procure the liberation of their religious leaders, one of whom was
their *teoteuctli*, or high priest, whose presence was indispensable in the
probable event of a new coronation.

Cortés, meanwhile, relying on the prospects of a speedy arrangement, was hastily taking some refreshment with his officers, after the
fatigues of the day, when he received the alarming tidings that the
enemy were in arms again, with more fury than ever; that they had
overpowered the detachments posted under Alvarado at three of the
bridges, and were busily occupied in demolishing them. Stung with
shame at the facility with which he had been duped by his wily foe, or
rather by his own sanguine hopes, Cortés threw himself into the
saddle, and, followed by his brave companions, galloped back at full
speed to the scene of action. The Mexicans recoiled before the impetuous charge of the Spaniards. The bridges were again restored; and
Cortés and his chivalry rode down the whole extent of the great
street, driving the enemy, like frightened deer, at the points of their
lances. But before he could return on his steps, he had the mortification to find that the indefatigable foe, gathering from the adjoining
lanes and streets, had again closed on his infantry, who, worn down
by fatigue, were unable to maintain their position, at one of the
principal bridges. New swarms of warriors now poured in on all sides,
overwhelming the little band of Christian cavaliers with a storm of
stones, darts, and arrows, which rattled like hail on their armour and
on that of their well-barbed horses. Most of the missiles, indeed,

glanced harmless from the good panoplies of steel, or thick quilted cotton; but, now and then, one better aimed penetrated the joints of the harness, and stretched the rider on the ground.

The confusion became greater around the broken bridge. Some of the horsemen were thrown into the canal, and their steeds floundered wildly about without a rider. Cortés himself, at this crisis, did more than any other to cover the retreat of his followers. While the bridge was repairing, he plunged boldly into the midst of the barbarians, striking down an enemy at every vault of his charger, cheering on his own men, and spreading terror through the ranks of his opponents by the well-known sound of his battle-cry. Never did he display greater hardihood, or more freely expose his person, emulating, says an old chronicler, the feats of the Roman Cocles. In this way he stayed the tide of assailants, till the last man had crossed the bridge, when, some of the planks having given way, he was compelled to leap a chasm of full six feet in width, amidst a cloud of missiles, before he could place himself in safety. A report ran through the army that the general was slain. It soon spread through the city, to the great joy of the Mexicans, and reached the fortress, where the besieged were thrown into no less consternation. But, happily for them, it was false. He, indeed, received two severe contusions on the knee, but in other respects remained uninjured. At no time, however, had he been in such extreme danger; and his escape, and that of his companions, were esteemed little less than a miracle.

The coming of night dispersed the Indian battalions, which, vanishing like birds of ill-omen from the field, left the well-contested pass in possession of the Spaniards. They returned, however, with none of the joyous feelings of conquerors to their citadel, but with slow step and dispirited, with weapons hacked, armour battered, and fainting under the loss of blood, fasting, and fatigue. In this condition they had yet to learn the tidings of a fresh misfortune in the death of Montezuma.

The Indian monarch had rapidly declined, since he had received his injury, sinking, however, quite as much under the anguish of a wounded spirit, as under disease. He continued in the same moody state of insensibility as that already described; holding little communication with those around him, deaf to consolation, obstinately rejecting all medical remedies, as well as nourishment. Perceiving his end approach, some of the cavaliers present in the fortress, whom the kindness of his manners had personally attached to him, were anxious to save the soul of the dying prince from the sad doom of those who perish in the darkness of unbelief. They accordingly waited on him, with Father Olmedo at their head, and in the most earnest manner implored him to open his eyes to the error of his creed, and consent to be baptised. But Montezuma—whatever may have been suggested to the contrary—seems never to have faltered in his hereditary faith, or to have contemplated becoming an apostate; for surely he merits that name in its most odious application, who, whether Christian or pagan, renounces his religion without conviction of its falsehood. Indeed, it was a too implicit reliance on its oracles, which had led him to give such easy confidence to the Spaniards. His intercourse with them had, doubtless, not sharpened his desire to embrace their communion; and the calamities of his country he might consider as sent by his gods to punish him for his hospitality to those who had desecrated and destroyed their shrines.

When Father Olmedo, therefore, kneeling at his side, with the uplifted crucifix, affectionately besought him to embrace the sign of man's redemption, he coldly repulsed the priest, exclaiming, "I have but a few moments to live; and will not at this hour desert the faith of my fathers." One thing, however, seemed to press heavily on Montezuma's mind. This was the fate of his children, especially of three daughters, whom he had by his two wives; for there were certain rites of marriage, which distinguished the lawful wife from the concubine. Calling Cortés to his bedside, he earnestly commended these children to his care, as "the most precious jewels that he could leave him." He besought the general to interest his master, the emperor, in their behalf, and to see that they should not be left destitute, but be allowed some portion of their rightful inheritance. "Your lord will do this," he concluded, "if it were only for the friendly offices I have rendered the Spaniards, and for the love I have shown them,—though it has brought me to this condition! But for this I bear them no ill-will." Such, according to Cortés himself, were the words of the dying monarch. Not long after, on the 30th of June, 1520, he expired in the arms of some of his own nobles, who still remained faithful in their attendance on his person. . . .

A New Explanation

J. H. ELLIOTT AND ANTHONY PAGDEN

In the whole account of the conquest of Mexico, nothing is more puzzling than the behavior of Montezuma. He was in the prime of life, in secure and undisputed control of an aggressive, warlike empire that could field hundreds of thousands of soldiers on his order alone. He had a considerable reputation for military leadership himself. Yet he was virtually paralyzed by the course of events.

The explanation that is presented is that Montezuma profoundly believed that Cortés was the agent of the Aztec god Quetzalcoatl and that Cortés acted on behalf of the god, incarnate in the person of his sovereign, Charles V. But was this the case? In the critical notes to the latest and best edition of the Cortés letters, the editor, Anthony Pagden, and the author of the introduction, J. H. Elliott, offer an alternative explanation. Elliott argues that Cortés's letters were not only reports on the events of the conquest but carefully crafted political apologies as well. He notes, quite correctly, that Cortés was operating without any real official authorization. He had been sent by Don Diego Velásquez, the Governor of Cuba, to investigate the loss of a small exploration fleet and to rescue any Spaniards being held captive in Yucatan. He was also authorized to explore and trade—but he had no permission to colonize. Yet he had founded the town-settlement of Vera Cruz, in large part so that he could be authorized by the town government (which was himself) to undertake an expedition to the interior. He had set out on that expedition on the basis of this contrived and specious authority.

Cortés had therefore defied his own immediate superior, Velázquez, and had potentially antagonized Velázquez's powerful friends at Court. He knew well enough the grave risks he was running. But to Cortés and his friends . . . the risks paled before the attractions of the anticipated prize. Nothing could more quickly obliterate the stigma of treachery and rebellion than a brilliant military success and the acquisition of fabulous riches. If new peoples were won for the Faith, and rich new lands won for the Crown, there was reason to hope that the original defiance of Velázquez would be regarded as no more than a peccadillo, and that Velázquez's friends and protectors would be silenced by a *fait accompli.* . . .

Success in arms, and resort to the highest authority of all, that of the king himself—these were the aims of Cortés and his fellow conspirators as they prepared in April, 1519, to compound their defiance of Velázquez by a landing which would mark the real beginning of their attempt to conquer an empire. They were concerned, like all conquistadors, with fame, riches, and honor. But behind the willful defiance of the governor of Cuba there existed, at least in Cortés's mind, a philosophy of conquest and colonization which made his action something more than an attempt at self-aggrandizement at the expense of Velázquez. He entertained, like so many Castilians of his generation, an exalted view of the royal service, and of Castile's divinely appointed mission. Both the divine and the royal favor would shine on those who cast down idols, extirpated pagan superstitions, and won new lands and peoples for God and Castile. . . .

But what seemed plausible enough in Mexico was bound to seem highly implausible in Cuba and at the Spanish Court. Clearly it was essential to win support in Spain for an action which Fonseca[4] and

---

[4]Juan Rodríguez de Fonseca, Bishop of Burgos, was Velásquez's relative and patron at the Spanish court and the royal councillor principally responsible for the affairs of the Indies during the previous reign.

his friends would certainly represent to the king as an act of open
rebellion. . . .

Everything now depended on the successful presentation of his
case at Court, where the Fonseca group would certainly do all in its
power to destroy him. If possible, Charles and his advisers must be
reached and won over before they had time to learn from Velázquez
himself of Cortés's act of rebellion. . . .

The first letter from Mexico, then, was essentially a political document, speaking for Cortés in the name of his army, and designed to
appeal directly to the Crown over the heads of Velázquez and his
friends in the Council of the Indies. Cortés was now involved in a
desperate race against time. Montejo and Puertocarrero[5] left for Spain
on July 26, 1519, with their bundle of letters and the gold; and unless,
or until, they could persuade Charles to sanction retrospectively the
behavior of Cortés and his men, Cortés was technically a traitor, liable
to arrest and persecution at the hands of an irate governor of Cuba,
fully empowered to act in the royal name. The danger was acute, and
the blow could fall at any time, perhaps even from within Mexico itself.
For there was still a strong group of Velázquez partisans in the expedition, and these men would do all they could to sabotage Cortés's plans.
But Cortés, who had his spies posted, was well aware of the dangers.
The friends of the governor of Cuba appear to have been plotting to
send him warning of the mission of Montejo and Puertocarrero, so that
he could intercept their ship. The plot was discovered, the conspirators
arrested, and two of them, Juan Escudero and Diego Cermeño, put to
death. . . . As long as Cortés could command the loyalties of his army—
and this would ultimately depend on his ability to capture and distrib-
ute the fabulous riches of Motecuçoma's empire—he was now reasonably safe from subversion within the ranks. . . .

Velázquez began to organize an army to be sent to Mexico against
Cortés. . . . At a time when a smallpox epidemic was raging in Cuba,
Velázquez felt unable to lead his army in person, and handed over the
command to one of his more reliable but less intelligent friends,
Pánfilo de Narváez. The army, twice the size of that of Cortés, set sail
from Cuba on March 5, 1520. . . . During the autumn and winter of
1519, therefore, at the time when Cortés was securing the submission
of Motecuçoma and had established himself precariously in Tenochtitlan, he was faced with the prospect of a military confrontation with
his immediate superior, the governor of Cuba. . . .

The outcome was likely to be determined on the battlefield, in an
internecine struggle of Spaniard against Spaniard, which could well
jeopardize and even destroy Cortés's uncertain hold over the Aztec
empire. But in the Spanish monarchy of the sixteenth century a

---

[5]Cortés's agents.

military solution could never be final. Legality was paramount, and the key to legality lay with the king.

Everything therefore turned on the success of Montejo and Puerto-carrero in Spain. They duly reached Seville at the beginning of November, 1519, only to find their country on the verge of revolt. Charles had been elected Holy Roman Emperor on June 28. Once elected, his immediate aim was to extract the largest possible subsidies from the Cortés[6] of the various Spanish kingdoms, and then to leave for Germany. When the procuradores[7] arrived in Seville, the emperor was still in Barcelona, heavily preoccupied with plans for his departure; and the Castilian cities were beginning to voice their dissatisfaction at the prospect of heavy new fiscal demands and an absentee king.

At this particular moment the chances of winning the emperor's support for a still-unknown adventurer on the other side of the world hardly looked very promising. . . . From Barcelona they [Montejo and Puertocarrero] moved across Spain in the tracks of the emperor, finally catching up with him at Tordesillas, near Valladolid, early in March. Here, seven months after leaving Vera Cruz, they could at last petition the emperor in person to confirm Cortés in his position as captain general and *justicia mayor*. . . .

Meanwhile, in Mexico, Cortés had seized the initiative, divided his forces, and moved to intercept Narváez's army. This was his situation at the time of the massacre of the Aztec lords at the religious festival. He defeated Narváez, conscripted the bulk of Narváez's men to his own cause, and returned to Tenochtitlan.

Narváez's defeat left the governor of Cuba a ruined and broken man. Cortés had defeated Velázquez—geographically his nearest enemy— but he was still without news from the Spanish Court. Moreover, his march to the coast to defeat Narváez had fatally weakened the Spanish position in Tenochtitlan. When Cortés got back to the capital on June 25 it was already too late. The behavior of Alvarado and his men in Tenochtitlan during Cortés's absence had precipitated an Indian uprising, and neither Cortés's troops, nor the diminished authority of Motecuçoma, proved sufficient to quell the revolt. Motecuçoma, rejected by his own subjects, died his strange death on June 30. During the course of the same night, the *noche triste*, the Spaniards made their famous retreat from Tenochtitlan. Cortés might have defeated the

---

[6]The *Cortes* were the legislative bodies of the Spanish kingdoms.
[7]The *procuradores* were the "agents" whom Cortés had sent from Mexico to the Spanish court.

governor of Cuba, but he had also lost the empire he had promised to Charles.

It was during the autumn months of 1520, while Cortés was preparing for the siege and reconquest of Tenochtitlan, that he wrote the Second Letter. This letter, like its predecessor from Vera Cruz, is both more and less than a straightforward narrative of events, for it, too, has an essentially political purpose. Cortés, when writing it, was influenced by three major considerations. In the first place, he still did not know what decision, if any, had been reached in Spain on his plea for retrospective authorization of his unconventional proceedings. In the second place, he had by now heard the news of Charles's election to the imperial throne. Finally, he had won a new empire for Charles and had proceeded to lose it. His letter, therefore, had to be so angled as to suggest that, at the most, he had suffered no more than a temporary setback . . . and that he would soon be in a position to render the most signal new services to a king who had now become the mightiest monarch in the world.

With these considerations in mind, Cortés carefully contrived his letter to convey a predominantly "imperial" theme. Its opening paragraph contained a graceful allusion to Charles's new empire in Germany, which was skillfully coupled with a reference to a second empire across the Atlantic, to which he could claim an equal title. This reference set the tone for the document as a whole. The fact that Cortés was no longer at this moment the effective master of the Mexican empire was no doubt inconvenient, but could be played down as far as possible. For the thesis of the letter was that Charles was already the *legal* emperor of this great new empire, and that Cortés would soon recover for him what was rightfully his.

The entire story of the march to Tenochtitlan and the imprisonment of Motecuçoma was related in such a way as to support this general thesis. Motecuçoma, by his speeches and his actions, was portrayed as a man who voluntarily recognized the sovereignty of Charles V, and voluntarily surrendered his empire into his hands. Whether Motecuçoma did indeed speak anything like the words which Cortés attributes to him will probably never be known for certain. Some passages in his two speeches contain so many Christian overtones as to be unbelievable coming from a pagan Aztec. Others, and in particular the identification of the Spaniards with the former rulers of Mexico wrongly banished from their land, may be an ingenious fabrication by Cortés, or may conceivably reflect certain beliefs and legends, which Motecuçoma himself may or may not have accepted. Whatever its origins, the story of the expected return of lords from the east was essential to Cortés's grand design, for it enabled him to allege and explain a "voluntary" submission of Motecuçoma, and the "legal" transfer of his empire—an empire far removed from the jurisdiction of the Audiencia of Santo Domingo and from the

Caribbean world of Diego Colón[8] and Velázquez—to its rightful ruler, Charles V.

Motecuçoma's death at the hands of his own subjects left Charles the undisputed master of the field. It was unfortunate that the Mexicans were now in open rebellion—a situation which could only be ascribed to the nefarious activities of the governor of Cuba, acting through his agent Pánfilo de Narváez. But although Narváez's invasion had nearly brought disaster, the tide had now been turned, because God was on the emperor's side. With divine help, and through the agency of that most loyal of lieutenants, Hernán Cortés, the land would soon be recovered; and what better name could be bestowed upon it than that of New Spain?

———————————

Anthony Pagden, the editor of the text, turns more specifically to the inexplicable behavior of Montezuma. He begins with the speech that Montezuma made as soon as Cortés and his men had been settled in their quarters in Tenochtitlan.

———————————

Both this speech and the one that follows . . . would seem to be apocryphal. Motecuçoma could never have held the views with which Cortés accredits him. Eulalia Guzmán (*Relaciones de Hernán Cortés*, I: 279 ff.) has pointed out the Biblical tone of both these passages and how their phraseology reflects the language of the *Siete Partidas*.[9] Cortés is casting Motecuçoma into the role of a sixteenth-century Spaniard welcoming his "natural lord," who in this case has been accredited with a vaguely Messianic past. Indeed the whole setting has a mythopoeic ring: Motecuçoma is made to raise his garments and to declare, "See that I am flesh and blood like you and all other men, and I am mortal and substantial," words reminiscent of those of Jesus to his disciples, "A spirit hath not flesh and bones as ye see me have" and of Paul and Barnabas to Lystra, "We also are men of like passions with you." (J. H. Elliott, "The Mental World of Hernán Cortés," pp. 51–53). There is evidence, however, that Motecuçoma did believe himself to be the living incarnation of Huitzilopochtli (see Durán, chaps. LIII–LIV; and Sahagún, bk. IV, chap. 10), and certainly such an identification would not have been alien to Mexica religious thought. Despite the absurdity of attributing such words and gestures to an Amerindian, it seems likely that Cortés's account of the events is based on partially understood information about the native mythologies. A number of modern commentators seem to believe the

———————————

[8]The son of Christopher Columbus, who had inherited the title of Admiral from his father.

[9]This is a thirteenth-century compilation of Castilian law.

thesis of Motecuçoma's speeches, namely, that the Mexica lived in fear of a vengeful Messiah, who would one day return from the east, and mistook Cortés for his captain. Later this Messiah, who in the words attributed to Motecuçoma is only a legendary tribal chieftain, becomes Quetzalcoatl, the "Plumed Serpent" lord of Tula, whose story as told by Sahagún bears some resemblance to the Cortés-Motecuçoma version of Mexica prehistory. There is, however, no preconquest tradition which places Quetzalcoatl in this role and it seems possible therefore that it was elaborated by Sahagún . . . from informants who themselves had partially lost contact with their traditional tribal histories.

The identification of Cortés with Quetzalcoatl is also the work of Sahagún (see bk. XII, chap. 4, pp. 11 ff.). Don Antonio de Mendoza, first viceroy of New Spain, however, said that Cortés was mistaken for Huitzilopochtli (Elliott, *op cit.,* p. 53), traditionally associated with the south, and about whom no Messianic legend is known to exist. It is possible that Mendoza was told this by Cortés himself, and "Uchilobos" was the only Mexica deity Cortés could name.

Cortés may have picked up a local legend and embellished it in an attempt to prove that Motecuçoma was himself an usurper and therefore had no right to the lands he ruled (cf. the Third Letter, n. 3). . . .

Where Cortés first heard the story is uncertain. Cervantes de Salazar (bk. 111, chap. 49) and Bernal Díaz (chap. 79) both say that it was in Tlaxcala but both are very vague (see also Muñoz Camargo, pp. 184–185). Professor Guzmán says that a similar legend was common in the Antilles. But perhaps the first contact was made in Yucatán, where a foliated cross appears on a number of Mayan buildings and seems to have been associated with Quetzalcoatl, called Kukulcan in Maya. . . . If it is unlikely that Motecuçoma took the Spaniards to be the vicars-on-earth of the "Plumed Serpent," it is even more unlikely that it would have in any way affected his attitude toward Cortés. Besides the improbability of any leader acting on a prophecy, Quetzalcoatl's cult was largely confined to the lowland regions beyond Popocatepetl and Iztaccihuatl and appears to have held little sway in central Mexico itself (*Códice Borgia*, 1: 67). Its cult center was Cholula, which, when it came under Mexica rule, was granted no special respect and even forced to venerate Huitzilopochtli. Nor, it might be added, did Cholula accord to Cortés the welcome he might be expected to receive as Quetzalcoatl's lieutenant. Motecuçoma was himself a priest of Huitzilopochtli; and, secure in the power of the tutelary deity of his race, it does not seem likely that he would have resigned his powers to the supposed avatars of an apotheosized Toltec chieftain.

The attitude of the Mexica toward the Spaniards can best be explained by the traditional immunity from harm enjoyed by all ambassadors—and Cortés claimed to be an ambassador albeit without an embassy. It is also possible that once Motecuçoma had realized Cortés's intentions, he deliberately drew him inland, not understanding that the sea could be a supply route for the Spaniards.... Motecuçoma may well have underestimated the Spanish powers of diplomacy and the state of unrest within his own empire. It was unfortunate for him ... that the Spaniards were in a position to play one Indian against another....

Questions for Review and Study

1. What were Cortés's hidden motives in his letter to Charles V detailing his conquest of Montezuma's empire?
2. How much credence do you place in the story that Montezuma and the Aztecs believed Cortés to be the agent of the god Quetzalcoatl? Explain.
3. How do you account for the surprising ease with which Cortés accomplished the conquest of Mexico?
4. Relate Cortés's activities upon arrival in Tenochtitlan.
5. Describe Cortés's preparation for departure from Tenochtitlan in the late summer of 1520.

Questions for Comparison

1. Compare Cortés and Da Vinci as expressions of the Renaissance spirit. How far removed were these men from the medieval concern for a unified Christian order? In what ways did each man still belong to the Middle Ages? To what degree did Christianity inspire their work? How did each display a "Faustian" exertion of the human will? What explicit or implied notions of progress are evident in their respective projects? Whose feats shed a more favorable light on Western culture?

Suggestions for Further Reading

In addition to *Hernándo Cortés*, translated and edited by J. Bayard Morris, which is excerpted in this chapter, there are two other editions: *Conquest*, with an introduction and commentary by Irwin R. Blacker and edited by Harry M. Rosen, and *Hernán Cortés*, translated and edited by A. R. Pagden with an introduction by J. H. Elliott, also excerpted in this chapter. Two other contemporary Spanish accounts of the conquest are recommended. *Cortés* is by Francisco López de Gómara. Although Gómara never actually visited the New World, he had access to Cortés's own papers and recollections. The other account, *The Bernal Díaz Chronicles,* is by one of the soldiers on the expedition, written many years later from his recollections (translated and edited by Albert Idell); another edition is Bernal Díaz del Castillo, *The Discovery and Conquest of Mexico, 1517–1521.* A contemporary Indian work is *1547–1577, A History of Ancient Mexico,* by Fray Bernardino de Sahagún. This is actually not a history but an account of the Aztec religion; it is, furthermore, largely a series of selections from the much more comprehensive edition of Fray Bernardino de Sahagún's *Florentine Codex,* edited by Arthur J. O. Anderson and Charles E. Dibble, a massive work in thirteen parts. The account of Cortés and Montezuma occurs in Part XIII, No. 14.

Of the modern accounts of the dramatic confrontation between Aztec and Spaniard, Montezuma and Cortés, the best is by R. C. Padden, *The Hummingbird and the Hawk.* A much less substantial and analytical popular work is *Cortés and Montezuma,* by Maurice Collis. An earlier work whose author tried to make some of the same analyses as Padden did is *Religious Aspects of the Conquest of Mexico,* by Charles S. Braden.

The standard modern biography of Cortés is by Salvador de Madariaga, *Hernán Cortés.* There is also a 1955 edition of this work, published by Henry Regnery Company of Chicago. A brief, popular, but competent biography is William Weber Johnson's *Cortés.* The only substantial modern biography of Montezuma is by C. A. Burland; his *Montezuma* is a brilliantly written if somewhat fictionalized account but solidly based on the standard sources. The masterwork on the entire history of the period is William H. Prescott's three-volume *History of the Conquest of Mexico.* There is also a one-volume abridgement of this work, *A History of the Conquest of Mexico,* dealing only with the career of Cortés.

Of the many works on the Aztecs themselves, probably the best general history is *The Aztecs,* by Nigel Davies. Rudolf A. M. van Zantwijk's *The Aztec Arrangement* is a detailed but somewhat difficult book on Aztec social organization by a great European anthropologist. *Aztecs* is Inga Clendinnen's attempt to reconstruct the social life and customs of the Aztecs on the eve of the Spanish conquest.

Two recent books are especially recommended. Richard L. Marks's *The Great Adventurer and the Fate of Aztec Mexico* is an excellent, evenhanded, up-to-date popular history. And *Conquest,* by Hugh Thomas, is the best and most comprehensive study since Prescott. (Titles with an asterisk are out of print.)

Braden, Charles S. *Religious Aspects of the Conquest of Mexico.* Durham, N.C.: Duke University Press, 1930.

Burland, C. A. *Montezuma, Lord of the Aztecs.* New York: Putnam, 1973.*

Clendinnen, Inga. *Aztecs: An Interpretation.* Cambridge: Cambridge University Press, 1991.

Collis, Maurice. *Cortés and Montezuma*. New York: Harcourt, Brace, 1954.*

Cortés, Hernándo. *Conquest: Dispatches of Cortéz from the New World*. Ed. Harry M. Rosen, with intro. and commentary by Irwin R. Blacker. New York: Grosset and Dunlap, 1962.*

———. *Hernán Cortés: Letters from Mexico*. Trans. and ed. A. R. Pagden, with intro. by J. H. Elliot. New York: Grossman, 1971.

———. *Hernándo Cortés: Five Letters*. Trans. and ed. J. Bayard Morris. New York: Norton, 1960.

Davies, Nigel. *The Aztecs: A History*. London: Macmillan, 1973.

De Gómara, Francisco López. *Cortés: The Life of the Conqueror by His Secretary*. Trans. and ed. Lesley Byrd Simpson. Berkeley and Los Angeles: University of California Press, 1964.

De Madariaga, Salvador. *Hernán Cortés, Conqueror of Mexico*. New York: Macmillan, 1941.

De Sahagún, Fray Bernardino. *1547–1577, A History of Ancient Mexico*. Trans. Fanny R. Bandelier. Glorieta, N.M.: The Rio Grande Press, 1976.

———. *Florentine Codex: General History of the Things of New Spain*. Ed. Arthur J. O. Anderson and Charles E. Dibble. Santa Fe, N.M.: The School of American Research; and Salt Lake City: The University of Utah, 1955–1982.

Diaz del Castillo, Bernal. *The Bernal Diaz Chronicles: The True Story of the Conquest of Mexico*. Trans. and ed. Albert Idell. Garden City, N.J.: Doubleday, 1957.*

———. *The Discovery and Conquest of Mexico, 1517–1521*. Trans. and ed. A. P. Maudslay, intro. Irving A. Leonard. New York: Farrar, Straus and Cudahy, 1956.

Johnson, William Weber. *Cortés*. Boston: Little, Brown, 1975.

Marks, Richard L. *The Great Adventurer and the Fate of Aztec Mexico*. New York: Knopf, 1993.

Padden, R. C. *The Hummingbird and the Hawk: Conquest and Sovereignty in the Valley of Mexico, 1503–1541*. Columbus: Ohio State University Press, 1967.

Prescott, William H. *History of the Conquest of Mexico*, 3 vols. Philadelphia: Lippincott, 1843, and five later editions.

———. *A History of the Conquest of Mexico*. Ed. Harry Block. New York: Heritage Press, 1949.

Thomas, Hugh. *Conquest: Montezuma, Cortés, and the Fall of Old Mexico*. New York: Simon and Schuster, 1994.

van Zantwijk, Rudolf A. M. *The Aztec Arrangement: The Social History of Pre-Spanish Mexico*. Norman: University of Oklahoma Press, 1985.

MARTIN LUTHER: PROTESTANT SAINT OR "DEVIL IN THE HABIT OF A MONK"?

c. 1483	Born
1505	Entered Augustinian Order
1510	Journey to Rome on business for his order
1512	Doctorate in Theology from University of Wittenberg
1513–1517	The Lectures on Scripture
1517	The Ninety-five Theses
1519	*On Christian Liberty*
1520	*On Good Works*
	Address to the Christian Nobility
	Babylonian Captivity of the Church
1521	Diet of Worms
1525	Married Katherina von Bora
	On the Bondage of the Will
1534	Published complete German Bible
1546	Died

On a summer day in the year 1505, a young German law student was returning to the University of Erfurt after a visit home. He was overtaken by a sudden, violent thunderstorm and struck to the ground by a bolt of lightning. Terrified, he cried out, "St. Anne, help me! I will become a monk." Such vows were usually quickly forgotten, but not this one, for the student was Martin Luther, the man who was to bring about the most profound revolution in the history of the Christian faith. Within a matter of weeks, he disposed of his worldly goods, including his law books, and joined the order of the Augustinian Eremites in Erfurt. His father was furious; his friends were dismayed. And historians and theologians since the sixteenth century have speculated about the motives that compelled him. But this is only one of the questions about Martin Luther that have fascinated scholars and made him the subject of more writing than any other figure in European history.

There was seemingly nothing in his youth or adolescence to account for his decision to become a monk. But once that decision was made, Luther was swept by such a tidal wave of religious intensity that it troubled even his monastic superiors. He prayed for hours on end; he subjected himself to such ascetic rigors that he almost ruined his health; and he confessed his sins over and over again. He was assaulted by what one modern scholar has aptly called "the terror of the holy." God was for him a terrible judge, so perfect and so righteous that sinful man could not even begin to deserve anything at His hands but eternal damnation. Martin Luther was beginning his search for "justification," the sense that somehow, against all odds, he might earn God's grace and escape damnation.

The terror of the holy remained, and the monastic life gave Luther no assurance that God's grace was close at hand. But the very religious disquiet that tormented the young monk also caused his superiors to single him out, for this was the stuff that the great figures of religion were made of—St. Francis, St. Bernard, St. Benedict. Moreover, Brother Martin, for all his inner turmoil, was a bright and capable young man and already well educated, a Master of Arts. Soon he was ordained a priest. He was sent on a matter of chapter business to Rome. And his education continued, but now in theology rather than law.

Then the Elector of Saxony, Frederick the Wise, approached the Erfurt Augustinians in search of faculty members for the newly founded university in his capital town of Wittenberg. Brother Martin was sent. In Wittenberg he taught the arts course, worked at his own studies, and assumed more than a fair share of the parish duties. By 1513 he earned his doctor's degree and began to teach theology. As he prepared a series of lectures on the Psalms, he began to gain new understanding of his texts. And then, while he was working out his lectures on the Epistles of St. Paul, he found meaning in the familiar passage from Romans 1:17 that he had never before perceived. "For therein is the righteousness of God revealed from faith to faith: as it is written, the just shall live by faith." Later Luther said, "This passage of Paul became to me a gate to heaven." Here was the "justification" he had sought so long in vain. People are justified by faith, by the simple act of belief in Christ, in a way that no amount of works, however pious and well intended, no amount of prayers or anguish or penance can ensure. Justification by faith was to become the cardinal doctrine of a new religious sect.

But Luther's inward revelation might never have led to a separate sect, much less a Reformation, except for a chain of events external to him. It began with a particularly scandalous sale of indulgences in the neighboring lands of the Archbishop of Mainz. The doctrine of indulgences was the basis of the church's profitable traffic in "pardons," as they were sometimes called, remissions of the temporal penalties for sin. Although the doctrine was an outgrowth of the sacrament of penance, many religious were troubled by it. To Luther, the indulgences that had been bought across the border by some of his parishioners and the outrageous claims for their effectiveness that were being made by the indulgence preacher, the Dominican Johann Tetzel, seemed a surpassingly bad example of the concept of "works," especially in light of his own increasing conviction that works could not work salvation in people—that only faith ("sola fides") could. In response to this scandalous situation, Luther was led to propose his ninety-five theses against indulgences. The document was dated October 31, 1517, the most famous date in Protestantism. The theses were written in Latin, intended for academic disputation, but somehow they were translated into German and found their way into print. Despite their dry, scholarly prose and formal organization, they became a popular, even an inflammatory manifesto. Ecclesiastical authorities, including the offended Archbishop of Mainz, complained to Luther's superiors and eventually to Rome. Luther was pressed to recant, but he refused. Instead, he clung stubbornly not only to his basic position on indulgences but to the ever more revolutionary implications of his belief in justification by faith. Within three years, he had come to reject much of the sacramental theory of the church, nearly all its traditions, and the authority of the pope. In 1520 he defied Pope Leo X's bull of condemnation; in the following year he defied the Emperor Charles V in the famous confrontation at the Diet of Worms. The Lord's good servant had become, in Charles's phrase, "that devil in the habit of a monk." The Catholic Luther had become the Protestant Luther.

The Protestant Luther

MARTIN LUTHER

The image of Luther the Protestant results most directly, of course, from Luther's deeds—his successful act of defiance against established church and established state, his uncanny ability not only to survive but to build around him a new political-religious community vital enough to maintain itself. Luther's Protestant image is also based upon the incredible quantity of his writings—tracts and treatises, sermons, commentaries, translations, disputations, hymns, and letters—nearly a hundred heavy volumes in the standard modern edition. But his image also rests upon an elaborate Protestant tradition that can be traced to Luther himself.

Luther was a voluble and expansive man. Even his formal treatises are rich in anecdotes from his own experience and filled with autobiographical detail. These qualities carried over into his talk, and Luther loved to talk. As the Reformation settled into a political and social reality and Luther married—for he rejected clerical celibacy along with the other doctrines of the old church—his kitchen table became the center of the Protestant world. In addition to his own large family, there were always people visiting—friends and associates, wandering scholars and ecclesiastics, professors and students, and religious refugees. After dinner, when the dishes were cleared and the beer steins passed around, they would talk, Luther usually taking the lead. He had opinions on practically everything—politics, people, theology, education, child rearing—and he would reminisce about his own life as well.

Some of the guests took notes on these conversations, and a great many of them have been preserved in a collection appropriately called the Tabletalk, *which comprises six volumes in the German Weimar edition. The following selections are from the* Tabletalk. *They are fragments of Luther's own recollections of his experiences of monasticism, his inward struggle to gain a sense of justification, and his defiance of the old church.*

He [Martin Luther] became a monk against the will of his father. When he celebrated his first mass and asked his father why he was angry about the step he took, the father replied reproachfully, "Don't you know that it's written, Honor your father and your mother [Exod. 20:12]?" When he excused himself by saying that he was so frightened by a storm that he was compelled to become a monk, his father answered, "Just so it wasn't a phantom you saw!" . . .

[Luther recalled] "later when I stood there during the mass and began the canon, I was so frightened that I would have fled if I hadn't been admonished by the prior. For when I read the words, 'Thee, therefore, most merciful Father,' etc., and thought I had to speak to God without a Mediator, I felt like fleeing from the world like Judas. Who can bear the majesty of God without Christ as Mediator? In short, as a monk I experienced such horrors; I had to experience them before I could fight them." . . . "I almost fasted myself to death, for again and again I went for three days without taking a drop of water or a morsel of food. I was very serious about it. I really crucified the Lord Christ. I wasn't simply an observer but helped to carry him and pierce [his hands and feet]. God forgive me for it, for I have confessed it openly! This is the truth: the most pious monk is the worst scoundrel. He denies that Christ is the mediator and highpriest and turns him into a judge.

"I chose twenty-one saints and prayed to three every day when I celebrated mass; thus I completed the number every week. I prayed especially to the Blessed Virgin, who with her womanly heart would compassionately appease her Son. . . .

"When I was a monk I was unwilling to omit any of the prayers, but when I was busy with public lecturing and writing I often accumulated my appointed prayers for a whole week, or even two or three weeks. Then I would take a Saturday off, or shut myself in for as long as three days without food and drink, until I had said the prescribed prayers. This made my head split, and as a consequence I couldn't close my eyes for five nights, lay sick unto death, and went out of my senses. Even after I had quickly recovered and I tried again to read, my head went 'round and 'round. Thus our Lord God drew me, as if by force, from that torment of prayers. To such an extent had I been captive [to human traditions]. . . .

"I wouldn't take one thousand florins for not having seen Rome because I wouldn't have been able to believe such things if I had been told by somebody without having seen them for myself. We were simply laughed at because we were such pious monks. A Christian was taken to be nothing but a fool. I know priests who said six or seven masses while I said only one. They took money for them and I didn't. In short, there's no disgrace in Italy except to be poor. Murder and theft are still punished a little, for they must do this. Otherwise no sin is too great for them." . . .

[As a young professor in Wittenberg] "the words 'righteous' and 'righteousness of God' struck my conscience like lightning. When I heard them I was exceedingly terrified. If God is righteous [I thought], he must punish. But when by God's grace I pondered, in the tower[1] and heated room of this building, over the words, 'He who through faith is righteous shall live' [Rom. 1:17] and 'the righteousness of God' [Rom. 3:21], I soon came to the conclusion that if we, as righteous men, ought to live from faith and if the righteousness of

---

[1]The tower was the "privy" of the cloister, and it was there that Luther suddenly saw the significance of justification by faith. Hence Lutheran scholarship refers to his *turmerlebnis*, or "tower experience."

God should contribute to the salvation of all who believe, then salvation won't be our merit but God's mercy. My spirit was thereby cheered. For it's by the righteousness of God that we're justified and saved through Christ. These words [which had before terrified me] now became more pleasing to me. The Holy Spirit unveiled the Scriptures for me in this tower. . . .

"That works don't merit life, grace, and salvation is clear from this, that works are not spiritual birth but are fruits of this birth. We are not made sons, heirs, righteous, saints, Christians by means of works, but we do good works once we have been made, born, created such. So it's necessary to have life, salvation, and grace before works, just as a tree doesn't deserve to become a tree on account of its fruit but a tree is by nature fitted to bear fruit. Because we're born, created, generated righteous by the Word of grace, we're not fashioned, prepared, or put together as such by means of the law or works. Works merit something else than life, grace, or salvation—namely, praise, glory, favor, and certain extraordinary things—just as a tree deserves to be loved, cultivated, praised, and honored by others on account of its fruit. Urge the birth and substance of the Christian and you will at the same time extinguish the merits of works insofar as grace and salvation from sin, death, and the devil are concerned.

"Infants who have no works are saved by faith alone, and therefore faith alone justifies. If the power of God can do this in one person it can do it in all, because it's not the power of the infant but the power of faith. Nor is it the weakness of the infant that does it; otherwise that weakness would itself be a merit or be equivalent to one. We'd like to defy our Lord God with our works. We'd like to become righteous through them. But he won't allow it. My conscience tells me that I'm not justified by works, but nobody believes it. 'Thou art justified in thy sentence; against thee only have I sinned and done that which is evil in thy sight' [Ps. 51:4]. What is meant by 'forgive us our debts' [Matt. 6:12]? I don't want to be good. What would be easier than for a man to say, 'I am a sinful man' [Luke 5:8]? But thou art a righteous God. That would be bad enough, but we are our own tormentors. The Spirit says, 'Righteous art thou' [Ps. 119:137]. The flesh can't say this: 'Thou art justified in thy sentence' [Ps. 51:4]. . . .

"God led us away from all this in a wonderful way; without my quite being aware of it he took me away from that game more than twenty years ago. How difficult it was at first when we journeyed toward Kemberg[2] after All Saints' Day in the year 1517, when I first made up my mind to write against the crass errors of indulgences! Dr. Jerome Schurff[3] advised against this: 'You wish to write against the

---

[2]A nearby monastery where, presumably, they were traveling on some routine parish business.

[3]A colleague of Luther's in the faculty of law.

pope? What are you trying to do? It won't be tolerated!' I replied, 'And if they have to tolerate it?' Presently Sylvester,[4] master of the sacred palace, entered the arena, fulminating against me with this syllogism: 'Whoever questions what the Roman Church says and does is heretical. Luther questions what the Roman Church says and does, and therefore [he is a heretic].' So it all began. . . .

"At the beginning of the gospel[5] I took steps only very gradually against the impudent Tetzel. Jerome, the bishop of Brandenburg, held me in esteem, and I exhorted him, as the ordinary of the place, to look into the matter and sent him a copy of my *Explanations*[6] before I published them. But nobody was willing to restrain the ranting Tetzel; rather, everybody ventured to defend him. So I proceeded imprudently while the others listened and were worn out under the tyranny. Now that I got into the matter I prayed to God to help me further. One can never pay the pope as he deserves."

Young Man Luther

ERIK H. ERIKSON

Erik H. Erikson, from whose book, Young Man Luther, A Study in Psychoanalysis and History, *the following selection is taken was a psychiatrist turned historian (d. 1994). In this selection he traces the development of Luther's personality. He also dwells on the evolution of his powerful preaching style and dwells on him as an inspired and popular lecturer and biblical exegete. And he concludes with Luther's perception of justification by faith, which was to become the centerpiece of his new theology.*

Martin's preaching and teaching career started in earnest in Wittenberg, never to be interrupted until his death. He first preached to his fellow-monks (an elective job), and to townspeople who audited his intramural sermons. He became pastor of St. Mary's. As a professor, he lectured both to monks enrolled in advanced courses, and to the students in the university. Forced to speak his mind in public, he realized the rich spectrum of his verbal expression, and gained the courage of his conflicted personality. He learned to preach to the

---

[4]Sylvester Prierias, a papal official and a Dominican, the first dignitary in Rome to attack Luther.

[5]Luther often used this phrase for the beginning of the Reformation.

[6]The book Luther wrote explaining and defending his ninety-five theses.

heart and to lecture to the mind in two distinct styles. His sermons were for the uplift of the moment; in his lectures, he gradually and systematically developed as a thinker.

Luther the preacher was a different man from Martin the monk. His posture was manly and erect, his speech slow and distinct. This early Luther was by no means the typical pyknic, obese and round-faced, that he became in his later years. He was bony, with furrows in his cheeks, and a stubborn, protruding chin. His eyes were brown and small, and must have been utterly fascinating, judging by the variety of impressions they left on others. They could appear large and prominent or small and hidden; deep and unfathomable at one time, twinking like stars at another, sharp as a hawk's, terrible as lightning, or possessed as though he were insane. There was an intensity of conflict about his face, which might well impress a clinician as reveal-ing the obsessive character of a very gifted, cunning, and harsh man who possibly might be subject to states of uncontrolled fear or rage. Just because of this conflicted countenance, Luther's warmth, wit, and childlike candor must have been utterly disarming; and there was a total discipline about his personality which broke down only on rare occasions. It was said about Luther that he did not like to be looked in the eye, because he was aware of the revealing play of his expression while he was trying to think. (The same thing was said of Freud; and he admitted that his arrangement for the psychoanalytic session was partially due to his reluctance "to be stared at.")

Martin's bearing gradually came to contradict the meekness de-manded of a monk; in fact, his body seemed to be leaning backward so that his broad forehead was imperiously lifted toward the sky; his head sat on a short neck, between broad shoulders and over a power-ful chest. Some, like Spalatin, the elector's chaplain and advisor, ad-mired him unconditionally; others, like the elector himself, Frederic the Wise, felt uncomfortable in his presence. It is said that Luther and the elector, who at times must have lived only a short distance from him and to whose cunning diplomacy and militant protection he would later owe his survival, "personally never met" to converse, even though the elector often heard him preach—and on some occasions, preach against him and the other princes.

As a preacher and lecturer, Luther combined a command of quota-tions from world literature with a pervading theological sincerity. His own style developed slowly out of the humanistic preoccupation with sources, the scholastic love of definitions, and the medieval legacy of (to us, atrocious) allegory. He almost never became fanciful. In fact, he was soon known for a brusqueness and a folksy directness which was too much for some of his humanist friends, who liked to shock others in more sophisticated ways: but Luther, horrors! was one who "meant it." It could not have endeared him to Erasmus that of all the animals which serve preachers for allegories and parables, Luther came to prefer the sow; and there is no doubt but that in later years his colorful earthiness sometimes turned into plain porcography. Nervous symptoms harassed his preaching; before, during, or after sermons he was on occasion attacked by dizziness. The popular German term of dizziness is *Schwindel*, a word which has a significant double meaning, for it is also used for the fraudulent acts of an impostor. And one of his typical nightmares was that he was facing a congregation, and God would not send him a *Konzept*.

But I think the psychiatrist misjudges his man when he thinks that endogenous sickness alone could have kept Luther from becoming a well-balanced (*ausgeglichen*) creature when his preaching brought him success. After all, he was not a Lutheran; or, as he said himself, he was a mighty bad one. On the frontier of conscience, the dirty work never stops, the lying old words are never done with, and the new purities remain forever dimmed. Once Luther had started to come into his own as a preacher, he preached lustily, and at times compulsively, every few days; when traveling, he preached in hospitable churches and in the marketplace. In later years when he was unable to leave his house because of sickness or anxiety, he would gather wife, children, and house guests about him and preach to them.

To Luther, the inspired voice, the voice that means it, the voice that really communicates in person, became a new kind of sacrament, the partner and even the rival of the mystical presence of the Eucharist. He obviously felt himself to be the evangelical giver of a substance which years of suffering had made his to give; an all-embracing verbal generosity developed in him, so that he did not wish to compete with professional talkers, but to speak to the people so that the least could understand him: "You must preach," he said, "as a mother suckles her child." No other attitude could, at the time, have appealed more to members of all classes—except Luther's preaching against taxation without representation which, in 1517, made him a national figure. By then, he had at his command the newly created machinery of communication. Within ten years thirty printers in twelve cities published his sermons as fast as he or the devoted journalists around him could get manuscripts and transcripts to them. He became a popular preacher, especially for students; and a gala preacher for the princes and nobles.

Luther the lecturer was a different man from either preacher or monk. His special field was Biblical exegesis. He most carefully studied the classical textbooks (*Glossa, Ordinaria*, and *Lyra*), and his important predecessors among the Augustinians; he also kept abreast of the humanist scholars of his time and of the correctives provided by Erasmus's[7] study of the Greek texts and Reuch-

---

[7]Desiderius Erasmus (1466?–1536) was the most famous humanist scholar of Luther's time. He corresponded with Luther breifly but later fell away from his support.

lin's[8] study of the Hebrew texts. He could be as quibbling a linguist as any scholasticist and as fanciful as any humanist. In his first course of lectures he tries the wings of his own thoughts; sometimes he bewilders himself, and sometimes he looks about for companions, but finally he soars his own lonesome way. His fascinated listeners did not really know what was happening until they had a national scandal on their hands, and by that time Luther's role had become so political and ideological that his early lectures were forgotten and were recovered only in the late nineteenth and early twentieth centuries. Because of Luther's habit of telescoping all of his theological prehistory into the events of 1517, when he became a celebrity, it has only been recognized in this century that his theology was already completed in outline when he burst into history. Then it became politics and propaganda; it became Luther as most of us know him.

But we are interested here in the beginnings, in the emergence of Martin's thoughts about the "matrix of the Scriptures." Biblical exegesis in his day meant the demonstration—scholarly, tortured, and fanciful—of the traditional assumption that the Old Testament was a prophecy of Christ's life and death. The history of the world was contained in the Word: the book of Genesis was not just an account of creation, it was also a hidden, an allegorical, index of the whole Bible up to the crowning event of Christ's passion. Exegesis was an ideological game which permitted the Church to reinterpret Biblical predictions of its own history according to a new theological line; it was a high form of intellectual and linguistic exercise; and it provided an opportunity for the display of scholastic virtuosity. There were rules, however; some education and some resourcefulness were required to make things come out right.

The medieval world had four ways of interpreting Biblical material: literally (*literaliter*), which put stress on the real historical meaning of the text; allegorically (*allegorice*), which viewed Biblical events as symbolic of Christian history, the Church's creation, and dogma; morally (*tropologice*), which took the material as figurative expression of proper behavior for a man of faith; and anagogically (*anagogice*), which treated the material as an expression of the life hereafter. Luther used these techniques for his own purposes, although he always tried to be sincere and consistent; for example, he felt that the demand for circumcision in the Old Testament foretold his new insight that outer works do not count; but this interpretation also expresses the idea that the covenant of circumcision stressed humility by its attack on the executive organ of male vainglory. Luther's ethical

---

[8]Johann Reuchlin (1455–1522) was the most eminent Hebrew scholar of northern Europe as well as being a distinguished Hellenist. He was linked with Luther in the popular press.

search gradually made him discard the other categories of exegesis and concentrate on the moral one: *tropologicem esse primarium sensum scripturae.*[9] The scriptures to him became God's advice to the faithful in the here and now.

The Book of Psalms was the subject of the first series of lectures given by the new *lector bobliae* in the academic year 1513–14. Tradition suggested that King David the Psalmist ought to be interpreted as an unconscious prophet whose songs prefigured what Christ would say to God or to the Church, or what others would say to or about Christ. Our point here is to establish the emergence of Lutherisms from the overripe mixture of neoplatonic, sacramental, mystical, and scholastic interpretations; but we must remember that the personal conflict and the theological heresy on which we will focus were firmly based in what was then scholarly craftsmanship and responsible teaching. Nothing could make this more clear than the fact that no eyebrows were raised at what Martin said: and that as far as he was concerned, what he said was good theology and dedicated to the service of his new function within the Church. Furthermore, despite the impression early Lutherisms give, Luther maintained in his sermons and in his lectures a disciplined dedication to his métier, and allowed his personality expression only in matters of divine conviction. When he discussed a certain depth of contrition in his lectures, he could confess simply, "I am very far from having reached this myself"; but on the day he was to leave for Worms to face the Emperor, he preached in the morning without mentioning his imminent departure for that historical meeting.

His series of lectures, at the rate of one lecture a week, extended over a two-year course. Luther took the job of being a professor rather unprofessionally hard. He meticulously recorded his changes of mind, and accounted for insights for which he found the right words only as he went along with editorial honesty. "I do not yet fully understand this," he would tell his listeners. "I did not say that as well the last time as I did today." *Fateamur nos proficere scribendo et legendo,* he pleaded: We must learn to become more proficient as we write and read. He does not try to hide his arbitrariness ("I simply rhymed the abstract and the concrete together"), or an occasional tour de force: "All you can do with a text that proves to have a hard shell is to bang it at a rock and it will reveal the softest kernel (*nucleum suavissimum*)." For these words he congratulated himself by marks on the margins. It is obvious that his honesty is a far cry from the elegant arbitrariness of the scholastic divines, and their stylized methods of rationalizing gaps between faith and reason. Luther's arbitrariness is part of a working lecture in which both rough spots and polish are made apparent. The

---

[9]"The tropological [figurative] is the primary sense of scripture."

first lectures on the Psalms impress one as being a half-finished piece of work; and Luther's formulations fully mutured only in the lectures on Paul's Epistles to the Romans (1515–16). But concerned as we are here with the solution of an extended identity crisis rather than with a completed theology, we will restrict ourselves to the first emergence of genuine Lutherisms in the lectures on the Psalms.

Rather dramatic evidence exists in Luther's notes on these lectures for the fact that while he was working on the Psalms Luther came to formulate those insights later ascribed to his revelation in the tower, the date of which scholars have tried in vain to establish with certainty. As Luther was reviewing in his mind Romans 1:17, the last sentence suddenly assumed a clarity which pervaded his whole being and "opened the door of paradise" to him: "For therein is the righteousness of God revealed from faith to faith: as it is written, *The just shall live by faith.*" The power of these words lay in a new perception of the space-time of life and eternity. Luther saw that God's justice is not consigned to a future day of judgment based on our record on earth when He will have the "last word." Instead, this justice is in us, in the here and now; for, if we will only perceive it, God has given us faith to live by, and we can perceive it by understanding the Word which is Christ. We will discuss later the circumstances leading to this perception; what interests us first of all is its relation to the lectures on the Psalms. . . .

When the lectures on the Psalms reached Psalm 71:2, Luther again faced the phrase, "Deliver me in thy righteousness," again preceded (Psalm 70) by "Let them be turned back for a reward of their shame that say, Aha, aha." But now his mood, his outlook, and his vocabulary had undergone a radical change. He twice quotes Romans 1:17 (the text of his revelation in the tower) and concludes

"*Justitia dei . . . est fides Christi*": Christ's faith is God's righteousness. . . .

This was the breakthrough. . . .

Luther between Reform and Reformation

ERWIN ISERLOH

A phenomenon of the last generation or so of Luther scholarship has been the emergence of a new, more balanced, and more charitable Catholic view of him. The polemical tone has almost disappeared, the shortcomings of the old church have

been recognized, and Luther himself is interpreted in ways other than simply as a bad Catholic and a worse monk, led by his own overweening hubris to an inevitable apostasy.

One of the best of the new Catholic critics is Erwin Iserloh, professor of church history at the University of Münster in Germany. The following selection is taken from his liveliest and most widely read book, The Theses Were Not Posted: Luther between Reform and Reformation. *It is, quite apart from its point of view, a stunning demonstration of how a thoughtful scholar may use a precise event to reach a general conclusion. The event in this case is the "primal image" of Luther nailing the ninety-five theses to the door of the castle church in Wittenberg, thereby defiantly proclaiming the beginning of his rebellion from the Catholic church. Iserloh presents evidence that this treasured picture appeared only after Luther's death, that it came not from Luther himself but from his younger associate Philipp Melanchthon, and that Melanchthon had not even witnessed the event. Iserloh goes on to point out that, far from an act of rebellion, Luther's handling of the matter of the theses shows him to have been, at this crucial point, both a good Catholic and a responsible theologian—in Iserloh's phrase, "an obedient rebel." Iserloh argues further that it was not necessary for Luther to have been driven to rebellion; he might well have been kept within the church to its great advantage, as well as his own.*

Our investigation of the sources and the reports concerning October 31, 1517, compels us to conclude that the drama of that day was notably less than what we would suppose from the jubilee celebrations which have been held since 1617 and from the Reformation Day festivals since their inception in 1668. In fact the sources rule out a public posting of the ninety-five theses.

Although October 31, 1517, lacked outward drama it was nevertheless a day of decisive importance. It is the day on which the Reformation began, not because Martin Luther posted his ninety-five theses on the door of the castle church in Wittenberg, but because on this day Luther approached the competent church authorities with his pressing call for reform. On this day he presented them with his theses and the request that they call a halt to the unworthy activities of the indulgence preachers. When the bishops did not respond, or when they sought merely to divert him, Luther circulated his theses privately. The theses spread quickly and were printed in Nürnberg, Leipzig, and Basel. Suddenly they were echoing throughout Germany and beyond its borders in a way that Luther neither foresaw nor intended. The protest that Luther registered before Archbishop Albrecht[10] and the inclusion of the theses with the letter eventually led to the Roman investigation of Luther's works.

Some will surely want to object: Is it not actually of minor impor-

---

[10]The Archbishop of Mainz, who had authorized the particular sale of indulgences.

tance whether Luther posted his theses in Wittenberg or not? I would answer that it is of more than minor importance. For October 31 was a day on which the castle church was crowded with pilgrims taking advantage of the titular feast of All Saints. Luther's theses on the door would have constituted a public protest. If Luther made such a scene on the same day that he composed his letter to Archbishop Albrecht, then his letter loses its credibility, even when we take into account its excessive protestations of submissiveness and humility as conventions of the time.

Above all, if Luther did post his theses, then for the rest of his life he knowingly gave a false account of these events by asserting that he only circulated his theses after the bishops failed to act.

If the theses were not posted on October 31, 1517, then it becomes all the more clear that Luther did not rush headlong toward a break with the church. Rather, as Joseph Lortz has never tired of repeating, and as Luther himself stressed, he started the Reformation quite unintentionally. In the preface to an edition of his theses in 1538 Luther gave a detailed picture of the situation in 1517. It is as if he wanted to warn the Protestant world against dramatizing the start of the Reformation with false heroics. First he stresses how weak, reticent, and unsure he was; then he tells of his efforts to contact church authorities. This is something he knows his readers cannot appreciate, since they have grown used to impudent attacks on the broken authority of the pope. . . .

If Luther did turn first to the competent bishops with his protest, or better, with his earnest plea for reform, and if he did give them time to react as their pastoral responsibilities called for, then it is the bishops who clearly were more responsible for the consequences. If Luther did allow the bishops time to answer his request then he was sincere in begging the archbishop to remove the scandal before disgrace came upon him and upon the church.

Further, there was clearly a real opportunity that Luther's challenge could be directed to the reform of the church, instead of leading to a break with the church. But such reform would have demanded of the bishops far greater religious substance and a far more lively priestly spirit than they showed. The deficiencies that come to light here, precisely when the bishops were called on to act as theologians and pastors, cannot be rated too highly when we seek to determine the causes of the Reformation. These deficiencies had far more serious consequences than did the failures in personal morality that we usually connect with the "bad popes" and concubinous priests on the eve of the Reformation. Archbishop Albrecht showed on other occasions as well how indifferent he was to theological questions, and how fully incapable he was of comprehending their often wide-ranging religious significance. For example, he expressed his displeasure over the momentous Leipzig debate of 1519 where famous professors were, as he saw it, crossing swords over minor points of no interest for true Christian men. This same Albrecht sent sizable gifts of money to Luther on the occasion of his marriage in 1525 and to Melanchthon after the latter had sent him a copy of his commentary on Romans in 1532.

A whole series of objections might arise here: Do not the indulgence theses themselves mark the break with the church? Do they not attack the very foundations of the church of that day? Or, as Heinrich Bornkamm wrote, do they not decisively pull the ground from under the Catholic conception of penance? Was a reform of the church of that day at all possible by renewal from within? Is not the Luther of the ninety-five theses already a revolutionary on his way inevitably to the Reformation as a division of the church?

Our first question must be whether Luther's indulgence theses deny any binding doctrines of the church in his day. And even if this be true, we cannot immediately brand the Luther of late 1517 a heretic. This would be justified only if he became aware of holding something opposed to the teaching of the church and then remained adamant in the face of correction. It is especially important to recall this in view of Luther's repeated assertions that the theses do not express his own position, but that much in them is doubtful, that some points he would reject, and no single one out of all of them would he stubbornly maintain. . . .

Still, a truly historical judgment on the theses will not consider their precise wording only. We must further ask in what direction they are tending and what development is already imminent in them. Luther's theses can only be understood in the context of late medieval nominalism. This theology had already made a broad separation of divine and human activity in the church. For God, actions in the church were only occasions for his saving action, with no true involvement of the latter in the former. Regarding penance and the remission of punishment, Luther simply carries the nominalist separation of the ecclesiastical and the divine to the extreme in that he denies that ecclesiastical penances and their remission even have an interpretive relation to the penance required by or remitted by God. I see here one root of Luther's impending denial of the hierarchical priesthood established by God in the church.

The theological consequences of the ninety-five theses were not immediately effective. The secret of their wide circulation and their electrifying effect was that they voiced a popular polemic. Here Luther touched on questions, complaints, and resentments that had long been smouldering and had often been expressed already. Luther made himself the spokesman for those whose hopes for reform had often been disappointed in a period of widespread dissatisfaction.

Theses 81–90 list the pointed questions the laity ask about indulgences. If the pope can, as he claims, free souls from purgatory, why then does he not do this out of Christian charity, instead of demanding money as a condition? Why does he not forget his building project and simply empty purgatory? (82) If indulgences are so salutary for the living, why does the pope grant them to the faithful but once a day and not a hundred times? (88) If the pope is more intent on helping souls toward salvation than in obtaining money, why is it that he makes new grants and suspends earlier confessional letters and indulgences which are just as effective? (89) If indulgences are so certain, and if it is wrong to pray for people already saved, why are anniversary masses for the dead still celebrated? Why is the money set aside for these masses not returned? (83) Why does the pope not build St. Peter's out of his own huge wealth, instead of with the money of the poor? (86) These are serious and conscientious questions posed by laymen. If they are merely beaten down by authority, instead of being met with good reasons, then the church and the pope will be open to the ridicule of their enemies. This will only increase the misery of the Christian people. (90)

Here Luther's theses brought thoughts out into the open that all had more or less consciously found troublesome. . . .

The rapid dissemination of his theses was for Luther proof that he had written what many were thinking but, as in John 7:13, they would not speak out openly "out of fear of the Jews" (WBr 1, 152, 17).

Luther regretted the spread of the theses, since they were not meant for the public, but only for a few learned men. Furthermore, the theses contained a number of doubtful points. Therefore he rushed the "Sermon on Indulgences and Grace" into print in March 1518 (W 1, 239–46) as a popular presentation of his basic point on indulgences, and he wrote the *Resolutiones* (W 1, 526–628 and LW 31, 83–252) as an extensive theological explanation of the theses. . . .

[The] prefatory statements accompanying the explanations of the theses have been singled out for a remarkable combination of loyal submissiveness, prophetic sense of mission, and an almost arrogant conviction of their cause. Meissinger saw here the maneuverings of a chess expert. This does not strike me as an adequate analysis. I see rather the genuine possibility of keeping Luther within the church. But for this to have happened the bishops who were involved, and the pope himself, would have to have matched Luther in religious substance and in pastoral earnestness. It was not just a cheap evasion when Luther repeated again and again in 1517 and 1518 that he felt bound only by teachings of the church and not by theological opinions, even if these came from St. Thomas or St. Bonaventure. The binding declaration Luther sought from the church came in Leo X's doctrinal constitution on indulgences, *"Cum postquam"* (DS 1447ff.), on November 9, 1518. . . .

The papal constitution declares that the pope by reason of the power of the keys can through indulgences remit punishments for sin by applying the merits of Christ and the saints. The living receive this remission as an absolution and the departed by way of intercession. The constitution was quite reticent and sparing in laying down binding doctrine. This contrasts notably with the manner of the indulgence preachers and Luther's attackers. . . .

Silvester Prierias, the papal court theologian, exceeded his fellow Dominican Tetzel in frivolity. For him, a preacher maintaining the doctrines attacked by Luther is much like a cook adding seasoning to make a dish more appealing. Here we see the same lack of religious earnestness and pastoral awareness that marked the bishops' reaction to the theses.

This lack of theological competence and of apostolic concern was all the more freighted with consequences, in the face of Martin Luther's zeal for the glory of God and the salvation of souls in 1517–18. There was a real chance to channel his zeal toward renewal of the church from within.

In this context it does seem important whether Luther actually posted his theses for the benefit of the crowds streaming into the Church of All Saints in Wittenberg. It is important whether he made such a scene or whether he simply presented his ninety-five theses to the bishops and to some learned friends. From the former he sought the suppression of practical abuses, and from the latter the clarification of open theological questions.

I, for one, feel compelled to judge Luther's posting of the ninety-five theses a legend. With this legend removed it is much clearer to what a great extent the theological and pastoral failures of the bishops set the scene for Luther to begin the divisive Reformation we know, instead of bringing reform from within the church.

Questions for Review and Study

1. Did Luther set out to found a new religious sect? Explain.
2. How did Luther formulate his important concept of justification by faith?
3. How did the indulgence scandal of 1517 contribute to the break in the church that became known as the Reformation?
4. How did Luther move from being an obedient rebel to being an enemy of the established church?
5. Why did Luther succeed where so many others failed?

Questions for Comparison

1. Compare and contrast the conversions of Constantine and Martin Luther. What were the social, political, and personal catalysts of their

conversions? How helpful is psychology in understanding their motives? In what personal changes did their transformations result? What were the historical effects of their choices? How had the church changed from Constantine to Luther's day, and what were the two men's relations to it? Were the two men's Christian faiths essentially similar?

Suggestions for Further Reading

Luther was himself a voluminous and powerful writer, and students should sample his writings beyond the brief excerpt from the *Tabletalk* presented in this chapter. The standard English edition of his works is in many volumes and sets of volumes, each edited by several scholars, elaborately cross-indexed and with analytical contents so that individual works are easy to find. The set *Martin Luther, Career of the Reformer*, vols. 31–34 is of special interest. Some of the same works will be found in another edition, Martin Luther, *Reformation Writings*, translated by Bertram L. Woolf.

The career of the young Luther, which is emphasized in this chapter, has been of particular interest to Luther scholars. Heinrich Boehmer's *Road to Reformation* is the standard work by a great German authority. The same ground is covered by Robert H. Fife in *The Revolt of Martin Luther*. DeLamar Jensen gives a detailed look at the terminal event in young Luther's career in *Confrontation at Worms*. Erik H. Erikson's *Young Man Luther* is a famous and controversial book that students find provocative. It is excerpted in this chapter.

Of the many works on Luther's theology and thought, two are recommended: *Luther's World of Thought*, by Heinrich Bornkamm, one of the most influential works of modern Luther literature, is fundamentally a theological rather than a historical work and is difficult but also important. For the background of the young Luther, see *Luther and the Mystics*, by Bengt R. Hoffman.

Of the many general biographical works, James Atkinson's *Luther and the Birth of Protestantism* places emphasis on his theological development. Probably the best and most readable of all the Luther biographies is *Here I Stand*, by Roland H. Bainton. Four books are recommended for the broader topic of Luther and his age. Two are very large and comprehensive—Ernest G. Schwiebert's *Luther and His Times* and Richard Friedenthal's *Luther*. The third, by A. G. Dickens, *The German Nation and Martin Luther*, is an attractive, authoritative extended essay. David C. Steinmetz's book *Luther in Context* is a collection of ten essays in which Luther's ideas are compared with such figures as Staupitz, Biel, and Hubmeier. Eric W. Gritach's *Martin*, while not a connected biography, is a study of aspects of Luther's life, personality, work, and influence by a great European authority. It is scrupulously based on Luther's own writings but reviews in a knowledgeable way the best modern scholarship. Two attractive, up-to-date biographies, *Martin Luther* and *Luther,* are by Walter von Loewenich and Heiko A. Oberman, respectively. See also Heiko Oberman's *The Reformation.*

For the still larger topic of Luther in relation to the Reformation, see A. G. Dickens, *Reformation and Society in Sixteenth-Century Europe;* Lewis W. Spitz, *The Renaissance and Reformation Movements;* and Harold J. Grimm, *The Reformation Era.* The new social history enters Lutheran-Reformation studies with Steven Ozment's *When Fathers Ruled.* A short book by R. W. Scribner, *The German Reformation,* surveys the recent trends of Lutheran and Reformation scholarship and has a fine annotated bibliography. An excellent recent book on a specialized topic is *Printing, Propaganda, and Martin Luther,* by Mark U. Edwards. (Titles with an asterisk are out of print.)

Atkinson, James. *Luther and the Birth of Protestantism.* Baltimore: Penguin, 1968.

Bainton, Roland H. *Here I Stand: A Life of Martin Luther.* Nashville: Abingdon Press, 1950.

Boehmer, Heinrich. *Road to Reformation: Martin Luther to the Year 1521.* Trans. John W. Doberstein and Theodore S. Tappert. Philadelphia: Muhlenberg Press, 1946.*

Bornkamm, Heinrich. *Luther's World of Thought.* Trans. Martin H. Bertram. St. Louis: Concordia, 1958.*

Dickens, A. G. *The German Nation and Martin Luther.* New York: Harper & Row, 1974.

———. *Reformation and Society in Sixteenth-Century Europe.* New York: Harcourt, Brace, 1966.

Edwards, Mark U. *Printing, Propaganda, and Martin Luther.* Berkeley: University of California Press, 1994.

Erikson, Erik H. *Young Man Luther: A Study in Psychoanalysis and History.* New York: Norton, 1958.

Fife, Ribert H. *The Revolt of Martin Luther.* New York: Columbia University Press, 1957.

Friedenthal, Richard. *Luther: His Life and Times.* Trans. John Nowell. New York: Harcourt, Brace, 1970.

Grimm, Harold J. *The Reformation Era.* 2nd ed. New York: Macmillan, 1973.

Gritach, Eric W. *Martin—God's Court Jester: Luther in Retrospect.* Philadelphia: Fortress Press, 1983.

Hoffman, Bengt R. *Luther and the Mystics: A Re-examination of Luther's Spiritual Experiences and His Relationship to the Mystics.* Minneapolis: Augsburg Press, 1976.

Jensen, DeLamar. *Confrontation at Worms: Martin Luther and the Diet of Worms. With a Complete English Translation of the Edict of Worms.* Provo, Utah: Brigham Young University Press, 1973.

Luther, Martin. *Martin Luther, Career of the Reformer,* Vols. 31–34. Philadelphia: Muhlenberg Press, 1957–1960.

———. *Reformation Writings.* Trans. Bertram L. Woolf. 2 vols. New York: Philosophical Library, 1953–1956.

Oberman, Heiko A. *Luther: Man between God and the Devil.* New Haven, Conn.: Yale University Press, 1989.

———. *The Reformation: Roots and Ramifications.* Grand Rapids: Eerdmans, 1994.

Ozment, Steven. *When Fathers Ruled: Family Life in Reformation Europe.* Cambridge, Mass.: Harvard University Press, 1983.

Schwiebert, Ernest G. *Luther and His Times: The Reformation from a New Perspective.* St. Louis: Concordia, 1950.

Scribner, R. W. *The German Reformation.* Atlantic Highlands, N.J.: Humanities Press International, 1986.

Spitz, Lewis W. *The Renaissance and Reformation Movements,* vol. 2. Chicago: Rand McNally, 1971.

Steinmetz, David C. *Luther in Context.* Bloomington: Indiana University Press, 1986.

von Loewenich, Walter. *Martin Luther, The Man and His Work.* Trans. Lawrence W. Denef. Minneapolis: Augsburg Press, 1986.

ELIZABETH I,
THE ARMADA, AND
"THE BLACK LEGEND"

1533	Born
1558	Succeeded to the throne
1559	"Elizabethan Settlement"—return to Edwardian Protestantism
1562–1563	Invasion of France failed, loss of Calais
1570	Papal bull excommunicating and deposing Elizabeth
1587	Execution of Mary Stuart
1588	Defeat of Spanish Armada
1596	Capture of Cadiz by Essex
1603	Died

"She had a sharp tongue, a vile temper, almost no feminine delicacy, and little or no feminine modesty. Of personal loyalty and affection she seems to have commanded little or none."[1] The woman thus so unflatteringly described was Elizabeth I, Queen of England; the describer, Conyers Read, the most eminent American scholar of Tudor England. And yet Read goes on to point out, as he did in a dozen other works, that Elizabeth was "Good Queen Bess" to the great bulk of her subjects and that she has held an unrivaled place in the affections of the English since the end of the sixteenth century. Most other modern Elizabethan scholars would agree. They would also agree that despite their own learned assessments of the importance of one aspect or another of Elizabeth's reign—her management of the economy, her relations with Parliament, her domestic religious settlement—the most enduring of all Elizabethan traditions is that of Elizabeth and her England pitted against the Spain of Philip II, culminating in the dramatic English victory over the Spanish Armada in the late summer of the year 1588.

This hardy tradition has its origin in the Armada fight itself and in the events surrounding it. English hostility to Spain was growing for a

---

[1]Conyers Read, "Good Queen Bess," *American Historical Review*, 31 (1926), 649.

number of reasons: sympathy for the beleaguered French Huguenots and the Protestants of Holland locked in their own desperate struggle with Philip; the undeclared sea war with Spain that English privateers and pirates had already been carrying on for a generation; as well as the gnawing fear of a domestic fifth column of Spanish spies and English Catholics ready to betray their country for the sake of their religion. Holinshed's famous *Chronicle,* for example, quotes a speech given by one "Maister Iames Dalton" in the year 1586 having to do with the designs of certain captive traitors and Spanish sympathizers, one of whom "vomited these prophane words out of his vncircumcised mouth; that it was lawfull for anie of worship in England, to authorise the vilest wretch that is, to séeke the death of hir highnese whose prosperous estate the italish préest and Spanish prince doo so maligne." Dalton goes on to decry "an inuasion long since pretended" and the popish threats "that would burn hir bones, and the bones of all such as loued hir, either alive or dead [and] that this was to de doone, when they held the sterne of gouernement; which shall be, when errant traitors are good subjects, and ranke knaues honest men."[2]

In the years immediately following the Armada, such sentiments were even more strongly voiced. Sir Walter Raleigh in his spirited account of "The Last Fight of the Revenge," written in 1591, spoke of "how irreligiously [the Spanish] cover their greedy and ambitious pretences with that veil of piety," and how they "more greedily thirst after English blood than after the lives of any other people of Europe, for the many overthrows and dishonours they have received at our hands, whose weakness we have discovered to the world, and whose forces at home, abroad, in Europe, in India, by sea and land, we have even with handfuls of men and ships over thrown and dishonoured."[3]

Thus, by the end of the sixteenth century, the major elements of what modern Hispanic scholars have come to call "The Black Legend" were substantially formed: Spain was England's implacable enemy, cruel in victory, craven in defeat; Spaniards were treacherous and cowardly, made more so by their "popery"; and, though outmanned and outgunned, English ships could either defeat Spanish ships or, if not, at least show how "beardless boys" could go to heroic death. The center of the legend was the Armada, which, "more than any other event, implanted anti-Hispanism in the English consciousness."[4] And Queen Elizabeth became the exemplar of the virtues of her nation and the symbol of its hostility to Spain.

---

[2]*Holinshed's Chronicle* (London, 1808; rpt. New York: AMS Press, 1965), IV, 920.

[3]Sir Walter Raleigh, *Selected Prose and Poetry,* ed. Agnes M. C. Latham (London: University of London–Athlone Press, 1965), pp. 85, 87.

[4]William S. Maltby, *The Black Legend in England: The Development of Anti-Spanish Sentiment, 1558–1660* (Durham, N.C.: Duke University Press, 1971), p. 84.

The Legendary Elizabeth

SIR FRANCIS BACON

Elizabeth's "Gloriana" image was a bit tarnished during the last years of her reign by grievances that had finally begun to surface, by the residue of unfulfilled hopes and unredeemed promises, and by a general restlessness after almost half a century of her rule. But the succession of her Stuart cousin James I shortly restored Elizabeth's luster. The Elizabethan Age and Elizabeth herself assumed heroic stature when compared with James I, "who feared his own shadow and manifested such unkingly habits as drivelling at the mouth, picking his nose, and closeting himself with pretty young men."[5] Yet it was not his personal habits, no matter how offensive, not even his penchant for playing at "kingcraft" or the muddle he made of the religious settlement that most alienated James's English subjects; it was his resolution to abandon the tradition of hostility to Spain, indeed to court a Spanish-Catholic alliance.

Sir Francis Bacon (1561–1626) was a functionary of James's court and one of the leading men of affairs in the new reign. But he had also been a figure of Elizabeth's court and a member of Parliament during the Armada. Though he had not advanced under Elizabeth as grandly as he thought his merits deserved, still, looking back to her reign, even the cold and analytical Bacon could not help being moved. In the summer of 1608, the year following his appointment by James as Solicitor General, Bacon wrote in Latin a memorial to Elizabeth that he titled "On the Fortunate Memory of Elizabeth Queen of England." He circulated the piece privately to a few friends but provided that it be published only after his death. Bacon was not only a stupendous genius but also a good judge of his own advantage.

"On the Fortunate Memory of Elizabeth Queen of England" is of considerable interest because it is the mature reflection of one who had been close to the center of events. The memorial is equally important because it shows a renewed interest in "the heroic Elizabeth" in the light of her unheroic successor and the new foreign and religious policies he was already considering. Bacon was writing a memorial not only to Elizabeth but to an age of giants now sadly past.

I account . . . as no small part of Elizabeth's felicity the period and compass of her administration; not only for its length, but as falling within that portion of her life which was fittest for the control of affairs and the handling of the reins of government. She was twenty-five years old (the age at which guardianship ceases) when she began to reign, and she continued reigning until her seventieth year; so that

---

[5]Lacey Baldwin Smith, *The Elizabethan World* (Boston: Houghton Mifflin, 1967), pp. 204–05.

she never experienced either the disadvantages and subjection to other men's wills incident to a ward, nor the inconveniences of a lingering and impotent old age. . . .

Nor must it be forgotten withal among what kind of people she reigned; for had she been called to rule over Palmyrenes or in an unwarlike and effeminate country like Asia, the wonder would have been less; a womanish people might well enough be governed by a woman; but that in England, a nation particularly fierce and warlike, all things could be swayed and controlled at the beck of a woman, is a matter for the highest admiration.

Observe too that this same humour of her people, ever eager for war and impatient of peace, did not prevent her from cultivating and maintaining peace during the whole time of her reign. And this her desire of peace, together with the success of it, I count among her greatest praises; as a thing happy for her times, becoming to her sex, and salutary for her conscience. . . .

And this peace I regard as more especially flourishing from two circumstances that attended it, and which though they have nothing to do with the merit of peace, add much to the glory of it. The one, that the calamities of her neighbours were as fires to make it more conspicuous and illustrious; the other that the benefits of peace were not unaccompanied with honour of war,—the reputation of England for arms and military prowess being by many noble deeds, not only maintained by her, but increased. For the aids sent to the Low Countries, to France, and to Scotland; the naval expeditions to both the Indies, some of which sailed all round the globe; the fleets despatched to Portugal and to harass the coasts of Spain; the many defeats and overthrows of the rebels in Ireland;—all these had the effect of keeping both the warlike virtues of our nation in full vigour and its fame and honour in full lustre.

Which glory had likewise, this merit attached,—that while neighbour kings on the one side owed the preservation of their kingdoms to her timely succours; suppliant peoples on the other, given up by ill-advised princes to the cruelty of their ministers, to the fury of the populace, and to every kind of spoliation and devastation, received relief in their misery; by means of which they stand to this day.

Nor were her counsels less beneficent and salutary than her succours; witness her remonstrances so frequently addressed to the King of Spain that he would moderate his anger against his subjects in the Low Countries, and admit them to return to their allegiance under conditions not intolerable; and her continual warnings and earnest solicitations addressed to the kings of France that they would observe their edicts of pacification. That her counsel was in both cases unsuccessful, I do not deny. The common fate of Europe did not suffer it to succeed in the first; for so the ambition of Spain, being released as it were from prison, would have been free to spend itself (as things then were) upon the ruin of the kingdoms and commonwealths of Christendom. The blood of so many innocent persons, slaughtered with their wives and children at their hearths and in their beds by the vilest rabble, like so many brute beasts animated, armed, and set on by public authority, forbade it in the other; that innocent blood demanding in just revenge that the kingdom which had been guilty of so atrocious a crime should expiate it by mutual slaughters and massacres. But however that might be, she was not the less true to her own part, in performing the office of an ally both wise and benevolent.

Upon another account also this peace so cultivated and maintained by Elizabeth is a matter of admiration; namely, that it proceeded not from any inclination of the times to peace, but from her own prudence and good management. For in a kingdom laboring with intestine faction on account of religion, and standing as a shield and stronghold of defence against the then formidable and overbearing ambition of Spain, matter for war was nowise wanting; it was she who by her forces and her counsels combined kept it under; as was proved by an event the most memorable in respect of felicity of all the actions of our time. For when the Spanish fleet, got up with such travail and ferment, waited upon with the terror and expectation of all Europe, inspired with such confidence of victory, came ploughing into our channels, it never took so much as a cockboat at sea, never fired so much as a cottage on the land, never even touched the shore; but was first beaten in a battle and then dispersed and wasted in a miserable flight with many shipwrecks; while on the ground and territories of England peace remained undisturbed and unshaken.

Nor was she less fortunate in escaping the treacherous attempts of conspirators than in defeating and repelling the forces of the enemy. For not a few conspiracies aimed at her life were in the happiest manner both detected and defeated; and yet was not her life made thereby more alarmed or anxious; there was no increase in the number of her guards; no keeping within her palace and seldom going abroad; but still secure and confident, and thinking more of the escape than of the danger, she held her wonted course, and made no change in her way of life.

Worthy of remark too is the nature of the times in which she flourished. For there are some times so barbarous and ignorant that it is as easy a matter to govern men as to drive a flock of sheep. But the lot of this Queen fell upon times highly instructed and cultivated, in which it is not possible to be eminent and excellent without the greatest gifts of mind and a singular composition of virtue. . . .

With regard to her moderation in religion there may seem to be a difficulty, on account of the severity of the laws made against popish subjects. But on this point I have some things to advance which I myself carefully observed and know to be true.

Her intention undoubtedly was, on the one hand not to force consciences, but on the other not to let the state, under pretence of conscience and religion, be brought in danger. Upon this ground she concluded at the first that, in a people courageous and warlike and prompt to pass from strife of minds to strife of hands, the free allowance and toleration by public authority of two religions would be certain destruction. Some of the more turbulent and factious bishops also she did, in the newness of her reign when all things were subject to suspicion—but not without legal warrant—restrain and keep in free custody. The rest, both clergy and laity, far from troubling them with any severe inquisition, she sheltered by a gracious connivency. This was the condition of affairs at first. Nor even when provoked by the excommunication pronounced against her by Pius Quintus (an act sufficient not only to have roused indignation but to have furnished ground and matter for a new course of proceeding), did she depart almost at all from this clemency, but persevered in the course which was agreeable to her own nature. For being both wise and of a high spirit, she was little moved with the sound of such terrors; knowing she could depend upon the loyalty and love of her own people, and upon the small power the popish party within the realm had to do harm, as long as they were not seconded by a foreign enemy. About the twenty-third year of her reign, however, the case was changed. And this distinction of time is not artificially devised to make things fit, but expressed and engraved in public acts.

For up to that year there was no penalty of a grievous kind imposed by previous laws upon popish subjects. But just then the ambitious and vast design of Spain for the subjugation of the kingdom came gradually to light. . . .

. . . It is true, and proved by the confession of many witnesses, that from the year I have mentioned to the thirtieth of Elizabeth['s reign] (when the design of Spain and the Pope was put in execution by that memorable armada of land and sea forces) almost all the priests who were sent over to this country were charged among the other offices belonging to their function, to insinuate that matters could not long stay as they were, that a new aspect and turn of things would be seen shortly, and that the state of England was cared for both by the Pope and the Catholic princes, if the English would but be true to themselves. . . .

. . . This so great a tempest of dangers made it a kind of necessity for Elizabeth to put some severer constraint upon that party of her subjects which was estranged from her and by these means poisoned beyond recovery, and was at the same time growing rich by reason of their immunity from public offices and burdens. And as the mischief increased, the origin of it being traced to the seminary priests, who were bred in foreign parts, and supported by the purses and charities of foreign princes, professed enemies of this kingdom, and whose time had been passed in places where the very name of Elizabeth was never heard except as that of a heretic excommunicated and accursed, and who (if not themselves stained with treason) were the acknowledged intimates of those that were directly engaged in such crimes, and had by their own arts and poisons depraved and soured with a new leaven of malignity the whole lump of Catholics, which had before been more sweet and harmless; there was no remedy for it but that men of this class should be prohibited upon pain of death from coming into the kingdom at all; which at last, in the twenty-seventh year of her reign, was done. Nor did the event itself which followed not long after, when so great a tempest assailed and fell with all its fury upon the kingdom, tend in any degree to mitigate the envy and hatred of these men; but rather increased it, as if they had utterly cast off all feeling for their country, which they were ready to betray to a foreign servitude. . . .

The "New" Elizabeth

JAMES ANTHONY FROUDE

James Anthony Froude (1818–1894), for all the criticism he received—his Oxford rival E. A. Freeman called him "the vilest brute that ever wrote a book"[6]—was surely one of the most influential historians "that ever wrote a book." The book on which both his reputation and his influence most firmly rest is his massive, twelve-volume History of England from the Fall of Wolsey to the Defeat of the Spanish Armada. *Froude began work on it about 1850, and it was published in two-volume installments roughly every other year between 1856 and 1870 to a rising chorus of popular acclaim. Ignoring the factual inaccuracies that bothered Froude's fellow scholars, the public was delighted by his preference for advocacy rather than objectivity. The people tended to agree with Froude that history proclaimed, or should proclaim, "the laws of right and wrong." Moreover, they agreed that right resided in the Church of England and wrong, more often than not, in the Church of Rome. If proof was needed for their prejudices—or his—it was abundantly available in the profusion of facts that crowded Froude's* History *and gave it an unequaled sense of authenticity. For Froude was one of the first modern British historians to go extensively to the original sources for his research; he was aided by the fact that only in his lifetime was the great mass of English public documents of the Tudor Age at last being systematically edited and published.*

---

[6]Quoted in F. Smith Fussner, *Tudor History and Historians* (New York: Basic Books, 1970), p. 55.

Froude considered the Tudor Age to be the pivot of all English history. The topical limits he set to his own great History *display his thesis. The fall of Wolsey and Henry VIII's break with Rome marked the start of the English Reformation; the defeat of the Spanish Armada marked the triumph of English Protestantism and the beginning of England's supremacy in the modern world. Like his lifelong friend Carlyle, Froude was more impressed with people than with large economic or social forces. Heroic people accomplish heroic deeds. Henry VIII was Froude's hero, standing stalwart and unblinking at the beginning of his narrative. At the other end stood the most heroic deed in English history, the defeat of the Armada. Yet careful research revealed that Elizabeth, Henry's daughter, was—at least by Froude's standards—considerably less than heroic. Where Henry had been defiant, Elizabeth preferred to negotiate. Where Henry had carried the fight to the enemy, Elizabeth was suspicious of fighting and more than reluctant to throw her resources into the great national effort against Spain. Even when the fight was inevitable, she was stingy of her support and vacillating in her resolve. Worst of all, Froude found her, at the most charitable, to be a guarded and circumstantial Protestant, perhaps even a crypto-Catholic. If Henry VIII was Froude's hero, Elizabeth was his burden. In order to reconcile his low opinion of Elizabeth with the importance he attached to the Armada, Froude made the triumph over the Armada a victory "in spite of" Elizabeth, the product of the patient policy of her great Protestant advisers and the selfless heroism of her seamen.*

It may be charged that Froude, more than most historians, took his conclusions to his sources and then found them there. But this failing is surely not unique with him. Even his severest critics today admit that Froude's History *is "one of the great masterpieces of English historical literature,"[7] that it is "a classic"[8] for its period, and that "more than any other nineteenth-century English historian James Anthony Froude set the nineteenth-century version of Tudor history."[9] An indispensable part of that version was Froude's equivocal image of the "new" Elizabeth.*

We turn now to the summation of Froude's account of Elizabeth and the Armada, from the conclusion of his History.

It had been my intention to continue this history to the close of Elizabeth's life. The years which followed the defeat of the Armada were rich in events of profound national importance. They were years of splendour and triumph. The flag of England became supreme on the seas; English commerce penetrated to the farthest corners of the Old World, and English colonies rooted themselves on the shores of the New. The national intellect, strung by the excitement of sixty years, took shape in a literature which is an eternal possession of mankind, while the incipient struggles of the two parties in the Angli-

---

[7]Conyers Read, *Bibliography of British History: Tudor Period, 1485–1603*, 2nd ed. (Oxford: Clarendon Press, 1959), p. 30.

[8]Ibid.

[9]Fussner, p. 55.

can Church prepared the way for the conflicts of the coming century, and the second act of Reformation. But I have presumed too far already on the forbearance of my readers in the length to which I have run, and these subjects, intensely interesting as they are, lie beyond the purpose of the present work. My object, as I defined it at the outset, was to describe the transition from the Catholic England with which the century opened, the England of a dominant Church and monasteries and pilgrimages, into the England of progressive intelligence; and the question whether the nation was to pass a second time through the farce of a reconciliation with Rome, was answered once and for ever by the cannon of Sir Francis Drake. The action before Gravelines of the 30th of July, 1588, decided the largest problems ever submitted in the history of mankind to the arbitrement of force. Beyond and beside the immediate fate of England, it decided that Philip's revolted Provinces should never be reannexed to the Spanish Crown. It broke the back of Spain, sealed the fate of the Duke of Guise,[10] and though it could not prevent the civil war, it assured the ultimate succession of the King of Navarre.[11] In its remoter consequences it determined the fate of the Reformation in Germany; for had Philip been victorious the League must have been immediately triumphant; the power of France would have been on the side of Spain and the Jesuits, and the thirty years' war would either have never been begun, or would have been brought to a swift conclusion. It furnished James of Scotland with conclusive reasons for remaining a Protestant, and for eschewing for ever the forbidden fruit of Popery; and thus it secured his tranquil accession to the throne of England when Elizabeth passed away. Finally, it was the sermon which completed the conversion of the English nation, and transformed the Catholics into Anglicans. . . .

. . . The coming of the Armada was an appeal on behalf of the Pope to the ordeal of battle and the defeat of Spain with its appalling features, the letting loose of the power of the tempests—the special weapons of the Almighty—to finish the work which Drake had but half completed, was accepted as a recorded judgment of heaven. The magnitude of the catastrophe took possession of the nation's imagination. . . . Had the Spanish invasion succeeded, however, had it succeeded even partially in crushing Holland and giving France to the League and the Duke of Guise, England might not have recovered from the blow, and it might have fared with Teutonic Europe as it fared with France on the revocation of the Edict of Nantes. Either Protestantism would have been trampled out altogether, or expelled

---

[10]The leader of the radical Catholic League in the French Wars of Religion.

[11]The sometime leader of the French Protestant Huguenots who became King Henry IV in 1594.

from Europe to find a home in a new continent; and the Church, insolent with another century or two of power, would have been left to encounter the inevitable ultimate revolution which is now its terror, with no reformed Christianity surviving to hold the balance between atheism and superstition.

The starved and ragged English seamen, so ill furnished by their sovereign that they were obliged to take from their enemies the means of fighting them, decided otherwise; they and the winds and the waves, which are said ever to be on the side of the brave. In their victory they conquered not the Spaniards only, but the weakness of their Queen. Either she had been incredulous before that Philip would indeed invade her, or she had underrated the power of her people; or she discerned that the destruction of the Spanish fleet had created at last an irreparable breach with the Catholic governments. At any rate there was no more unwholesome hankering after compromise, no more unqueenly avarice or reluctance to spend her treasure in the cause of freedom. The strength and resources of England were flung heartily into the war, and all the men and all the money it could spare was given freely to the United Provinces and the King of Navarre. The struggle lasted into the coming century. Elizabeth never saw peace with Spain again. But the nation throve with its gathering glory. The war on the part of England was aggressive thenceforward. One more great attempt was made by Philip in Ireland, but only to fail miserably, and the shores of England were never seriously threatened again. Portugal was invaded, and Cadiz burnt, Spanish commerce made the prey of privateers, and the proud galleons chased from off the ocean. In the Low Countries the tide of reconquest had reached its flood, and thenceforward ebbed slowly back, while in France the English and the Huguenots fought side by side against the League and Philip. . . .

[Yet] for Protestantism Elizabeth had never concealed her dislike and contempt. She hated to acknowledge any fellowship in religion either with Scots, Dutch, or Huguenots. She represented herself to foreign Ambassadors as a Catholic in everything, except in allegiance to the Papacy. Even for the Church of England, of which she was the supreme governor, she affected no particular respect. She left the Catholics in her household so unrestrained that they absented themselves at pleasure from the Royal Chapel, without a question being asked. She allowed the country gentlemen all possible latitude in their own houses. The danger in which she had lived for so many years, the severe measures to which she was driven against the seminary priests, and the consciousness that the Protestants were the only subjects she had on whose loyalty she could rely, had prevented her hitherto from systematically repressing the Puritan irregularities; but the power to persecute had been wanting rather than the inclination. The Bishops with whom she had filled the sees at her accession were chosen necessarily from the party who had suffered under her sister. They were Calvinists or Lutherans, with no special reverence for the office which they had undertaken; and she treated them in return with studied contempt. She called them Doctors, as the highest title to which she considered them to have any real right; if they disputed her pleasure she threatened to unfrock them; if they showed themselves officious in punishing Catholics, she brought them up with a sharp reprimand; and if their Protestantism was conspicuously earnest, they were deposed and imprisoned. . . .

To permit the collapse of the Bishops, however, would be to abandon the Anglican position. Presbytery as such was detestable to Elizabeth. She recognised no authority in any man as derived from a source distinct from herself, and she adhered resolutely to her own purpose. So long as her own crown was unsafe she did not venture on any general persecution of her Puritan subjects; but she checked all their efforts to make a change in the ecclesiastical system. She found a man after her own heart for the see of Canterbury in Whitgift; she filled the other sees as they fell vacant with men of a similar stamp, and she prepared to coerce their refractory "brethren in Christ" into obedience if ever the opportunity came.

On the reconciliation of the Catholic gentry, which followed on the destruction of the Spanish fleet, Elizabeth found herself in a position analogous to that of Henry IV of France. She was the sovereign of a nation with a divided creed, the two parties, notwithstanding, being at last for the most part loyal to herself.

Both she and Henry held at the bottom intrinsically the same views. They believed generally in certain elementary truths lying at the base of all religions, and the difference in the outward expressions of those truths, and the passionate animosities which those differences engendered, were only not contemptible to them from the practical mischief which they produced. On what terms Catholics and Protestants could be induced to live together peaceably was the political problem of the age. Neither of the two sovereigns shared the profound horror of falsehood which was at the heart of the Protestant movement. They had the statesman's temperament, to which all specific religions are equally fictions of the imagination. . . .

To return to Elizabeth.

In fighting out her long quarrel with Spain and building her Church system out of the broken masonry of Popery, her concluding years passed away. The great men who had upheld the throne in the days of her peril dropped one by one into the grave. Walsingham died soon after the defeat of the Armada, ruined in fortune, and weary of his ungrateful service. Hunsdon, Knollys, Burghley, Drake, followed at brief intervals, and their mistress was left by herself, standing as it seemed on the pinnacle of earthly glory, yet in all the loneliness of greatness, and unable to enjoy the honours which Burghley's policy had won for her. The first place among the Protestant powers, which had been so often offered her and so often refused, had been forced upon her in spite of herself. "She was Head of the Name," but it gave her no pleasure. She was the last of her race. No Tudor would sit again on the English throne. . . . She was without the intellectual emotions which give human character its consistency and power. One moral quality she possessed in an eminent degree: she was supremely brave. For thirty years she was perpetually a mark for assassination, and her spirits were never affected, and she was never frightened into cruelty. She had a proper contempt also for idle luxury and indulgence. She lived simply, worked hard, and ruled her household with rigid economy. But her vanity was as insatiable as it was commonplace. No flattery was too tawdry to find a welcome with her, and as she had no repugnance to false words in others, she was equally liberal of them herself. Her entire nature was saturated with artifice. Except when speaking some round untruth Elizabeth never could be simple. Her letters and her speeches were as fantastic as her dress, and her meaning as involved as her policy. She was unnatural even in her prayers, and she carried her affectations into the presence of the Almighty. . . .

Vain as she was of her own sagacity, she never modified a course recommended to her by Burghley without injury both to the realm and to herself. She never chose an opposite course without plunging into embarrassments, from which his skill and Walsingham's were barely able to extricate her. The great results of her reign were the fruits of a policy which was not her own, and which she starved and mutilated when energy and completeness were needed. . . .

But this, like all other questions connected with the Virgin Queen, should be rather studied in her actions than in the opinion of the historian who relates them. Actions and words are carved upon eternity. Opinions are but forms of cloud created by the prevailing currents of the moral air. Princes, who are credited on the wrong side with the evils which happen in their reigns, have a right in equity to the honour of the good. The greatest achievement in English history, the "breaking the bonds of Rome," and the establishment of spiritual independence, was completed without bloodshed under Elizabeth's auspices, and Elizabeth may have the glory of the work. Many problems growing out of it were left unsettled. Some were disposed of on the scaffold at Whitehall, some in the revolution of 1688; some yet survive to test the courage and the ingenuity of modern politicians.

Elizabeth and the "Invincible" Armada

GARRETT MATTINGLY

Twentieth-century Elizabethan scholarship has largely forsaken the "standard" view of Elizabeth that, more than anyone else, Froude helped to frame. Froude's Elizabeth is both too simple and too doctrinaire: Elizabeth was neither. There have been literally hundreds of special studies and monographs on various aspects of Elizabeth's reign and even a number of biographies. But despite this profusion of writing, there is not yet a comprehensive general interpretation of her for our time or an entirely satisfactory biography.

The same cannot be said, however, of the Armada, for that great and popular adventure found its definitive twentieth-century interpretation in the work of Garrett Mattingly, professor of history at Columbia University until his death in 1962. In addition to the sources that Froude had used to such advantage, Mattingly had access to even more and better British sources, for the process of editing and publishing the public documents of the Tudor Age had continued, and new archives and collections had been opened. French and Netherlandish archives were available to him, as well as collections in Italy and Spain. Thus Mattingly had the advantage of a rounded collection of materials that earlier scholars, whether English or Spanish, had not had. And he had the disposition to write a balanced account, free of the special pleading and the special point of view that were ultimately Froude's greatest flaws.

The following excerpt is taken not from Mattingly's slim and elegant masterpiece, The Armada,[12] *but from a carefully abbreviated account that he prepared for the Folger Shakespeare Library monograph series, entitled* The "Invincible" Armada and Elizabethan England. *It was his last work.*

Not surprisingly, the work deals primarily with the Armada rather than with Elizabeth. But many elements of a contemporary view of Elizabeth—even though that view has not entirely coalesced—can be discovered. Mattingly admires Elizabeth's grasp of foreign policy, which reached beyond a simplistic hostility to Spain. He admires her courage to resist the opinions of her naval advisers that the war should be carried to Spanish waters, opinions that she seemed to be almost alone in opposing. The queen's courage was the greater when we realize, as Mattingly points out, that she was already past "the peak of her popularity and prestige." Finally, Mattingly admires the tenacity that enabled Elizabeth to maintain the peace, no matter how tenuously, for thirty years and that led her into war only when it could be fought on her terms. The victory over the Armada was indeed Elizabeth's victory, and, in the words of Froude, she may have the glory of it.

---

[12](Boston: Houghton Mifflin, 1959).

Probably no event in England's military history, not even the battles of Trafalgar and Waterloo, not even the battle of Hastings, has been so much written about, celebrated, and commented upon as the repulse of the Spanish Armada by English naval forces after nine days of dubious battle from the Eddystone to Gravelines in the summer of 1588. The repulse foiled decisively, as it turned out, the Spanish plan to invade England with the Duke of Parma's army of the Netherlands, covered and supported by a Spanish fleet, and reinforced by the troop transports and supply ships it convoyed. At first the significance of the repulse was by no means clear. As it became clearer, the chroniclers of both combatants tended to magnify, oversimplify, and distort the event. English writers, pamphleteers, and historians hailed the victory, first as a sign of God's favor to the champions of the Protestant cause, later as evidence of the manifest destiny of an imperial people. . . .

. . . By now, through the efforts of two generations of historians, Spanish and English, most of the mistakes about the Armada campaign and the Anglo-Spanish naval war have been corrected and a more balanced emphasis restored. So far, however, no general account of the correction has been drawn up. Let us attempt one here.

We shall have to begin with the long period of uneasy peace, cold war, and "war underhand," undeclared and peripheral, before the actual outbreak of major hostilities. In general, historians both English and Spanish have tended to assume that since war was coming anyway the sooner it came the better, and that any policy that postponed its coming was feeble, shortsighted, and mistaken. Most English historians have been certain that Elizabeth should have unleashed her sea dogs against the Spanish colossus long before she did and have blamed or excused her for feminine weakness, gullibility at the hands of smooth Spanish diplomats, and miserly reluctance to spend money. The chorus of blame begins in the correspondence of the leading Puritans of her own day. They were always bewailing to one another the Queen's vacillation, her stubborn refusal to subsidize Protestant leaders on the Continent as liberally as they would have liked to be subsidized, her obstinate belief that peace with the armies of Antichrist could still be preserved. The chorus of blame swelled through the centuries until it culminated in the thundering voice of James Anthony Froude, who could as little conceal his boundless, uncritical admiration for the male vigor of Henry VIII, who led England into one vainglorious, financially ruinous war after another, as he could his scorn for the feminine weakness of Henry's daughter Elizabeth, who preferred to save money and stay out of trouble. Since Froude, the chorus of blame has subsided somewhat, but its echoes are still distinctly audible. . . .

. . . Elizabeth . . . and her peace party had reasons more cogent (if any reasons can be more cogent) than prudence and economy. No ruler of this century was more sensitive to the economic interests of his subjects. She knew the importance of an outlet in the Netherlands—Antwerp for choice—for the vent of English cloth, on which, after agriculture, the prosperity of her realm depended. If there was a tradition of more than a hundred years of alliance with Spain, the tradition of alliance with Flanders, with "waterish Burgundy," was as old as any coherent English foreign policy at all. In Flanders, Zeeland, and Holland were the ports not only through which English goods could most cheaply and safely reach the Continent, but from which an invasion of England could be launched most quickly and easily. And on the frontier of Flanders lay France, divided for the moment by religious civil wars, but in area, population, productivity, and centralized power easily the greatest state in Europe. Somebody had to guard the Netherlands from France—if not Spain, then England.

Elizabeth preferred to have the Spanish bear the burden. . . .

There was still one tie between Elizabeth and Philip stronger than profitable trade, old alliances, or strategic necessities. That was the life of Mary Queen of Scots. For nearly twenty years Mary Stuart had been part guest, part prisoner of her cousin. Since she was a devout Catholic and the next in succession to the English throne, she had always been the center of plots by English Catholics. . . . But with each plot the outcry for Mary's life grew stronger, and at last Elizabeth could no longer resist the clamor. When in February, 1587, the ax fell, the die was cast. As soon as Philip heard the news and had taken his characteristic time to ponder the consequences, he began to put the creaky machinery of his painfully devised plans for the invasion of England into high gear.

His plans were further delayed by Drake's brilliant raid down the Spanish coast. On the whole that raid has been duly appreciated and well described, but perhaps for the sake of dramatic narrative the emphasis on its importance has been somewhat distorted. . . .

The real damage Drake did the Spaniards was afterward, by his operations off Cape St. Vincent. His mere presence there, though he found no one to fight with, kept the Spanish fleet from assembling. But more, he swept up along the coast a swarm of little coasting vessels, most of them laden with hoops and barrel staves ready to be made into casks for the food and drink of the invasion fleet. Without tight casks made of seasoned wood, provisions spoiled and wine and water leaked away. Drake burned the seasoned barrel staves. They were almost all the fleet at Lisbon was expecting, far more than it could ever collect again. This was the secret, mortal wound. Drake knew exactly what he was doing, but most of his biographers seem not to have appreciated it. . . .

After a description of the Spanish preparations for the Armada, Mattingly continues.

If Spanish historians have been too severe with their admiral and not critical enough of his sovereign, English historians have usually made the opposite mistake. From October, 1587, on, the English commanders by sea, Drake and Hawkins and finally even Lord Howard of Effingham, the Lord Admiral, had clamored to be let loose on the coast of Spain. If the smell of booty to be won by the sack of undefended Spanish towns had anything to do with their eagerness, they did not say so to the Queen. What they proposed was that they blockade the Spanish coast, fight the Spanish when they came out, perhaps prevent their sortie, or even destroy them in port. On the whole, English naval historians have warmly approved their plan and condemned the Queen for squelching it. Perhaps they were thinking of Nelson's ships, or Collingwood's. Elizabethan ships had not the same sea-keeping qualities. If they had taken station off Lisbon in November, by April they would have been battered and strained, sails and spars and rigging depleted, crews decimated or worse by ship's fever and scurvy, and provisions exhausted. Even if none of them had foundered, and such foundering was not unlikely, the English fleet would have been in no condition to face an enemy for weeks, perhaps for months. And the cost in pounds, shillings, and pence would have been staggering. Elizabeth, who had kept a wary eye on naval accounts for forty years, knew this. What she probably did not know was that had the fleets met off the Spanish coast and the English adopted the same tactics they later used off the Eddystone, as they surely would have done, they would have fired every shot in their lockers before they had done the Spanish any appreciable harm, and would have been obliged to scuttle home in search of more munitions, while the Spanish could have marched grandly into the Channel. Partly by prudence and partly by luck, Elizabeth's preference that the battle, if there had to be one, should be fought in home waters was a major contribution to English victory. . . .

. . . About the strength and composition of the two fleets there is actually very little doubt. The Armada sailed from Lisbon with 130 ships. . . . Opposing this force, English lists show 197 ships. Actually, not all of these saw action; some of them, though not so many nor such large ships as in the Spanish fleet, were mere supply ships, practically noncombatants, and a good many, a slightly higher percentage than in the Armada, were under a hundred tons, incapable of carrying guns heavier than a six-pounder and useful mainly for scouting and dispatch work. The first line of the English fleet was twenty-one Queen's galleons of two hundred tons and upward, roughly comparable in size and numbers with the ten galleons of Portugal and ten galleons of the Indian Guard which made up the Spanish first line, but tougher, harder hitting, and, on the whole, bigger.

The myth of the little English ships and the huge Spanish ones has long since been refuted by naval historians, without, of course, being in the least dispelled. Taking the official tonnage lists of the two first lines, the biggest ship in either fleet is English, and the rest pair off in what seems like rough equality. . . . We do know that in comparison with their English adversaries the Spanish were seriously undergunned. . . . In such guns, especially the culverin type, firing round shot of from four to eighteen pounds for three thousand yards or more, the English were superior by at least three to one. . . .

There follows a detailed description of the battle, the stiff Spanish discipline, the long-range gun battles that did little but deplete shot and powder supplies, and the crucial failure of Parma to "come out" with his barge-loads of soldiers to board the waiting fleet. They were blockaded by the Dutch in the tidal waters, safe from the deep-water Spanish fleet. Then came the English attack on the Armada mounted with fire ships and fire power and finally the famous storm in the channel that permitted the Armada to "escape" to the north and to its ultimate destruction, sailing around the British Isles in a desperate and futile attempt to return home.

When, on the thirtieth anniversary of her reign, the Queen went in state to St. Paul's, where the captured Spanish banners had been hung up, the kneeling, cheering throngs hailed her as the victorious champion of her kingdom and their faith. The next few years were probably those of Elizabeth's greatest popularity, at least around London, and this was almost certainly due to her having come forward at last as the open champion of the Protestant cause, to her gallant conduct in the months of danger, and to the victory, by divine intervention almost everyone believed, which crowned her efforts. It is probable, too, that the victory gave a lift to English morale. It may be that a good many Englishmen, like a good many other Europeans, though not like Elizabeth's sea dogs, had doubted that the Spanish could ever be beaten. Now they knew that they could. The thoughtful and the well-informed understood, however, that England had not won a war, only the first battle in a war in which there might be many more battles. England was braced for the struggle.

Questions for Review and Study

1. What were the main features of Bacon's characterization of Elizabeth?
2. How did Froude's picture of Elizabeth differ from that of Bacon?
3. What are the main lines of Mattingly's account of the preparations for and the defeat of the Spanish Armada?

Questions for Comparison

1. Compare and contrast the reigns of Charlemagne and Elizabeth I of England. What were the ideological and spiritual bases of the power each inherited? What were its social and economic sources? What obstacles to kingdom- or empire-building did each ruler face? Whose task was harder? Who proved more successful? How much had the geopolitical realities of Europe and the tasks of statecraft changed from Charlemagne to Elizabeth's time? On whom did government more squarely rest?
2. Compare the reigns of England's Elizabeth I and France's Louis XIV. What challenges and achievements defined their respective reigns? Do these rulers seem to have sought prosperity or glory (or both) for their countries? Were the two aims compatible? How important were religious issues to these early modern monarchs? How do their personal qualities seem to have affected their rule? Did Elizabeth and Louis's reigns betray the aggressive or despotic tendencies that so many republicans have judged inherent to monarchy? Did early modern dynasties have any advantages over more recent forms of government?

Suggestions for Further Reading

The central problem of Elizabethan scholarship has been to disentangle the historical Elizabeth from the Elizabeth of legend. This chapter is really about an aspect of that process, for the defeat of the Spanish Armada was a powerful force in creating the Elizabeth legend. The historical Elizabeth still tends to elude scholars, but of all the books on her, the best modern work is still probably Sir John E. Neale's *Queen Elizabeth I*, reprinted a dozen times since its publication in 1934. Of the newer books on Elizabeth, the best by far is *Elizabeth Tudor*, by Lacey Baldwin Smith. But students may prefer Elizabeth Jenkins's *Elizabeth the Great* a lively, personal-psychological biography, or the attractive, heavily illustrated text by Neville Williams, *The Life and Times of Elizabeth I*. Two additional competent and straightforward biographies are also recommended: *Elizabeth I and the Unity of England,* by Joel Hurstfield, and Paul Johnson's *Elizabeth I*. Jasper Ridley's *Elizabeth I* is a readable, if somewhat superficial, biography, not too flattering to the queen. Students may find interesting Carolly Erickson's *The First Elizabeth,* a general biography that has a tinge of contemporary feminism. Especially recommended is Alison Plowden's *Elizabeth Regina,* the culminating work in a series of books on Elizabeth, this one dealing precisely with the period of her life emphasized in this chapter. Wallace T. MacCaffrey's *Elizabeth I* is a relatively new but conventional biography of Elizabeth. In her *Elizabeth I,* Susan Erye argues that Elizabeth fashioned her own image as queen. Carole Levin's *"Heart and Stomach of a King"* is a carefully research but somewhat naive book dealing with the world of gossip and rumor that attached to the queen.

Among the great monuments in modern Tudor scholarship are the studies of two of the men around Elizabeth by Conyers Read: *Mr. Secretary Walsingham and the Policy of Queen Elizabeth, Mr. Secretary Cecil and Queen Elizabeth,* and *Lord Burghley and Queen Elizabeth.* These books are detailed and complex. Students may prefer the lighter and briefer work by Neville Williams, *All the Queen's Men.* Two works on Elizabeth and her age are especially recommended: A. L. Rowse's *The England of Elizabeth,* the first of two volumes on the Elizabethan Age, the massive and lively work of a controversial and dynamic British scholar, and Lacey Baldwin Smith's *The Elizabethan World.* On the broader topic of Tudor England, the basic work is G. R. Elton's *England under the Tudors;* but students should also see A. J. Slavin's *The Precarious Balance,* an important revisionist study of the internal structure of Tudor England.

The standard work on the Armada is by Garrett Mattingly, *The Armada,* eminently readable and exciting. Felipe Fernandez-Armesto's *The Spanish Armada* is an up-to-date work that supplements Mattingly. For more detailed diplomatic history background, the best work is probably by R. B. Wernham's *Before the Armada,* and for a closer look at the technical-naval aspects of the Armada, see Michael A. Lewis's *The Spanish Armada.* An excellent revisionist account of the Armada is David A. Howarth's *The Voyage of the Armada.* There is a definitive biography of Don Alonso Perez de Guzman by Peter Pierson, *Commander of the Armada.* For an account of the growth of the English anti-Spanish sentiment, see William S. Maltby's *The Black Legend in England.* For the diplomatic linchpin in the whole background of the Armada, see the large and thoroughly readable biography *Mary, Queen of Scots,* by Antonia Fraser, and *Danger to Elizabeth,* by Alison Plowden, a work on a related topic. (Titles with an asterisk are out of print.)

Elton, G. R. *England under the Tudors.* Rev. ed. London: Methuen, 1974.

Erickson, Carolly. *The First Elizabeth.* New York: Summit Books, 1983.

Erye, Susan. *Elizabeth I: The Competition for Representation.* New York: Oxford, 1993.

Fernandez-Armesto, Felipe. *The Spanish Armada: The Experience of the War in 1588*. Oxford and New York: Oxford University Press, 1988.

Fraser, Antonia. *Mary, Queen of Scots*. New York: Delacorte Press, 1969.

Howarth, David A. *The Voyage of the Armada: The Spanish Story*. New York: Viking, 1981.

Hurstfield, Joel. *Elizabeth I and the Unity of England*. Teach Yourself History Library. New York: Macmillan, 1960.*

Jenkins, Elizabeth. *Elizabeth the Great*. New York: Coward, McCann and Geoghehan, 1958.

Johnson, Paul. *Elizabeth I: A Biography*. New York: Holt, Rinehart and Winston, 1974.*

Levin, Carole. *"Heart and Stomach of a King": Elizabeth I and the Politics of Sex and Power*. Philadelphia: University of Pennsylvania Press, 1994.

Lewis, Michael A. *The Spanish Armada*. New York: Crowell, 1960.

MacCaffrey, Wallace T. *Elizabeth I*. London: E. Arnold, 1993.

Maltby, William S. *The Black Legend in England: The Development of Anti-Spanish Sentiment, 1558–1660*. Durham, N.C.: Duke University Press, 1971.

Mattingly, Garrett. *The Armada*. Boston: Houghton Mifflin, 1959.

Neale, Sir John E. *Queen Elizabeth I*. London: Cape, 1961.

Pierson, Peter. *Commander of the Armada: The Seventh Duke of Medina Sidonia*. New Haven, Conn.: Yale University Press, 1989.

Plowden, Alison. *Elizabeth Regina: The Age of Triumph, 1588–1603*. New York: Times Books, 1980.

———. *Danger to Elizabeth: The Catholics under Elizabeth I*. New York: Stein and Day, 1973.

Read, Conyers. *Lord Burghley and Queen Elizabeth*. New York: Knopf, 1960.

———. *Mr. Secretary Cecil and Queen Elizabeth*. New York: Knopf, 1955.

———. *Mr. Secretary Walsingham and the Policy of Queen Elizabeth*, 3 vols. Hamden, Conn.: Archon Books, 1925, 1967.

Ridley, Jasper. *Elizabeth I: The Shrewdness of Virtue*. New York: Viking, 1988.

Rowse, A. L. *The England of Elizabeth: The Structure of Society*. New York: Macmillan, 1950.

Slavin, A. J. *The Precarious Balance: English Government and Society, 1450–1640*. New York: Knopf, 1973.*

Smith, Lacey Baldwin. *The Elizabethan World*. Boston: Houghton Mifflin, 1967.

———. *Elizabeth Tudor: Portrait of a Queen*. Boston: Little, Brown, 1975.

Wernham, R. B. *Before the Armada: The Emergence of the English Nation, 1485–1588*. New York: Harcourt, Brace and World, 1966.*

Williams, Neville. *All the Queen's Men: Elizabeth I and Her Courtiers*. New York: Macmillan, 1972.*

———. *The Life and Times of Elizabeth I*. New York: Doubleday, 1972.

LOUIS XIV: "THE SUN KING"

1638	Born
1643	Succeeded to throne under a regency
1661	Beginning of Louis's personal government
1667–1668	War of Devolution
1689–1697	War of the Grand Alliance
1701–1714	War of the Spanish Succession
1715	Died

In 1661, on the death of the regent Cardinal Mazarin, the personal reign of Louis XIV of France began. Though he was just twenty-three years old, Louis had already been nominally the king for almost twenty years. And he was to rule for more than another half century, through one of the longest, most brilliant, most eventful, and most controversial reigns in the history of modern Europe.

It had been the aim of Cardinal Richelieu, the great first minister of Louis's father, "to make the king supreme in France and France supreme in Europe." And to an extent Cardinal Richelieu, as well as his successor, Cardinal Mazarin, had been successful. France was the richest and most populous nation in Europe. Its army had surpassed that of Spain as Europe's most formidable military machine. And the two wily cardinals had gained for France a diplomatic ascendancy to match her military might. It remained for Louis XIV to complete their work. In the process he became the archetype of divine-right monarchical absolutism, justifying later historians' labeling of the age that he dominated as the Age of Absolutism. Louis took the sun as his emblem, as he himself wrote, for its nobility, its uniqueness, and "the light that it imparts to the other heavenly bodies," and as "a most vivid and a most beautiful image for a great monarch."[1]

---

[1]Louis XIV, . . . *Mémoires for the Instruction of the Dauphin*, trans. Paul Sonnino (New York: Free Press, 1970), pp. 103–04.

From the beginning of his personal rule, Louis XIV intended to make the other states of Europe—"the other heavenly bodies"—swing in the orbit of his sun. In 1667 he began the so-called War of Devolution to claim the disputed provinces of the Spanish Netherlands for his Spanish wife. He fought a series of wars with Spain and the Empire, the Dutch, and the English, culminating in the great European conflict, the War of the Spanish Succession (1701–1714), to set his grandson on the throne of Spain and create a Bourbon "empire" to dominate the Continent. In the course of these wars, he gained the hostility of most of Europe and was finally brought to terms in 1713 at the Peace of Utrecht. Even though Louis was reported on his deathbed to have said, "I have loved war too much," he had, nevertheless, come closer to making France supreme in Europe than had any ruler before Napoleon.

Louis XIV disliked Paris. From early in his reign, he made increasing use of the royal estate of Versailles, built between 1623 and 1683, some ten miles out of the city, as his principal residence and the locus of the court. Versailles grew in size and magnificence to become the most visible symbol of and the most enduring monument to Louis's absolutism. An English visitor, Lord Montague, sniffily called it "something the foolishest in the world," and thought Louis himself "the vainest creature alive."[2] But Versailles was far from foolish and, though vain indeed, Louis XIV was a consummate realist. Versailles was not simply a symbol of his absolutism; it was a working part of it. The function of Versailles was to help make the king supreme in France.

Royal supremacy was, in Louis's reign as before, most clearly threatened by the power and independence of the great nobility. On the very eve of Louis's personal rule, he, his mother, Mazarin, and the court had been faced with an uprising, called the Fronde (1648–1652), led by the great Princes of the Blood. Though it failed, Louis never forgot the Fronde. It became his deliberate policy to keep the great nobility at Versailles, separated from their provincial estates and the roots of their political power, and to redirect their interests and their energies. It may be argued that the elaborate court behavior that developed at Versailles, with its perpetual spectacles and entertainments, its endless adulteries and affairs, its incredible tedium and banality—and its perpetual attendance upon the king—was really a device to neutralize the power of the great nobility while the king governed with the aid of a succession of ministers, appointed by him, answerable to him alone, and capable of being dismissed by him without question. It has been suggested by more than one scholar

---

[2]Quoted in John C. Rule, "Louis XIV, Roi-Bureaucrate," in *Louis XIV and the Craft of Kingship,* ed. John C. Rule (Columbus: Ohio State University Press, 1969), p. 42.

that Louis XIV was the archetype not only of the absolute monarch but of the "royal bureaucrat." The court life at Versailles was surely the most glittering side-show ever staged. But it was a show that fascinated the very people who played their parts in it; and it has fascinated—and distracted—observers ever since.

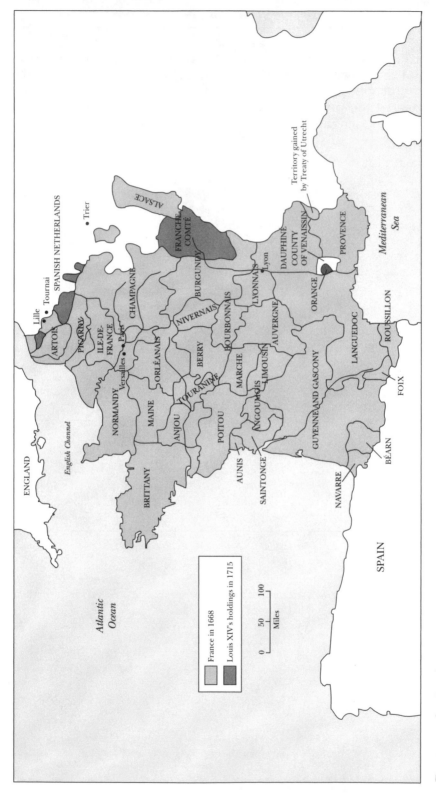

France under Louis XIV

The *Memoirs*

LOUIS, DUC DE SAINT-SIMON

The sources for the reign of Louis XIV are an embarrassment of riches—an enormous volume of public documents and official records, reports, and inventories and such a mass of royal correspondence that it still has not been completely edited. Many of the figures of the court wrote letters as prodigiously as the king, and almost as many wrote memoirs as well. Of these the most important are the memoirs of Louis de Rouvroy, Duc de Saint-Simon.

Saint-Simon was born at Versailles in 1675 and lived there for the next thirty years. Through much of that time—and throughout the rest of his long life—he kept his memoirs with a compulsive passion. In one edition, they run to forty-three volumes, and a complete text has yet to be published. Saint-Simon's memoirs are important not only for their completeness but also for the perspective they give on the age of Louis XIV. Saint-Simon fancied himself a chronicler in the tradition of Froissart or Joinville and saw his literary labor as preparing him in the knowledge of "great affairs" "for some high office." But preferment never came. Saint-Simon was never more than a minor figure of the court, moving on the fringes of the affairs that his memoirs so carefully record.

Saint-Simon blamed the king for his neglect—as he quite properly should have, for nothing happened at Versailles without the wish of the king, and the king simply disliked Saint-Simon. Saint-Simon also accused the king of demeaning the old aristocracy to which Saint-Simon so self-consciously belonged. This complaint is the nagging, insistent theme that runs like a leitmotif through the memoirs. Saint-Simon believed that Louis deliberately preferred "the vile bourgeoisie" to the aristocracy for high office and great affairs. Although the claim is somewhat exaggerated, it is indeed true that Louis preferred the lesser nobility for his bureaucrats because they had no separate power base beyond the king's preferment.

But while Saint-Simon hated his king, he was also fascinated by him, for, like it or not, Louis was the center of the world in which Saint-Simon lived. He set the fashion in dress, language, manners, and morals. Even his afflictions inspired instant emulation: after the king underwent a painful operation, no fewer than thirty courtiers presented themselves to the court surgeon and demanded that the same operation be performed on them.

Saint-Simon hated Versailles nearly as much as he hated the king, and he described it with the same malicious familiarity—its size, its vulgarity, its inconvenience and faulty planning. But he also described the stifling, debasing, desperate style of life that it dictated for the court nobility so grandly imprisoned there.

One modern scholar has called Saint-Simon "at once unreliable and indispensable."[3] We can correct his unreliability, however, by consulting other sources, and

---

[3]Peter Gay, in the introductory note to Louis, Duc de Saint-Simon, *Versailles, the Court, and Louis XIV*, ed. and trans. Lucy Norton (New York: Harper & Row, 1966), p. vii.

he remains indispensable for the picture he gives us of the "other side" of royal absolutism.

We turn now to Saint-Simon at Versailles *for Saint-Simon's appraisal of Louis XIV.*

He was a prince in whom no one would deny good and even great qualities, but he had many others that were petty or downright bad, and of these it was impossible to determine which were natural and which acquired. Nothing is harder to find than a well-informed writer, none rarer than those who knew him personally, yet are sufficiently unbiased to speak of him without hatred or flattery, and to set down the bare truth for good or ill.

This is not the place to tell of his early childhood. He was king almost from birth, but was deliberately repressed by a mother who loved to govern, and still more so by a wicked and self-interested minister, who risked the State a thousand times for his own aggrandisement. . . .

. . . After Mazarin's death, he had enough intelligence to realize his deliverance, but not enough vigour to release himself. Indeed, that event was one of the finest moments of his life, for it taught him an unshakable principle, namely, to banish all prime ministers and ecclesiastics from his councils. Another ideal, adopted at that time, he could never sustain because in the practice it constantly eluded him. This was to govern alone. It was the quality upon which he most prided himself and for which he received most praise and flattery. In fact, it was what he was least able to do. . . .

. . . The King's intelligence was below the average, but was very capable of improvement. He loved glory; he desired peace and good government. He was born prudent, temperate, secretive, master of his emotions and his tongue—can it be believed?—he was born good and just. God endowed him with all the makings of a good and perhaps even of a fairly great king. All the evil in him came from without. His early training was so dissolute that no one dared to go near his apartments, and he would sometimes speak bitterly of those days and tell how they found him one night fallen into the fountain at the Palais Royal. He became very dependent on others, for they had scarcely taught him to read and write and he remained so ignorant that he learned nothing of historical events nor the facts about fortunes, careers, rank, or laws. This lack caused him sometimes, even in public to make many gross blunders.

You might imagine that as king he would have loved the old nobility and would not have cared to see it brought down to the level of other classes. Nothing was further from the truth. His aversion to noble sentiments and his partiality for his Ministers, who, to elevate themselves, hated and disparaged all who were what they themselves were not, nor ever could be, caused him to feel a similar antipathy for noble birth. He feared it as much as he feared intelligence, and if he found these two qualities united in one person, that man was finished.

His ministers, generals, mistresses, and courtiers learned soon after he became their master that glory, to him, was a foible rather than an ambition. They therefore flattered him to the top of his bent, and in so doing, spoiled him. Praise, or better, adulation, pleased him so much that the most fulsome was welcome and the most servile even more delectable. . . .

Flattery fed the desire for military glory that sometimes tore him from his loves, which was how Louvois[4] so easily involved him in major wars and persuaded him that he was a better leader and strategist than any of his generals, a theory which those officers fostered in order to please him. All their praise he took with admirable complacency, and truly believed that he was what they said. Hence his liking for reviews, which he carried to such lengths that he was known abroad as the "Review King," and his preference for sieges, where he could make cheap displays of courage, be forcibly restrained, and show his ability to endure fatigue and lack of sleep. Indeed, so robust was his constitution that he never appeared to suffer from hunger, thirst, heat, cold, rain, or any other kind of weather. He greatly enjoyed the sensation of being admired, as he rode along the lines, for his fine presence and princely bearing, his horsemanship, and other attainments. It was chiefly with talk of campaigns and soldiers that he entertained his mistresses and sometimes his courtiers. He talked well and much to the point; no man of fashion could tell a tale or set a scene better than he, yet his most casual speeches were never lacking in natural and conscious majesty.

He had a natural bent towards details and delighted in busying himself with such petty matters as the uniforms, equipment, drill, and discipline of his troops. He concerned himself no less with his buildings, the conduct of his household, and his living expenses, for he always imagined that he had something to teach the experts, and they received instruction from him as though they were novices in arts which they already knew by heart. To the King, such waste of time appeared to deserve his constant attention, which enchanted his ministers, for with a little tact and experience they learned to sway him, making their own desires seem his, and managing great affairs of State in their own way and, all too often, in their own interests, whilst they congratulated themselves and watched him drowning amidst trivialities. . . .

From such alien and pernicious sources he acquired a pride so colossal that, truly, had not God implanted in his heart the fear of the

---

[4]Michel Le Tellier, Marquis de Louvois (1641–1691), Louis's great minister of war.

devil, even in his worst excesses, he would literally have allowed himself to be worshipped. What is more, he would have found worshippers; witness the extravagant monuments that have been set up to him, for example the statue in the Place des Victoires, with its pagan dedication, a ceremony at which I myself was present, and in which he took such huge delight. From this false pride stemmed all that ruined him. We have already seen some of its ill-effects; others are yet to come. . . .

The Court was yet another device to sustain the King's policy of despotism. Many things combined to remove it from Paris and keep it permanently in the country. The disorders of the minority[5] had been staged mainly in that city and for that reason the King had taken a great aversion to it and had become convinced that it was dangerous to live there. . . .

The awkward situation of his mistresses and the dangers involved in conducting such scandalous affairs in a busy capital, crowded with people of every kind of mentality, played no small part in deciding him to leave, for he was embarrassed by the crowds whenever he went in or out or appeared upon the streets. Other reasons for departure were his love of hunting and the open air, so much more easily indulged in the country than in Paris, which is far from forests and ill-supplied with pleasant walks, and his delight in building, a later and ever-increasing passion, which could not be enjoyed in the town, where he was continually in the public eye. Finally, he conceived the idea that he would be all the more venerated by the multitude if he lived retired and were no longer seen every day. . . .

The liaison with Mme de La Vallière,[6] which was at first kept secret, occasioned many excursions to Versailles, then a little pasteboard house erected by Louis XIII when he, and still more his courtiers, grew tired of sleeping in a low tavern and old windmill, after long, exhausting hunts in the forest of Saint-Léger and still further afield. . . .

Gradually, those quiet country excursions of Louis XIV gave rise to a vast building project, designed to house a large Court more comfortable than in crowded lodgings at Saint-Germain, and he removed his residence there altogether, shortly before the death of the Queen.[7] Immense numbers of suites were made, and one paid one's court by asking for one, whereas, at Saint-Germain, almost everyone had the inconvenience of lodging in the town, and those few who did sleep at the château were amazingly cramped.

The frequent entertainments, the private drives to Versailles, and the royal journeys, provided the King with a means of distinguishing

---

[5]A reference to the Fronde.
[6]One of Louis's early mistresses.
[7]The Spanish princess Maria Theresa died in 1683.

or mortifying his courtiers by naming those who were or were not to accompany him, and thus keeping everyone eager and anxious to please him. He fully realized that the substantial gifts which he had to offer were too few to have any continuous effect, and he substituted imaginary favours that appealed to men's jealous natures, small distinctions which he was able, with extraordinary ingenuity, to grant or withhold every day and almost every hour. The hopes that courtiers built upon such flimsy favours and the importance which they attached to them were really unbelievable, and no one was ever more artful than the King in devising fresh occasions for them. . . .

. . . He took it as an offence if distinguished people did not make the Court their home, or if others came but seldom. And to come never, or scarcely ever, meant certain disgrace. When a favour was asked for such a one, the King would answer haughtily, "I do not know him at all," or, "That is a man whom I never see," and in such cases his word was irrevocable. . . .

There never lived a man more naturally polite, nor of such exquisite discrimination with so fine a sense of degree, for he made distinctions for age, merit and rank, and showed them in his answers when these went further than the usual *"Je verrai,"*[8] and in his general bearing. . . . He was sometimes gay, but never undignified, and never, at any time, did he do anything improper or indiscreet. His smallest gesture, his walk, bearing, and expression were all perfectly becoming, modest, noble, and stately, yet at the same time he always seemed perfectly natural. Added to which he had the immense advantage of a good figure, which made him graceful and relaxed.

On state occasions such as audiences with ambassadors and other ceremonies, he looked so imposing that one had to become used to the sight of him if one were not to be exposed to the humiliation of breaking down or coming to a full stop. At such times, his answers were always short and to the point and he rarely omitted some civility, or a compliment if the speech deserved one. The awe inspired by his appearance was such that wherever he might be, his presence imposed silence and a degree of fear. . . .

In everything he loved magnificently lavish abundance. He made it a principle from motives of policy and encouraged the Court to imitate him; indeed, one way to win favour was to spend extravagantly on the table, clothes, carriages, building, and gambling. For magnificence in such things he would speak to people. The truth is that he used this means deliberately and successfully to impoverish everyone, for he made luxury meritorious in all men, and in some a necessity, so that gradually the entire Court became dependent upon his favours for their very subsistence. What is more, he fed his

---

[8]"We shall see."

own pride by surrounding himself with an entourage so universally magnificent that confusion reigned and all natural distinctions were obliterated.

Once it had begun this rottenness grew into that cancer which gnaws at the lives of all Frenchmen. It started, indeed, at the Court but soon spread to Paris, the provinces, and the army, where generals are now assessed according to the tables that they keep and the splendour of their establishments. It so eats into private fortunes that those in a position to steal are often forced to do so in order to keep up their spending. This cancer, kept alive by confusion of ranks, pride, even by good manners, and encouraged by the folly of the great, is having incalculable results that will lead to nothing less than ruin and general disaster.

No other King has ever approached him for the number and quality of his stables and hunting establishments. Who could count his buildings? Who not deplore their ostentation, whimsicality, and bad taste? . . . At Versailles he set up one building after another according to no scheme of planning. Beauty and ugliness, spaciousness and meanness were roughly tacked together. The royal apartments at Versailles are beyond everything inconvenient, with backviews over the privies and other dark and evil-smelling places. Truly, the magnificence of the gardens is amazing, but to make the smallest use of them is disagreeable, and they are in equally bad taste. . . .

But one might be forever pointing out the monstrous defects of that huge and immensely costly palace, and of its outhouses that cost even more, its orangery, kitchen gardens, kennels, larger and smaller stables, all vast, all prodigiously expensive. Indeed, a whole city has sprung up where before was only a poor tavern, a windmill, and a little pasteboard château, which Louis XIII built so as to avoid lying on straw.

The Versailles of Louis XIV, that masterpiece wherein countless sums of money were thrown away merely in alterations to ponds and thickets, was so ruinously costly, so monstrously ill-planned, that it was never finished. Amid so many state rooms, opening one out of another, it has no theatre, no banqueting-hall, no ballroom, and both behind and before much still remains undone. The avenues and plantations, all laid out artificially, cannot mature and the coverts must continually be restocked with game. As for the drains, many miles of them still have to be made, and even the walls, whose vast contours enclose a small province of the gloomiest, most wretched countryside, have never been completely finished. . . . No matter what was done, the great fountains dried up (as they still do at times) in spite of the oceans of reservoirs that cost so many millions to engineer in that sandy or boggy soil.

A Rationalist View of Absolutism

VOLTAIRE

Voltaire (1694–1778) was the preeminent figure of what modern scholars call the Enlightenment, or the Age of Reason. He was also one of the greatest and most influential of early modern historians. Among Voltaire's most important books was The Age of Louis XIV *(1751), which he conceived as one of the earliest instances of what we would nowadays call "cultural history." His intention in writing this book was to illuminate the great achievements of Louis's "age"—as the title announces—rather than the king himself. Indeed* The Age of Louis XIV *is usually published as part of Voltaire's later* Essay on the Morals and the Spirit of Nations *(1756). But Louis the king was as impossible for Voltaire to ignore as he had been for Saint-Simon, and as he has been for historians of his age ever since.*

Voltaire knew and cultivated many of the survivors of Louis's court, some of them important figures. He collected their letters and memoirs and those of other contemporaries—in short, he had much of the equipment of modern historical research. Although Voltaire also had strong and independent views on the past, as on most other subjects, his portrait of Louis XIV is surprisingly balanced. He does not evade Louis's faults, nor does he exploit them. Indeed, Voltaire seems rather to have admired the king, both as a person and as a ruler. We must remember, however, that, though a rationalist, Voltaire was not a revolutionary. He thought highly of what has come to be called Enlightened Despotism. At the time he completed The Age of Louis XIV, *for example, Voltaire was in Berlin as the guest, tutor, and "friend in residence" of Frederick the Great of Prussia.*

We must remember, too, that Voltaire was a French patriot who shared Louis XIV's love for the glory of France. We do not even find him denouncing Louis's militarism, so often the target of more recent criticism. Voltaire was especially mindful of the unprecedented domination of French culture in Europe during the age of Louis XIV and of the extent to which Louis himself exemplified that culture. Voltaire admired Louis's sound domestic economy and the diligence with which he worked at his craft of kingship, and he had considerable sympathy for his trials as a person. The picture that Voltaire gives us of Louis XIV is altogether a very different one from that created by Saint-Simon.

Louis XIV invested his court, as he did all his reign, with such brilliancy and magnificence, that the slightest details of his private life appear to interest posterity, just as they were the objects of curiosity to every court in Europe and indeed to all his contemporaries. The splendour of his rule was reflected in his most trivial actions. People are more eager, especially in France, to know the smallest incidents of his court, than the revolutions of some other countries. Such is the effect of a great reputation. Men would rather know what happened in the private council and court of Augustus than details of the conquests of Attila or of Tamerlane.

Consequently there are few historians who have failed to give an account of Louis XIV's early affection for the Baroness de Beauvais, for Mlle. d'Argencourt, for Cardinal Mazarin's niece, later married to the Count of Soissons, father of Prince Eugene; and especially for her sister, Marie Mancini, who afterwards married the High Constable Colonne.

He had not yet taken over the reins of government when such diversions occupied the idleness in which he was encouraged by Cardinal Mazarin, then ruling as absolute master. . . . The fact that his tutors had allowed him too much to neglect his studies in early youth, a shyness which arose from a fear of placing himself in a false position, and the ignorance in which he was kept by Cardinal Mazarin, gave the whole court to believe that he would always be ruled like his father, Louis XIII. . . .

In 1660, the marriage of Louis XIV was attended by a display of magnificence and exquisite taste which was ever afterwards on the increase. . . .

The king's marriage was followed by one long series of fêtes, entertainments, and gallantries. They were redoubled on the marriage of *Monsieur,* the king's eldest brother, to Henrietta of England, sister of Charles II, and they were not interrupted until the death of Cardinal Mazarin in 1661.

The court became the centre of pleasures, and a model for all other courts. The king prided himself on giving entertainments which should put those of Vaux in the shade.

Nature herself seemed to take a delight in producing at this moment in France men of the first rank in every art, and in bringing together at Versailles the most handsome and well-favoured men and women that ever graced a court. Above all his courtiers Louis rose supreme by the grace of his figure and the majestic nobility of his countenance. The sound of his voice, at once dignified and charming, won the hearts of those whom his presence had intimidated. His bearing was such as befitted himself and his rank alone, and would have been ridiculous in any other. . . .

The chief glory of these amusements, which brought taste, polite manners, and talents to such perfection in France, was that they did not for a moment detach the monarch from his incessant labors. Without such toil he could but have held a court, he could not have reigned: and had the magnificent pleasures of the court outraged the miseries of the people, they would only have been detestable; but the same man who gave these entertainments had given the people bread during the famine of 1662. He had bought up corn, which he sold to the rich at a low price, and which he gave free to poor families at the gate of the Louvre; he had remitted three millions of taxes to the people; no part of the internal administration was neglected, and his government was respected abroad. The King of Spain was obliged to allow him precedence; the Pope was forced to give him satisfaction; Dunkirk was acquired by France by a treaty honourable to the purchaser and ignominious to the seller; in short, all measures adopted after he had taken up the reins of government were either honourable or useful; thereafter, it was fitting that he should give such fêtes . . . that all the nobles should be honoured but no one powerful, not even his brother or *Monsieur le Prince.* . . .

Not one of those who have been too ready to censure Louis XIV can deny that until the Battle of Blenheim[9] he was the only monarch at once powerful, magnificent, and great in every department. For while there have been heroes such as John Sobieski and certain Kings of Sweden who eclipsed him as warriors, no one has surpassed him as a monarch. It must ever be confessed that he not only bore his misfortunes, but overcame them. He had defects and made great errors, but had those who condemn him been in his place, would they have equalled his achievements? . . .

. . . It was the destiny of Louis XIV to see the whole of his family die before their time; his wife at forty-five and his only son at fifty; but a year later we witnessed the spectacle of his grandson the Dauphin, Duke of Burgundy, his wife, and their eldest son, the Duke of Brittany, being carried to the same tomb at Saint-Denys in the month of April 1712, while the youngest of their children, who afterwards ascended the throne, lay in his cradle at death's door. The Duke of Berri, brother of the Duke of Burgundy, followed them two years later, and his daughter was carried at the same time from her cradle to her coffin.

These years of desolation left such a deep impression on people's hearts that during the minority of Louis XV I have met many people who could not speak of the late king's bereavement without tears in their eyes. . . .

The remainder of his life was sad. The disorganisation of state finances, which he was unable to repair, estranged many hearts. The complete confidence he placed in the Jesuit, Le Tellier, a turbulent spirit, stirred them to rebellion. It is remarkable that the people who forgave him all his mistresses could not forgive this one confessor. In the minds of the majority of his subjects he lost during the last three years of his life all the prestige of the great and memorable things he had accomplished. . . .

On his return from Marli towards the middle of the month of August 1715, Louis XIV was attacked by the illness which ended his life.

---

[9]Marlborough's great victory (1704) for England and her allies in the War of the Spanish Succession.

His legs swelled, and signs of gangrene began to show themselves. The Earl of Stair, the English ambassador, wagered, after the fashion of his country, that the king would not outlive the month of September. The Duke of Orleans, on the journey from Marli, had been left completely to himself, but now the whole court gathered round his person. During the last days of the king's illness, a quack physician gave him a cordial which revived him. He managed to eat, and the quack assured him that he would recover. On hearing this news the crowd of people that had gathered round the Duke of Orleans diminished immediately. "If the king eats another mouthful," said the Duke of Orleans, "we shall have no one left." But the illness was mortal. . . .

Though he has been accused of being narrow-minded, of being too harsh in his zeal against Jansenism,[10] too arrogant with foreigners in his triumphs, too weak in his dealings with certain women, and too severe in personal matters; of having lightly undertaken wars, of burning the Palatinate and of persecuting the reformers—nevertheless, his great qualities and noble deeds when placed in the balance eclipse all his faults. Time, which modifies men's opinions, has put the seal upon his reputation, and, in spite of all that has been written against him, his name is never uttered without respect, nor without recalling to the mind an age which will be forever memorable. If we consider this prince in his private life, we observe him indeed too full of his own greatness, but affable, allowing his mother no part in the government but performing all the duties of a son, and observing all outward appearance of propriety towards his wife; a good father, a good master, always dignified in public, laborious in his study, punctilious in business matters, just in thought, a good speaker, and agreeable though aloof. . . .

The mind of Louis XIV was rather precise and dignified than witty; and indeed one does not expect a king to say notable things, but to do them. . . .

Between him and his court there existed a continual intercourse in which was seen on the one side all the graciousness of a majesty which never debased itself, and on the other all the delicacy of an eager desire to serve and please which never approached servility. He was considerate and polite, especially to women, and his example enhanced those qualities in his courtiers; he never missed an opportunity of saying things to men which at once flattered their self-esteem, stimulated rivalry, and remained long in their memory. . . .

It follows from what we have related, that in everything this monarch loved grandeur and glory. A prince who, having accomplished as

---

[10]A sect named after the Flemish theologian Cornelis Jansen that was, though Catholic, rather Calvinistic in many of its views. Jansenism was bitterly opposed by the Jesuits, who finally persuaded Louis XIV to condemn it.

great things as he, could yet be of plain and simple habits, would be the first among kings, and Louis XIV the second.

If he repented on his death-bed of having lightly gone to war, it must be owned that he did not judge by events; for of all his wars the most legitimate and necessary, namely, the war of 1701, was the only one unsuccessful. . . .

His own glory was indissolubly connected with the welfare of France, and never did he look upon his kingdom as a noble regards his land, from which he extracts as much as he can that he may live in luxury. Every king who loves glory loves the public weal; he had no longer a Colbert[11] nor a Louvois, when about 1698 he commanded each comptroller to present a detailed description of his province for the instruction of the Duke of Burgundy. By this means it was possible to have an exact record of the whole kingdom and a correct census of the population. . . .

The foregoing is a general account of what Louis XIV did or attempted to do in order to make his country more flourishing. It seems to me that one can hardly view all his works and efforts without some sense of gratitude, nor without being stirred by the love for the public weal which inspired them. Let the reader picture to himself the condition to-day, and he will agree that Louis XIV did more good for his country than twenty of his predecessors together; and what he accomplished fell far short of what he might have done. The war which ended with the Peace of Ryswick[12] began the ruin of the flourishing trade established by his minister Colbert, and the war of the succession completed it. . . .

. . . Nevertheless, this country, in spite of the shocks and losses she has sustained, is still one of the most flourishing in the world, since all the good that Louis XIV did for her still bears fruit, and the mischief which it was difficult not to do in stormy times has been remedied. Posterity, which passes judgment on kings, and whose judgment they should continually have before them, will acknowledge, weighing the greatness and defects of that monarch, that though too highly praised during his lifetime, he will deserve to be so for ever, and that he was worthy of the statue raised to him at Montpellier, bearing a Latin inscription whose meaning is *To Louis the Great after his death.*

---

[11] Jean Baptiste Colbert (1619–1683), Louis's great minister of finance.
[12] The War of the League of Augsburg (1688–1697).

Louis XIV
and the Larger World

PIERRE GOUBERT

The historiography of Louis XIV is almost as vast as the original sources and almost as intimidating. Few figures in European history have been more variously or more adamantly interpreted. As W. H. Lewis has said, "To one school, he is incomparably the ablest ruler in modern European History; to another, a mediocre blunderer, pompous, led by the nose by a succession of generals and civil servants; whilst to a third, he is no great king, but still the finest actor of royalty the world has ever seen."[13] And such a list does not exhaust the catalogue of Louis's interpreters.

There is at least one contemporary revisionist school that has turned again to "the world of Louis XIV," not the limited world that Saint-Simon saw—the world of the court and the hated prison of Versailles—but the larger world of economic and social forces beyond the court. One of the best exponents of this school is the French historian Pierre Goubert, from whose Louis XIV and Twenty Million Frenchmen *the following selection is taken. Goubert is essentially an economic historian, occupied with such things as demographic trends, price and wage fluctuations, gross national products, and the like. In this book he is concerned with Louis XIV as an able bureaucratic manager rather than as strictly an autocrat; as a king whose foreign policy was often governed not by his own absolutist theories, but by the realities of economics, and whose domestic policies were limited by the dragging, inertial resistance to change of the inherited institutions of his own nation.*

As early as 1661, as he declared in his *Mémoires,* Louis meant to have sole command in every sphere and claimed full responsibility, before the world and all posterity, for everything that should happen in his reign. In spite of constant hard work, he soon found he had to entrust the actual running of certain departments, such as finance or commerce, to a few colleagues, although he still reserved the right to make major decisions himself. There were, however, some aspects of his *métier de roi* to which he clung absolutely and persistently, although his persistence was not invariably absolute. Consequently, it is permissible to single out a kind of personal sphere which the king reserved to himself throughout his reign, although this sphere might vary, while the rest still remained, as it were, under his eye.

---

[13]W. H. Lewis, *The Splendid Century: Life in the France of Louis XIV* (Garden City, N.Y.: Doubleday, 1957), p. 1.

As a young man, Louis had promised himself that his own time and posterity should ring with his exploits. If this had been no more than a simple wish, and not an inner certainty, it might be said to have been largely granted.

As a hot-headed young gallant, he flouted kings by his extravagant gestures and amazed them by the brilliance of his court, his entertainments, his tournaments, and his mistresses. As a new Augustus he could claim, for a time, to have been his own Maecenas. Up to the year 1672, all Europe seems to have fallen under the spell of his various exploits and his youthful fame spread even as far as the "barbarians" of Asia. For seven or eight years after that, the armies of Le Tellier and Turenne[14] seemed almost invincible while Colbert's youthful navy and its great admirals won glory off the coast of Sicily. Then, when Europe had pulled itself together, Louis still showed amazing powers of resistance and adaptability. Even when he seemed to be ageing, slipping into pious isolation amid his courtiers, he retained the power to astonish with the splendours of his palace at Versailles, his opposition to the Pope, and the will to make himself into a "new Constantine," and later by allying himself with Rome to "purify" the Catholic religion. When practically on his death bed, he could still impress the English ambassador who came to protest at the building of a new French port next door to the ruins of Dunkirk. . . .

For precisely three centuries, Louis XIV has continued to dominate, fascinate, and haunt men's minds. "The universe and all time" have certainly remembered him, although not always in the way he would have wished. From this point of view, Louis' personal deeds have been a great success. Unfortunately, his memory has attracted a cloud of hatred and contempt as enduring as that which rises from the incense of his worshippers or the pious imitations of a later age.

In his personal desire to enlarge his kingdom, the king was successful. The lands in the north, Strasbourg, Franche-Comté and the "iron belt"[15] are clear evidence of success. In this way Paris was better protected from invasion. But all these gains had been made by 1681 and later events served only to confirm, rescue or reduce them. . . .

As absolute head of his diplomatic service and his armies, from beginning to end, he was well served while he relied on men who had been singled out by Mazarin or Richelieu, but he often made a fool of himself by selecting unworthy successors. He was no great warrior. His father and his grandfather had revelled in the reek of the camp and the heady excitement of battle. His preference was always for

---

[14]Le Vicomte Henri de Turenne (1611–1675), one of Louis's generals. A holdover from Louis's father's reign, Turenne was the French hero of the Thirty Years' War and the war against Spain.

[15]A reference to the fortifications—the *frontière de fer*—of the Marquis de Vauban (1663–1707), Louis's master military and siege engineer.

impressive manoeuvres, parades, and good safe sieges rather than the smoke of battle, and as age grew on him he retreated to desk strategy. Patient, secretive, and subtle in constructing alliances, weaving intrigues, and undoing coalitions, he marred all these gifts by ill-timed displays of arrogance, brutality, and unprovoked aggression. In the last analysis, this born aggressor showed his greatness less in triumph than in adversity, but there was never any doubt about his effect on his contemporaries, whose feelings towards him were invariably violent and uncompromising. He was admired, feared, hated, and secretly envied. . . .

More often than not, and permanently in some cases, administrative details and the complete running of certain sectors of the administration were left to agents appointed by the king and responsible to him. Louis rarely resorted to the cowardly expedient of laying the blame for failure on his subordinates. Not until the end of his life, and notably in the case of the bishops, did he indulge in such pettiness. Everything that was done during his reign was done in his name and Louis' indirect responsibility in matters he had delegated was the same as his direct responsibility in his own personal spheres. Moreover, the two sectors could not help but be closely connected.

A policy of greatness and prestige demanded an efficient and effective administration as well as adequate resources, both military and financial. . . .

In order to disseminate the king's commands over great distances and combat the complex host of local authorities, a network of thirty intendants had been established over the country. These were the king's men, dispatched by the king's councils and assisted by correspondents, agents and *subdélégués* who by 1715 were numerous and well organized. By this time the system was well-established and more or less accepted (even in Brittany). It met with reasonable respect and sometimes obedience. Sometimes, not always, since we only have to read the intendants' correspondence to be disabused swiftly of any illusions fostered by old-fashioned textbooks or history notes. The difficulties of communications, the traditions of provincial independence, inalienable rights and privileges, and the sheer force of inertia all died hard. Lavisse used to say this was a period of absolutism tempered by disobedience. In the depths of the country and the remote provinces, the formula might almost be reversed. Nevertheless, there is no denying that a step forward had been made and that the germ of the splendid administrative systems of Louis XV and of Napoleon was already present in the progress made between 1661 and 1715. . . .

In one adjacent but vital field, ministers and jurists laboured valiantly to reach a unified code of French law, giving the king's laws priority over local custom and simplifying the enormous tangled mass of statute law. . . .

The navy, rescued from virtual oblivion by Colbert, who gave it arsenals, shipwrights, gunners, talented designers, its finest captains, and fresh personnel obtained by means of seaboard conscription, distinguished itself particularly from 1672 to 1690. . . .

The greatest of all the king's great servants were those who helped him to build up an army, which in size and striking force was for the most part equal to all the other armies of Europe put together. They were first Le Tellier and Turenne and later, Louvois and Vauban. Many others of less fame, such as Chamlay, Martinet, Fourilles, and Clerville would also deserve a place in this unusually lengthy roll of honour if the historian's job were the awarding of laurels, especially military ones. The fighting strength was increased at least fourfold, discipline was improved, among generals as well as officers and men, and a civil administration superimposed, not without a struggle, on the quarrelsome, short-sighted and in many cases incompetent and dishonest military one. New ranks and new corps were introduced; among them the artillery and the engineers, as well as such new weapons as the flintlock and the fixed bayonet, and a new military architect, Vauban, all helped to make the army more efficient. Most important of all, the army at last possessed a real *Intendance* with its own arsenals, magazines, and regular staging posts. Uniforms became more or less general, providing employment for thousands of workers. The first barracks were an attempt to put an end to the notorious custom of billeting troops on civilian households. The Hôtel des Invalides[16] was built, on a grand scale. The instrument which these invaluable servants placed at their master's disposal was almost without parallel in their time, a genuine royal army, growing ever larger and more diversified, modern, and disciplined. . . .

An ambition to astonish the world with magnificence and great armies is all very well so long as the world is prepared to be astonished.

At the beginning of his reign, when Louis surveyed the rest of Europe, he saw nothing but weakness and decline. Some of his observations, as regards Spain and Italy, were perfectly correct. In others, he was mistaken. He stupidly underestimated the United Provinces, as though a small, bourgeois, and Calvinist population were an inevitable sign of weakness. Yet another observation was swiftly belied by the changes which occurred in two highly dissimilar entities: England and the Empire.

Louis XIV found himself baulked at every turn by the diplomacy and dogged courage, as well as by the seapower and the immense wealth of the United Provinces. It is no longer fashionable to believe

---

[16]Now a military museum and the site of Napoleon's tomb but originally intended as an old soldiers' home.

that the "Golden Age" of the Dutch was over in 1661. For a long time after that, their Bank, their Stock Exchange, their India Company, their fleets, and their florins remained as powerful as ever. The invasion of 1672 weakened them only temporarily and even in 1715 . . . their wealth, currency, and bankers remained powerful and respected and often decisive. Their policy was not yet tied directly to England's. It was simply that they no longer enjoyed undivided supremacy: another nation's economy had reached the same level and was about to overtake them.

Louis XIV always did his best to ignore economic factors, but they would not be denied and they took their revenge. . . .

Louis found other forces of opposition within the borders of his kingdom . . . the ancient, traditional, and heavily calculated weight of inertia possessed by that collection of "nations," *pays, seigneuries,* fiefs, and parishes which together made up the kingdom of France. Each of these entities was accustomed to living independently, with its own customs, privileges, and even language, snug in its own fields and within sound of its own bells. The king consecrated at Rheims was a priest-king to be revered and almost worshipped, but from afar. . . .

If, dazzled by the splendours of Versailles, we let ourselves forget the constant presence of these seething undercurrents, we will have understood nothing of the France of Louis XIV and of the impossible task which the king and his ministers had set themselves, or of the massive inertia which made it so difficult. . . .

For some years now, younger historians of a certain school have tended to ignore the bustle of individuals and events in favour of what they call revealing, measuring, defining, and illustrating the great dominant rhythms which move world history as a whole. These rhythms emerge as largely economic. . . . From 1600 onwards, the quantities of silver reaching Spain from America grew less and less until by 1650 the imports were only a fifth of what they had been in 1600. A probable revival of the mines of central Europe was insufficient to make up the deficit. First gold, and then silver, grew scarce, giving rise to hoarding. Copper from Sweden or Japan (via Holland) tended to take their place, but it was a poor substitute. The whole age of Louis XIV was an age that Marc Bloch has called "monetary famine.". . .

Historians and economists have long been aware that the seventeenth century as a whole and the period from 1650 to 1690 in particular, or even 1650–1730, was marked by a noticeable drop in the cost of basic foodstuffs as well as of a great many other things—a drop quite separate from annual "accidents." Landed incomes, offices, and possible moneylending, all seem to have been affected by the same general reduction. . . .

There remains a strong impression that the period of Louis' reign was one of economic difficulties, suffering both from sudden, violent crises and from phases of stagnation and of deep depression. It is not easy to govern under such conditions especially when, like the king and most of his councillors, one is unaware of them. But what they tried to do and sometimes, despite such obstacles, achieved, remains nonetheless worthy of interest and even admiration.

It is possible, therefore, that France under Louis XIV may have been unconsciously subject to powerful economic forces which are still much disputed and not fully understood. Social, demographic, mental, and other factors, wholly or partly incomprehensible to the rulers, may have played their part also. . . .

About the great mass of French society and its slow, ponderous development we know almost nothing, only a few glimmers here and there. . . .

It is true that Louis XIV, like most men who grew up between 1640 and 1660, was incapable of rising beyond the limits of his education, let alone of taking in, at one glance, the whole of the planet on which he lived, to say nothing of infinite space. A king to the depths of his being, and a dedicated king, he had a concept of greatness which was that of his generation: military greatness, dynastic greatness, territorial greatness, and political greatness which expressed itself in unity of faith, the illusion of obedience, and magnificent surroundings. He left behind him an image of the monarchy, admirable in its way, but already cracking if not outworn at the time of his death.

Questions for Review and Study

1. In Saint-Simon's account of Louis XIV, how do his own prejudices show themselves?
2. Is Voltaire admiring or critical of Louis XIV? Explain.
3. Is Pierre Goubert admiring or critical of Louis XIV? Explain.
4. In what respects was Louis XIV a great king?

Questions for Comparison

1. Compare the French rulers Louis XIV and Napoleon. How did they variously symbolize French greatness? What were their relations to the rest of Europe? On what authority (ideologically speaking) did these rulers hold power? Which social classes stood to gain or lose from their rule? Were they simply products of their times, or did they in some sense create their times by force of character? Who was more successful? What were their respective relations to the French Revolution?
2. Compare the reigns of England's Elizabeth I and France's Louis XIV. What challenges and achievements defined their respective reigns? Do these rulers seem to have sought prosperity or glory (or both) for

their countries? Were the two aims compatible? How important were religious issues to these early modern monarchs? How do their personal qualities seem to have affected their rule? Did the reigns of Elizabeth and Louis betray the aggressive or despotic tendencies that so many republicans have judged inherent to monarchy? Did early modern dynasties have any advantages over more recent forms of government?

Suggestions for Further Reading

The best biography of Louis XIV is *Louis XIV,* by John B. Wolf, a comprehensive, analytical, and persuasive book. Another work, *The Age of Louis XIV,* by an eminent French historian, Pierre Gaxotte, can also be recommended, but it is not as readable as Nancy Mitford's *The Sun King,* a handsome book on Louis and the daily life at Versailles, the court intrigues and decisions of government—a lively and witty, if somewhat superficial, book by a popular British novelist and biographer. Three brief biographies can also be recommended: *Louis XIV and the Greatness of France,* by Maurice Ashley, and the *Louis XIV* of Vincent Buranelli and of Oliver Bernier. A recent well-written political biography is *Louis XIV and the French Monarchy* by Andrew Lossky.

Louis XIV, no matter how he is judged, is the central figure in seventeenth-century Europe. Some works on that century and the age of Louis XIV are therefore necessary to understand the Sun King. *Europe in the Seventeenth Century,* by David Ogg, and *The Seventeenth Century,* by G. N. Clark, have long been the standard works of, respectively, the narrative and institutional history of the period. A famous interpretive book, somewhat like Clark's, is *The Splendid Century* by W. H. Lewis, but it is livelier and more entertaining. More comprehensive and much more far-ranging in subject is Maurice Ashley's *The Golden Century.* Of the same sort but more popular is Ragnhild Hatton's *Europe in the Age of Louis XIV.* J. B. Wolf's *Toward a European Balance of Power, 1620–1715,* deals almost entirely with the central role of Louis XIV's France in the evolution of that important political-diplomatic concept. Students interested in the intellectual history of Louis's France should consult the small but well-done work by Edward John Kearns, *Ideas in Seventeenth-Century France.*

Through the last generation or so, seventeenth-century studies and the study of Louis XIV have passed through a major crisis of revision. One of the early works reflecting this is by J. B. Wolf, *The Emergence of the Great Powers, 1685–1715,* a brilliant synthesis of narrative, analysis, and modern research. Students should read more extensively in the important work by Pierre Goubert, *Louis XIV and Twenty Million Frenchmen,* excerpted in this chapter. Readers interested in this sort of work might be interested in the vast, two-volume compendium of French institutional history by the great French authority Roland E. Mousnier, *The Institutions of France under the Absolute Monarchy.* There are four sets of readings that represent much of the newer research and interpretation of Louis XIV: *Louis XIV and the Craft of Kingship,* edited by John C. Rule; two texts edited by Ragnhild Hatton, *Louis XIV and Absolutism* and *Louis XIV and Europe;* and *Sun King,* edited by David Lee Rubin. An important revisionist book is *Power and Faction in Louis XIV's France,* in which Roger Mettam argues that Louis was actually an ineffective king in his domestic policy. Finally, students may be interested in an important thesis book on the so-called general crisis of the seventeenth century, *The Struggle for Stability in Early Modern Europe,* in which Theodore K. Rabb argues that the crisis was a search for a principle of authority. (Titles with an asterisk are out of print.)

Ashley, Maurice. *The Golden Century: Europe 1598–1715.* New York: Praeger, 1969.

———. *Louis XIV and the Greatness of France.* Teach Yourself History Library. New York: Macmillan, 1948.

Bernier, Oliver. *Louis XIV: A Royal Life.* New York: Doubleday, 1987.

Buranelli, Vincent. *Louis XIV.* Rulers and Statesman of the World Series. New York: Twayne, 1966.

Clark, G. N. *The Seventeenth Century.* 2nd ed. Oxford: Clarendon Press, 1961.*

Gaxotte, Pierre. *The Age of Louis XIV.* Trans. Michael Shaw. New York: Macmillan, 1970.

Goubert, Pierre. *Louis XIV and Twenty Million Frenchmen.* Trans. Anne Carter. New York: Pantheon, 1970.

Hatton, Ragnhild. *Europe in the Age of Louis XIV.* New York: Harcourt, Brace and World, 1969.

———, ed. *Louis XIV and Absolutism.* Columbus: Ohio State University Press, 1976.

———, ed. *Louis XIV and Europe.* Columbus: Ohio State University Press, 1976.

Kearns, Edward John. *Ideas in Seventeenth-Century France: The Most Important Thinkers and the Climate of Ideas in Which They Worked.* New York: St. Martin's Press, 1979.

Lewis, W. H. *The Splendid Century: Life in the France of Louis XIV.* New York: Doubleday, 1953, 1957.

Lossky, Andrew. *Louis XIV and the French Monarchy.* New Brunswick, N.J.: Rutgers, 1994.

Mettam, Roger. *Power and Faction in Louis XIV's France.* Oxford: Blackwell, 1988.

Mitford, Nancy. *The Sun King.* New York: Harper & Row, 1966.*

Mousnier, Roland E. *The Institutions of France under the Absolute Monarchy, 1598–1789.* vol. 1, *Society and the State.* Trans. Brian Pearce. Vol.

2, *The Organs of State and Society.* Trans. Arthur Goldhammer. Chicago: University of Chicago Press, 1979, 1984.

Ogg, David. *Europe in the Seventeenth Century.* 8th ed. London: Macmillan, 1961.*

Rabb, Theodore K. *The Struggle for Stability in Early Modern Europe.* New York: Oxford University Press, 1975.

Rubin, David Lee, ed. *Sun King: The Ascendancy of French Culture during the Reign of Louis XIV.* Washington: Folger Shakespeare Library and Associated University Presses, 1992.

Rule, John C., ed. *Louis XIV and the Craft of Kingship.* Columbus: Ohio State University Press, 1969.

Wolf, John B. *The Emergence of the Great Powers, 1685–1715.* Rise of Modern Europe Series. New York: Harper & Row, 1951.*

———. *Louis XIV.* New York: Norton, 1968.*

———. *Toward a European Balance of Power, 1620–1715.* Chicago: Rand McNally, 1970.

(*Acknowledgments continued from page iv*)

HOMER: Portrait: Culver Pictures. Aristotle, "The Poetics," © 1934. Reprinted by permission of Everyman's Library, David Campbell Publishers, Ltd. Milman Parry, "Homer and Oral Tradition," from © Oxford University Press 1970. Reprinted from *The Making of Homeric Verse: The Collected Papers of Milman Parry*, edited by Adam Parry (1970) by permission of Oxford University Press. William A. Camps, "How the Stories Are Told," from © W. A. Camps, 1980. Reprinted from "An Introduction to Homer" by W. A. Camps, by permission of Oxford University Press.

SOCRATES: Portrait: Alinari/Art Resource, New York. Aristophanes, "The Clouds" from *The Clouds*, translated by William Arrowsmith. English translation copyright © 1959 by William Arrowsmith. Reprinted with the permission of New American Library, a division of Penguin Books USA Inc. Moses Hadas and Morton Smith, "The Image of Socrates" from *Heroes and Gods*. Copyright © 1965 by Moses Hadas and Morton Smith. Reprinted with the permission of HarperCollins Publishers, Inc.

ALEXANDER THE GREAT: Portrait: Stock Montage. Arrian, excerpt from *The Life of Alexander the Great by Arrian*, translated by Aubrey de Selincourt. Copyright © 1958 by The Estate of Aubrey de Selincourt. Reprinted with the permission of Penguin Books, Ltd. Plutarch excerpts from "On the Fortune of Alexander" from *Moralia*, Volume VI, translated by Frank C. Babbitt. Copyright 1936 by the President and Fellows of Harvard College. Reprinted with the permission of Harvard University Press. W. W. Tarn, "Alexander the Great and the Unity of Mankind," *Proceedings of the British Academy* 19 (1933). Copyright 1933. Reprinted with the permission of The British Academy. N. G. L. Hammond, "The New Alexander" from *Alexander the Great: King, Commander, and Statesman*. Copyright © 1989 by N. G. L. Hammond. Reprinted with the permission of BCP/Gerald Duckworth, Ltd.

JULIUS CAESAR: Portrait: Christie's, London/Superstock. Suetonius, "The Life of Caesar" from *The Lives of the Twelve Caesars*, edited and translated by Joseph Gavorse. Copyright 1931 and renewed © 1959 by Modern Library. Reprinted with the permission of Random House, Inc. Ronald Syme, "Caesar the Politician" from *The Roman Revolution*. Copyright 1939. Reprinted with the permission of Oxford University Press.

CONSTANTINE: Portrait: Stock Montage. Peter Brown, "Constantine and the 'Great Thaw' " from *The World of Late Antiquity*, A.D. *150–750*, pp. 86–88. Copyright © 1971 by Thames and Hudson, Ltd., London. Reprinted with the permission of W. W. Norton & Company, Inc. and Thames & Hudson, Ltd.

CHARLEMAGNE: Portrait: Culver Pictures. Einhard, "The Emperor Charlemagne" from *The Life of Charlemagne by Einhard*, translated by Samuel Epes Miller. Copyright © 1960. Reprinted with the permission of The University of Michigan Press. Heinrich Fichtenau, "A New Portrait of the Emperor" from *The Carolingian Empire: The Age of Charlemagne*, translated by Peter Munz (Toronto: University of Toronto Press/Medieval Academy Reprints for Teaching Volume I, 1978), pp. 25–29, 31–34, and 44–46. Reprinted with the permission of the author. F. L. Ganshof, "A More Somber Light" from *Speculum: A Journal of Medieval Studies* 24 (1949): 523–527. Copyright 1949. Reprinted with the permission of The Medieval Academy of America.

ELEANOR OF ACQUITAINE: Portrait: Bettmann. William, Archbishop of Tyre, "Eleanor and the Chroniclers" [first part] from *A History of Deeds Done Beyond the Sea,* Volume II, translated by E. A. Babcock and A. C. Krey. Copyright 1943 by Columbia University Press. Reprinted with the permission of the publishers. John of Salisbury, "Eleanor and the Chroniclers" [second part] from *The Historical Pontificals of John of Salisbury,* edited and translated by Marjorie Chinball, pp. 52–53. Copyright © 1956. Reprinted with the permission of Oxford University Press, Inc. Amy Kelly, "Eleanor, the Queen of Hearts," from *Eleanor of Aquitaine and the Four Kings.* Copyright 1950 by the President and Fellows of Harvard College, renewed © 1978 by J. Margaret Malcolm. Reprinted with the permission of Harvard University Press. Marion Meade, "Eleanor the Regent" from *Eleanor of Aquitaine.* Copyright © 1977 by Marion Meade. Reprinted with the permission of Dutton, an imprint of New American Library, a division of Penguin Books USA Inc.

DANTE: Portrait: Culver Pictures. Henry Osborn Taylor, "The Historical Dante" from *The Medieval Mind: A History of the Development of Thought and Emotion in the Middle Ages,* Fourth Edition. Copyright 1925 by the President and Fellows of Harvard College. Reprinted with the permission of Harvard University Press. Philip McNair, "Dante's Relevance Today," *The Listener* 74, no. 1892 (July 1, 1965). Copyright © 1965 by Philip McNair. Reprinted with the permission of the author.

LEONARDO DA VINCI: Portrait: AP/World Wide Photos. John Herman Randall Jr., "The Place of Leonardo da Vinci in the Emergence of Modern Science," *Journal of the History of Ideas* 14 (1935): 193–195. Reprinted with the permission of The Johns Hopkins University Press. Ladislao Reti, "The Problem of Prime Movers" from C. D. O'Malley, *Leonardo's Legacy: An International Symposium.* Copyright © 1969 by the Regents of the University of California. Reprinted with the permission of University of California Press.

HERNÁN CORTÉS: Portrait: Culver Pictures. "The Second Letter to Emperor Charles V" from Anthony Pagden, ed., *Letters from Mexico.* Copyright © 1986 by Yale University. Reprinted with the permission of Yale University Press. J. H. Elliott and Anthony Pagden, "A New Explanation" from Anthony Pagden, ed., *Letters from Mexico.* Copyright © 1986 by Yale University. Reprinted with the permission of Yale University Press.

MARTIN LUTHER: Portrait: Marburg/Art Resource, New York. "The Protestant Luther" from *Luther's Works,* Volume 54, edited and translated by Theodore G. Tappert. Copyright © 1965 by Fortress Press. Reprinted with the permission of Augsburg Fortress. Erik H. Erikson, excerpt from *Young Man Luther: A Study in Psychoanalysis and History* by Erik H. Erikson. Copyright © 1958, 1962 and renewed 1986, 1990 by Erik H. Erikson. Reprinted by permission of W. W. Norton & Company, Inc. Erwin Iserloh, "Luther Between Reform and Reformation" from *These These Were Not Posted,* translated by Jared Wicks, S.J. Copyright © 1968 by Beacon Press. Reprinted with the permission of Beacon Press.

ELIZABETH I: Portrait: Bridgeman Art Library, London. Garrett Mattingly, "Elizabeth and the 'Invincible' Armada" from *The Invincible Armada and Elizabethan England.* Copyright © 1963 by the Folger Shakespeare Libary. Reprinted with the permission of Associated University Presses.

LOUIS XIV: Portrait: Giraudon/Art Resource, New York. Louis, Duc de Saint-Simon, "The Memoirs" from Lucy Norton, *The Memoirs of M. le Duc de Saint-Simon.* Copyright © 1958 by Hamish Hamilton, Ltd. and Harper & Brothers. Reprinted with the permission of the publishers. Voltaire, "A Rationalist View of Absolutism" from *The Age of Louis XIV,* translated by Martyn P. Pollack. Copyright © 1926. Reprinted with the permission of Everyman's Library/David Campbell Publishers, Ltd. Pierre Goubert, "Louis XIV and the Larger World" from *Louis XIV and Twenty Million Frenchmen,* translated by Anne Carter. Copyright © 1970 by Anne Carter. Reprinted with the permission of Pantheon Books, a division of Random House, Inc.

Social/Economic *(continued)*

1519	Magellan's voyage around the world begins
1560–1600	Increased use of coal as a power source
1607	Founding of Jamestown, the first permanent English colony in North America
c. 1698	Development of the steam engine
1709	Terrible famine throughout Europe

Cultural/Intellectual

B.C.

1280	**Moses leads exodus of the Jewish people from Egypt**
c. 800	**Epic poems ascribed to Homer**
c. 600	Sappho, Greek lyric poet
496?–406	Sophocles, Greek tragic playwright
c. 428–348	Plato, Greek philosopher and student of Socrates
399	**Trial and conviction of Socrates**
384–322	Aristotole, Greek philosopher and student of Plato
106–43	Cicero, Roman orator, essayist, and statesman
c. 50	**Caesar's** *Commentaries*

A.D.

c. 6 B.C.– c. A.D. 30	Jesus, founder of Christianity
55?–120?	Tacitus, Roman historian and politician
c. 85–165	Ptolemy, Greco-Egyptian mathemetician, astronomer, and geographer
412–424	Augustine composes *City of God*
451	Council of Chalcedon recognizes papal authority in deciding dogmatic questions
610	Muhammad begins preaching at Mecca
c. 850	Great age of Byzantine culture
c. 1000	Beginning of extensive construction of churches in the Romanesque style
1054	Schism between the Eastern and Western churches
1073–1085	Gregory VII pope; climax of the Investiture Controversy
1160–1200	Building of Notre Dame cathedral, Paris; development of the Gothic style of architecture
c. 1182–1226	St. Francis of Assisi
1231	Pope Gregory IX institutes the Inquisition
c. 1266–1274	Aquinas writes *Summa Theologica*
1309	Papacy at Avignon
1313–1321	**Dante composes** *Divine Comedy*
1341	Petrarch crowned poet laureate at Rome
1378–1417	Great Schism; popes at Rome and Avignon
1386–1400	Chaucer writes *Canterbury Tales*
1495–1498	**Da Vinci paints** *The Last Supper*
1501–1504	Michelangelo sculpts *David*